BANK ORGANIZATION AND OPERATION

American Institute of Banking
SECTION AMERICAN BANKERS ASSOCIATION
22 East 40 Street   New York, N. Y.

Copyright 1937
by
American Institute of Banking
Section American Bankers Association

First printing, August 1937
Second printing, October 1937
Third printing, June 1938
Fourth printing (revised), August 1939

PREFACE

BANK Organization and Operation is one of a series of three courses on banking included in the curriculum of the American Institute of Banking. While this course is the first of the group, it is not elementary. As a prerequisite to a thorough understanding of the theoretical and administrative aspects of banking discussed in Banking II and Banking III, the student must have a comprehensive knowledge of the process by which our banking system carries on the millions of banking transactions that take place each day.

Banking I is a working manual of the practical operations of a bank, department by department. It explains the complex systems by which it is possible to clear checks all over the country, to receive deposits and make loans, and to perform the numerous functions of the modern bank safely and expeditiously and without excessive cost. The subject matter is amplified by means of suitable forms.

The author of the text, George D. Bushnell of the American National Bank and Trust Company of Chicago, has had wide experience in practical banking, both as a bank executive and as an instructor, having taught this subject in Chicago Chapter of the Institute for a number of years. The present edition of Banking I was taught in manuscript form in Mr. Bushnell's classes during the chapter year 1936-1937.

In building this course, the Institute received the active cooperation of the Bank Management Commission of the American Bankers Association, which appointed a committee to review the manuscript and offer criticisms and suggestions. The Institute is deeply indebted to the Commission for its services, and particularly to the committee, which consisted of G. Fred Berger, Norristown-Penn Trust Company, Norristown, Pennsylvania; Arch W. Anderson, Continental Illinois National Bank and Trust Company, Chicago, Illinois; and Fred B. Brady, Commerce Trust Company, Kansas City, Missouri.

HAROLD STONIER
National Educational Director

Contents

CHAPTER	PAGE
I. BANKS AND BANKING	7
II. BANK ORGANIZATION PROCEDURE	39
III. DEPOSITS AND THE RECEIVING FUNCTION	79
IV. THE RECEIVING FUNCTION AND THE PAYING FUNCTION	139
V. THE CLEARING PRINCIPLE. ANALYSIS OF ACCOUNTS	181
VI. THE TRANSIT DEPARTMENT	225
VII. THE COLLECTION DEPARTMENT. THE SAVINGS DEPARTMENT. THE SAFE DEPOSIT COMPANY	267
VIII. BANK ACCOUNTING AND AUDITING	313
IX. THE LOANING FUNCTION	350
X. THE LOAN AND DISCOUNT DEPARTMENT. THE FOREIGN DEPARTMENT	387
XI. TRUST FUNCTIONS	424
XII. BANK EXAMINATION. THE STATEMENT OF CONDITION	448
APPENDIX	469
ILLUSTRATIONS	475
INDEX	477

Bank Organization and Operation

CHAPTER I

BANKS AND BANKING

The Purposes of This Chapter:
1. To outline the reasons for the public interest in banking.
2. To explain the principal functions exercised by banks.
3. To indicate the various classifications of banks.

IT IS often said that the United States is a nation of business superlatives. Its business enterprises are larger and more varied than those of any other country in the world. "Largest in the world," "most extensively used," and similar phrases commonly describe the results of American endeavor. It is recognized that Americans demand more, use more, and produce more than citizens of other nations. There is no nation so widespread in so many major activities, among them agriculture, mining, manufacturing, and trade.

The American people not only use more modern business facilities and conveniences than other nations in proportion to population but use them to a *greater extent*. It is not only that we have more automobiles, telephones, railroads, and the like, but that they are more extensively used by our population than are those same facilities in other countries. These facts are material evidences of the constructive American ambition that has brought us from a minor, insignificant position to a commanding one among the nations of the world.

The purpose of calling attention to these facts at the beginning of a study of Bank Organization and Operation is not to "point with pride" to the accomplishments of the past or to the part banks have played in assisting agriculture, trade, and industry. It is rather to emphasize the constructive challenge that these facts present to individual bankers, to banking institutions, and to the banking system as a whole.

Banking and the Public Interest—There are thousands [1] of banks in the United States of varying size, type, and scope. They range in size from those of modest proportions in small villages and communities, with resources in the thousands, to metropolitan banks ranking among the largest in the world, with resources in the billions. Some banks conduct their business at a single location; others have a multitude of branch offices scattered over the city, trade area, or state in which the main office is situated. There are banks that provide only savings facilities, or only commercial services, or only trust services. There are others that provide all these facilities and services through a departmentalized organization.

The type, the size, the location, and the extent of facilities of these thousands of banks are determined by the needs and demands of their customers and by a code of laws which has grown up over the years. These needs and desires vary greatly. Millions of wage earners are primarily interested in the savings services of banks. Farmers, merchants, manufacturers, jobbers, and a host of others need and use commercial banking services. Both individuals and corporations find trust services effective and economical. Within the framework of banking law, a bank's customers, both actual and prospective, directly affect the size, the type, and the extent of services of that bank. The cumulative effect of all these customer-bank relationships

---

[1] As of June 30, 1938—15,287. See Table I, Appendix.

is seen in the banking laws, the banking practices, and the major characteristics of the entire banking system.

With millions of bank customers employing the deposit and checking facilities, the loan facilities, the collection services, and numerous other services, the importance of banking becomes an established fact. If these services were no more than convenient and economical, they would still play a prominent part in the efficient conduct of trade and commerce because of the extent to which they are used. But banking functions have progressed far beyond the stage of convenience; they have become *necessities* to millions of customers, since most of the facilities provided by banks are not duplicated by other agencies. The very few that are offered by others are either only partially performed or performed within a limited range.

The consequences of banking services and facilities are likewise of vital significance to additional millions who are not customers of banks, for every individual or business enterprise, in dealing with a commercial customer of a bank, is indirectly affected by those services. Business deals of non-customers with customers frequently depend upon the relationship between the customers and the bank. If the customer-bank relationship is satisfactory, business firms with which a customer deals will find their transactions promptly and properly completed. It is the same with bank-customer relationships of a personal or thrift nature. The reserve funds of an individual ordinarily are not destined for his use alone, but for the protection of his family and other dependents and of his creditors as well. Thus the *public at large* has a *direct interest* in banking; its well-being is subject to the success or failure of the individual banks and to the adequacy or inadequacy of the banking system as a whole. This effect of banks upon customers and non-customers is so marked that banking has long been recognized as being imbued with a public interest.

The interdependence of banking and the public has been demonstrated repeatedly in the banking history of this and other countries, not only in the dim past but in very recent times. It was dramatically demonstrated in the United States by the bank moratorium in 1933. During the moratorium even the most casual observer saw clearly that business and banking were inseparable, for the business and trade of the entire nation were paralyzed when deprived of the ordinary facilities of banks. Recognizing this public interest, all groups concerned should strive to improve banking conditions by working toward constructive objectives.

Banking Objectives—The primary joint objective of bankers, banking associations, governing and supervising authorities, and the public at large has been, and continues to be, the elimination of practices that are detrimental to the stability of individual banks and to the success of the entire banking system. In effect, each group demands certain conditions particularly desirable to itself. The foremost interest of the public is the *safety of funds* entrusted to banks and efficient service at reasonable cost. The primary objective of governing and supervising authorities is the *prevention of bank failures* and the promotion of an effective banking system. The principal objective of bankers, banking associations, and owners of banks is *profit* obtained by a *conservative performance of banking functions*. Supervising authorities rely upon examination and regulation, and their knowledge of banking conditions is used to advantage in the framing of laws and regulations. Bankers and bankers associations emphasize study and application of conservative principles in bank management and operation. They also contribute substantially to the formulation of laws and regulations and to the public dissemination of information as to what constitutes good banking.

These constructive efforts are not limited to group or organization activities; individuals in banks, for example, contribute to the welfare of their own bank and of the banking system by the study and application of the many factors involved in adequate, conservative, and profitable banking. The benefits so derived are personal as well as general, for the individual improves his own position, prepares for added responsibilities, and, incidentally, for increased remuneration.

The Study of Bank Organization and Operation—A general knowledge of banking requires an approach from many angles. An understanding of the broad principles of business economics, of the law of contracts and negotiable instruments (Law I and Law II in the Institute curriculum), of the more specialized phases of banking (Trust Business and Credit Administration), and of other subjects included in the Institute Standard and Graduate series is a necessary supplement to the practical work of the individual banker. Among the many Institute courses, there are three that may be regarded as almost a unit—Bank Organization and Operation, Money and Banking, and Bank Administration.

It might be said that Money and Banking (Banking II) explains the "why" of banking—the broad facts concerning it and the economic and financial laws as they are applied to, or fulfilled by, banking. A knowledge of the subject matter of this course is essential if the major problems of the individual bank are to be considered intelligently. Bank Administration (Banking III) is devoted to a consideration of the principles and policies best adapted to meet the problems of the individual institution; it explains the "what" of banking.

No matter how complete a banker's knowledge of fundamental economic and financial laws may be, and no matter how well he can translate those laws into suitable policies for an individual bank, the real test of that knowledge and ability is the successful application of laws and policies to the millions of banking transactions taking place each day. Therefore, a third viewpoint is necessary. Bank Organization and Operation (Banking I) deals with the systems and methods by means of which bank policies are converted into action; it has to do with the "how" of banking.

Customer Contact or Customer Relations—Among the changing practices of banking are those concerned with customer relations—the ways and means by which banks endeavor to promote a better knowledge and understanding of the functions which banks perform in our economic life. The attitude of the modern bank in its customer contacts, or customer relations, is noticeably different from the attitude that formerly prevailed. Today the advertising of a bank and its services is a matter of common practice and is recognized as a constructive and essential part of banking procedure; yet in earlier times such publicity was considered unseemly if not actually unethical. Direct solicitation of business by representatives of banks, formerly considered unprofessional, is now an integral part of banking activities. Bankers, as well as the informed public, are alert to the benefits arising from the creation of new ways and means of service and new applications of facilities to the needs of customers, and they recognize clearly that such a course is advantageous to all concerned.

In their advertising, banks call attention not only to their financial stability and to their experienced and well regarded management but also, very directly, to the efficiency of their services. For example, the efficient operation of a service such as the collection of checks has been, and will continue to be, an excellent means of obtaining new business to the satisfaction and profit of both the customer and the bank.

Contacts with customers, or customer relations, continue to play an important part in the management and operating policies of banks, for a satisfied bank customer is no less productive of profit to a bank than is a satisfied business customer to a retail store or to a manufacturer or to any other kind of business enterprise. In creating good will by the efficient, courteous, and economical transaction of a customer's commercial banking business, a bank creates additional opportunities to serve the customer in ways which he has not used before but which are adapted to his needs and are profitable to the bank. The student of banking must therefore be alert to the benefits of good customer relations based upon an extensive, constructive, and profitable utilization of banking services and facilities.

Principles and Operations—Certain rules of practice have been developed as a guide to the establishment and conduct of banks under circumstances favorable to the best interests of all concerned. These may well be called "principles of banking." Many of these rules—such as the minimum reserve requirements—are embodied in national and state banking laws; others are included in the by-laws of banks; still others appear as policies established by the boards of directors of banks. Many rules and regulations formulated by such organizations as clearing house associations, state bankers associations, and national bankers associations have been voluntarily adopted by banks in an endeavor to improve steadily and consistently the practice of banking.

These principles require able judgment on the part of the management, competent personnel, and adequate equipment if banking transactions are to be performed to the satisfaction of both the customer and the bank. Constant study of the changing problems of each department is necessary in order that transactions may be carried out accurately and economically. This phase of banking, known as *bank operations,* involves the practical application of the principles of banking to the millions of transactions passing through the banks daily.

The Importance of Bank Operations—Banking is frequently referred to as a profession. Certainly experience has demonstrated that specialized knowledge, professional training, able judgment, and a strict standard of integrity are essential to the successful conduct of any bank; but knowledge, training, and judgment are effective only when the mechanics of operation are efficient. Banking is a business, subject to the principles of business efficiency. Bank operations constitute the mechanics of banking—the production, or business, side. Just as the management of a manufacturing plant is dependent on efficient production, so a bank's management expects that its policies will be carried out effectively on a competitive basis with other banking organizations.

That the primary importance of bank operations is not yet realized by some bankers is perhaps due to the fact that the emphasis on the profit possibilities of operations is comparatively new, whereas in industry it has long been recognized. It was not always so in industry, however, for in earlier times industry's main problem was the conversion of raw materials into finished products to meet a ready demand. As a result of competition to meet the needs and changing desires of the public, the production phase of industry has been brought, step by step, to an efficient state. The outstanding example today of an effective combination of management and production (or mechanical operation) is the automobile industry in this country. Committed to a policy of a better product at lower cost, the automobile industry has shown by experience that management and production are inseparable components in successful business undertakings.

A bank sells a *service,* or a combination of services, and not a *product.* Not many years ago the main problem of a bank was comparable to that of the manufacturer of former times. If a bank could obtain deposits, it could use those deposits, together with the capital funds of the stockholders, in a wide range of earning assets. Provided losses on these principal earning assets (loans and investments) could be kept within moderate limits, the bank was considered prosperous; at that time economy in operations was of secondary importance.

Gradually, however, additional banking facilities were developed to meet the needs or desires of bank customers; the volume of business increased; and the cost of equipment, space, and personnel became factors of major importance. Recently the declining volume of commercial loans and lower interest rates, together with the factors mentioned, have emphasized the importance of economy and efficiency in operations.

Successful banks today regard management and operations as natural complements and accord to each the recognition and support to which it is entitled. Without any diminution of the established fact that integrity, judgment, and knowledge are essential to successful banking and that management today is facing greater problems than ever before, it is also recognized that the mechanics of banking—the production of service and economy and efficiency of operation—have assumed a major role in banking.

The Principal Functions of Banks—The general function of banks is to create and to service a medium of exchange. A medium of exchange is something that can be generally and satisfactorily used as money.[1a] For the purpose of studying

---

[1a] In this country checks drawn on banks constitute the greater portion (in terms of volume) of the mediums of exchange. When a bank lends money, it sets up the amount on its books as a deposit against which the borrower draws checks. Thus the bank, practically speaking, *creates* the medium of exchange. This medium requires *servicing* in that the bank must be able to convert it into currency on demand, must eventually collect it, and must clear the checks resulting, keep the books in balance, and so forth. Incidentally, banks also service currency (official money) by counting, sorting, and checking the bills and coins as they pass through the bank.

bank organization and operation, this *general* function—to create and to service a medium of exchange—will be divided into five *specific* functions, as follows:

1. To receive deposits to be used according to banking practice
2. To make loans to qualified applicants and to invest funds
3. To transfer money and credit
4. To provide a medium of exchange
5. To hold property for others and to act on their behalf (the trust function).

From the economic standpoint, then, banks may be said to create some mediums of exchange and to service all mediums of exchange. These functions are performed through the loan and investment activities of banks, through the use of facilities for the deposit and withdrawal of funds by customers, and through the handling by the banks of practically all money in circulation. The extent to which an individual bank participates in the performance of these functions, both in manner and in volume, depends upon the acceptable requirements of its customers. The nature of the principal line of business in the community in which the bank is located, the type of bank, the general condition of business, all will affect the relative importance of these functions from time to time; but over a given period the banking system, by the convenience and economy of its operations, facilitates trade and commerce and assists in the completion of business transactions— in short, makes possible the present methods of American business.

The Deposit Function—The first of the specific banking functions to be developed was the *deposit function*. While it existed to a limited extent in ancient times, the origin of the present deposit function dates back to the revival of trade following the so-called dark ages. Invariably, as trade and commerce developed within a country or between countries, the protection of gold and silver coin and other valuables of small bulk became a pressing problem to traders—in England, in France, in Holland, and in other countries.

Confronted with this problem, merchants and traders looked about for persons of integrity and responsibility who were in a position to provide physical protection for cash and other valuables of small bulk. The persons who could generally meet these requirements at that time were the goldsmiths. As a class they were honest and financially responsible. The nature of their business required them to keep on hand supplies of precious metals and jewels. For the protection of such supplies, the goldsmiths used strong iron-bound chests, fitted with staunch locks. As a further measure of protection, the apprentices who lived and worked in the combination home and shop of the goldsmith acted as guards.

The factors of character and financial responsibility were regarded as primarily essential in the custodian of funds, and the protective features offered by the custodian were of secondary importance. Experience since then has served to emphasize the importance of the double requirement, and today it is more strongly entrenched in our banking system than ever before.

Having selected as safe, reliable, and convenient a place as could be found, the merchant left with the goldsmith a sealed bag containing the coin or other valuables. The receipt issued for this transaction called for the return of the identical bag with its contents undisturbed. A fee was paid the goldsmith for the protection rendered. The entire transaction was merely one of protection, similar to the modern safekeeping facilities of trust companies and commercial banks.

Today, as we look at the museum exhibits of the strong boxes of those earlier days and compare them with our modern steel vaults, equipped with intricate locks and alarms, protected by trained guards, and further protected by insurance, we can realize how much progress has been made in the problem of the physical protection of money.

This purely safekeeping arrangement, requiring the return of the identical coin or valuables left with the goldsmith, soon became a *deposit agreement*. Gradually, instead of returning the identical funds, the goldsmith, by agreement, returned funds of equal value, in the meantime using the money for loaning purposes.

Referring to the proposal to form a public bank introduced in the British House of Commons in 1691, one banking historian says:

"Up to this time the so-called bankers were really pawnbrokers. The country people found it expedient to leave their small savings for safe keeping with goldsmiths and other city merchants, whose shops included among their fittings strong boxes which defied thieves. These clever people soon found that instead of keeping these savings locked up, they could make loans on ample security to anyone, from the King down at an interest which paid them well." [2]

The Loaning Function—Early loaning practices were actually pawnbroker transactions. For the repayment of a loan, the goldsmith depended on the value of the property pledged and in his possession. Loans based on the business of the individual and not specifically secured by pledge of personal property were almost unknown. This situation has been reversed through the years; in American banking today unsecured loans, developed in conformity with the habits and practices of business, are an important part of the business of banks.

From earliest loaning operations, the principle that loans

---

[2] Selfridge, H. Gordon, The Romance of Commerce; John Lane Company, New York, 1918

are made at the risk of the banker and that the profit earned or the loss sustained is his concern alone has been clearly understood. Regardless of profit or loss resulting from the employment of the funds in loans, the goldsmith was obligated to return the sums to his depositors according to the agreements made, just as the bank today is obligated to return funds to its customers according to agreement, regardless of whether profits or losses have resulted from the use of the funds.

While the motive prompting these early bankers to accept deposits was the profit to be obtained, the ultimate result of the loans was to assist in the carrying on of trade and commerce, to benefit the merchants as well as the bankers, and to encourage the growth of the community and country by making the production and movement of goods more efficient and economical, as is the case today.

The Transfer of Funds—As trade within a country or between countries expanded, there arose the problem of transferring funds from one point to another as needed. In early days, merchants traveling from one part of the continent to another had to carry cash to pay for their purchases. Not only was this an added cost and danger, but it was a deterrent to the rapid development of trade. Guards had to be provided to protect the money on the way. This at best only lessened the danger, for a strong band of outlaws could overcome the guards.

Even in fairly recent times the transportation of money has been a major problem. For many years after the discovery of gold in California in 1848, the transportation of that gold and of money was a matter of great concern. Individuals established services for the protection and transportation of gold and money, among them the founders of one of the leading California banks.

While there are still problems in the transfer of currency today, they are few in comparison with those of earlier days. The Federal Reserve System and the commercial banks of the country, with their facilities for the shipment of coin and currency, have minimized the risk and cost of transportation. Other occasions that require the transfer of actual currency are met by companies which are organized to provide such service and protection at reasonable fees. These companies, of excellent reputation and equipped with fleets of armored cars, trained guards, and protective insurance, do an extensive business in the transportation of cash. Large chain store systems, oil companies with numerous service stations, and similar concerns are constant users of such transport services. These and other bank customers often retain the transport companies for the entire handling of their cash receipts, including collecting, proving, sorting, and depositing them.

In addition to the transfer of actual coin and currency, credit is transferred by telegraph (the wire transfer system) and by the use of the circulating mediums created and serviced by banks.

The Circulating Medium—Transportation of cash is inconvenient and generally expensive. If, instead of the cash itself, an order representing cash proves to be acceptable, the cost and inconvenience incident to the transfer of actual currency are greatly reduced, and such a medium of circulation can be expanded extensively. This situation was appreciated by the merchant-bankers of early times, who, as they increased in number and in importance and established branches or representatives in other cities and countries, began to make use of informal intercompany orders instead of shipping cash from one place to another. Organizations such as the House of Rothschild developed this system to a very high degree. Gradually the service was extended to their customers, and this was the beginning of the modern checking system. An example of the use of these informal orders was the arrangement which existed between the House of Fugger in Germany and its representative in Rome. A German merchant who deposited gold with the head office in Germany received an order on the representative in Rome. With this order the merchant could travel in safety; he had no need to carry gold with him, and yet he could obtain gold on his arrival in Rome where he had use for it.

Today, whether the individual or business concern to whom money is due is located in the same city as the debtor or a thousand miles away, payment of bills may be made by check because of the services rendered by banks in providing for the use of orders in place of money and in arranging for the collection of those orders. Actual currency is now the "small change" of business, for, according to estimates, over 90% of the daily financial transactions are settled by the use of checks or drafts.

Trust Functions—In recent years the problems incident to the handling of both real and personal property have grown to such proportions that individuals as well as business organizations have found it desirable to utilize the services of special institutions, known as trust institutions. Trust functions, exercised by banks in conformance with established principles and careful practices, have opened up a wide field of profitable service. The nature of the facilities of banks makes the extensive, economical, and safe fulfilment of trust services a logical adjunct to commercial banking and savings banking.

Although trust banking, by the nature of its operations, is essentially different in major respects from commercial banking, fiduciary functions are being exercised more and more by commercial banks. The separate trust department in the commercial bank was a logical development. Customers like to do business with an institution that renders good service, and when their commercial and savings banking requirements are satisfactorily met and their contacts with the officers and employees of those departments are pleasant and friendly, they are inclined to consult the bank about their trust problems as well and as a result customers will be inclined to conduct their entire business—commercial, savings, and trust—with the same institution.

Foreign Banking and Exchange—Many of the larger metropolitan banks maintain a special department which handles transactions in foreign credits, transfers of balances, the purchase and sale of exchange, and other financial operations arising from international trade or travel. While foreign banking and exchange operations are a distinct and separate field, they are often included in commercial banking organization services, since the customers of the commercial department are also customers of the foreign department. In this study of bank organization and operation, foreign banking and exchange can be considered only briefly, and principally in connection with other banking operations.

Classification of Banks—Banks may be classified in several ways, each classification being based on some particular characteristic (charter, type of business, and so forth), although there may be and is considerable overlapping. The four major classifications are:

1. Source of authority—state banks and national banks
2. Membership in the Federal Reserve System—member banks and non-member banks
3. Kinds of services rendered—commercial banks, savings banks, and trust companies
4. Form of organization—unit banks, branch banks, chain banks, and group banks.

State Banks and National Banks—Until the National Bank Act was passed, most American banks were state banks. They received their powers from, and were subject to regulation by, the state in which they were located. American banks were first established by special laws of the state, and each bank had to be authorized to operate by a special act of the state legislative body. As banks increased in number and importance, the states passed general banking laws which governed all state banks. These laws included the rules and regulations under which new banks could be established, as well as the controls to be exercised thereafter. Today there is only one state, Delaware, in which banks are still individually chartered by special act of the legislature. In the remaining states, banks are chartered and regulated by general banking laws.

The National Bank Act was passed during the Civil War (June 3, 1864) and provided for the chartering of banks under the supervision of federal authorities. These *national* banks may be located in any state and are operated under the direction of the Comptroller of the Currency. Chartered by the Federal Government and subject to identical rules and laws regardless of location, national banks have greater uniformity in operation and powers than state banks (consisting of forty-eight varieties), the capital, powers, and supervision of which are established under the laws and regulations of the state in which they are located. This distinction between national banks and state banks was particularly marked for many years in that the bank name indicated the scope of operations permitted the institution in a particular locality. The diagram of bank control (Figure 1) shows the lack of a common basis of control for national banks and state banks before the formation of the Federal Reserve System.

Federal Reserve Banks—Federal Reserve banks were established in 1914 to provide a more elastic currency, to centralize

24 BANKS AND BANKING

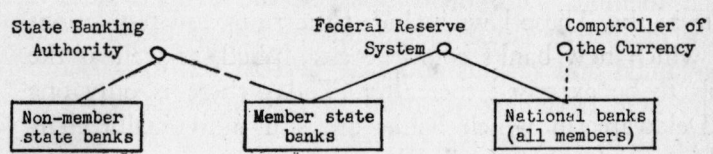

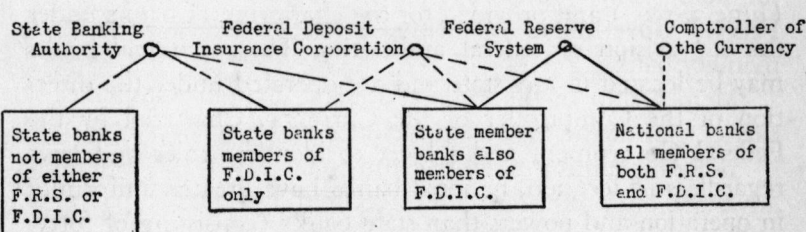

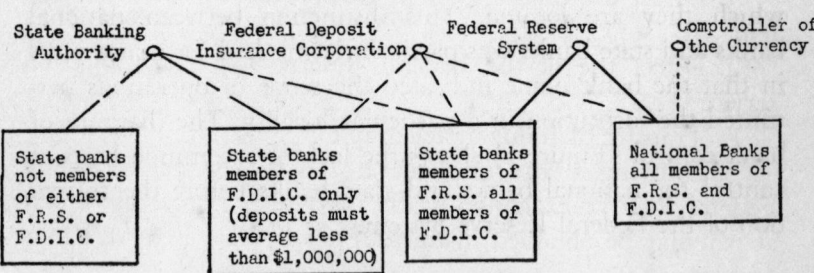

FIGURE 1. BANK CONTROL

the gold reserves of the country, to establish more effective supervision of banking, and to provide a means of rediscounting commercial paper. The United States is divided into twelve Federal Reserve districts, each with a Federal Reserve bank centrally located in a major city and with branches in other important cities of the district. These districts, with the Federal Reserve banks and their branches, are shown in Figure 2.

Each member bank owns stock in the Federal Reserve bank of its district equal in amount to 3% of the member bank's capital and surplus and may be required to subscribe up to 6%. On December 31, 1938, the paid-in capital stock of the Federal Reserve banks (all owned by member banks) totaled $134,575,000.

Federal Reserve banks do not come in direct contact with the public except to a very limited extent in connection with Federal Government financing. Their main contact is with member banks.

Membership in the Federal Reserve System automatically carries with it the following facilities and privileges:

1. Rediscounting eligible commercial paper and obtaining advances on promissory notes secured by eligible paper or other acceptable collateral
2. Obtaining currency and coin when needed
3. Direct use of the Federal Reserve check collection system
4. Direct use of the Federal Reserve non-cash collection service
5. Transfer of funds by telegraph
6. Drawing drafts on Federal Reserve banks, including Federal Reserve exchange drafts for which immediate credit at par may be obtained in thirty-seven Federal Reserve banks and branches
7. Use of the emblem signifying membership
8. Membership in the Federal Deposit Insurance Corpora-

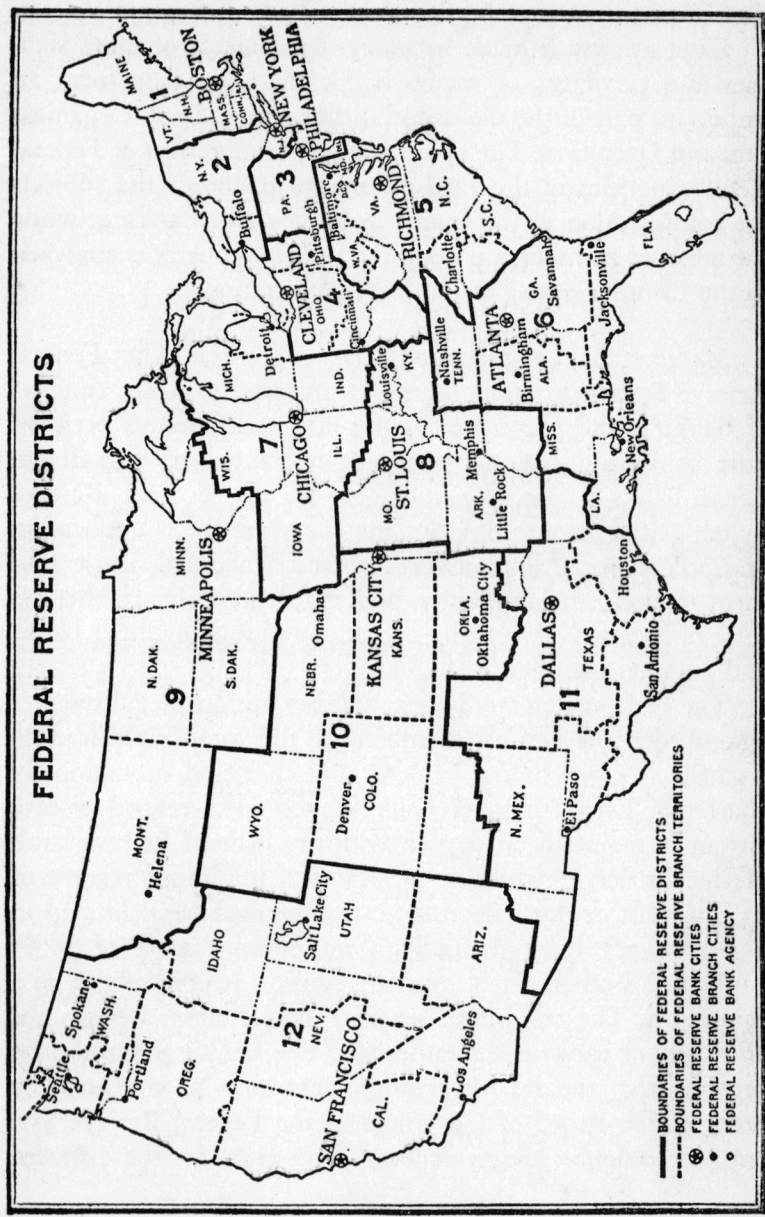

Figure 2. Federal Reserve Districts

tion by virtue of membership in the Federal Reserve System.

Extensive use is made by many departments of these facilities and privileges of membership; therefore they form an important part of the discussion in this text in Bank Organization and Operation. The broad and important effect of Federal Reserve policies in the field of finance is one of the subjects for consideration in the course in Money and Banking, while the effect of membership upon the individual bank is analyzed in the Institute course in Bank Administration.

Member Banks and Non-Member Banks—The Federal Reserve System brought increased uniformity in the conduct of banking and eliminated many of the differences between state banks and national banks. It is compulsory for all national banks to become members of the Federal Reserve System. State banks may become members upon application and acceptance. All members, state and national, must conform to uniform laws, rules, and regulations; hence there is little difference between the operations of state member banks and national member banks.

The Federal Reserve System requires uniform legal reserves against deposits for all members of the same classification, regardless of whether a bank is state-chartered or nationally chartered. Every member bank located in a central reserve city must maintain on deposit with the Federal Reserve bank of the district in which it is located a minimum reserve of 13% against *demand* deposits; every member bank located in a reserve city must maintain a minimum reserve of 10%; banks in all other places must maintain a reserve of 7% as a minimum. The minimum reserve against *time* deposits for *all classes* of banks is the same, 3%. The Banking Act of 1935 provides that the reserve requirements may be increased, by order of the Board of Governors of the Federal Reserve System, up to double the percentages here given for the different classes of deposits.[3] The minimum, however, cannot be set below these basic reserves. Varying the amount of reserves is one of the measures of control of prices and business activity which is entrusted to the Federal Reserve System. The subject will be discussed in the Institute text Money and Banking.

All other rules and regulations of the Federal Reserve System—such as eligible paper requirements, reports and regulations, transfer of funds, collection facilities, and the like—apply to both state member banks and national banks regardless of location. The effect of the application of uniform regulations to both national banks and state member banks is shown in the second part of the bank control diagram (Figure 1).

Non-members consist entirely of state banks that have not joined the system—small banks, for the most part. From the standpoint of volume of banking business, as measured by deposits, loans, investments, and all other activities, the banking of the United States is predominantly performed by members of the Federal Reserve System.

The extent of the banking business carried on by member banks is indicated by the resources of the members as of June 30, 1938.[4] At that time the number of national banks totaled 5,242, and all, of course, were members of the Federal Reserve System. The state member banks totaled 1,096, ranging from banks of $25,000 capital to some of the largest banks in the country. By number, approximately 41% of all commercial banks in the United States were members of the system. That the non-member banks were small banks and performed a minor part in American banking may be seen from the fact that the member banks represented about

---
[3] See Table II, Appendix.
[4] Figures taken from Twenty-Fifth Annual Report of the Board of Governors of the Federal Reserve System Covering Operations for the Year 1938, p. 7 (See Table I, Appendix.)

70% of the banking resources of the country. Of the four groups represented in the third portion of Figure 1, the state non-member banks (shown at the extreme left) were representative of only 30% of the banking resources on June 30, 1938, although 59% of the banks by number of units.

The fourth section of Figure 1 shows the provision of the Banking Act of 1935 for membership after July 1, 1942. From present indications it is probable that membership will be further augmented before that date both by number of member banks and by total banking resources.

Federal Deposit Insurance Corporation—By authority of the Banking Act of 1933, a corporation was formed for the purpose of providing further protection for bank depositors, principally those with small deposits. This was done by creating a fund (1) through payments from banks participating in the plan and (2) through subscription to the capital stock of the corporation on the part of the Treasury of the United States and the Federal Reserve banks. Provision was made for additional funds through the borrowing power granted to the corporation by law.

All members of the Federal Reserve System are required to become members of the Federal Deposit Insurance Corporation. Banks which are not members of the Federal Reserve System may become members of the Federal Deposit Insurance Corporation upon application, examination, and acceptance, and they are then subject to its rules and regulations. Figure 1 indicates the position of all banks with regard to membership and regulation by the corporation.

The Banking Act of 1935 revised the status of members of the Federal Deposit Insurance Corporation that were not members of the Federal Reserve System, by requiring that all state non-member banks with average deposits of $1,000,000 or over must become members of the Federal Reserve System by

July 1, 1942 or forfeit their participation in the Federal Deposit Insurance Corporation plan.[4]

The original capital funds for the corporation were provided by the Treasury of the United States, which purchased $150,000,000 of stock, and by the Federal Reserve banks, which were required to subscribe an amount equal to one-half their surplus as of January 1, 1933 (this totaled approximately $139,000,000). The additional working funds are provided by the members of the Federal Deposit Insurance Corporation on the basis of an annual assessment of 1/12 of 1%, payable semiannually, on the average deposit liability of insured banks over a six-month period (Banking Act of 1935, Sec. 101 (h) (1)).

The practice of the Federal Deposit Insurance Corporation is to take over the liquidation of an insured bank whenever necessary and, as soon as possible, to repay the insured depositors from the fund. The present plan provides that each depositor of a participating bank shall be insured to a maximum of $5,000 of deposits.

Commercial Banks, Savings Banks, and Trust Companies —On the basis of the type of service rendered, banks may be divided into three main groups—commercial banks, savings banks, and trust companies.

Commercial banks are those designed primarily to receive deposits, to make loans, to transfer money and credit, and to supply a circulating medium to individuals and business enterprises. Their primary object is to fulfil the short term financial needs of trade and commerce and so assist in the promotion of agriculture, trade, and industry.

Savings banks engage principally in the receiving of time deposits from persons of thrift, who place their funds in the

---

[5] This provision is the subject of heated political controversy and may be altered or amended before the effective date.

BANKS AND BANKING 33

Mutual Savings Banks and Private Banks—Many savings institutions, particularly in the eastern states, are conducted on a mutual basis, each depositor sharing in the dividends declared in proportion to the amount he has on deposit. Such banks have no stated capital and therefore no stockholders. Each depositor is a proportionate owner of the bank in addition to being a depositor. His principal right is that of sharing in the earnings declared as dividends. Usually only a portion of the earnings is so disbursed; the remainder is left in the form of surplus, undivided profits, and reserves, which, over a period of time, create large amounts of excess earnings by accumulation. These excess earnings are used by the bank in the same way that an incorporated institution uses its capital and surplus. To be eligible for membership in the Federal Reserve System, a mutual savings bank must have surplus and undivided profits at least equal to the amount of capital required to organize a national bank in the same locality.

Through the National Association of Mutual Savings Banks, an organization composed of mutual savings banks of the United States and dedicated to their interests, some very interesting figures are available on the scope of operations of these banks. The January 1, 1939 report showed 543 mutual savings banks operating in 17 states. On that date these banks had total deposits of $10,235,431,452 and total depositors of 15,156,553. The 100 largest mutual savings banks had total deposits of $7,194,520,315. Of these 100 banks, 54 were located in the state of New York, 18 in Massachusetts, 5 in Pennsylvania, 3 in Rhode Island, 9 in Connecticut, 3 in New Jersey, 2 in Maryland, and 1 each in Delaware, Maine, Minnesota, New Hampshire, Ohio, and Washington.

From the standpoint of total deposits, mutual savings banks represent the largest group of unincorporated banking institutions.

The number of *private* unincorporated banks has been

greatly reduced in recent years for the reason that the national banking laws and most state laws now require the incorporation of banks. In a recently published consolidated capitulation for December 1938 statements, private banks totaling 186 were listed in 13 states. This complete comparison is shown in Table III of the Appendix.

Personal Loan Institutions and Departments—There are many banking institutions that specialize in small loans to individuals. These loans may be secured by acceptable collateral or by the guaranty or indorsement of one or more reliable persons. Such institutions, when properly managed, fulfil an important banking need that often is not met by other banking institutions. These small loans range in amount from $50 to $1,000, the average amount being nearer the lower figure. To handle them profitably, a particular method of operation has been devised. The period for which a loan is made is ordinarily twelve months (or less), and the borrower repays it in equal monthly instalments. Because it is specially organized to handle a volume of small loans, the personal loan institution is able to make a profit. The cost of handling such loans by a bank not specially equipped for the purpose would amount to more than the interest received.

Many commercial banks encourage people seeking small loans to make use of the services of personal loan institutions. Some commercial banks, however, operate special small loan departments with satisfactory results, and the tendency seems to be for an increasing number of banks to enter this field.[6] A further discussion of the personal loan department will be found in Chapter IX.

The Problem of Bank Operations—At first glance it may

---

[6] The subject is discussed more thoroughly in the Institute text Bank Administration (Banking III).

seem almost impossible to establish methods or forms of operation that can be adapted to the activities of all banks—large and small; country, town, and city; state and national; member and non-member; unit, chain, group, and branch. When the activities of such specialized types as savings banks and trust companies are added, the problem appears even more difficult.

A particular type of banking transaction, however, generally calls for identical treatment no matter what the size, kind, or location of the bank performing it may be. The crossroads country bank, faced with the problem of forwarding five checks to other parts of the country for payment, follows the same *general rules* as the city bank with its daily volume of a hundred thousand similar items. In the country bank the problems of personnel and equipment may be small compared with those of the metropolitan bank, but both will follow the rules that experience has shown to be most satisfactory. For example, in collecting checks in other parts of the country, both institutions have the same goal; each desires safe, prompt, and economical conversion of the items into collected balances at its institution or at a designated correspondent bank. The general rules that govern the handling of the check from its entrance into the bank through the deposit channel to its ultimate payment are the same for all institutions.

The problem of operations, then, is not one of deciding which of many principles should be followed, for the principles are well established. It is rather the application of systems, methods, equipment, and personnel in accordance with those principles and the adaptation of such systems and methods to the problems of the institution in question. In succeeding chapters it will be noticed that while there are many methods, systems, and types of equipment in use, the principles involved are the same for the large, the medium sized, and the small bank, for all types of banks, and for banks in all parts of the United States.

One more fact should be kept clearly in mind. It is not to be expected that operations once established can be continued indefinitely, since changing problems within an institution sometimes require a modification of existing systems and methods, and even, on occasion, the adoption of entirely new ones, in order to maintain the operations of the bank on an economical and efficient basis.

Questions Based on Chapter I

1. Why are banks vested with a public interest?
2. What are the purposes of banking study in the courses of the American Institute of Banking?
3. Why are bank operations important?
4. What are the principal functions of banks?
5. How are banks classified as to the type of service performed?
6. What are the principal forms of organization used by banks?
7. What is the main purpose of the Federal Deposit Insurance Corporation?
8. What are the facilities and privileges of membership in the Federal Reserve System?
9. To what extent is banking in the United States carried on by banks that are members of the Federal Reserve System?
10. Who owns the capital stock of the Federal Reserve banks?

Questions for Outside Investigation

1. Is your bank a member of the Federal Reserve System?
2. Is your bank a member of the Federal Deposit Insurance Corporation?
3. Is your bank a branch bank? a unit bank? a group bank?
4. What Federal Reserve bank facilities does your bank use daily (if it is a member bank)?
5. Does your bank have a commercial department? a savings department? a trust department?

Assignment

After studying the chart on bank control (Figure 1), make a similar chart showing the position of your own bank with regard to present controls.

CHAPTER II

BANK ORGANIZATION PROCEDURE

The Purposes of This Chapter:
1. To outline the steps involved in the organization of a bank.
2. To explain the external controls exerted upon banking and the effects of those controls.
3. To discuss the internal controls exercised over banking procedure and the sources of authority for them.
4. To enumerate the duties and responsibilities of a bank's stockholders, directors, and officers.

THE idea of organizing a bank generally originates with a small group of business men who believe that their community is capable of supporting a new institution. As in the case of other business ventures, the organizers of a bank rely upon the profit they will make—the return from the money and effort they invest—to repay them for the work and risks they assume in organizing and operating the bank. They have every reason to expect that they will realize a profit if the bank is operated on a basis of service to customers within the limits of recognized conservative management. The expectation of profit, without extraordinary risks, through service to the business and trade of the community is what motivates them in undertaking the venture.

The community may never before have had a bank, it may have grown both in population and trade to a point where the need for banking facilities is apparent, and the chances of success may be so good that the organization of a bank is the logical business move; or, even with existing facilities, the organization of another bank may seem desirable.

In the years immediately following the bank moratorium

in 1933, banks were established in many communities which in normal times had supported banks but which, because of the severity of the depression, had been deprived of banking facilities. Sizable towns that had previously supported two or three banks and entire counties or trade areas left without banking facilities by the debacle of 1931-1932 offered opportunities for the formation of new banks to take the place of those that had been swept away. The banks chartered in the United States during the period from 1933 to 1936 were almost without exception replacements in communities which in the past had demonstrated their ability to support banks and where the need for banking service still existed. It is one of the important duties of the chartering authority to discourage the organization of banks in localities where there is not sufficient business in prospect to provide adequate income for a bank.

Bank Organization Preliminaries—Whatever may be the reason for thinking that a new bank will be successful, once the organizers have decided that the project is worthy of serious action, they then proceed, at first informally, to discuss what banking services will be needed, what type of institution will best suit the requirements of their prospective customers, and what location will be most convenient for the new institution.

Overoptimistic appraisals or incomplete surveys have in the past resulted in the chartering of institutions for which there was no justification. Unwise chartering of banks is most likely to occur at times when bank deposits are much increased and money rates are higher than average. Excess deposits are very often the result of increased commodity prices, which are reflected in increased loan and discount levels.

To cite a specific example of overchartering: Several years ago a certain town in one of the western states with a population of about 1,200 had one bank. For many years the deposits in that bank grew steadily though not spectacularly. They had reached about $1,250,000 when a period of rapidly rising land and grain prices began. Land doubled in price within two years; corn, wheat, and other grains sold at nearly double their previous prices. Naturally the bank's deposits increased as a result of these unusual and (as it turned out) temporary conditions. When the bank's deposits reached the $2,000,000 mark, a second bank was organized in the belief that the increase in deposits was a permanent condition. However, within two years prices receded and deposits decreased, with the result that neither bank prospered.

Sometimes, however, steady growth or unusual circumstances result in a permanent increase in the business of a community so that additional banks may be established with profit. In recent years the opening of new oil fields in Texas, the building and operation of refineries, and the extension of bus lines and railroads as a result of the development of business have made new banks necessary in localities where previously there was little or no need for banking conveniences.

It should be noted that while, theoretically, chartering authorities have always *taken into consideration* the need for a proposed institution, today they are inclined to *insist* upon convincing proof of that need before permitting a new bank to open. In addition to securing the approval of the chartering authority, it is wise to secure the approval of the Federal Deposit Insurance Corporation. The *need* for a bank is the main consideration of the corporation, for reasons which will be made apparent in the discussion of the corporation later in the text.

The organizers of a bank often obtain preliminary information by canvassing individuals and merchants in the locality for the purpose of gaining support for the proposed bank; in this way they ascertain not only the general public's reaction to the proposed organization but also the amount of business that the bank may expect to do if it is established.

In localities where in normal times one or more banks have operated successfully, the record of those banks, particularly as to type of business, volume of deposits, and average earnings, is valuable. Such records, of course, must be considered in the light of current conditions, for it may be that, because of fundamental changes, the community no longer needs the banking services it previously required.

Coincident with this investigation, the group prepares a list of prospective stockholders, among whom are included those whose connections will be valuable in bringing to the bank business from other sources as well as their own.

When the need for a bank has been satisfactorily proved and the organizers are sure that they can raise the required or desired amount of capital, they make formal application for a charter, the first step to take in attempting to qualify under either state or national authority for the right to operate. For purposes of illustration, let us suppose that the organizers have decided to make application for a national charter.

The Application—The *application* for a national charter must be submitted to the *Comptroller of the Currency*. It sets forth the need for a bank, together with the information substantiating this assertion; it lists the names of proposed stockholders and the amount of stock each has agreed to purchase; and it gives full information regarding the general reputation and financial standing of each proposed director. In addition, it states the desired name of the new bank, the proposed location, and other pertinent data.

The name chosen must not conflict with that of any other bank operating in the locality or be such as to confuse the public. It *must* contain the word *national* and *may not,* in the case of a new bank, include the words "United States," "federal," or "reserve." If the name requested meets these requirements, it is temporarily reserved pending the Comptroller's action on the application.

The nature and scope of the services to be rendered are also included in the application—and, in fact, any other information which might be of assistance to the Comptroller in appraising the need for the bank, its probable conformance to laws and regulations, and the integrity and financial responsibility of its organizers.

Investigation and Approval—The office of the chief national bank examiner in the district in which the organizers propose to locate their bank makes a full report on the need for a new bank, its prospects for successful operation, the character of the organizers, and other matters of importance in connection with the application, so that the Comptroller may have adequate information upon which to make a decision.

If the decision is favorable, the name is reserved for an extended period of time, and the organizers are authorized to complete the remaining steps in the organization procedure.

Articles of Association—*Articles of association* are now drawn up and signed by at least five individuals. These articles contain the following information: the name and location of the bank, the names of the members of the initial board of directors (if not definitely named, their selection is at least provided for), the powers of the board of directors, the date of the regular annual meeting of the stockholders, the amount of the capital stock, its par value, and the manner in which it is divided, and provisions for amending the articles of association. In completing these articles, the organizers avail themselves of the assistance of the district examiner's office in order to be certain that they are meeting all the requirements. The articles, together with the organization certificate (signed by the same persons who signed the articles of association), are then sworn to and filed with the Comptroller.

Obtaining the Charter—After all the organization details have been completed and the necessary papers have been forwarded to Washington, the Comptroller, if he is satisfied that the laws and regulations have been fully met, issues a charter, which empowers the banking institution to begin business immediately.

Governing authorities are much more strict today in their inspection of the need for new banking facilities than they used to be. The Banking Act of 1935 granted the Federal Deposit Insurance Corporation broad powers in determining its membership, and those powers, in turn, have a very important bearing upon the chartering of banks, both state and national. The organizers of proposed banks generally consider that acceptance for membership in the Federal Deposit Insurance Corporation is a prerequisite for complete success; hence they defer applying for a charter until their membership in that organization is definitely assured.

Chartering by States—A detailed study of the bank chartering methods followed by the several states would be too lengthy to include in this course. In general, the procedure required by state authorities is similar to that required by national authorities. The care exercised in the chartering of banks, the restrictions placed upon them from the beginning of their existence, and the regulations and controls exercised over them during their entire life are in general the same for both national banks and state banks.

In Chapter I mention was made of the fact that the regulations of the Federal Reserve System and of the Federal Deposit Insurance Corporation tend to produce uniformity in banking throughout the country. Uniformity, however, is not the result of regulation alone; the trend toward uniformity is noticeable from the very day a bank is organized. Prospective organizers of banks must consider the question of membership in the Federal Reserve System and in the Federal Deposit Insurance Corporation along with other matters of policy. Therefore, they will be guided by the regulations which the new bank must follow if it is to be admitted to membership in the Federal Reserve System and in the Federal Deposit Insurance Corporation. If the organizers contemplate such memberships, they must be certain that their capital stock is sufficient to meet Federal Reserve membership requirements and that in all other matters subject to regulation by either the Federal Reserve System or the Federal Deposit Insurance Corporation they will have the approval of the governing authorities of those bodies.

There is another important factor to be considered in some states. By a provision of the Banking Act of 1935, the double liability of stockholders, after July 1, 1937, may be abolished by a national bank upon six months' public notice. Double liability has in the past been a common requirement of stockholders in both state and national banks; it made them liable, in the event of the bank's liquidation, for an amount equal to the par value of the stock they held, provided that it was found necessary to make up any deficiency to depositors or other creditors of the bank. Under the double liability requirement, a person owning a share of stock having a par value of $100 might be liable for an additional $100 if that amount was needed.

Many states have either modified or eliminated this feature, but in others double liability still holds. Some states require increased surpluses or make a stockholder responsible for additional liability only to the extent that surplus does not equal capital. Continued double liability without modification is often a major factor in the selection of a national charter in preference to a state charter. In Illinois, where the double liability rule is still in effect and where rulings on the length of time during which liability rests upon former stockholders (sometimes long after the stock has been sold to others) are severe, to say the least, only one new state bank was chartered in the three-year period from 1933 to 1936 as against seventy national banks. Among those granted national charters were several state banks which relinquished their state charters for that purpose.

Completion of Opening Plans—After obtaining a charter, the organizers of a bank must next establish it as a going concern. While a great many tentative arrangements can be made pending the granting of the charter, there will still be many details to be worked out. In transforming the bank from an idea into an actuality, all those concerned must cooperate to the fullest extent.

A meeting of the stockholders must be held for the adoption of by-laws. The by-laws must of course be consistent with the articles of association and must be in conformity with banking laws; they should reflect the general policy of the bank and the scope of its activities. To be certain that the by-laws are in regular and proper form, stockholders should employ an attorney skilled in banking law.

After the adoption of by-laws, the stockholders proceed to select from among their number the members of the board of directors.

The board of directors then meets to select the officers of the bank, to designate their duties beyond the general outlines contained in the by-laws, to arrange for banking quarters, to authorize the purchase and installation of equipment, and to approve other major expenditures. The entire board and the committees selected from among its members work closely with the officers in making decisions and in mapping out the necessary lines of action.

The essential policies are formulated by the board of directors at the very outset, to serve as guides to the officers and employees. Upon the operating officers and staff rests the burden of creating an organization that will function smoothly and effectively. This task involves a multitude of details, some of wide application and others of only departmental importance; but all must be well executed if the organization is adequately to serve its purpose.

The banking quarters must be arranged to accommodate conveniently the business anticipated, and suitable space must be assigned to departments. Cages, counters, and other equipment must be installed; vaults and protective devices must be set up and thoroughly tested; and furniture and office supplies must be purchased.

Bank layouts are frequently planned in advance by the use of scale floor plans. Each piece of furniture and equipment is drawn to scale and fitted on this floor plan so that the actual installations may be effective. In the case of new bank buildings (and remodeled quarters for that matter), the board of directors may employ specially trained architects and firms that specialize in bank planning. By virtue of knowledge and experience, they are able to make the best possible use of the space available. Responsibility for the layout is usually assigned to one of the bank's officers, who may, if necessary, be assisted by a committee of the board of directors. Such centralization of responsibility has been found very satisfactory.

The division of the work of the new bank into departments or sections, the selection of equipment, the adoption and printing of forms, the planning of systems and methods of handling banking transactions—these and many other matters must be settled before the bank is ready for business. Many of them are management problems, others operating problems.

The hiring of a trained personnel is another task that requires detailed care and attention, for the more efficient the staff is at the start, the fewer will be the delays and difficulties even though these are inevitable in a new organization.

The problem of operations in the early life of an institution is one of almost constant change. However accurate the estimates as to the amount and nature of the contemplated business may seem to be, the actual results may be very different; hence those charged with the responsibility for operations must continually revise and adjust their methods as needs change and must be prepared to adopt entirely new ones on short notice. As the activities of the institution gradually take definite shape, more permanent plans can be adopted.

General Powers of Banks—Among the important general powers of banks are:

1. The right to receive deposits and to pay interest on them, subject to the limitations imposed by law
2. The right to accept drafts and bills of exchange arising out of the importation, exportation, and domestic shipment of goods, and to accept drafts and bills for creating dollar exchange
3. The right to hold sufficient real estate for the transaction of business
4. The right to take title to real estate as security for debts previously contracted
5. The power to make loans on improved real estate within the limits prescribed by banking law
6. The power to act as trustee, executor, administrator, or guardian of estates and to act as trustee, registrar, agent, and paying agent for corporations (if qualified to exercise trust powers)
7. The right to own an interest (within prescribed limits) in a company in the safe deposit business

8. The right to operate domestic branches, as permitted by law

9. The right to operate foreign branches if authorized by the Board of Governors of the Federal Reserve System to do so (in the case of a member bank)

10. The right to make commercial loans and secured loans, subject to the general limitations as to total advances to any single borrower in proportion to capital and surplus, and subject to the collateral regulations provided by law

11. The right to invest in various kinds of bonds and other obligations within the limits (particularly in the case of savings banks) of certain legal standards of eligibility.

To these powers should be added various others that arise out of membership in the Federal Reserve System and in the Federal Deposit Insurance Corporation.

Bank Control—Because of the broad effect of banking upon the public interest, special banking laws and regulations are in effect both nationally and in each of the forty-eight states. These laws are not mere legal guides or combinations of broad regulations, as in the case of laws applicable to other types of business; on the contrary, they are specific, and strict compliance with their provisions is required. The control of banks by banking laws and regulations is an *external control* in contrast to the *internal control* exercised by each bank's own stockholders, directors, and officers. External control establishes general regulations and places general limitations upon the conduct of banking, while internal control particularizes those regulations and limitations to the individual institution and adds others. The internal or voluntary controls which banks impose upon themselves have a cumulative effect which eventually becomes a factor in banking generally. A clear conception of both external and internal bank control is essential to the operating man, for operations must directly reflect both of these sources of control in actual practice. Systems, methods, and operation activities must all be consistent with external controls and, in addition, must conform to the internal or voluntary restrictions placed upon the institution by its stockholders, directors, and officers.

Many external controls have developed from internal controls; that is, many regulations and laws are directly the result of the voluntary practices of banks. Just as the present status and use of negotiable instruments and the laws regulating them are the result of the gradual development of such instruments over a long period of time (beginning with the initial and limited use of orders and promises to pay and becoming more complicated through custom and usage), so are many of the present banking laws the outgrowth of custom and usage based on experience. These customary procedures became crystallized, over a period of time, into general banking practice and finally were adopted as law.

A major criticism of law making for banks has been that too often those who make the laws do not thoroughly understand banking procedure and so do not appreciate the advantages that experience and knowledge of banking facts will bring. In other instances, national and state authorities have cooperated with the well organized legislative committees of bankers associations, such as the American Bankers Association and many state associations, in producing satisfactory legislation. In this way the practical experience of banks and bankers can be incorporated in laws and regulations.

External Control—The study of external control is not confined to any particular phase of banking study. The effects of the various external controls exercised over banking are as significant in the field of economics as in the field of money and banking; both are directly affected by the status of that large branch of finance, commercial banking. The effects of external control on bank management are seen in the policies adopted by banking institutions—indeed, in the form of organization of the individual banks. External control also determines the systems, methods, and general procedure of bank organization and operation.

For the purposes of this study, external control may be classified as follows:

1. Chartering or organization—laws and regulations applying to the chartering of banks; laws and regulations applying to membership in the Federal Reserve System and in the Federal Deposit Insurance Corporation
2. Laws and regulations governing the bank after chartering—minimum reserves against deposits; maximum loans to one customer; duties and liabilities of stockholders, directors, and officers
3. Examination privilege
4. Statement calls and reports
5. Special laws or regulations, such as state laws governing corporate trust activities.

Chartering and Membership Requirements—In addition to the national banking laws, there are the laws of the various states relating to the chartering of banks. Certain requirements common to all states must be met by the organizers of a proposed bank before they open for business. In each state the duty of enforcing these requirements is delegated to some one official. In some states this official is designated as the "superintendent of banks"; in others he has the title of "state banking commissioner" or "state examiner," or the duties may be assigned to some other officer—the state auditor, for example. This state supervisory official often is given wide latitude, beyond the technical requirements that may prevail, for the exercise of his own judgment in passing upon applications for bank charters.

Among the chartering requirements are some which are common to almost all the states. Practically all the states have minimum capital stock requirements; that is, they require that all banks within their jurisdiction must have at least a designated amount of capital stock. This minimum requirement for capitalization is sometimes a set minimum and sometimes a varying amount graduated according to the population of the community in which the bank is to be located.

A compilation of state chartering requirements appeared in the July 1936 issue of the Bankers Monthly. Many interesting comparisons may be made from this data, one of which shows the differences in the capital requirements of the forty-eight states. A brief summary follows.

Four states have no legal minimum capitalization.

Four states have a minimum capitalization requirement of $10,000.

Three states have a minimum of $15,000.

Four states have a minimum of $20,000.

Twenty-two states have a minimum of $25,000.

One state has a minimum of $30,000.

One state has a minimum of $35,000.

Eight states have a minimum of $50,000.

One state has a minimum of $100,000.

Seven of the forty-eight states have no graduated scale of capital requirements, while the remaining forty-one have varying requirements depending on the size of the town or city in which the bank is to be located.

Minimum capital requirements on a graduated scale have long been a part of chartering procedure in the national banking system. At present the minimum required is $50,000 for banks located in towns with a population of 6,000 or less; in towns with a population of from 6,000 to 50,000, the minimum is $100,000; in cities of 50,000 and over, the minimum is $200,000.

The graduated scale of state requirements is similar. In North Carolina, for example, banks located in towns with a population of 3,000 or less must have a capital of at least $25,000; in towns with a population of from 3,000 to 10,000, the minimum is $30,000; in cities with a population of from 10,000 to 25,000, the minimum is $50,000; and in cities with a population above 25,000, the minimum is $100,000.

Another common requirement is that of a minimum surplus account, either to be created at the time of the chartering of the bank or to be built up from earnings (or both). The minimum surplus requirement is stated in terms of its proportion to a bank's capital stock. The survey made by the Bankers Monthly shows that nine states have no minimum surplus requirement in proportion to capital stock, one has a 5% requirement, four states have a 10% requirement, fifteen states require 20% to 25%, and so on up to a surplus equal to the capital stock. Vermont requires a surplus equal to 10% of deposits. Colorado requires capital plus surplus to be at least 10% of the average daily deposits during the preceding year. The state of Connecticut requires an initial surplus equal to 100% of capital stock, which is the largest initial surplus requirement set up by any state.

National banks are required to apply a portion of earnings to surplus each half year until surplus equals the amount of capital. Eleven states require that a portion of earnings be added to surplus until a specified surplus figure is reached. These proportions vary from 10% to 50% of earnings, and the desired surplus ranges from 20% to 100% of capital.

State laws generally prohibit the payment of any fee or commission in connection with the sale of an original issue of bank stock, and penalties are set for violation of this rule. State laws also require that the capital stock of a bank be paid for in cash or its equivalent either at the time of the opening of the bank or within a specified time shortly thereafter.

In many states the supervisory authority or his representatives must investigate the character and standing of the proposed organizers before giving official approval. The experience and record of the proposed directors and officers are often included in this appraisal.

Major considerations in some states are the need for the proposed bank and its probable success. The tendency today is toward more thorough investigation of one or both of these factors.

In each state some forms of organization are permitted and others prohibited, either by statute or by policy and practice. Thus, in some states private commercial banks are permitted to operate, while in other states they are not; in some states branch banking is permitted, but in others it is prohibited.

Both the Federal Reserve System and the Federal Deposit Insurance Corporation have certain powers which they may exercise in connection with the acceptance or rejection of applications for membership. These powers should be added to those of state and national chartering authorities in summing up the external controls exercised over banks. Briefly, the Federal Deposit Insurance Corporation has the right of investigation and approval for membership in the corporation. The Board of Governors of the Federal Reserve System, in acting upon an application of a state bank for membership in the system, gives special consideration to:

1. The financial history and condition of the applicant bank
2. The general character of the bank's management
3. The adequacy of its capital structure
4. Future prospects for earnings
5. The needs of the community in which the bank is located
6. Whether the corporate powers of the bank are consistent with the purposes of the Federal Reserve Act.

Upon its acceptance as a member, a state bank must subscribe to the capital stock of the Federal Reserve bank of its district (as described in Chapter I). Other regulations and rules assumed with membership are described next.

Laws and Regulations Governing a Bank after Chartering —When the laws and regulations which apply to the chartering of a bank have been complied with, the new bank at once becomes subject to the laws and regulations that will govern its major activities during its entire existence. Most important of these is the series of laws and regulations, both state and national, governing the minimum reserves to be maintained against both demand deposits and time deposits. These reserves must be in the form of either cash or balances with acceptable depositories.

Reserve requirements are expressed in terms of a percentage of the deposits—demand or time. A member bank must carry its entire reserves as a deposit with the Federal Reserve bank of the district in which it is located. The state regulations apply chiefly to banks that are not members of the Federal Reserve System; in the case of state member banks, the reserve regulations of the Federal Reserve System are generally acceptable also to state banking authorities unless the laws of a particular state require strict compliance with its reserve regulations. In many states no condition is placed upon the substitution of Federal Reserve requirements for state requirements; therefore, when a state bank in such a state becomes a member of the Federal Reserve System, the reserve requirements of the system are considered sufficient to comply with the state law. The reserve regulations of the Federal Reserve System apply to all national banks as a matter of course.

The maximum amount that may be loaned to any one borrower, in proportion to the bank's capital, is generally established by law. This restriction recognizes the law of probability as applied to bank loans. If *one-third* of the capital and surplus of a bank is loaned to a single borrower and that borrower becomes financially involved, the loss to the bank may affect its solvency. If the maximum in proportion to capital and surplus that can be loaned is 10% (as provided in the national banking laws), then the maximum loss through insolvency of the borrower will be only *one-tenth* of total capital and surplus instead of *one-third*. Moreover, by the law of probability, *three* borrowers, each with loans of *one-tenth* of capital and surplus, are much less likely to become involved to the same extent as *one* borrower owing *one-third* of capital and surplus. The subject of *diversification,* both in amounts and in kinds of loans, is covered in the course in Bank Administration (Banking III).

Some of the duties and liabilities of directors and officers are often specified in the laws and regulations. Certain responsibilities are mandatory, and severe penalties for their violation are provided. These duties are set forth in the banking laws and regulations in order that there may be no misunderstanding on the part of a bank's officers and directors as to their individual responsibilities. For example, a sworn statement of a bank's condition must be submitted to the supervising authority upon demand. The laws and regulations covering this provision designate the officers who must certify to the statement; in addition, two or more directors are generally required to swear to the correctness of the statement. These officers and directors are then held strictly accountable for any false representations contained in the sworn statement.

The number of shares that a stockholder must own in order to qualify as a director is often specified by law. It is only reasonable to expect that a director who has a financial interest of some consequence in the bank through the ownership of stock will perform his duties more conscientiously than one who has little financial interest. For this reason, banking laws generally require that directors must own a designated minimum amount of stock and that this stock must be owned outright—not pledged to secure a loan or only partially paid for. In some states the stock certificate, as evidence that this requirement has been met, must be filed with the cashier or treasurer of the bank.

At times the result at which an existing law or regulation aims may better be achieved by the substitution of some other method of regulation. A law which for many years was binding upon both state banks and national banks was the law providing for the double liability of stockholders. This double liability, as already stated, has been eliminated for stockholders of national banks as of July 1, 1937 and has either been eliminated or modified by many states. In place of double liability, the tendency is toward the requirement of a larger surplus as a protection for depositors.

Banking laws definitely specify what can and what cannot be done by banks and establish the regulatory powers to be exercised by the proper authorities in enforcing the laws. Regulations issued by supervising authorities have the full force of law. There are many regulations in force, ranging from those which inaugurate major policy changes to those which merely clarify banking laws. The Banking Act of 1935 empowered the Comptroller of the Currency to issue regulations regarding the investments of member banks. In accordance with this power, the Comptroller issued detailed regulations applying to all securities purchased by member banks for their investment accounts. This regulation, which went into effect February 15, 1936, is an example of the inauguration of a major banking policy by regulation.

From time to time existing banking laws are amended, or new banking laws are enacted, and banks must conform to the major or minor changes made. The Banking Act of 1933 prohibited (with minor exceptions) the payment by member banks of interest on demand balances. The same act limited the interest to be paid on time deposits to the rates established from time to time by the governing body of the Federal Reserve System.[1] The Banking Act of 1935 further clarified these requirements by directing that the governing bodies of the Federal Reserve System and the Federal Deposit Insurance Corporation should classify and define time accounts and demand accounts.

The Examination Privilege—Another important control over banking provided by both national and state laws is the examination of banks by representatives of the supervising authorities. The purpose of an examination is threefold: (1) to ascertain the bank's solvency or insolvency; (2) to ascertain whether it is violating any of the banking laws; and (3) to discover and correct errors in management or operation which, if not checked, might lead to disastrous results. These examinations are made at least twice a year and more frequently if special circumstances require it. Often the examining force is divided into groups according to districts.

National banks are subject to examination by representatives of the Comptroller of the Currency. The country is divided into districts, each under the direction of a chief national bank examiner. The examination reports are forwarded to the Comptroller's office, where they are reviewed. A copy of the report is sent to the board of directors of the examined bank and must be formally acknowledged. As a result of the examination, the Comptroller frequently makes suggestions and recommendations to the bank. If unsatisfactory conditions are not corrected in due time, action is taken by the Comptroller's office to enforce compliance with the recommendations made. Recent amendments to the National Bank Act provide that officers or directors who persist in

---

[1] See Table IV of Appendix for changes since November, 1933.

unsafe and unsound practices may be removed by the Board of Governors of the Federal Reserve System. State examination procedure is much the same as that of the national supervising authorities.

Both the Federal Reserve System and the Federal Deposit Insurance Corporation have the right to examine their members. By mutual agreement among the various bank examining authorities—national (or state), Federal Reserve, and Federal Deposit Insurance—the examination of one authority is often accepted by the others, a copy of the examination report being forwarded to each authority entitled to receive it; or, in the case of state member banks, a joint examination is made.

Statement Calls and Reports—The supervising authority is required to call for sworn statements of condition. The number and frequency of these "calls" are often established by law. The procedure followed in connection with the statement call and the significance of the items appearing in the statement of condition will be discussed in some detail in a subsequent chapter. Other reports (such as earnings reports) are also required by law.

Special Laws and Regulations—To do more than touch briefly upon the laws and regulations of banking would be to enter the field of banking law, which is a subject for study in itself. Besides the numerous general laws and regulations that apply to commercial banking, there are laws and regulations that apply to specific functions or departments. The investment of trust funds and in some states the investment of savings funds are regulated by law; the conditions under which trust departments may be operated by commercial banks are specified by law. These special laws and regulations are the subject of careful consideration from the standpoint of both bank management and bank operations.

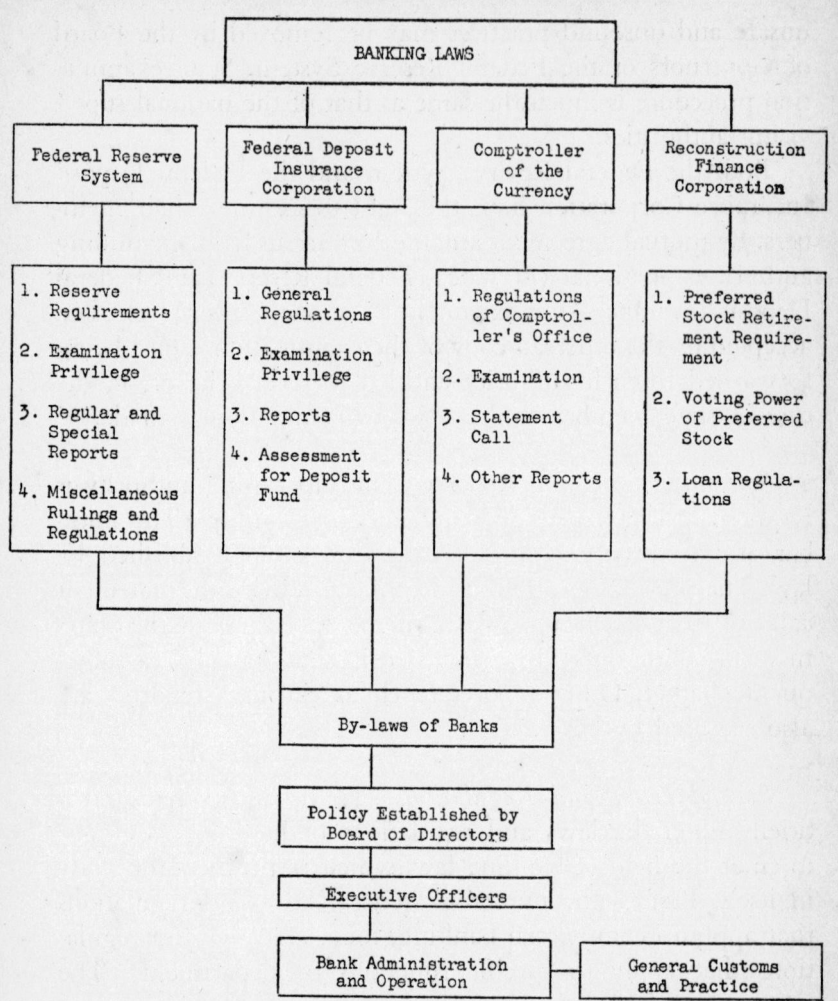

FIGURE 3. EXTERNAL CONTROL OF NATIONAL BANKS

External control, then, begins with the first step taken in the organization of a bank and governs its entire life. External control is exercised even in the liquidation of a bank and

BANK ORGANIZATION PROCEDURE

continues to be exercised until the last obligation of the bank is fulfilled as well as may be under the circumstances. (The chart reproduced as Figure 3 shows the general external controls which are applied to national banks.) A chart showing the principal bank supervisory relationships taken from the Twenty-Fifth Annual Report of the Board of Governors of the Federal Reserve System appears in the Appendix.

Internal Control—Internal control, also, begins with the formation of the bank, for it is the organizers who decide on the type of bank (whether commercial, savings, or trust) and on the form of organization (unit, branch, or chain) within the limits permitted by law. These general decisions are set forth in the by-laws of the bank, together with a statement of the bank's objectives, the provisions for stockholders' meetings, a list of the members of the first board of directors, a statement of the general duties of the officers, and similar matters. The stockholders exercise internal control in a *direct* way by their authority to approve or disapprove major changes. Changes in capitalization, proposed mergers with other institutions, and added functions or departments are all matters of internal control that ordinarily require the approval of the stockholders. Indirectly, the stockholders also have a part in the formulation of the bank's policies, for it is they who elect the board of directors, and the board in turn manages the bank. The election of directors is held at the annual stockholders' meeting, and the stockholders either approve the directors individually by reelecting them to the board or disapprove them by electing others to fill their places.

Executive Control—While some of the duties of the officers are designated in the by-laws (and of course legal limitations apply in any case), most of their duties are assigned or delegated by the board of directors. The *board of directors* elects the officers, who hold their positions subject to the board, for the board can terminate an officer's employment at any time. The extent of the board's internal control is evident in all the major activities of the bank—loans, investments, trust activities, operations, and so on.

The *officers,* by virtue of the powers granted them by the board of directors, determine policies and actions of a specific nature, and they, in turn, delegate many of their duties and responsibilities to department managers and other employees. A general summary of the duties and responsibilities commonly assigned to bank officers is given later in the chapter.

Department managers establish policies and supervise activities which apply to their particular department and which conform to the general policies of the bank already established. Department managers are responsible for operating procedure, and upon their intelligent and careful analysis of departmental problems and upon their use of methods, personnel, and equipment depend the successful operation of the department as a unit and the bank's general operations.

Effect of Clearing House and Other Associations upon Internal Control—Banks cooperate to a large extent with other banks through *voluntary associations.* These voluntary associations, not provided for by banking law, exercise a very important control over the policies and operations of banks, for having agreed to abide by the rules or having adopted the suggestions of such an association, the individual bank considers faithful compliance with those rules or suggestions as important as faithful compliance with its own internal regulations. The beneficial effects of the adoption of clearing house association rules will be shown in Chapter V.

National and state bankers associations exist for the purpose of promoting activities or agreements that will benefit the banks individually and the banking system as a whole.

The American Bankers Association—The American Bankers Association plays a major role in the conduct of banking in the United States. Through the activities of its several divisions, departments, commissions, committees, and sections, it promotes better banking, wages unceasing war against the menace of bank robbery and fraud, encourages clearing house association activities, and studies problems pertaining to state banks, national banks, trust companies, and savings banks. Through the American Institute of Banking, its educational section, a knowledge of the theory and practice of banking is made available to bank employees. The work of the Institute, its support by the parent organization, and its contacts with banking problems, all combine to provide courses of study in the field of banking that are not duplicated by any other educational institution or system.

By means of its official publications and through annual meetings and special meetings, the American Bankers Association informs its members of important and current phases of banking, obtains the opinions of individual bankers, and compiles and distributes to its members the results of its study of banking problems. In short, the Association aims to foster any constructive activity that will improve American banking or assist individual banks and bankers.

The Association of Reserve City Bankers—Under the National Bank Act certain cities were designated as reserve cities, and banks in other localities kept their reserve funds on deposit in banks in those cities. The problems peculiar to reserve banks are the chief concern of an association known as The Association of Reserve City Bankers. This association has done excellent work in connection with the study of monetary and management problems and banking practices.

State Associations—State bankers associations concentrate

their efforts on the problems of their members within the state. Their activities are so many and varied that it is impossible to attempt a discussion of them in this course. One of the most impressive activities of state associations in the past few years has been the war they have diligently waged against bank robbery. The results which they have obtained through voluntary cooperation in fighting this menace are a tribute to the effectiveness of bankers associations in providing protection which sometimes cannot be obtained in any other way.

Special Associations—One of the most important special associations which supplement the work of bankers associations is the Robert Morris Associates. This association devotes its efforts to the study of credits and to the voluntary adoption by its members of a code of ethics covering bank credit policies and actions.

Another important special association is the Financial Advertisers Association, which has as its aim the betterment of advertising, publicity, new business methods, and public relations. Included in its membership are commercial banks, savings banks, trust companies, investment houses, building and loan associations, advertising agencies, and financial publications.

Other special associations, such as auditing associations, savings associations, trust associations, and safe deposit company associations—whether they are national, state, or local—make similarly important contributions to constructive control through the voluntary cooperation of their members.

The benefits to be derived from and the cost of membership in these various associations, as far as the individual bank is concerned, are subjects for bank management and are discussed in detail in Banking III.

A typical chart of the internal control of a bank is shown in Figure 4.

BANK ORGANIZATION PROCEDURE

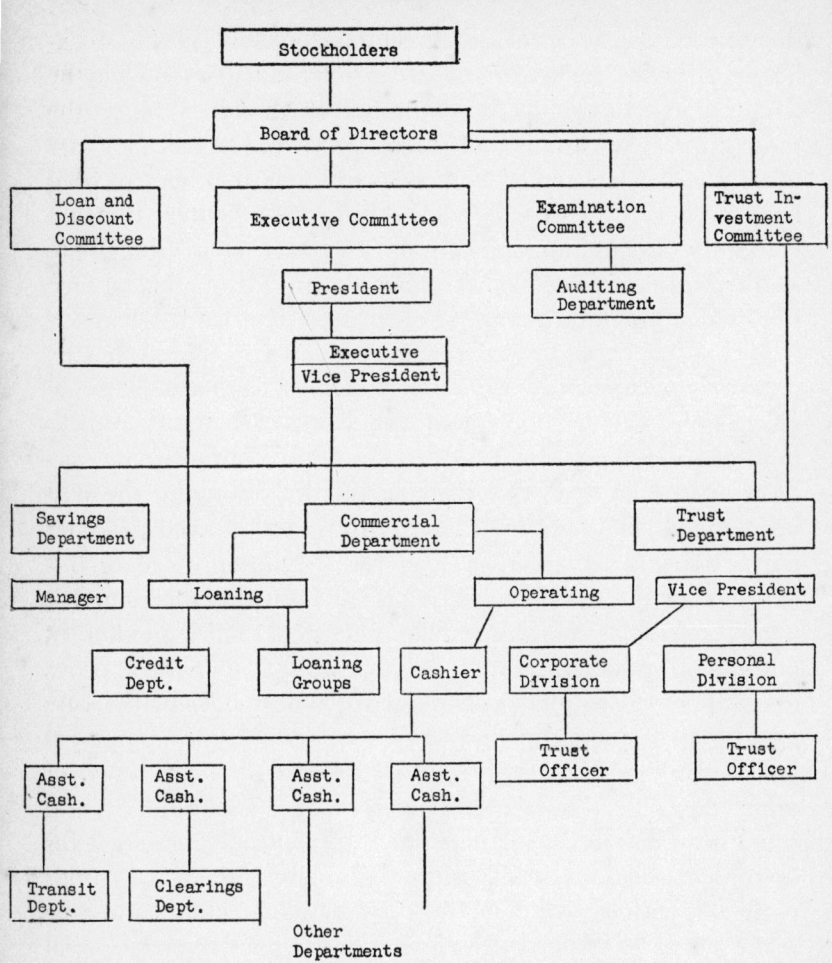

FIGURE 4. INTERNAL CONTROL

The Stockholders—The stockholders are the owners of the bank and, in the event of liquidation, are entitled to share in the net assets in proportion to the number of shares they own; the stockholders are also entitled to share in the profits in like proportion when those profits are distributed in the form of dividends by the board of directors. As owners, the stockholders provide for the *management* of the bank through the selection of certain of their number as directors. Since the number of stockholders is often large and since they are usually widely scattered, it is not practicable for them to hold frequent meetings to pass on the important matters that are constantly arising, and as a group they are not in position to keep closely in touch with the bank's current affairs. In fact, many stockholders prefer to take no active part whatever, regarding their holdings as an investment to be protected by others.

The by-laws provide for an annual meeting of the stockholders for the purpose of electing the directors for the succeeding year. A report of the progress made during the past year and of prospects for the coming year, as well as other matters of importance that must receive the approval or disapproval of the stockholders, is presented at this meeting.

Various occasions arise when the stockholders, either in regular or special meetings, must be called upon to approve or disapprove actions contemplated by the bank. In the case of a proposed consolidation with another institution, for example, the details are generally arranged for by the board of directors, subject to the approval of the stockholders, and action on the proposal is taken at a special meeting called for that purpose. Similarly, any changes in the nature of the bank's more important operations or in its capital structure must be approved by the stockholders at either a regular or a special meeting.

While the stockholders as a group are not active in the affairs of a bank, those owning large blocks of stock keep themselves informed on its affairs, often by serving as directors or officers. Until a few years ago, bank stocks were not actively traded, and the roster of a bank's stockholders showed little change from year to year. Although the boom period in the late 1920's brought wider distribution of bank stocks and more active trading, the tendency at present is again toward fewer changes in stockholder lists.

The Board of Directors—*The board of directors of a bank is charged with the responsibility of determining policies for the conduct of the bank's business.* The policies formulated by the board are, of course, supplementary to the requirements imposed by law and to those set forth in the bank's by-laws; they may be changed from time to time as modifications are deemed necessary because of changed conditions. In addition to establishing the bank's policies, the board of directors *selects the bank's officers* and thus designates the individuals who are actually to put the policies into operation.

The by-laws of the bank usually prescribe the general duties of the various officers, but the board of directors outlines those duties more specifically and may confer upon the officers certain powers that are ordinarily exercised by the directors themselves.

Having established the bank's policies and selected its official personnel, the board of directors is then responsible for seeing that the policies are properly executed.

Since the board is generally composed of men who have their own business to conduct and hence can devote only a part of their time to the bank's affairs, a division of responsibility is essential. Thus the directors function not only as a unit but individually as well through the board committees. Committees composed of board members are appointed to see that certain policies adopted by the board are carried out. The committees report to the board as a whole. In practice, the board of directors of a bank meets once a month upon a regular date (often the second Tuesday in the month), and the appointed committees meet regularly at more frequent intervals.

Although committees may be appointed for any number of purposes, at least three problems of management are so generally present that the committees to which they are assigned may be considered permanent.

The *executive committee* works closely with the bank's executive officers and is responsible for broad managerial policies and actions.

Loans, discounts, and investments constitute the work of the *discount committee*. Especially large loans or investments contemplated by the officers are often subject to the approval of the discount committee and are then referred to the entire board of directors for final decision.

The *examination committee* works with the auditing department to insure proper protective accounting and operation. Department examinations and reports, with suggested changes for the improvement of accounting practices and methods, are made by this committee, and, when necessary, they are referred to the entire board.

Other committees operate on either a permanent or a temporary basis as conditions warrant. Such problems as extensive alterations and consideration of new quarters for the bank are referred to a *building committee,* which is usually temporary. If the bank has a trust department, a separate *trust investment committee* passes on suggested investments and is included among the permanent committees.

The board of directors represents the stockholders and is responsible to them for the proper conduct of the institution. The board is also responsible to the governing authorities and to the depositors for the proper execution of its duties.

The number of directors varies with the size of the institution, with its policies, and with the scope of its operations. According to the present requirement for Federal Reserve member banks, the number shall not be less than five nor more than twenty-five. Less than the minimum would presumably be inadequate; more than the maximum would be unwieldy.

The position of the board of directors as the bank's managing body is frequently emphasized by court decisions involving the powers or responsibilities of officers and directors. A certain decision in the state of New York clearly indicated the position of the board of directors. The case in point arose out of guaranties made by the senior executives of certain banks in New York City on behalf of their institutions. These were guaranties of the deposit liability of a local bank and were made in an endeavor to quiet public apprehension toward that bank. The decision to guarantee the deposits was admittedly made at a time of great stress, under circumstances which demanded quick action, and during the depression when changes were sudden and drastic. The court ruled, however, that regardless of the obviously constructive intentions of those senior bank executives and regardless of the emergency that prevailed, the obligation of guaranty could be assumed by a bank only through specific and formal action on the part of its board of directors in a duly called and conducted meeting.

The Officers and Their Duties—While an official title generally conveys some idea of the duties of the officer who holds that title, it is not necessarily true that a particular title carries with it the same duties in all banking institutions, for the duties of an officer are determined by a bank's by-laws and by its board of directors. Thus, a cashier in one institution may be a loaning officer, although generally the duties of cashier are along operating lines. The following brief summary of official duties is merely an indication of the customary division of work and responsibility; the duties mentioned are commonly, though not necessarily, assigned to the officers named.

The *president* of a bank is its senior executive officer, and problems of major importance in connection with the fulfilment of policies established by the board of directors come before him; he is a member and often chairman of the board and presents to it such matters as may require action. In recent years a new title has come into use—that of *executive vice president*. That officer ordinarily works directly under the president and performs the same general duties as the president.

The *vice presidents* act as senior department executives or as loaning officers. The trust department, for example, ordinarily is under the supervision of a vice president charged with the management of that division of the bank. Vice presidents in the commercial department of the bank make loans, sign contracts on behalf of the bank, and pass upon matters having to do with commercial accounts. The commercial accounts of a bank often are divided among the vice presidents; that is, each vice president has a certain number of accounts, both borrowing and non-borrowing, under his direction, and his close contact with them enables both the customers and the bank to be served to the fullest extent.

The *assistant vice presidents* work under the vice presidents, assisting them in loaning activities and other duties.

The *cashier* of a bank, often titled vice president and cashier, is the operating head. He is responsible for the efficient coordination of methods, equipment, space, and personnel, to the end that maximum efficiency in operation may at all times be maintained. The cashier supervises these various activities through junior officers and department heads. The cashier, by law, has a very definite responsibility, for he is the official designated to maintain custody and control of the bank's assets. His name and title are used in many transactions between banks and customers—and often on receipts issued by the bank.

The *assistant cashiers* work directly under the cashier. Particular departments are often assigned to them, such as the transit department or the clearings department. An assistant cashier supervises the department of which he is in charge, approving or disapproving important departmental matters. Assistant cashiers also act as "counter" men; in this capacity they approve new accounts, pass upon requests for the cashing of checks, handle signature changes and account authorizations and other matters needing official consideration.

The *secretary* is principally concerned with the affairs of the bank as a whole; he acts as recorder in the board meetings, signs documents pertaining to the bank, and keeps the records of the stockholders' meetings. In trust companies the titles "treasurer" and "assistant treasurer" are often used instead of "cashier" and "assistant cashier."

The *comptrollers* and *auditors* in a commercial bank are also important and necessary officers. The duties of the auditor will be discussed in connection with the auditing department under the subject of bank accounting; the comptroller's duties will be considered in the discussion of methods and systems of bank operations.

Each department performing a major function of banking, such as the trust department or the savings department, has its own officers who have duties peculiar to the work of that department. In the trust department there are *trust officers, assistant trust officers,* and *assistant secretaries,* in addition to the vice presidents who are assigned to the department. The duties of these officers will be described in a later chapter in connection with a discussion of the work of these special departments.

The officers in any division, such as the commercial department, ordinarily confine their activities to their own division, even though they have general powers to bind the bank by contract. While the powers that may be exercised by a given officer are determined by the bank's by-laws and by its board of directors, custom dictates the scope of his activity as well. For example, trust matters are not referred to commercial department officers, and commercial department decisions are not made by trust officers.

Each bank has its own allocation of powers and responsibilities, varying with the relative importance of the facilities provided. For an understanding of the manner in which these responsibilities are allocated and controlled, the typical internal control chart (Figure 4) will be found useful.

Operating Coordination—A general picture of the position of banks in relation to business, the types and kinds of banks, the external and internal controls, the procedure in establishing a bank, and some of the general powers, duties, and responsibilities of a bank's stockholders, directors, and officers have now been considered. Before proceeding to study how the various banking functions are performed through bank operations, the student should have a clear idea of the importance of operations and the duties of the various departments and individuals.

The orderly performance of operations depends upon (1) the efficient organization and operation of each department and (2) the cooperation of the various departments with one another. The fullest contribution of the receiving teller department to operating efficiency depends quite as much on its satisfactory contacts with the distribution or clearings department, the bookkeeping department, and the transit department as on its own efficiency in receiving deposits. For this reason, whenever a revision of methods within a department is contemplated, adjustments between that department and other departments, or revisions within other departments, must be considered and made if necessary.

Each bank has informal or formal time limits governing

work which must pass from one department to another in the course of the day. In small organizations the workers in one department come into such close contact with those in other departments that it is apparent to each individual that if he is delinquent in performing his duties, some one else will be inconvenienced. In larger organizations, the size of departments, the distances between them, and the fact that many workers within a given department have no contact with those in other departments all combine to make necessary some method of impressing upon them the interdependence of the work of the various departments.

One way to accomplish this correlation of departments is by a schedule of "deadlines," or time limits, at which point certain work must be completed by one department and ready for the next. One bank posts in a prominent place in each department a large chart showing the *time schedule of operations*. This chart is within the view of all workers and serves as a constant reminder of the necessity of their dispatching their duties promptly. Such a chart is illustrated in Figure 5.

According to the set-up of this chart, the division of the mail starts the day's work at 8:00 a.m. Incoming mail is sorted, and the mail deposits are then turned over to a group of clerks for verification and further sorting. Immediately after the work of the department starts, the mail deposits are set aside and the sorting and proving group finds a first "run" or batch of deposits ready for it at 8:30 a.m. From then on until the deadline at 9:30 a.m., these mail deposits are steadily given to the proving group. By 10:15 a.m. all mail deposits must be proved and sorted, totals must be verified, and the work must be in the hands of the clearings department for inclusion in the daily exchange, which takes place at 10:30 a.m. The checks drawn on the bank itself must be in the bookkeeping department for the morning posting, and the transit checks must reach that department on time.

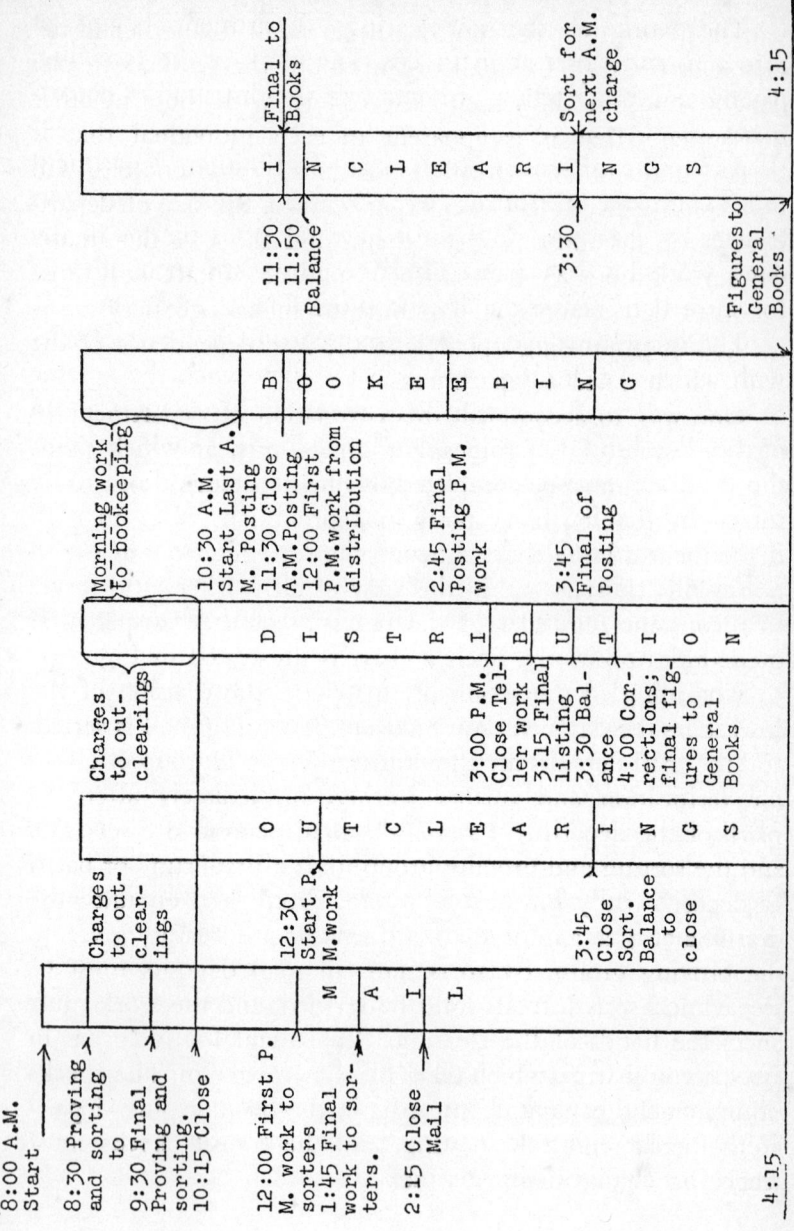

FIGURE 5. TIME SCHEDULE OF OPERATIONS

The work of the out-clearings department begins at 8:30 a.m. and closes at 10:15 a.m. The work of the receiving, paying, and other tellers goes through the distribution department.

As to the afternoon work, the distribution department must complete all sorting by 3:00 p.m., must balance its batches by 3:30 p.m., and must have the total figures of the day's work by 3:45 p.m.; fifteen minutes are then allowed for corrections before the afternoon deadline at 4:00 p.m.

The interesting part of this time schedule is the regularity with which the deadlines are met. On days when the volume of work is less than usual, departments finish slightly ahead of the time limit. On days when the volume of work is large, the deadlines may be slightly exceeded, but delays are minimized by the flexibility of personnel and by the provisions made for extra temporary help when needed. Over a period of a year, the operations of this bank conformed so surprisingly to these time limits that the chart is considered an accurate guide for the staff.

The interdependence of departments is shown by the following incident. A certain bank recently found it necessary to modernize its bookkeeping department. It installed new and faster bookkeeping machines which increased the number of checks posted per hour by approximately 18%. It was obvious that the checks would have to go to the bookkeeping department in sufficient and steady volume if full advantage was to be taken of the increased speed.

After careful consideration, the force in the distribution department was increased by the addition of two clerks. This increased the rate of transfer of items from that source to the bookkeeping department. Prior to the installation of the new equipment, the work from the in-clearings group had come to the bookkeeping department faster than it could be posted; hence no changes were needed to maintain an efficient relationship between the in-clearings department and the bookkeeping department under the new system. It was found necessary for one mail teller to start an hour earlier each day in order to keep up with the increased speed required of items going from the mail department to the bookkeeping department. Minor adjustments were also made in other interdepartmental contacts.

The net result of the study and preparation made before the new bookkeeping equipment was installed was that the schedule of operations worked not only as smoothly and orderly as before but also at an accelerated speed and with a substantial saving in cost.

Questions Based on Chapter II

1. Describe the first step to be taken in the organization of a bank.
2. What use is made of the application for a charter?
3. Outline the main requirements for a charter.
4. What are the general powers of a bank?
5. In what ways are banks controlled?
6. What are the principal methods of bank control exercised by supervising authorities?
7. Who are the owners of a bank?
8. Who manages the bank and establishes its policies?
9. Name the principal banking associations, and show what effect they have upon bank control.
10. Enumerate the titles of the principal officers of commercial banks. In general, what are the duties and responsibilities of each?

Questions for Outside Investigation

1. Under what authority is your bank chartered?
2. What are the state laws in your state with regard to minimum capitalization? to surplus? to branch banking?
3. Is your bank a member of the American Bankers Association? of the state bankers association?
4. Is the cashier in your bank (if it has one) a loaning officer? Do the assistant cashiers supervise departmental operations?
5. How many members are there on the board of directors of your bank?
6. What official titles discussed in this chapter are used in your bank?

Assignment

As a business man in the town of Warren, you are asked to join a group interested in opening a bank. The town has a population of 5,000 and prior to January 1933 had two banks, a state bank and a national bank. The state bank closed in 1932, the national bank in January 1933.

1. What general investigation would you suggest for the purpose of ascertaining the possible need for a bank?
2. What type of bank would you favor—commercial, savings, or trust company? Why?
3. What capital and surplus will be required of the bank if it is organized under the laws of your state? under national laws?
4. In a brief statement, not to exceed 200 words, give your conclusions as to the advisability of proceeding with the organization details, and give your reasons for those conclusions.

CHAPTER III

DEPOSITS AND THE RECEIVING FUNCTION

The Purposes of This Chapter:
1. To outline the requirements of negotiable instruments.
2. To list and explain the powers that banks have in connection with various types of accounts.
3. To explain the duties of the receiving teller and the principal systems used in receiving teller operations.

*A*NY *business agreement which is enforceable in law is known as a contract.* Contracts play a major part in banking; in fact, all business transactions between banks and their customers are based on contractual agreements. Every account in the bank, every loan made, every collection accepted, and every trust activity is subject to general or special contracts. Thus a knowledge of contracts is of primary importance to the banker. The Commercial Law (Law I) course of the American Institute of Banking is largely devoted to the study of contracts, particularly in relation to banking.

Negotiable Instruments—A negotiable instrument is a special form of contract used in connection with money payments. By custom and law, it has become a form of contract with very definite privileges and responsibilities on the part of all parties concerned. Negotiable instruments, it is estimated, are used for over 90% of the money payments made in the United States each day. The Institute course Law II is devoted entirely to the study of negotiable instruments.

In carrying on its operations, a bank places complete reliance on the protection given it as a party to a negotiable instrument, and it is careful to use systems and methods that insure the fulfilment of its obligation as a party to a negotiable instrument. Thus it is possible for a bank to handle thousands of these instruments—checks, drafts, and notes—in the ordinary routine of collection and yet be certain that all duties and responsibilities in connection with them have been adequately met.

Since Banking I deals with methods and systems of operation designed to meet the requirements of negotiable instruments, a brief outline of the subject is necessary at this point; more detailed information concerning the significance of negotiable instruments will be found in the Institute course Law II.

Negotiable instruments are divided into two general classes: *orders* to pay, or drafts, and *promises* to pay, or notes and acceptances.

Drafts—The requisites of orders to pay (that is, drafts or bills of exchange) are definitely established. An order to pay must meet the following requirements:

1. It must be in writing and signed by the maker or drawer.
2. It must contain an unconditional order addressed by one party to another for payment to a third party.
3. It must be an order to pay a sum certain in money.
4. The order must be payable on demand or at a fixed or determinable future date.
5. It must be payable to order or to bearer.

The parties to a draft or bill of exchange are the *drawer* (the party issuing and signing the order), the *drawee* (the party to whom it is addressed), and the *payee* (the party in whose favor it is drawn). *A demand draft drawn on a bank is called a check;* it is the most commonly used of all forms of drafts or bills of exchange. In the case of a check the customer of the bank is the *drawer,* the bank is the *drawee,* and the party to whom the check is payable is the *payee.*

In addition to the use of drafts (particularly checks) for

DEPOSITS AND THE RECEIVING FUNCTION 81

payments without reference to the transactions for which they are used, drafts are used to expedite transactions between buyer and seller. The seller "draws on" the purchaser for the amount involved in accordance with the time agreements applying to the transaction. When the draft is used without supporting papers, it is called a *clean draft;* when papers or documents are attached, it is called a *documentary draft.*

Documentary drafts are widely used in export and import trade and in the movement of commodities within a country. By the use of the proper documents attached to a draft, the seller or shipper of goods can assure himself of payment before control of the goods (represented by the documents) is obtained by the purchaser. The documents are delivered and control passes to the purchaser upon either payment or acceptance of the draft, whichever is required by the seller or shipper. By these simple methods, trade can be promptly, safely, and economically carried on to an extent not otherwise possible.

Banks, because of the nature of their organization and operation, provide the means by which checks, drafts, notes, and acceptances can be used to the best advantage.

Acceptances—An acceptance is a time draft which the drawee has agreed to pay when due. Acceptance of a draft is accomplished by writing across the face of the instrument the word "accepted," followed by the signature of the accepting party and the addition of the date and the place payable. The party accepting the draft thus acknowledges the debt and promises to pay it where and when it is due, and the instrument then becomes a *promise to pay.* The usual form of an acceptance is shown in Figure 6.

There are two general classes of acceptances: the *trade acceptance* and the *bank acceptance.*

Trade Acceptances—In many countries it is customary to

embody the arrangements agreed upon between buyer and seller in the form of an acceptance. The seller of goods then has a promise to pay which may be indorsed and discounted at his bank under agreed credit arrangements; that is, a loan may be obtained by the use of the acceptance. Acceptances were rarely used in this country until the provisions of the Federal Reserve Act encouraged their use by making them, when properly drawn by parties of well regarded credit, acceptable for rediscount at the Federal Reserve banks. The number and amount of acceptances have increased because of this added advantage.

A trade acceptance is created by the purchase and delivery of goods. A trade acceptance must originate in an actual trans-

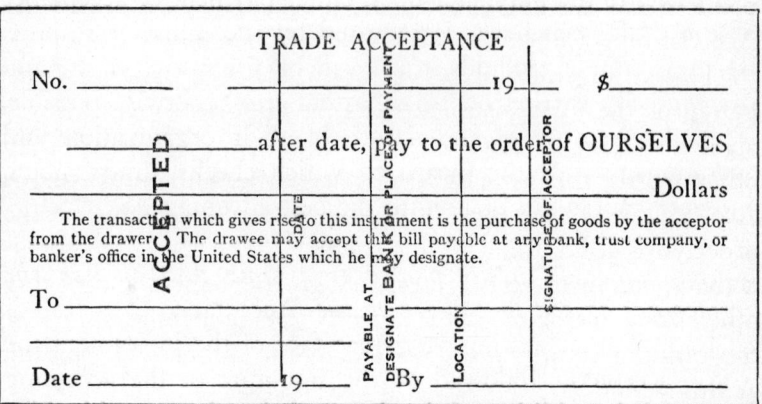

FIGURE 6. TRADE ACCEPTANCE

action and may not be used for the collection of past due accounts or for any other sort of collection. In the case of the trade acceptance, it is also presumed that the nature of the transaction for which the acceptance is executed is such that a substantial part (if not all) of the obligation will be liquidated during the life of the acceptance by proceeds from the resale of the goods by the purchaser. A partially or totally

DEPOSITS AND THE RECEIVING FUNCTION 83

self-liquidating transaction is thus created. The following illustration of a typical domestic trade acceptance operation will show how simple and effective the use of a trade acceptance can be.

The Ace Canning Company of Highland, Wisconsin cans peas, corn, and other vegetables. One of its customers is the Campbell Wholesale Grocery Company of Canton, Oklahoma, a company with an excellent credit standing. The Ace Canning Company receives an order from the Campbell Wholesale Grocery Company for goods costing $1,017.40. The bill is not to be paid immediately. The Campbell Wholesale Grocery Company expects to sell the goods to its retail customers within the succeeding ninety days, and from the proceeds it plans to pay for the cost of the goods; therefore it asks the Ace Canning Company to extend credit for ninety days.

This arrangement is satisfactory to the Ace Canning Company, for the First National Bank of Highland, Wisconsin is always willing to discount well rated trade acceptances. In other words, the bank will advance the selling price to the Ace Canning Company. This is fortunate, for at the time the order is received, the canning company is at the height of its activity, employing a full force, buying vegetables, and paying other costs incident to the "pack." In short, the funds of the canning company are needed in the business of canning at this period.

In order not to be deprived of the use of the money for the ninety days and yet meet the request of the buyer, a draft for $1,017.40, with a bill of lading covering the shipment of the goods, is sent through the collection department of the First National Bank of Highland to its correspondent bank in Canton, Oklahoma, with instructions to deliver the bill of lading (and thus control of the goods) to the Campbell Wholesale Grocery Company upon its acceptance of the draft.

The accepted draft (or acceptance) is returned to the Ace

Canning Company and is then discounted by the local bank. A few days before the end of the ninety days, the acceptance is sent by the First National Bank to its correspondent bank in Canton for collection, the acceptance is presented and paid on the due date, and the transaction is completed. Thus by the use of the acceptance method through ordinary banking facilities, a sale has been assured, the terms of payment requested have been granted, and the transaction has been carried through to completion.

Bank Acceptances—When a draft is accepted by a bank, it is called a bank acceptance. By accepting the draft, the bank lends its credit to the customer for whose account the acceptance is made. Bank acceptances are used most widely in foreign trade, where the seller is willing to accept the obligation of a bank but might not wish to make direct credit arrangements with the customer for whose account the bank executes the acceptance. Bank acceptances are highly rated; they command preferred interest rates for the advance or promise of payment and are very convenient and satisfactory in use.

To illustrate: The Norval Coffee Company of New Orleans wishes to buy a shipment of coffee from the South American Trading Company at Barranquilla, Colombia upon four months' terms. The amount involved is $2,347.10. The Norval Coffee Company arranges with the Gulf National Bank of New Orleans to accept a draft for that amount. The arrangement between the coffee company and the bank is made possible by the bank's knowledge of the company's standing.

When the coffee is shipped, a draft for $2,347.10 is drawn on the Gulf National Bank, and this draft, with documents attached, is presented by the South American Trading Company at its bank in Barranquilla for discount. That bank forwards the draft to the Gulf National Bank of New Orleans for acceptance. The draft, which has now become a bank acceptance, may be sold in the open market. When the bank acceptance falls due, the Gulf National Bank pays it with funds supplied by the Norval Coffee Company.

Thus a sale has been made, and on the terms agreed upon, by means of a bank's promise to pay. The details of the steps involved in an acceptance operation will be described more completely in connection with the discussion of letters of credit in a later chapter.

Notes—Negotiable promissory notes are the most widely used of all promises to pay. As evidences of debt, they constitute a large proportion of the total loans and discounts of banks—advances of money and credit upon promise of repayment.

To be *negotiable,* a promissory note must meet the following requirements:

1. It must be in writing and signed by the maker.
2. It must contain an unconditional promise made by one party to another party.
3. It must specify a sum certain in money.
4. It must be a promise to pay on demand or at a fixed or determinable future date.
5. It must be payable to order or to bearer.

The party promising to pay is called the *promissor* (or *maker*); the party to whom it is payable is called the *payee.*

Negotiation—The process of transferring a negotiable instrument from one party to another in such a manner that the second party becomes the holder is called *negotiation.* Negotiation consists of the physical transfer of the instrument, after indorsement by the proper party, with the *intention* to transfer. The party transferring the instrument is called the *transferor,* and the person receiving it is called the *transferee.*

The important general characteristic of negotiation is the

protection afforded a *holder in due course*. A holder in due course is the party who receives a negotiable instrument by indorsement and delivery, for value, and without notice of any defect in the instrument. If a party becomes a holder in due course, he is entitled to payment according to the terms of the instrument, regardless of the defenses to the instrument that a prior party may have.

To clarify the explanation, let us consider a simple transaction. R. D. Cousin, a customer of the First State Bank, wishes to discount a note for $100, payable to him and signed by R. B. Sunden. The note is due ninety days from the date of the note and is payable at the Second National Bank.

To discount the note, Cousin indorses it, obtains the approval of a loaning officer of the First State Bank, and presents the note to the discount teller. The teller, as a representative of the bank, gives value for the note by crediting the account of R. D. Cousin. As far as the bank knows, there is nothing to prevent the payment of the note by the maker at maturity. The bank has received it in the proper way, has paid value for it, and therefore *is a holder in due course, is entitled to collect the $100 from Sunden regardless of any claims the maker, Sunden, may have against Cousin.*

When one considers the thousands of loan and discount transactions handled by the banks of the country daily, some appreciation of the importance of the protection given a holder in due course is obtained. In order that a bank may be assured of the protection afforded a holder in due course and that its responsibilities in meeting the requirements of the law of negotiable instruments will be fulfilled, great care is exercised in the selection and training of its personnel and in the adoption of methods and systems.

Presentation and Payment—The place of payment is usually stated in a note or draft, and on the due date the instrument must be presented at that place within business hours. If a note or draft is payable at a bank, presentment must be made during banking hours; but if the maker has no funds in the bank (or insufficient funds) during banking hours, presentment may be made afterward on the same day. If no place of payment is specified, the instrument should be presented at the place of business of the maker, or at his residence, or, if these addresses are unknown, at the last known place of business or residence.

The obligations of the parties to a negotiable instrument are very clearly defined by law. In order to fulfil his responsibilities, the *maker* must pay the obligation at the time when and at the place where it is due. A *holder in due course* must pay value for an instrument; he must receive it from the previous indorser with the full intention of that indorser to transfer the instrument; and he must properly indorse it and be responsible for its presentation at the place of payment on the due date (the only exception being when delay or non-presentment is excused because of circumstances beyond the control of the holder).

The maker may waive the requirement of presentation either by express or by implied agreement if he desires.

The Indorser—An indorser ordinarily is responsible to subsequent holders in the event of non-payment of a draft (or acceptance) or a note provided the instrument has been properly presented. If for any reason the indorser does not wish to assume this responsibility, he must execute a particular kind of indorsement informing all subsequent indorsers of his position. This is called a qualified indorsement.

An indorser's liability is of particular importance to banks. Any item which a bank presents for payment and which is not paid is returned to the last indorser, who is required to reimburse the bank. This last indorser is in most cases the customer of the bank who has deposited or discounted the item, although, of course, he may be a non-customer for whom a check has been cashed. By custom and by specific agreement between a bank and its customers, the bank reimburses itself for an item on which payment has been refused by *charging the account* of the customer—that is, deducting the amount from the customer's balance. The item is then returned by mail to the customer, together with a memorandum of the charge against his account. This procedure is followed in order that the customer may take steps to obtain payment from other indorsers if desired.

While the charge-back of items that have been deposited or discounted is a procedure well established by law and practice, the same rules do not always apply when checks are cashed for customers. The courts in some states have held that a returned check which was cashed for a customer and not deposited to his account is *not chargeable* against the account. If this rule applies in the state in which a particular bank is located, extra precautions should be taken to protect the bank's position. All too frequently banks fail to realize the position in which they may be placed unless such special care is exercised.

Intervening Indorsements—While most checks received by a bank, whether deposited or cashed by customers, bear only the customer's indorsement, some checks bear *prior* or *intervening* indorsements as well. The bank, of course, by its own indorsement stamp, guarantees all indorsements when forwarding the items for presentation. It is a relatively simple matter to guarantee a customer's indorsement, whether the customer be an individual, a corporation, a partnership, or an association, since the bank has full information regarding the authority of each customer, furnished in the resolution or other form of authority (to be explained later in this chapter).

If the intervening indorsers are individuals, the problem is not particularly difficult, for barring forgery or incapacity of the individual to indorse (which is infrequent), the intervening individual indorsements are sufficient authority in themselves. But if an intervening indorser is a corporation, the bank does not know whether the parties executing the indorsement for the corporation are authorized to do so, and therefore it may be guaranteeing an indorsement that is not authorized or binding. This point is mentioned to emphasize the significance of the guaranty assumed by the bank and the conditions that call for special attention.

Kinds of Indorsements—There are five principal kinds of indorsements, each of which is used for a particular purpose.

1. An *indorsement in blank* (or *general* indorsement) consists simply of the signature of the indorser on the back of the instrument. If this signature is the *first* indorsement, it should agree exactly with the name of the payee shown on the face of the instrument. A check made payable to George J. Jones should be indorsed George J. Jones, not Geo. J. Jones or G. J. Jones.

If the first indorsement does not agree with the name of the payee on the face of the instrument, it is called an *irregular* indorsement.

The effect of a blank indorsement is to make the instrument negotiable simply by delivery. This is the form of indorsement most commonly used on checks presented at the paying teller's window for payment.

2. A *special* indorsement specifies the party to whose order the instrument is to be paid. The following is an illustration of such an indorsement.

Pay to the order of
John J. Smith
(signed)   George J. Jones

This form of indorsement is used on checks mailed to a bank for deposit to a customer's account; it is also used on notes and acceptances sent to a bank for rediscount. Finance companies often use the indorsement "Pay to the Order of Any Bank or Banker," which requires the indorsement of a bank immediately following, thus eliminating the chance that the item may be indorsed and cashed by irresponsible parties.

3. A *restrictive* indorsement prevents further negotiation of the instrument (except in the course of collection), by making this indorsement the last one; for example:

>Pay to the order of Blank
>National Bank for deposit only
>John J. Jones Company

This form of indorsement is a familiar one to the receiving teller and to the mail division as well, since it is widely used on checks sent to the bank for deposit to a customer's account.

4. A *qualified* indorsement is made by the addition of the words "without recourse" or similar expression to the signature of the indorser. It has the effect of relieving the indorser of the liabilities that usually accompany an indorsement. In other words, the indorsement implies that while the party transferring the instrument has the right to do so, he does not assume the liability of an indorser.

If, in connection with a collection or similar matter, a check is erroneously made payable to one bank when it should be made payable to another bank, the first bank may indorse *without recourse* to the second bank rather than delay the completion of the transaction; in other words, the first bank is willing to negotiate the check but not to assume responsibility in the event of non-payment.

5. A *conditional* indorsement imposes upon any subsequent indorsers the responsibility of determining whether or not the

condition included in the indorsement has been fulfilled; for example:

> Pay to the order of John J. Jones
> if the repairs on my house are
> completed by March 1
> (signed)   George R. Smith

The condition puts subsequent indorsers on notice; it puts them in the position of holding funds received by cashing the check subject to the rights of previous indorsers. The section of the Negotiable Instruments Law applying to conditional indorsements states that the drawee (the bank upon which a check is drawn) may elect to pay the check by disregarding the condition or may refuse to pay the check because of the condition imposed upon indorsers. If a check drawn on one bank is cashed at the paying teller's window of *another* bank, the position of the latter bank may be that of an indorser. A still different position is assumed if a check is deposited and the bank acts as agent for the customer in collecting it. Conditional indorsements are rarely used, principally because of the unusual positions (at variance with the general protection accorded holders in due course) in which they may place the parties to the instrument.

Ordinarily, banks will not accept conditionally indorsed instruments for collection and will not cash them, because, regardless of the bank's position technically, any litigation which might ensue would be a source of annoyance and expense.

Protest—In order to have an independent record that he has properly presented the item for payment, a holder in due course may make the instrument subject to *protest* if it is not paid. Protest consists simply in the presentation of a dishonored instrument, with a demand for its payment, by some one legally authorized so to act. Protest is generally made by a notary public, who has no interest in the obligation aside from its presentation and payment.

In practice, an item subject to protest is first presented for payment through the usual channels. If payment is refused, the instrument is then given to a notary (usually an employee of the bank), who presents it in person and demands payment. If payment is still refused, the notary formally *protests* the item. A special *form of protest* is used for noting in a formal manner the non-payment of an instrument. This form recites that the item has been presented and is unpaid (for the reason given). The form is signed and sealed, and all interested parties, including the maker and all indorsers, are notified that protest has been made.

The purpose of protest is to establish the fact that an instrument has been properly presented for payment; its effect is to bind the indorsers to their responsibilities and at the same time to provide proof of presentation to the maker. In order to hold indorsers or other parties, a foreign bill of exchange—a bill arising in one state and payable in another—*must* be protested. A domestic bill of exchange *may* be protested if dishonored.

The Deposit Function

Deposit Defined—Technically, the term "deposit" may have several different meanings. A deposit may be money or valuables left with a bank for safekeeping; it may be securities left with a trust department for exchange; it may be funds set aside for particular purposes. As ordinarily used in commercial banking, a deposit means *a sum of money or credit left with a bank to be used according to banking practice.* When money or credits are left with a commercial bank under special arrangements, the transactions are referred to by special names, such as *safekeeping, escrows,* and *special deposits.*

DEPOSITS AND THE RECEIVING FUNCTION 93

The term *deposits* is also commonly used by commercial banks to mean *balances to the credit of*. When bankers speak of *commercial deposits* or *savings deposits,* they mean the total funds due the customers of the bank by the commercial department or the savings department, as the case may be. These terms and meanings are commonly used in connection with a bank's statements of condition.

Banking, the same as other lines of business and trade, has its own terminology for describing its methods, systems, and operations, and its use of certain terms differs from ordinary usage. Funds placed to a customer's account in the bookkeeping department by other departments are called *credits,* deposits received by mail from other banks are called *cash letters,* credits received by telegraph are termed *wire transfers,* and so on. Banking terms have definite meanings and special significance to those in the banking business. Therefore, as these terms are used in connection with the discussion of the various bank operations, they will be explained in order that the student may have a clear understanding of the banking language so widely used.

Deposits are received by the bank through four channels: (1) through the receiving teller department—deposits left by customers (or their representatives) in person; (2) deposits received by mail; (3) transfer of funds by telegraph; and (4) credits received from other departments—interdepartment credits. Regardless of the channel through which a deposit is received, there are basic duties connected with its acceptance that must be fulfilled.

Use of Deposits—To the extent that *a bank can attract deposits—either of cash or credits resulting from its own loans or those of other banks—it can expand its volume of earning assets proportionately and hence its profits*. Earning assets consist of the loans and investments in which the bank's funds are employed, and the interest received from loans and investments is the main source of a commercial bank's income.

Stockholders provide the initial bank funds in the form of capital stock subscriptions. An additional amount is set aside and maintained permanently in the surplus account. Surplus comes either from funds provided specifically for that purpose at the time a bank is organized or from net profits after the payment of declared dividends each year (or both). It is common practice for a new bank to sell its capital stock at a price above its stated (or par) value. The difference between the par value and the selling price is used to build up a surplus account. Suppose that stock with a par value of $100 a share is sold for $125 a share; $100 goes into the capital account and $25 into the surplus account (or part into surplus and part into undivided profits). As earnings accumulate, they are added to the surplus account from time to time in round amounts.

Banking laws deal separately with *capital, surplus,* and *undivided profits.* Capital, we have seen, is established on a definite basis and must not be impaired. Surplus is a protection to capital. It is created according to banking laws and banking practice from profits in the main, and while seldom disturbed, it can be used to absorb losses or increased to meet the needs of the bank for additional funds. Undivided profits are not subject to regulation by law; they are created according to the policy of the individual bank and ordinarily represent the remainder of profits after reserves, dividends, and the like have been deducted. Banking laws usually make the capital and surplus of a bank the basis for determining the legal limit of credit that may be extended to a single borrower.

Deposits received from customers supply the greater portion of the funds which a bank employs in earning assets. Capital and surplus, though substantial in amount, are usually only a fraction of the total amount of deposits. The combined capital and surplus, for example, may represent only one-tenth of the total funds of the bank, which means that for every dollar of the stockholders' funds in use, there are nine dollars of depositors' money. The ratio varies, naturally; while some banks have a ratio of less than 1 to 10, most banks have a higher one.

The Federal Deposit Insurance Corporation and the Reconstruction Finance Corporation have definitely indicated their attitude regarding the proper ratio of stockholders' funds to deposits. These agencies favor and encourage a ratio of 1 to 7 or 1 to 8.

The growth of deposits over a period of time is regarded by the executives of a bank as indicative of successful management and continued confidence on the part of customers. Over a period of time a bank should show a rather consistent increase in deposits, thereby providing additional funds with which to make loans and investments.

Kinds of Deposits—The two general classifications of deposits are demand deposits and time deposits.

A *demand deposit* is one which gives the customer the right to receive payment of part or all of the amount due him at any time upon a properly written order, generally in the form of a check.

In the case of a *time deposit,* the depositor *may* be required to give written notice a specified number of days prior to withdrawal of the funds. To classify a deposit as a time deposit, a bank *must* have the notice privilege (under most banking laws), even if this privilege is not exercised.

In savings accounts, which constitute the largest group of time deposits, banks *must* require written notice thirty or sixty days prior to the date upon which withdrawal is to be made. (The word *must* is important, for if that requirement is not included in the agreement between the bank and its customers, the accounts cannot be considered as *time* accounts.) In commercial accounts, which represent the largest group of demand deposits, no prior notice of withdrawal is required.

The most widely accepted distinction between time deposits and demand deposits is that stated in the Federal Reserve regulations and applied to member bank reserves. The rule established by these regulations is that any deposits which may be withdrawn on demand or on *less* than thirty days' notice are classed as demand deposits, while those requiring thirty days' notice (or more) are classed as time deposits.

The relative inactivity of time deposits and the right of banks to require notice prior to withdrawals make it possible for banks to employ such funds in long term investments and from the greater income thus received to pay interest to depositors for the use of the funds, in contrast to the nonpayment of interest on demand deposits by certain classes of banks or the lower rate paid on demand deposits by banks that are not members of the Federal Reserve System or of the Federal Deposit Insurance Corporation. Federal Reserve regulations require presentation of the passbook for the withdrawal of time deposits unless payment is made to the depositor himself. In actual practice (as will be noted in the discussion of the savings department) payments are seldom made without presentation of the passbook, and then only under special arrangements.

The Banking Act of 1933 prohibited the payment of interest on demand deposits by members of the Federal Reserve System and also authorized the regulation of the maximum rate of interest that may be paid on time deposits by member banks. The Banking Act of 1935 made provision for a similar regulation by the Federal Deposit Insurance Corporation, applicable to those of its members that are not members of the Federal Reserve System.

From a reserve standpoint, the difference between the

activity of time deposits and demand deposits has long been recognized by laws establishing legal reserves. For members of the Federal Reserve System the basic reserve against time deposits is 3%, while the basic reserve against demand deposits is 13%, 10%, or 7% depending upon whether a bank is classified as a central reserve city, a reserve city, or a country bank. State regulations, also, provide higher reserves against demand than against time deposits. While present legislation provides for changes in the legal reserves for member banks through determination by the Board of Governors of the Federal Reserve System (see Chapter I), relative differences between time and demand deposit reserves remain the same.[1]

From an internal standpoint, deposits may be classified in a number of ways—as to the purpose of the deposit, as to the type of organization making the deposit, as to the influence of the deposit on the policies and operations of the bank, and so on—but the most important classifications are on the basis of (1) *time* or *demand* and (2) *public* or *private*.

Public and Private Deposits—The two main sources from which deposits are received may be described as public and private. The Federal Government and its subdivisions (states, counties, municipalities, school districts, and other governmental subdivisions) furnish what are termed *public* funds. Deposits from individuals, partnerships, associations, and corporations are called *private* funds.

The distinction between these two classes of funds is based largely upon their difference in character. A bank assumes that deposits received from its individual or corporate customers will result in the maintenance of rather steady balances and that the relationship will extend over a period of years.

Since public funds are generally receipts of money from taxes and since their use is largely provided for in advance by

---
[1] See Table II, Appendix.

salaries, interest on or maturity of bonds, or other general expenses of the political subdivision, balances of public funds fluctuate more than those of private funds. Public funds often require minimum interest payments and the posting of surety bonds or securities in order to protect the deposit. Public funds also depend to some degree upon political connections; hence they are likely to be changed from one bank to another with change of the party in power. Most states prohibit the securing of private funds by the pledge of assets.

Banks generally consider their growth in terms of private funds and so make a distinction in their statements of condition between deposits received from *public sources* and those received from *private sources*.

Certificate of Deposit—A *certificate of deposit* is a receipt for money deposited; it contains a statement of the arrangement between the bank and the customer as to the time of payment and the interest to be paid (if any). The funds are not subject to the usual arrangements governing checking or savings accounts. There were formerly two principal kinds of certificates of deposit: (1) the demand certificate and (2) the time certificate with a maturity date ranging from thirty days to six months or more according to agreement. The provision of the Banking Act of 1933 requiring the elimination of interest on demand deposits made the use of demand certificates less advantageous than previously.

Customers use time certificates of deposit for funds that are needed for a definite purpose at a future date. Interest is paid in the meantime, and the funds are available when desired.

A certificate of deposit may be either non-negotiable or negotiable depending upon the state law. A negotiable certificate of deposit is payable to order or to bearer and is treated exactly the same as other negotiable instruments.

In banks where the number of certificates of deposit issued is small, one of the tellers is designated to maintain the records in addition to his regular work—the collection teller, for example. The same teller also issues and records the cashier's checks or drafts of the bank. In large banks the volume of certificates of deposit is usually sufficient to justify a separate cage or department to issue and keep the records for cashier's checks, drafts, and certificates of deposit. The teller who handles this work is known as a *draft teller*.

The records kept for these three classes of items are similar; the register used is called a cashier's check register, a bank draft register, or a certificate of deposit register, as the case may be. Each certificate, check, or draft is numbered and must be accurately accounted for. When a certificate of deposit is issued, descriptive information (consisting of the name of the party to whom the certificate is payable, the date of issue, the amount, the rate of interest, and the maturity date) is listed in columns opposite the number of the certificate. By using numbered certificates and accounting for each one, including those that are "voided" (that is, those on which a mistake has been made and therefore not issued), the bank can have the work of the teller or the department easily checked and balanced.

When a certificate is paid, it is canceled and filed for audit reference, and entries of the payment and the date of payment are made in the register. By this simple but complete record it is possible to balance the amounts outstanding in certificates of deposit at any time. An illustration of this form of register is shown in Figure 7.

The same method is used in the case of the cashier's check register and the draft register, with the omission of the unnecessary items of maturity date and interest rate.

New Accounts—Just as a customer may select the bank with which he will do business, so can a bank select the cus-

NUMBER	DATE ISSUED	PAYABLE TO THE ORDER OF	DUE DATE	AMOUNT	INT.	DATE PAID

FIGURE 7. CERTIFICATE OF DEPOSIT REGISTER

tomers with whom it will make contracts of banking relationship. A bank cannot be required to accept deposits or accounts offered and uses this selective privilege to insure business of the type and kind desired.

In any business agreement, difficulties can be avoided by a thorough understanding of their privileges and responsibilities on the part of all concerned at the very outset of their relationship. By carefully explaining the conditions at the time each account is offered, a bank may eliminate many accounts that might prove unsatisfactory, and it may induce others to do their part in maintaining a satisfactory connection.

When a customer violates his agreement by drawing against insufficient or uncollected balances, for example, the bank may close the account and sever the relationship. Although seldom used, this is an important privilege of banks.

To insure careful selection of customers, experienced members of the bank's staff (officers or others thoroughly familiar with the work) are assigned the duty of opening accounts. Forms and routines are established to impress upon a prospective customer the responsibilities as well as the privileges of a bank account.

In some banks there may be little necessity for routine investigation since the prospective customers may be known to the officers. In other institutions where definite information is essential, all new accounts must go through the process of investigation and approval. By this selection of business, unsatisfactory accounts are reduced to a minimum.

The procedure in opening accounts is similar for all banks regardless of size or location. When an account is offered, the new account representative obtains the necessary information from the prospective customer immediately. This information may be entered on a *new account sheet,* similar to the one illustrated in Figure 8, or in places provided on the signature card (or both).

NEW ACCOUNT

Name of account.................................Date opened...................19........

Business address............................... Business telephone................

Residence address............................. Residence telephone..............

Business........................ Inc.......... Partnership .... Ind.........

Character of first deposit.........................Amount..............................

Character of account; business....................Personal..........................

Probable balance............................Special instructions..................

Other bank accounts...

Last account with..

Reason for change...

Associated accounts...

....

Introduced by..

References ....

....

....

Account assigned to group...

Remarks ....

Mail statements to..Will call..............

Account accepted by...

Signature cards received by...

Resolution or other authority received by..

FIGURE 8. NEW ACCOUNT FORM

The references and other data are verified before the account is definitely accepted. This checking is done either by the bank's officers or new business representatives or by the credit manager or credit department. The information requested furnishes a complete record of the applicant and so forms a basis for judging the desirability or undesirability of the account. (The methods by which this information is obtained and analyzed are a development of credit work and will be discussed in connection with the work of the credit department.)

The importance of a favorable record for customers accepted cannot be overemphasized, for banks depend upon the honesty and integrity of customers to a large degree. The following incident illustrates the wisdom of careful selection. Recently the canceled checks of the customers of a bank in a midwestern city were completely destroyed by fire, and the bank could not produce evidence of the checks paid against the accounts except by the entries on the ledger records. Nevertheless, the claims made by customers beyond the ledger records were so slight that the total loss to the bank as compared with total deposits was almost negligible.

It has been necessary in recent years to add one more requirement to that of the reputation of the customer. Banks have found that if they are to make a profit from services rendered, there must be a direct relationship between the amount a customer keeps on deposit and the activity of his account. Below a certain balance the activity of an account may cost more than the income to be derived from the employment of the funds in earning assets, or an excess number of transactions may run the cost beyond the income. Therefore, banks generally establish a minimum as to the amount of balance to be carried and specify the number of transactions a month that will be permitted on such a balance. Balances below this minimum and activity beyond the prescribed limit are subject to charges to the customer at regular rates. It is essential that this procedure be clearly understood by the prospective customer.

Some banks prefer to accept only accounts that they have reason to believe will maintain at least the minimum balance. Other banks levy pro rata charges upon excess activity or lower-than-minimum balances. On the opening of an account, a bank endeavors to ascertain as accurately as possible just how closely the account will conform to pattern; otherwise the account may be carried at a loss to the bank, or ill will may result from the imposition of a service charge. The problem of service charges and analysis will be discussed further under "analysis of accounts."

New Business—One method by which banks obtain new business is direct solicitation by officers and employees. Before actual solicitation is made, however, a prospective customer is thoroughly investigated to be certain that he is the type desired. Bank customers are an excellent source of new business. Because of their acquaintanceship or friendship with officers and employees and their knowledge of the bank's requirements, they are often the means of bringing to the bank a substantial amount of business of the desired kind; in fact, cultivation of new business by customers is one of the most fertile of all new business channels. Business also comes to a bank because of its convenient location or favorable reputation, although in localities where there is more than one outstanding institution, new business is more often the result of solicitation either by the bank's representatives or by its customers.

It is essential that a uniformly favorable impression be made on customers. The neatness of a bank's quarters and the reputation of its management have much to do with creating a favorable impression, but a factor of major importance is the alert, courteous, and careful attention given by officers and employees to the transactions handled for customers. A large percentage of the bank's personnel comes in direct contact with its customers. A customer expects, and rightly so, that his business will be handled *efficiently* and *confidentially,* and by fulfilling his expectations the bank creates good will and increases its business. Of course, the officers and employees not only must be thoroughly informed as to their own department and duties but also must know something of the services rendered in all other departments. An alert, well informed, and efficient staff creates good will and brings increased profit to the bank through economical operations.

Many banks insist that their personnel study new operating systems and methods in order to be up to date at all times. In many banks, also, each new employee must become thoroughly familiar with the general outline of the bank's operations by studying the handbooks prepared for that purpose. In other banks meetings of operating groups are held regularly to discuss and make decisions regarding proposed improvements in methods and systems.

Just as a well informed and courteous employee is a vital factor in the profitable conduct of a bank, so a discourteous or poorly informed employee may undo the constructive work of many others. Upon the person or department in charge of personnel rests the responsibility of discovering those best equipped to meet the public and those less fitted to do so; and by making suitable adjustments, the personnel supervisor is able to eliminate the undesirables from contact with the public.

The Deposit Relationship—The relationship between a bank and its customers is created by a series of contracts, imposing upon bank and customer alike definite obligations and responsibilities.

It is as important for a customer to understand these definite responsibilities as it is for the bank. By fulfilling his duties and responsibilities, a customer can be certain that any delay or loss occasioned by the bank's negligence will be repaid by it, and the bank has a right to expect and receive similar treatment from a customer if he neglects to fulfil his duties and the bank thereby suffers inconvenience or loss.

To illustrate this point, let us consider the obligations assumed by a bank in paying checks against an account. The bank must be certain, among other things, that the drawer's signature is authorized, that it is genuine, that the check has not been altered, and that it is not post-dated. If these and other tests are not successfully applied, the bank suffers whatever loss may result from its negligence. Similarly, a customer who violates his responsibility by not having sufficient funds on deposit to meet the checks drawn against his account will find those checks dishonored through non-payment by the bank.

Authority to Make Contracts—Contracts are based on the power of the parties to make the contractual agreements; therefore the authority of a customer to assume the responsibilities required by his contracts with the bank must be known by the bank to be full and complete.

The authority of a bank to make contractual agreements is established by the powers granted it in the charter, by the powers set forth in the by-laws, or by the actions of the bank's board of directors. The individuals selected to exercise this authority are designated either by the board of directors or by the executive officers of the bank who are empowered to act on its behalf.

Kinds of Accounts—The particular authority necessary in each group of accounts and the manner in which this authority is obtained are standardized. By following definite procedures, banks easily obtain full and complete authority from every customer.

For the purpose of showing the different kinds of authority required, accounts may be classified into five main groups.
1. Individual accounts
   a. *One individual only*
   b. *Alternate* or *survivorship* (two or more individuals, each signature authorized alone, the balance of the account to the survivor)
   c. *Joint* (two or more signatures, a combination of signatures required)
2. *Partnership* accounts
3. *Corporation* accounts
4. *Club, church,* and *association* accounts
5. *Trustee* accounts

Individual Accounts—In the law of contracts, a distinction is made between individuals who are regarded as *legally competent,* or able to make contracts, and *incompetents*—those who because of youth or incapacity from insanity or other causes either are not permitted to make contracts or are limited to contracts for the necessities of life. The segregation of competents from incompetents is not a difficult problem, for the majority of individuals who wish to become customers are known by the bank, either personally or through their connections, to be legally able to make the necessary contracts.

If an individual is not known, his status is determined from the references given in the new account routine.

It is unusual in small towns for an individual who is not known to the bank to attempt to open an account. Identification as well as qualification is a simple matter of routine in such localities. In larger centers the problem is more difficult, and when proof of qualification and identification is needed, the bank will not open an account until the investigation proves that the individual is competent and fully identified.

In the case of an account for one individual only, the agreement of a competent person to abide by the rules and regulations of the bank is sufficient authorization. Generally, the individual simply signs the signature card and thus accepts the agreement included as part of the signature card form (see Figure 9, front and reverse side). For other kinds of individual accounts (alternate and joint), the signatures of competent parties on the signature card constitute full acceptance of the terms.

In addition to the authority itself, there must be absolute identification of the authorized party. The mere use of a name is not sufficient. The bank must be certain that the individual is the person he claims to be; otherwise fraud could be committed through illegal use of funds deposited in the name of one person and withdrawn by an impostor. To be amply protected, a bank must be fully assured of the identity of all customers.

The identity of a customer is assured by the use of an *identification card,* upon which a specimen of his signature is obtained. The card is then sent to the bank where the prospective customer formerly maintained an account or to the company or concern with which he is connected for verification of the signature. As explained in the description of the new account sheet, identification is made certain by detailed investigation.

The account for *one individual* is the simplest of all accounts, for one person only has the right to use the funds. A variation of this type is the *alternate* or *survivorship* account, where two or more persons are authorized to withdraw funds and checks are valid with any one of the authorized signatures. By the terms of the agreement, the balance in the account becomes the property of the remaining person or persons upon the death of any of the parties; hence the use of the term

DEPOSITS AND THE RECEIVING FUNCTION

Authorized Signature of

_____

For Blank State Bank, Morrison, Illinois

_____

_____

See reverse side for conditions on which deposits are accepted and checks honored, to which the undersigned agrees.

_____

Identified by_____ Date_____

Opened by_____ Approved by_____

(FRONT)

In receiving items for deposit or collection, this bank acts only as depositor's collecting agent and assumes no responsibility beyond the exercise of due care. All items are credited subject to final payment in cash or solvent credits. This bank will not be liable for default or negligence of its duly selected correspondents nor for losses in transit, and each correspondent so selected shall not be liable except for its own negligence. This bank or its correspondents may send items, directly or indirectly, to any bank, including the payor, and accept its draft or credit as conditional payment in lieu of cash; it may charge back any item at any time before final payment, whether returned or not, also any item drawn on this bank not good at close of business on day deposited.

BLANK STATE BANK

(REVERSE SIDE)

FIGURE 9. SIGNATURE CARD

survivorship in connection with this type of account. In order to avoid confusion, banks frequently find it advisable to limit the participation in a survivorship account to a maximum of three individuals.

In certain states (Pennsylvania, for example) survivorship accounts, except where they are carried for husband and wife, are taxable in the estate of the deceased to the extent of the interest the estate had in the account.

The *joint* account represents an arrangement between two or more individuals in which a combination of signatures is required for withdrawals. This type of account is also known as a *two-name* account, a *three-name* account, and so on, indicating the number of names necessary for withdrawals. As in the alternate account, a reasonable limitation as to the number of participants is advisable.

Partnership Accounts—In the partnership form of organization, *each partner is ordinarily responsible for the business contracts of the other partners, and one partner can therefore bind all the other partners to a contract.* The acts must be within the scope of the partnership business, however; hence a bank not only must be certain that a partnership exists but must know the purposes of the partnership and the limitations on its operations. A copy of the partnership agreement is sometimes filed with the bank, and the authority of the partners is ascertained from that agreement. If the agreement is complicated or not entirely clear, the attorney for the bank will study it carefully and state his opinion for the bank's information and protection. The original partnership agreement may be required for this purpose.

In order to simplify the assembling of the necessary information, a *partnership form* of application is often provided by the bank for such accounts. By executing this form, the partners inform the bank fully of the required facts and empower it to recognize the authority conferred upon the representatives of the partnership.

Corporate Accounts—The source of authority in a corporation is its board of directors, whose authority to bind the corporation by contract is very broad, being limited only by the charter and the by-laws of the corporation. The board of directors elects the officers of the corporation, assigns general and special duties to them, and as a board directly approves many contracts in which the company is engaged. When opening an account for a corporation, a bank, in order to be certain that it is receiving proper authority from the corporation, must have a copy of the official resolution of the board of directors authorizing the account and must have a certified list of the officers empowered to transact business with the bank.

In order to obtain all the necessary information and proof of authority, banks use what is called a *resolution form,* prepared by their attorneys. This form, when filled out, is approved by the board of directors of the corporation and is attested by the corporation's secretary, who attaches or impresses the seal of the corporation. The resolution form which is here reproduced is typical. As may be seen, it invests the designated officers with full and complete authority to do all the things necessary in the corporation's relationship with the bank.

Sometimes the authority of the officers is conferred upon them by the by-laws of the corporation; when this is the case, a certified copy of the sections of the by-laws containing that authorization is obtained by the bank in place of the resolution.

Since the resolution constitutes the bank's record of the authority of the officers of the corporation, it is very important that the resolution, as well as any other pertinent documents, be carefully filed and reviewed from time to time, in order to be certain that with changing conditions revisions have not been overlooked and that the resolution is neither incomplete nor out of date. The filing and review of resolution forms may be done by the cashier or some other officer in a moderate sized bank and by a resolutions division in a large institution. The responsibility for the care and revision of resolutions is often combined with the care and revision of signature cards.

Resolution Form for Corporate Accounts

I, ..., do hereby certify that I am the secretary of ...., a corporation duly and legally organized and existing under and by virtue of the laws of the State of ...., and that I am the custodian of the records and the seal of said corporation; that at a meeting of the board of directors of said corporation duly and legally called and held in accordance with the law and the by-laws of said corporation, on the ...... day of ......, A.D. 19.., at which said meeting a majority and quorum of the board of directors of said corporation was present, the following resolution was adopted by the affirmative vote of a majority of the whole board of directors of said corporation, to wit:

BE IT RESOLVED by the board of directors of ....
....

1. That the INSTITUTE STATE BANK be and it is hereby designated as one of the depositaries of the funds of this corporation, and that the officers or employees of said corporation are hereby authorized to indorse, in the name of this corporation, for the purpose of deposit and collection in and with said bank, checks, drafts, notes, and other like obligations, issued or drawn to and owned by said corporation, and it is further resolved that indorsements for deposit and collection may be by the written or stamped indorsement of the corporation without designation of the party making the indorsement.

2. That said bank be and it is hereby authorized to pay out the funds of this corporation on deposit with it from time to time upon checks, drafts, or other orders for the payment of money, drawn upon said depositary and signed in the name of this corporation by its .... or .... and countersigned by its .... or ...., whether

said checks are payable to cash, bearer, or the order of the corporation, or to any third party, or to the order of any signing or countersigning officer of the corporation or any other corporation officer, in either their individual or official capacity, without further inquiry or regard to the authority of said officer(s) and/or other person(s), or the use of said checks, drafts, and orders, or the proceeds thereof.

3. That the .... and .... or .... and .... of this corporation be and they are hereby authorized from time to time to borrow money from said bank in such amounts, for such length of time and at such rate of interest and upon such other terms and conditions as said officer or officers may deem expedient, and to evidence the indebtedness thereby created by executing and delivering in the name and on behalf of this corporation promissory notes, judgment promissory notes, and other like obligations of this corporation, signed in the name of this corporation by the officer or officers designated above; and said officer or officers is or are further authorized to discount with said bank the notes, bills receivable, acceptances, and other obligations issued to or owned by the said corporation, and to indorse the same for such purpose; and to pledge or hypothecate as security to said bank for the payment of any of said notes and/or any other obligations of this corporation to said bank, any of the notes, bonds, stocks, bills receivable, accounts receivable, conditional sales contracts, chattel mortgages, warehouse receipts, and/or other documents, accounts, securities, and/or any other property now or hereafter belonging to this corporation, and to execute and deliver any and all indorsements or instruments of assignment or transfer which may be necessary or proper in such cases effectually to transfer to the said bank the property so hypothecated or delivered.

4. That the said bank shall not be in any manner whatsoever responsible for or required to see to the application of any of the funds of this corporation deposited with it, checked out, or borrowed from it, or secured by the discount of notes and other obligations to it as hereinbefore provided, and all such transactions shall be conclusively presumed to be legally binding upon this corporation.

5. That ...., the secretary of this corporation, shall file with the said bank a certified copy of this resolution under the corporate seal of this corporation and shall also file with the said bank a certified list of the persons at the present time holding the offices of ...., ..., and .... in this corporation, and it shall be conclu-

sively presumed that the persons so certified as holding such offices continue respectively to hold the same until the said bank is otherwise notified in writing by the secretary of this corporation.

6. That this resolution shall be in full force and effect and binding upon this corporation until it shall have been rescinded, and written notice of such rescission under the corporate seal shall have been delivered to said bank.

And I do further certify that the above resolution has not been in any wise altered, amended, or rescinded and is now in full force and effect.

I do further certify that the names and genuine signatures of the present officers of said corporation are as follows and that the genuine signatures of those above authorized to sign for the corporation appear on the accompanying cards:

President	Secretary
Vice President	Treasurer
Vice President	Assistant Treasurer

IN WITNESS WHEREOF I have hereunto set my hand and affixed the corporate seal of said corporation, this ...... day of ...., A.D. 19...

.... Secretary

I, ..., a director of said corporation, do hereby certify that the foregoing is a correct copy of a resolution passed as therein set forth.

.... Director

Club, Church, and Association Accounts—Many organizations are formed as unincorporated associations for special or charitable purposes and not for profit. Ordinarily, such associations are characterized by informal organization with few regulations, they are governed by by-laws containing broad general powers, and their activities are carried on by officers elected at general meetings of the members. When an account is opened for an organization of this sort, the bank must be certain that the officers have been properly elected and must know the extent of their powers; a copy of the by-laws of the association and a report of the meeting at which the officers were elected will meet the requirements. Although the accounts in this group are for the most part of modest proportions, there are a few large unincorporated associations in this country which maintain bank balances of considerable size; particular care must be exercised by a bank to be sure that complete and proper information and authority are received.

Trustee Accounts—Many circumstances make it desirable or convenient for individuals or corporations to be given possession of the property of others and to act on their behalf in various ways. When an individual or a corporation has possession but not ownership of the property, the arrangement is called a *trust,* and the individual or corporation holding the property is known as a *trustee.* The nature of the authority of a trustee and the extent of that authority are determined by an agreement or by a court order.

The authority exercised by a trustee may range from broad and extensive powers to small and very limited ones, with all manner of variations. While the powers of an individual who opens an account are limited only by the general regulations regarding contracts, such is not the case with a trustee account. When a trustee account is offered, a bank is automatically *put on notice* that the only way to be certain of the nature of the trust and of the authority conferred upon the trustee is to examine the trust agreement carefully. Some trusts are established by voluntary agreement between the interested parties, others by direction of a court of law.

Let us suppose that Martin, Johnson, and Curtney are engaged in a joint operation and that they find it convenient to designate Smith, as trustee, to deposit funds in the bank and to draw checks in payment of expenses incurred in connection with the venture. Smith, then, controls the funds of the three, and although he has possession of them, actually none of the funds belong to him. He desires to open a trustee account in the First State Bank. The bank knows that he is acting for others, but it does not know to what extent and in what ways he may be authorized to act. In verifying Smith's authority, the bank first asks for the original agreement in order to ascertain the nature of the trustee relationship which exists; or the bank may supply Smith with a form and require him to have it properly completed and authenticated before opening the account. If the standard form supplied by the bank is used, all the necessary points are covered, and the bank knows exactly what authority is conferred upon the trustee. If the original agreement or an acceptable certified copy is submitted, the bank's questions may be completely answered by an examination of the document. In case doubt arises as to the arrangement, powers, authority, or identification of the trustee, the entire matter is referred to the bank's attorney for decision.

Courts of law are constantly establishing trustee relationships for companies or individuals who, for one reason or another, come under their direction. These vary from the extensive relationships pertaining to large corporations, such as railroads, to the modest and limited activities of trustees for individuals of small means. In creating trustee arrangements, the court recites the powers of the trustee or trustees named with regard to the funds they will control. The limitations of these powers are definitely set forth in the court order and are a permanent part of the court records. In opening an account for a trustee established by a court, a bank simply obtains a certified copy of the order establishing the trust and thus receives full and complete information.

The Signature Card—A bank obtains its authorization to accept the signatures of certain individuals for the withdrawal of funds, indorsements, and other actions by one of the means already described. In order to be certain that funds are being paid out on the order of authorized persons or that other actions are being taken by their order, the bank keeps specimens of customers' signatures on file for ready reference on *signature cards* provided for that purpose. These cards form an important part of the mechanics of banking.

Signature cards not only furnish a means of recording authorized specimen signatures for identification; they also serve as an acceptance of the rules and regulations of the bank by those signing the cards. In the case of an individual account, the signature card constitutes the *complete authority itself* as well as the *record* of the authority granted the bank.

Figure 9 shows a form of signature card that is widely used, although differing state laws and differing policies of institutions may require variation in its form or contents.

The signature cards must be carefully filed and must be revised from time to time in order that they may always be up to date and complete. Usually two or more cards are filled out for each account or photostat copies are made. One card is placed in a central file, so that all authorized signatures may be found at that place. A second card is filed with the paying teller unit, which needs to refer to the signatures more frequently than other units.

In branch banks specimen signatures are often provided for the head office as well as the branch in which the account is kept; these additional specimens may be provided by use of photostatic or other reproducing devices.

One of the duties of the individual in charge of the master

(or central) file is that of reviewing the file periodically so that new or additional signatures may be obtained as desired. Any individual's signature changes somewhat from time to time; therefore it is essential that a current specimen be on file. The individual in charge of signature cards also has the responsibility of seeing that when changes in the official roster of corporations occur, the proper specimen signatures are filed with the bank.

If the business of a bank does not warrant the use of a new account sheet, the signature card alone is used. In this case, a customer's business connections and affiliations, business address, former banking connections, references, telephone number, and other miscellaneous information are entered on the signature card.

The Deposit Slip—As already explained, deposits or credits to customers' accounts come from four sources: (1) deposits of cash and checks at the receiving teller windows, (2) deposits received by mail, (3) transfer of funds by telegraph, and (4) credits received from other departments of the bank. For the third and fourth sources, a special *internal* form is often used. A *transit* form is commonly used for deposits received by mail (this form and its uses will be explained in the discussion of the transit department). A *deposit slip* (or deposit ticket) is used for all deposits received at the receiving teller windows, and sometimes for deposits received by mail. *The deposit slip is a memorandum of the cash and other funds presented for deposit; it also serves as a record that the deposit has been received.* Since it is an original record, it should be made up by the customer, preferably in his own handwriting.

One form of deposit slip (Figure 10) has columns for the listing of checks and other items and space for the listing of cash (currency and coin). Such an itemized list must accompany all deposits taken in by the receiving teller; the deposit

INSTITUTE NATIONAL BANK

―――――――

―――――――

――― 193 ―

Depositors will please note that all deposits are received subject to the conditions specified on the back of this ticket.

CHECKS ON THIS BANK	CHECKS ON OTHER BANKS	CASH
	Total checks on this bank	
	Total checks on other banks	
	Total cash	
	TOTAL DEPOSIT	

FIGURE 10. DEPOSIT SLIP

slip not only is evidence of the credit to a customer's account but also is used for comparison with the listing and totaling of the items made by the bank.

The deposit slip used in some banks is further divided into columns for checks drawn upon the customer's bank, checks drawn on other local banks, New York City items, and all other out-of-town checks. By means of this division into groups, the bank can check the deposit against the departments to which the items are sent from the receiving teller. This form of deposit ticket is shown in the batch system illustration (Figure 13, Chapter IV). To facilitate the identification of items, the American Bankers Association transit number of the bank upon which each item is drawn is noted opposite the amount.

The correct listing and totaling of items by the customer eliminates the time and trouble that the bank must otherwise spend in correcting errors. Banks endeavor to have their customers prepare deposit slips carefully, not only to save the time of the staff but also to avoid delays and inconveniences to customers who may have to wait until corrections are made and then adjust their own records accordingly.

The wide use of adding machines in business has been a great help in this respect, for most customers list the items by adding machine and thus avoid errors. To check the importance of this practice, a large bank recently made a survey of the errors in deposit slips. As a result of this survey over a period of a year, it found that over 95% of the mistakes were made in deposits of ten items or less, those in which the items were not machine-listed or totaled.

When correction of a deposit slip is necessary, the change is indicated either by a stamp on the deposit slip and a notation of the error (such as, "check listed as $101.10 should be $110.10") or by a separate correction memorandum attached to the slip, a copy of which is sent to the customer.

DEPOSITS AND THE RECEIVING FUNCTION

After the deposit slip is used by the receiving teller and by the distribution, analysis, and bookkeeping departments for their work, it is filed away in a permanent file.

The Passbook—The bank gives a customer a receipt for every deposit made. This receipt may be in the form of an entry in the *passbook,* by a *duplicate deposit slip,* or by an *advice of credit.* For a deposit made at the receiving teller's window, a passbook entry or a duplicate deposit slip is used; for a deposit by mail or an interdepartment credit, an advice of credit is commonly used, although if the customer transacts his business at a particular department, a passbook entry or a duplicate receipt may be used instead.

The passbook is simply a small booklet with ruled pages for entries. Some of the rules and regulations of the bank under which deposits are received are printed on the first page or two of the book. In the back of the book there is a section in which collections may be entered. Originally, the passbook was used as the customer's record of his account, in addition to serving as a record of the deposits made. In the earlier days of American banking when only a small number of checks were written by the average customer, and when the accounts were not very active, the passbook served the purpose which the bank statement serves today. Periodically, each customer brought his passbook to the bank for balancing; the checks drawn against the account since the date of the last balance were entered, as were the deposits and credits, and a new balance was set down. Thus the customer had in his passbook a detailed and complete copy of the bank's record of his account.

As the number of customers and banking transactions increased and as the customers became more widely scattered, the passbook method of balancing accounts proved inconvenient and was abandoned. Instead, a copy of the ledger account was given to the customer at regular intervals, ordinarily once a month.

In commercial banking today the passbook is simply a receipt book. Many customers make little use of it even for that purpose, since their deposits are usually made by mail or by wire transfer. A few banks are eliminating the passbook for commercial accounts and replacing it with other receipt forms. In the savings department, the inactivity of accounts permits the use of the passbook to advantage, and deposits, withdrawals, and balance are recorded as each transaction occurs.

If the depositor does not have his passbook with him when making a deposit at the teller's window, he makes out two deposit slips, one to be used in the regular way and the other to be used as a receipt. When the passbook is used, the teller enters in it the amount of the deposit, the date, and his initials. When *duplicate deposit slips* are used, the teller stamps a notation on the face of the second slip and signs or initials this duplicate deposit slip as a receipt. A common form of duplicate stamp follows:

DUPLICATE
October 10, 1936
Institute State Bank

Teller

Figure 11 is an illustration of an advice of credit. The customer's name and address, the date of the deposit, and the amount are entered, and the advice is initialed or signed by the person receiving the deposit. By the use of outlook (or window) envelopes, these advices may be mailed without the additional typing of the customer's address. Some banks use an advice of credit memorandum instead of the duplicate deposit slip; in others both a credit memorandum and a duplicate deposit slip are used. A carbon copy of the advice serves the same purpose within the bank as the duplicate deposit slip.

```
            INSTITUTE NATIONAL BANK
                                              _____19__
  We credit your account as follows:
  $_____Your letter of_____
                                    John H. Selden, Cashier
  To_____
     _____
     _____
```

FIGURE 11. ADVICE OF CREDIT

Cash and Collection Items—All items handled by a bank are classified according to the way in which the bank accepts them for credit to its customers' accounts. *Cash items are those that the bank will accept for immediate credit*—checks, drafts, or other items that will increase the balance of a customer's account immediately by the amount of the items deposited. Nearly all checks are cash items. For instance, a check of the R.B.C. Company of San Francisco, drawn on the Golden Gate State Bank of that city, payable to the Better Manufacturing Company, a customer of the Institute State Bank, would ordinarily be treated as a cash item.

Collection items usually consist of drafts with documents attached, notes, and acceptances. *The amount of a collection item is not placed to the customer's credit until the item has been presented for payment and the funds have actually been received by the bank.* A trade acceptance, payable to the Better Manufacturing Company, accepted by the R.B.C. Company, due May 12, and entered for collection May 4, would be a typical collection item. A draft due on demand, with an attached bill of lading to be delivered upon payment of the draft, would also be classed as a collection item.

Some items have characteristics of both cash and collection items. In other words, the bank is willing to give immediate credit because the item is due on demand and acceptable in every other way, but special handling through collection channels is necessary because there are documents or securities attached. Some banks call these items *cash collections,* indicating that immediate credit is given but that special attention is required.

A typical cash collection item would arise as the result of the shipment of United States Government bonds by an investment house, upon order, to a bank in another city, with an attached demand draft for the amount involved. Such an item cannot pass through the ordinary transit department routine, for the facilities of the transit department are not designed to provide the special attention required by the attached securities. Immediate credit is given, but the item is forwarded to the out-of-town bank by the collection department, by registered or insured mail, with special instructions.

Characteristics of Cash and Collection Items—With minor variations among banks, or in a few cases among customers of the same bank, the differences between cash and collection items may be summarized as follows:

1. Cash items are due on demand; that is, they must be either paid or refused as soon as they are presented at the place of payment.

2. A large proportion of collection items are not due on demand but in the near future. (As already noted, cash collection items due on demand are subject to special arrangements.)

3. Cash items have no documents, securities, or other accompanying papers attached.

4. Many collection items have warehouse receipts, securities, and other papers attached.

5. The instructions necessary for the presentation of cash items are simple and uniform for practically all items.

6. The instructions necessary for collection items are more detailed, each collection requiring individual instructions.

The extent to which cash items can be handled by routine methods and the large number of items that are subject to the same instructions enable the clearings and transit departments to operate on a large volume, low-cost-per-item basis. In contrast, the individual attention and special handling required for each collection item demand that the collection department be organized on the basis of a lower volume per person, resulting in a higher cost basis. This point is further discussed in the description of the organization and operation of the collection department (Chapter VI).

One type of item, *coupons,* merits special mention. Some coupons are due at the time they are brought to the bank, and the bank knows that they will unquestionably be paid; hence they are treated as *cash items.* Government bond coupons are an example; in some banks such coupons are accepted by the receiving teller for deposit or are paid by the paying teller. Coupons not yet due and those with which the bank is not familiar are treated as collection items.

Where the volume of coupons or bonds presented for collection or payment justifies the expense, a special department or a section of the collection department is established to handle coupons and bonds exclusively. The work of this department or division is discussed in Chapter VI.

Most departments in a commercial bank handle cash items. The receiving teller, the paying teller, the clearings department, and the transit department are all organized upon the basis that items handled by them are those for which immediate credit is given, and the departmental operations are governed accordingly. For example, the clearings department operates on a basis of daily completion of work; its records are temporary and simple. The collection department, in contrast, is organized to handle items that will not be credited until they are actually collected, and it has uncompleted transactions outstanding continually. Therefore its records are more complicated than those of the clearings department and are not temporary in nature.

The Duties of the Receiving Teller—The average customer has no conception of what is being done at the teller's window to meet his needs and those of the bank. All he realizes is that when he has his turn at the window, he hands in his deposit ticket and items, perhaps passes the time of day while the teller is looking over the deposit, then gets back his passbook or other receipt, and goes on his way. All he sees from the outside is the line of customers at the windows making deposits and getting receipts for them in a steady and smoothly moving line; he does not realize that the teller is actually passing upon each and every deposit before accepting it on behalf of the bank. On the other side of the teller's window is the trained teller, rapidly, accurately, and courteously verifying, checking, and receipting for the deposits—following a well defined and responsible procedure.

The receiving teller, as the representative of the bank in receiving and receipting for deposits, is constantly in contact with the customers of the bank, and the prompt, accurate, and courteous manner in which he dispatches his duties creates good will and confidence on the part of customers. The duties of the receiving teller are five in number. In many banks each teller performs all of them without assistance from other individuals or departments. In other institutions, some of this work is handled by the proof or distribution department in order to make the operation of receiving deposits more economical and effective and to enable the teller to attend to more customers at the window. The five main duties of the receiving teller are:

1. To verify the amount of the cash and to see that it is all genuine money
2. To see that all items submitted for deposit are actually cash items
3. To see that all items are properly indorsed
4. To verify the total of the deposit
5. To issue a receipt for the deposit.

Without exception, these five duties are performed for every deposit, whether large or small and whether made at the receiving teller's window, by mail, by special messenger, or in any other way.

Besides the operation of receiving deposits, the teller must charge the cash and items to the other departments that handle them further, and his records must balance with those of the other departments.

In order to facilitate the work of the teller, the receiving cage is equipped with a drawer for currency, divided into sections for ready sorting. A coin machine is also provided, in which the teller can place coins and make change as desired by pressing the proper keys.

When a deposit is offered at the window, the first step of the teller is to verify the amount of the cash—that is, to see that the cash by actual count equals the amount shown on the deposit slip. While counting the cash, the teller watches for counterfeit currency or coins, for the law requires that such coins or currency be turned over to the government agency engaged in the protection of money against fraud. Whoever holds the money suffers a loss, since it is illegal to pass on counterfeits to others. If counterfeit money is offered in a deposit, the amount is deducted from the total of the deposit, the money is stamped as counterfeit and turned over to the Secret Service Division of the Federal Government, and the customer is informed of the counterfeit immediately. If the counterfeit is not detected at the time the deposit is made, the bank suffers the loss, since counterfeit currency or coin, when intermingled with other money, cannot be identified with the depositor.

So alert and well trained are tellers that the amount of counterfeit money undetected at the window is very small. The teller nevertheless must always be on his guard. Counterfeiters seem to work in spurts, concentrating on passing bad money in communities on an extensive scale for a short period of time, and carelessness on the part of the teller for even a brief time may prove costly.

An exception is made to the rule that currency must be *proved* at the time of deposit if the bank has an arrangement with a customer for accepting packaged currency and coin, stamped with the name of the depositor. In such a case the packaged currency or coin is accepted without verification but subject to count and correction later on. This arrangement is of benefit to the customer since he does not have to wait at the window for verification; it is also advantageous to the bank, for the count can be made at times of comparative inactivity at the window or by other tellers or departments. This arrangement provides for the identification of the money *until verified by the bank,* and the bank's count is accepted by the customer without question.

The second and third duties of the receiving teller can be accomplished by one operation. The teller can determine at a glance whether or not an item is a *cash* item, and by simply turning over each item as he goes through the stack, he can ascertain whether or not it is properly indorsed.

Bank customers often use a stamp provided by the bank

for indorsing items. The form used is the *special* indorsement mentioned earlier in the chapter; it serves both as an indorsement and as an identification in the event that the item must be traced for any reason. It is a simple matter for the teller, in looking over the items, to see that they are stamped or otherwise indorsed.

Where special instructions are to be followed for deposits of certain customers, the receiving teller must have such instructions before him so that he may refer to them readily. For example, deposits of branch offices of companies located in other cities are often made to the credit of the parent company and acknowledgments are made directly to the main office.

The next step in the receiving procedure is the verification of the total of the deposit. This operation requires more time than any of the others. It is an operation, however, that can be done elsewhere, and so various methods are used to assist the teller in this duty, even to the extent of passing on the work to another individual or department. If the average deposit has a small number of items or the peak load of the teller is not too concentrated, the teller will be able to prove all deposits without assistance and without delay. In small banks one teller may perform this duty easily.

If the practice is followed of having two tellers on duty in the receiving teller cage, often one teller will verify the deposit totals on an adding machine while the other is on duty at the window. A variation of this procedure is the use of an adding machine operator just behind the cage; this operator verifies the deposits for one or two receiving tellers and assembles the figures in the receiving teller's proof as well. Some other division of the work may be found expedient. In a southern bank, for example, the teller proves all deposits with eight or fewer items, while deposits with more than eight items are turned over to a central proof department for verification of totals.

The volume of deposits is usually so heavy in large banks and so many of the customers are corporations with numerous items in each deposit that the teller does none of the work of verifying the totals, this duty being assumed by the interior proof or central proof or distribution department (these and various other names are used interchangeably to refer to the same operation or department).

Reference has been made to the fact that, in addition to receiving deposits, the receiving teller must charge the deposit items to the proper departments and balance the day's work with each of them. This is called the *receiving teller's proof*.

Receiving Teller's Proof—In the deposits the receiving teller finds cash, checks on his own bank, checks on other local banks, checks on out-of-town banks, and miscellaneous items, such as coupons. When he has finished his duties in connection with them, he routes the cash and items to other departments for subsequent disposal. Cash goes to the head paying teller; checks on the teller's own bank (called "us" checks) go to the bookkeeping department; checks on other local banks, to the clearing house department; checks on out-of-town banks, to the transit department; and miscellaneous items, to other departments.

It is a characteristic of the receiving teller function that the work is on a daily basis; that is, the cycle of work is completed each business day. At the start of the day the teller has no carry-over work from the previous day; all he has to account for is the cash charged to him by the paying teller. This cash is given to the receiving teller for making change or for break-up and sorting; often it is charged from the head paying teller each morning. If the system used provides for a fund which the teller keeps constantly under his control, frequent adjustments and check-ups must be made by the head paying teller or by the audit department.

DEPOSITS AND THE RECEIVING FUNCTION

At the end of the day, the receiving teller turns over to the head teller the *counter cash* he received at the beginning of the day, together with the cash he has taken in with the deposits. This balance with the head teller may be made directly or through the batch or block system (described in the following chapter).

TELLER		DATE	
Debits			Credits
	Head Paying Teller		
	Exchange		
	Clearings A.M.		
	Clearings P.M.		
	New York		
	Transit		
	Mail Teller		
	Country Books		
	Bookkeeping A to L		
	Bookkeeping M to Z		
	Over	Short	

FIGURE 12. RECEIVING TELLER'S PROOF

Besides balancing the cash, the teller balances the deposit items with each department. The teller is charged with the total amount of deposits received, and the totals of all items sent to other departments must equal this deposit total.

If the block system is not used, each teller accounts for his operations directly with each department. The record of these transactions is called the receiving teller's *proof,* a sample of which is shown in Figure 12. If the block system is used, the receiving teller balances his cash directly with the paying teller through the block verification, and the rest of the balancing is done by the proof department.

Other Receiving Teller Duties—In recent years other duties have been assigned to receiving tellers, primarily because of the fact that they often are in a position to perform such duties better than other individuals or departments. One duty is the calculation of *float,* which is noted on the deposit slip by the teller at the time the deposit is accepted. Float is a term used to designate the amount of the balance of an account which is in the process of collection (this term will be explained in detail in the study of the transit department). Another duty is the deduction of exchange charges in those cities where such charges are made. The receiving teller figures the exchange, collects it, and makes a separate exchange list daily which is balanced with the paying teller at the close of business. Other minor duties may be performed, such as accepting orders for printed checks for customers, verifying balances, and the like.

Receiving Teller Problems—The receiving teller division must be organized to maintain maximum efficiency in the face of wide fluctuations in volume. From the bank that has a large number of accounts with frequent deposits at the window to the bank where deposits by the average customer are either less frequent or of larger amounts (or both), there are innumerable variations that will determine the method best suited to handle the work promptly, economically, and efficiently. The ideal situation, of course, would be the steady flow of business during banking hours each day, with approximately the same number of transactions each business day. This is never the case, however. Some banks have fewer *peak loads,* or exceptionally busy times, than others; but experience is the only gage of the variations for any bank, and systems and methods must be arranged according to the particular problem of the individual bank.

There are certain hours during the business day when the number of deposits made is two or three times as great as at other hours. There are some days in the week when the general activity during the entire day is much greater than on other days. There are days in the month when each bank has to service an increased number of customers. These periods of accelerated activity—daily, weekly, or monthly—are the peak periods, and receiving tellers must be able to serve customers as efficiently at these times as in ordinary periods.

While the banks in any given community tend to experience the same peak times, yet it is the customers who determine just what constitutes the particular problem of each bank, either because the general group of customers differs from the groups in other banks or because a few customers cause unusual activity on certain days or at certain hours during the day. This situation is one that demands careful consideration. Although little can be done in the way of regulating the time that customers will make deposits, since each naturally selects the time most convenient to him, it is interesting to note that efforts in this direction have had some effect. A bank in one of the midwestern cities was able to level off the deposit peak by a direct and well planned appeal to its customers to make Saturday deposits at an earlier hour than they had been in the habit of making them. By this appeal the bank was able gradually to spread the Saturday peak over two hours instead of one—a decided operating advantage.

Perhaps this experience may point the way to the improvement of receiving teller operations by demonstrating to customers what a difference it makes in the work of the bank to have a steadier flow of deposits during banking hours and how much faster a customer can transact his business if this is the case. Many customers could no doubt be induced to change the time of making their deposits if they could be made to realize that it is to their advantage to do so.

Receiving Teller Systems—There are four main systems used in receiving teller divisions. One is the *alphabetical system,* in which each receiving teller or cage receives the deposits of customers whose last names begin with letters coming in the alphabetical division from "A" to "D," for example. This system is especially effective when the accounts in the various alphabetical divisions have approximately the same activity. By the adjustment of alphabetical groups, the activity can be spread with approximate equality for each receiving teller.

Another system is the *numerical division.* This system is used almost exclusively in savings banks or savings departments. Accounts are numbered and each teller receives deposits from a group of consecutively numbered accounts. This numerical system will be explained in more detail in the discussion of the savings department.

Another method is the *general cage* system. In this system a single cage with several windows is used for receiving teller work. Deposits are made at any window without regard to the alphabetical or other designation of the accounts. Where flexibility is highly necessary, this method can be applied satisfactorily. Many large banks as well as smaller ones find it well adapted to their needs.

The fourth method is the *unit teller* system. Both receiving and paying are done by the same teller for a group of accounts. The unit system is widely used in savings banks and savings departments and also in many commercial banks and commercial departments. If the bank is of moderate size, often the unit tellers receive deposits and pay checks for all customers without designation as to groups. In a community of 10,000 population in the Middle West, one of its two banks uses the unit system successfully. The total deposits of this bank are $1,782,456 of which $1,000,000 represents commercial accounts. The receiving and paying are handled at four windows. The tellers at the first two windows receive and pay on commercial accounts. The teller at the fourth window receives and pays on savings accounts. The teller at the third window receives and pays on either commercial or savings accounts; however, since he has duties to perform in other departments, he operates the window only at the busy hours of the day.

By having one of the regular commercial tellers prove deposits and sort and package cash during slack periods, the receiving and paying can be handled by one commercial teller. As the business increases, two commercial tellers are used; and when the rush period comes, the third teller is added.

While the four systems—alphabetical, numerical, general cage, and unit teller—are all in general use, the possible variations to suit particular problems are many. Often a bank augments its regular alphabetical system with special cages that are used as *unit* or *general* cages.

Another problem in the operating of departments and divisions such as the receiving teller division is how to make the best use of banking floor space. Many departments, such as clearings and transit, can be operated equally well in other parts of the bank building, on other floors, without any decrease in effectiveness.

Night Depository Service—In some communities many bank customers find it advisable to keep their places of business open evenings, and the danger of holding receipts of checks and cash until the following morning is a real one. To solve this problem, banks provide a service called the *night depository* service. A specially constructed chute is built on the outside of the banking quarters, and this chute leads directly into a safe within the bank. The chute may be opened on the outside only with a key; after the chute is unlocked, a cylinder can be rotated and an opening for the deposit appears.

A customer who wishes to use the night depository service fills out an application containing an agreement to abide by the rules for the use of the service. The customer is then given a key to the outside chute and is charged for it. A pouch or bag is also charged to the customer. This bag is numbered, and a record is made of the customer to whom it is given.

In making a deposit, the customer lists the items on a deposit slip and totals them in the usual manner. He then places the checks, currency, and deposit slip in the bag, seals it, and deposits it in the night depository chute, using the key furnished by the bank to unlock and lock the chute.

There are two procedures generally followed in handling the deposit after it is in the night depository safe. In one procedure, double or even triple custody of the safe is provided; that is, two or three persons are required to work the combinations. The bags are then taken to a receiving teller or special cage, where the teller opens the bag in the presence of another teller or clerk, verifies the deposit, puts the cash and items through the usual routine, and sends a receipt to the customer. In the second procedure, the customer is required to come in and open the bag and make the deposit in person, after the safe has been opened.

Some banks provide this night depository service as a convenience, without charge to their customers; others impose a moderate monthly fee for its use.

Questions Based on Chapter III

1. What are the requisites of an order to pay?
2. What is the most commonly used kind of draft?
3. Define a negotiable promissory note. Where is it widely used in a bank?
4. Discuss the importance of the Negotiable Instruments Law to the operating procedure of a bank.
5. What are the two general classifications of deposits used in commercial banking?
6. What is a certificate of deposit?
7. What is the source of authority for corporation accounts? In what manner is it obtained by a bank?
8. What must a bank know in connection with trustee accounts in order to be certain of its position?
9. Explain the purpose of the signature card; the deposit slip.
10. Distinguish between cash items and collection items. What are some of the general characteristics of each?

Questions for Outside Investigation

1. What persons are authorized to accept new accounts for your bank?
2. Who has charge of the revision of signature cards, resolutions, and other authority forms?
3. Is a new account sheet used in your bank for information purposes? or the signature card? or both?
4. What type of receiving teller system is used in the commercial department of your bank?
5. At what hours and on what days do the receiving tellers in your bank experience peak loads?

Assignment

1. Using the deposit tickets of *your own bank,* make up the deposits listed below, correcting errors (if any) *by the method used in your bank.*

2. Assuming that these are deposits of customers of the Institute State Bank, prove the deposits by the batch or block system.

Smith & Jones......	$1,026.05	check drawn on a New York City bank
	420.10	check drawn on a local bank
	110.04	check drawn on the Institute State Bank
	40.00	currency
Total	$1,596.19	
R. B. Stone........	$ 42.43	check on San Francisco
	10.12	check on the Institute State Bank
Total	$ 52.55	
R. D. Beckett......	$ 462.10	check on New Orleans
	410.04	check on a local bank
	105.05	currency
Total	$ 977.19	
J. J. Schroeder, Inc..	$ 27.35	check on Dallas, Texas
	104.62	check on a local bank
	42.41	currency
	689.37	check on Boston
	84.10	check on the Institute State Bank
Total	$ 947.85	
Hayes & Hayes.....	$ 710.10	check on the Institute State Bank
	87.78	check on Milwaukee
	110.10	currency
	49.94	check on St. Louis
Total	$ 957.92	
Paradise Theatre...	$ 101.01	check on the Institute State Bank
	987.31	currency
Total	$1,088.32	

CHAPTER IV

THE RECEIVING FUNCTION AND THE PAYING FUNCTION

The Purposes of This Chapter:
1. To explain the operation of the batch (or block) proof system.
2. To describe the duties and activities of the mail division.
3. To explain the duties of the paying teller and to describe the steps taken in the paying of a check.

THE receiving operation that requires the most time is the verification of the customer's total as shown on the deposit slip. This verification must be done by actually adding all the items, including cash, and proving the total computed by the customer. It may be a short and simple operation if the number of items on the deposit slip are few. In that case the teller can quickly make the verification while the customer is at the window and before entering the amount in the passbook. If there are few customers in line, the teller, by the use of a small adding machine in his cage, can even take time to verify the deposits containing a large number of items.

In many banks, where the volume of deposits is large or the deposit activity somewhat uneven, the duty of proving the deposit is shifted from the receiving teller to some other individual or department. This arrangement enables the teller to attend to a large number of customers at the window, eliminates delays, and reduces the number of receiving windows needed. It reduces the amount of floor space required, which is an important economy.

Proving the Deposit—A simple and effective principle is used in the verification of deposits. If every one of a group of deposits is correct, the sum of all will be correct and the entire group can be proved simultaneously at a considerable saving of time and work. The application of this principle results in the so-called *batch* (or *block*) proof. The department doing the work is called the *proof* (or *distribution* or *central proof*) department. Another term commonly used is *interior proof*. All these terms, as well as others which may be found, refer to the same department and the same sort of process.

In verifying the total, the teller balances the transaction between the customer and the bank. The teller must then balance the items and cash comprising the deposit with the other departments to which the items are sent for disposition. Checks that are drawn on his own bank go to the bookkeeping department; those on other local banks, to the clearings department; those on other towns and cities, to the transit department; and the cash, to the head paying teller.

In the application of the block system, the balancing between the receiving teller and the customer and between the receiving teller and all the departments *is done in one operation.*

The Batch System—The simplest operation of the batch system is by the use of a proof clerk for each receiving teller cage, or one clerk for several cages depending upon the amount of work passing through each cage. Using an adding machine, the proof clerk lists the amounts of the deposits in one column on a large sheet. In separate columns he lists the amounts of cash, checks drawn on his own bank, checks drawn on other local banks, and checks drawn on all other banks. If coupons or other items are accepted at the receiving window, a miscellaneous column is also included. Instead of proving across—that is, adding cash, "us" checks, clearings, and transits for each separate deposit—and then comparing this amount with the total given by the customer, the proof clerk adds each column, recapitulates the totals, and compares the result with

THE RECEIVING FUNCTION AND THE PAYING FUNCTION 141

the total of deposits. If all the deposits are correct, the totals will verify that fact. Thus in one operation ten or twenty deposits are *proved*. Moreover, the totals of items sent to the several departments are set up by this operation, and these totals are used for verification between the receiving teller and the departments concerned.

The typical batch sheet shown in Figure 13 illustrates this operation. Instead of having the actual cash passed on to the proof clerk or proof department, *cash tickets* are used, each one being a memorandum of the cash received in a deposit.

Some banks use *cash books* instead of cash tickets. The purpose of the cash book is to provide a permanent record of the various cash items handled by each teller against which a later check can be made whenever necessary. These cash books may be posted either in the receiving teller department or by the batch department.

One of the most advantageous features of the batch system is its flexibility, ranging from partial or occasional use in rush hours to continuous and constant use. The experience of a bank located in a town in an agricultural section will serve to show how the system may be operated on special occasions to excellent advantage. This bank is the only one in the town, which is the county seat and has a population of 2,500. It is subject to an unusually high peak period on Saturday, and while the quarters are adequate for normal business, no extra cages are available for the peak receiving period.

Prior to the use of the block system, customers waited in line to make deposits on Saturday evening so long that they became irritated, and the tellers were so busy that they did not have sufficient time to verify the deposits properly. This condition naturally resulted in mistakes and differences between the bank's records and those of depositors. Other departments of the bank also suffered from the additional burden placed on the tellers. After the close of banking hours

142 THE RECEIVING FUNCTION AND THE PAYING FUNCTION

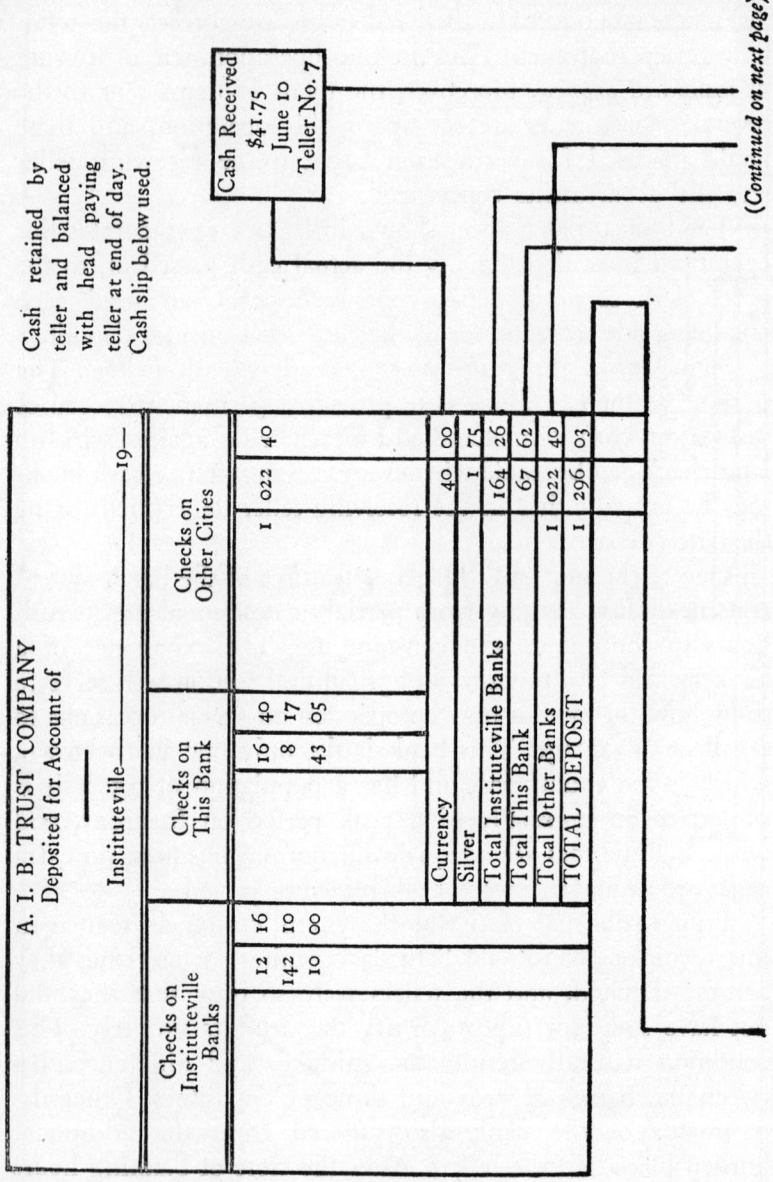

(Continued on next page)

The size of the department varies with volume. In a moderate sized bank, two or three persons can handle the work, while in large banks the department is usually so large that it is divided into groups, each handling the work of certain tellers.

The distribution department is characterized by accuracy, speed, and ability to carry peak loads. It must be able to handle a large volume in a short time. In Chicago, for example, the time for clearing is 10:30 a.m. on week days. For banks located in the downtown financial district, this means that the final deadline at the clearings department for including items in the daily trade is 10:15 or 10:20. The banks open for business at 9:00 a.m. There is a rush between this hour and the deadline, then a short lull, then another peak, and so on through the day.

Specially developed adding machines are used in most proof departments. By the use of these machines, batches of items are listed and totaled, and the subtotals are carried forward to a final section total, thus greatly simplifying the department proof.

A machine devised for this work in recent years deserves comment because it indicates the extent to which mechanical ingenuity is assisting bank operations. The machine is described in more detail in the chapter on clearings operations; hence at this point it is sufficient merely to note that by means of a revolving drum in the machine, a selective mechanism, and adding devices, checks are listed, totaled, and sorted to subdivisions of departments and deposits are proved in one operation. This machine seems to be particularly effective for banks with a large volume of items or unusual peak loads.

The Mail Division—Some individual or department in each bank is charged with the responsibility of properly sorting and distributing the incoming mail and of collecting and mailing the outgoing mail. In small banks this work is performed by one person, who finds it necessary to devote only a part of his time to the work, assisting in various departments at other times. In larger institutions the volume of items is so great that a special department is required.

Another task assigned to the mail department is that of maintaining a messenger division for the purpose of delivering checks and other items, presenting items received by the collection department, and making the necessary trips to the clearing house association and other local banks. More properly, and often actually, the mail division should be called the mail and messenger division. This division, then, has four main duties:

1. The collection and distribution of incoming mail
2. The collection and dispatch of outgoing mail
3. The maintenance of adequate messenger service
4. The exercise of receiving teller duties when the mail deposits are handled by the department.

Incoming mail is carefully sorted and distributed to the various departments and officers of the bank. Mail is picked up frequently at the post office in order that the work of other departments may not be delayed. Generally, the mail department starts earlier each morning than the other departments so that the distribution of mail may be completed before general working hours.

Outgoing mail is also scheduled. The staff of the department may be divided into groups for handling the different classes of mail—regular, special delivery, insured, and registered. The work of collecting and mailing the outgoing mail begins in the early afternoon. Letters are collected at regular intervals from officers' desks and departments; they are stamped, sealed, and often delivered to the post office each hour until all the day's mail is out.

In large banks part of the established routine of the collection of out-of-town checks and other items is the routing, both as to collection points and as to train and plane schedules. By scheduling outgoing mail to make these connections, a day is often saved in the time of collection. The mail department in such cases must be prepared to maintain a service to meet these arrangements, and often the responsibility for such special arrangements is definitely assigned to a member, or members, of the department.

There are many operations which require messenger service. The return of unpaid clearings to the sending bank, the presentation of items by the collection department, the delivery of statements to customers, the mailing of letters that must reach the post office at definite times, and many other similar tasks must be performed by the members of the bank's messenger force.

The duties of messengers are assigned by the head of the mail division, and often messengers have regular trips or *runs* to make daily. Since the messenger, in his capacity as such, is the bank's representative and since he comes in contact with customers of the bank, other business firms and individuals, and other banks, the impression created by his conduct and appearance has an importance that is recognized by all progressive institutions. A neat appearance, an alert manner, and courteous action are expected of him at all times. He must, above all, note his instructions carefully, understand them, and carry them out precisely. If he has the slightest doubt as to the proper procedure in a particular case, he should check with his superior to make sure that he is doing the proper thing. Many banks start all employees as messengers.

Whether or not any receiving teller duties are assigned to the mail department depends largely upon the number of out-of-town commercial or bank accounts, for such customers make deposits by mail habitually. If the number of mail deposits is not large, they are distributed directly to the receiving tellers to be handled in the same way as over-the-counter deposits. Where the mail deposits are large, the mail division is organized to verify and to charge the deposits in the same manner as do the receiving tellers. The prompt and accurate handling of mail deposits enables the bank to have the items ready for the clearings. If the other departments receive the items from the mail teller before the counter deposits begin to come in, there is a more even and a steadier flow of work. Reference to the time schedule of operations reproduced in Figure 5, Chapter II, will show that the mail division greatly assists the other departments by starting its work early.

For various reasons, banks located in large centers have a great number of accounts of other banks. They also have many accounts from out-of-town industries. The deposits to these accounts are made almost entirely by mail or by telegraphic transfer. In the mail deposits there are always a large number of local clearing items; thus it is doubly important for the mail tellers to be efficiently organized.

In recent years various attempts have been made to decrease the rush periods at the receiving windows or to increase the bank's deposits by encouraging *banking by mail*. Some of these attempts have been quite successful. One metropolitan institution has developed this service to such an extent that over 10% of its daily deposits from *local* customers are made by mail. The bank provides prepared forms and envelopes and makes special efforts to render the procedure convenient. The taking of this 10% load from the windows had a particularly significant effect in this bank, for its deposit growth has been so rapid as to tax space, equipment, and personnel. Not only has the crowded condition at the receiving windows been reduced, but since the mail deposits can be handled at earlier hours in the morning and under more favorable circumstances, the bank finds that the change has been satisfactory and profitable from an operating standpoint.

THE RECEIVING FUNCTION AND THE PAYING FUNCTION 149

Mail Division Organization—The mail work can be handled in most banks with a small or part-time force, the clerks working on the incoming and outgoing mail when they can be spared from their duties in other departments. Often an hour or so a day is sufficient for the incoming mail to be sorted and distributed and for the outgoing mail to be collected and mailed. If that is the case, one clerk will start sorting before banking hours each day and will distribute the mail early in the morning; he will then gather and mail the outgoing mail in the afternoon.

In other institutions one or more full-time clerks are required for the mail work. This is particularly true if there are registered or special delivery mail problems. In one bank studied, the person designated as mail clerk was found to be kept busy handling nothing but incoming and outgoing mail. From 8:00 to 9:30 a.m. he is engaged in sorting and distributing mail; from 9:30 to 11:30 he is engaged in proving mail deposits, sorting and distributing the late in-mail, and collecting the first out-mail. His lunch hour is from 11:30 to 12:30. At 12:30 he starts collecting and mailing the out-mail, including registered and special delivery, and he makes the last pick-up at 3:30 p.m. After that time mail is handled by the transit clerk.

To give the student some realization of the task that confronts the mail department of a city bank, the following outline of the work of the mail department in a large bank is given.

This department starts work at 6:30 a.m., when a force of twenty men report for incoming mail work. All mail is first sorted; mail designated on the envelope for delivery to a particular department or individual is distributed unopened, while all mail addressed generally to the bank is opened and sorted. Whenever the contents of a piece of mail furnishes no indication as to the department or individual for whom it is intended, it is sent around the bank by messenger until the proper department or individual is located.

By 8:00 a.m. there is sufficient work to require a force of eighty persons. This force proves deposits by the batch system; it is assisted by the twenty clerks from the early shift and by twenty machine operators for a peak period from 8:00 a.m. to 10:15 a.m., the deadline for local clearings. After this hour about one-fourth of the force is shifted to other departments.

The early shift is through work at 2:00 p.m. and the regular force handles the outgoing mail. A special cage is maintained in the mail department for receiving and sending registered and special delivery mail.

The activities of one section, the deposit proof division, indicate the scope of this department. Over a period of a year, this division handled a *daily average* of 1,946 credits and 37,663 debits.

Mail Department Equipment—The equipment of the mail department varies according to the volume of mail, the volume of items handled in mail teller work, the peak periods, and the amount of registered and special delivery mail.

If the department proves mail deposits, the supply of sorting racks and adding machine equipment must be adequate. A cage must be provided for registered and special delivery mail. In some banks where the number of registered pieces is small, the paying teller may do the work. An ordinary volume of mail can be sealed and stamped by hand. A larger volume may demand, for efficient operation, the use of a machine, or machines, for the sealing of envelopes. In addition, a metered system of stamping postage is frequently used. By imprinting on the envelope the amount of the postage and the number of the user of the machine, this metered postage machine has the double advantage of doing away with the handling of stamps and of providing an accurate postage check through the meter total. Where a large volume of mail must be handled at some period during the day, the rapidity and ease with which the metered system works is very evident.

The Paying Function

The Paying Teller Department—The paying teller department has two main duties: (1) *to act as custodian of the cash kept on the bank's premises* (under direction of the head paying teller); (2) *to be responsible for the proper cashing of checks presented at the window.* In some banks the paying teller also "pays" checks presented through the clearings. Paying tellers are selected for their experience, knowledge, and accuracy, for after the checks are cashed the tellers have much less opportunity to correct errors than do the workers in other bank operations. If an error in a deposit is not detected by the receiving teller at the time the deposit is made, it is often corrected through the operation of the batch or block system, or it may be found by other verification activities. After a check is paid, however, it is almost impossible to locate an error.

At the end of the day the paying teller balances what he has left in the way of currency and coin against what he had at the start, plus any additional money received and less payments made. If his cash proves and he has previously balanced with the various departments to which the items have been sent after being paid, he is sure that all transactions have been accurately performed. If, however, his cash does not prove at the end of the day and he has to check his transactions over again, it is difficult to ascertain just where or in what transaction the error was made.

Protection of the Cash—The head paying teller, as custodian of the cash on hand, has the problem of accounting for the cash and also the problem of so adjusting the work and operations as to minimize the threat of robbery. In meeting this problem he is assisted in every possible way by mechanical aids, for no well managed bank neglects to provide (within reason) alarms, safety devices, and the like which will protect the cash and prevent exposing the paying teller or others to undue danger.

First in importance is the vault equipment. Modern vaults are both burglarproof and proof against danger from fire, flood, or other catastrophe. The vault door with its time lock control, the inner compartments fitted with combination locks, and the wired alarm system that operates whenever the vault is tampered with provide physical protection from the time the cash is put away until the next business day when the vault is opened. Moderate sized banks find that a good vault, with wired alarm and a night watchman, provides sufficient protection for out-of-banking hours. Larger banks employ outside watch systems in addition to their own force, and these extra watchmen check at regular intervals to see that all is well.

The protection of cash in vaults during the hours when the cash is locked in is not a difficult problem; it becomes a question of efficient equipment and alarms. The chief problem is during the day when the main vault is open, when the working cash of the bank is distributed to various cages, and when customers and others are passing through the bank lobby. It is then that the criminal is most likely to attempt a hold-up.

There are a number of ways in which this danger from daylight banditry can be minimized. Vault equipment with additional safes under time locks may be used for currency; as the time elapses the locks are reset if the currency in the particular safe is not needed. Tear gas guns, bulletproof glass at tellers' windows, alarms conveniently located in cages, all aid in stopping raids. Space does not permit of an explanation of the many useful devices for the protection of cash; so many kinds of devices are available that a selection can be made to fit any situation. The insurance against loss by robbery that is habitually carried by banks is costly under the most favorable circumstances, but insurance companies charge higher premiums if the means used to protect the cash are inadequate.

The head paying teller can do much to minimize the possibility of losses by the manner in which he supplies cash to other tellers and departments. By seeing that each teller has a sufficient amount but no more than necessary in his cage, the head teller can keep the amount outside the vault at a reasonable figure, providing additional cash during the day as needed or taking back excess cash from tellers and departments. By thus regulating the amount of currency in the various cages, the paying teller keeps close and competent control of the bank's cash.

From the standpoint of internal control, it is customary for more than one person to be present at the opening and closing of vaults or safes, often the head payer and a member of the auditing department. By dual control—that is, the use of two men who have knowledge of combinations—a better protection is afforded than is possible with only one custodian. From the head payer's standpoint this is advantageous, for he has a verification at the opening and closing of the vaults that everything is in proper order.

Protective Work of State and County Associations—Much credit is due to state, county, and other bankers associations for their work against bank robbery and fraud. The limitations of regular local police and the mobility of robbers because of fast cars and excellent roads combine to handicap the banker in a small or moderate sized community. The forays of robbers became so prevalent in some parts of the country at one time that insurance rates became prohibitive. Led by local and state associations, a fight was waged upon these bandits, mainly through the cooperation of local citizens in trained vigilante groups, through the spreading of alarms by telephone, and through the blockade of roads with the cooperation of agencies in other towns and counties.

In some states, a state police force is established, and recent legislation by Congress has widened the operation of federal law-enforcing agencies. Members of the Federal Reserve System and of the Federal Deposit Insurance Corporation come under the wing of federal protection, and the offender against these banks has not only the local and state agencies to combat but the national as well.

The bankers associations also broadcast information on frauds that are attempted and descriptions of criminals operating in their territory. Through the combined efforts of banks in posting rewards for the capture and conviction of these criminals and through the cooperation of association members in presenting evidence at trials, the losses from both robbery and fraud have been greatly reduced.

Currency Service—Through the service of banks in connection with currency and coin, many conveniences not duplicated by other institutions are offered to the public at large. New currency is put into circulation and old, mutilated, retired, or counterfeit money is retired from circulation through the banks. *By the diligence of bank tellers, an important check is placed upon counterfeit money,* for banks are always informed of counterfeit money in circulation and are on the alert to detect it.

The Bank's Cash—Any bank that is a member of the Federal Reserve System is required to carry its entire legal reserve in the form of a collected balance with the Federal

Reserve bank of its district; therefore, the money which a member bank has on hand in its vaults or cash drawers for the cashing of checks, making up payrolls, and the like cannot be counted as legal reserve. An adequate amount of currency and coins of proper denominations must be on hand at all times to meet the requirements of customers, and the decision as to the amounts and denominations required must depend largely upon the knowledge and experience of the head paying teller. The needs of customers vary widely, and to meet them the head payer must consider also the location of the bank and its accessibility to funds from correspondent and Federal Reserve banks.

In a city where a Federal Reserve bank or branch is located, a member can obtain currency in the proper denominations, as needed, by drawing upon its balance. If a bank is located at some distance from its Federal Reserve bank or branch, the time element becomes important. Currency shipments are constantly being made both between banks and between banks and customers, and the time required for these transfers of actual currency and coin must be given consideration so that the supply will at all times be neither inadequate nor excessive. If the cash on hand is frequently inadequate, inconvenience and sometimes the expense of emergency currency shipments will result. On the other hand, banks do not like to have too large an amount of cash on hand, since the additional insurance premiums covering its protection against loss from bank robbery may run into a considerable sum of money.

The amount of cash kept on hand for ordinary daily purposes is called the *working fund*. In many banks this fund is under the control of the head paying teller, who charges out to the other tellers each morning the amounts needed for change or for payment purposes. During the day, if necessary, he supplies them with additional funds or has excess returned.

Each teller should have sufficient currency for customers' needs, but excessive amounts in the cage especially during banking hours should be avoided. All cash is returned to the head paying teller each night. Receiving tellers turn in the currency and coins deposited, the collection department turns in the cash received from its collections, the loan and discount department turns in the cash payments of interest and principal on notes, and so on.

Besides the working fund, additional cash is kept in the vaults for unusual requests or unanticipated demands. This is known as the *vault cash;* it is packaged and sealed and rarely handled except when examinations are made to verify the amount. So rarely is this fund disturbed that it is often under dual control—usually the head paying teller and the auditor —and changes in the vault cash often must be officially approved. For accounting purposes, a separate control account for the vault cash is carried on the general books.

The Handling of Money—To facilitate handling, currency and coins are packaged in convenient standard amounts. Currency is packed in bundles of various amounts from $100 up, and each bundle is kept together with a heavy paper strap upon which is printed the amount and the denomination contained in the package. This strap also bears the initials of the teller who actually counted and placed the money in the package, so that if there is any error, it can be traced back to the person responsible. To be readily accessible, these packages are generally stacked in compartments or racks.

The various coin denominations (cents, nickels, dimes, quarters, and half dollars) are wrapped in rolls of heavy manila paper in standard amounts, and each roll is stamped or initialed by the teller putting up the package. A change machine is used for odd amounts of coins. This machine delivers the desired amount when the proper keys are depressed.

THE RECEIVING FUNCTION AND THE PAYING FUNCTION 157

A drawer divided into compartments for various denominations is used for loose currency.

In cashing a check for $204.52, for instance, a customer might request $100 in $10 bills, $100 in $5 bills, and the balance in currency and change. To make this amount, the paying teller would use a package of $100 in $10's, $100 in $5's, $4 from the currency drawer, and the balance from the coin changer.

The Proving and Packaging of Money—The work of counting, sorting, and packaging currency and coins is ordinarily done entirely by the paying tellers. Occasionally, however, the receiving tellers and others may assist in the work. If a large volume of currency is handled, a separate cage or division, called a *currency cage,* is established. The work of this division is devoted entirely to verifying, packaging, and otherwise handling currency. Automatic counting and packaging machines and other devices are used.

Since the care and attention required in handling currency is costly, banks make service charges to customers for handling currency in great quantities. Currency for payrolls, shipments to correspondents, and other requests of a similar nature must be handled without interference with the daily routine. In order that the bank may make adequate charge for the extra work, the head paying teller calculates the cost involved in handling deposits composed chiefly of cash—such as those of a bus company which deposits a large amount of coins daily.

Currency Services of Federal Reserve Banks—While the banks service the currency needs of the country, directly or indirectly they depend upon the facilities of the Federal Reserve banks and branches for currency and coins and for the retirement of mutilated currency and lightweight coins. One

158   THE RECEIVING FUNCTION AND THE PAYING FUNCTION

of the privileges of membership in the Federal Reserve System is that of obtaining currency and coin, when needed, from a Federal Reserve bank or branch without cost for shipping or handling.

Currency transactions between a member bank and the Federal Reserve bank of its district are similar to the relationship between a bank and its customer. When a customer wishes currency, he draws a check against his account and cashes it. Similarly, when a member bank wishes currency, it draws a draft against its balance at the Federal Reserve bank and cashes it.

When a member bank finds that the currency on hand is in excess of its needs, that excess currency is deposited with the Federal Reserve bank, just as a commercial customer deposits cash with his bank.

A member bank also, by telephone or telegraph, authorizes the charging of its account and the shipment to it of currency of suitable denominations. The cost of shipping currency to and from a member bank is defrayed by the Federal Reserve bank.

Without going into detailed statistics, it is interesting to note the figures on volume of operations of the Federal Reserve banks and branches, as reported in the Annual Report of the Board of Governors of the Federal Reserve System for the year 1938.

In the following table, "pieces" refers to two or more handled as a *single* item.

Number of Pieces Handled	*1938*
Currency received and counted	2,089,987,000
Coins received and counted	2,676,248,000

Amounts Handled	*1938*
Currency received and counted	$8,883,728,000
Coins received and counted	$ 271,128,000

Non-member banks use the Federal Reserve facilities indirectly, in that a non-member bank calls upon its correspondent bank for currency and the correspondent bank, in turn, depends upon the Federal Reserve bank for its supply.

Mutilated currency and lightweight coins are sent to the Federal Reserve banks for redemption and retirement.

Some idea of the magnitude of this service may be obtained from a consideration of the organization of the coin division of one of the Federal Reserve banks. Coin is received from member and non-member banks (for credit to member bank accounts); coin is paid out upon drafts on the Federal Reserve bank indorsed by authorized messengers, or coin is paid out in exchange for other cash. Such authorized signatures are kept on file in the same manner as are authorized signatures in a commercial bank.

The necessary records are kept, orders received by telephone or wire are verified and filled, and shipments are made by a force consisting of (1) a coin teller or supervisor; (2) a shipping clerk, who is also assistant to the coin teller; (3) a receiving teller; (4) five or six coin counters, depending upon the volume handled; (5) a typist; and (6) a part-time teller from another department.

Coins are placed in a circular pan and are fed into a coin counting machine. As they go through, a register totals the count and a bag attached at the lower part of the machine catches the coins. These bags are stamped with the amount and denomination of the coins and sealed; they are then ready for delivery to member banks.

In addition to the coin division, there is a complete and well manned currency division to meet the requests for currency.

Currency Services of Correspondent Banks—Banks located in financial centers in the various parts of the country provide currency services to their correspondent banks and to their commercial customers for payroll and other purposes. In some centers banks find that the currency work—sorting, packaging, providing payroll funds, shipments of currency, and the like—can all be done by a special paying teller. In one bank, for example, the special paying teller handles all these requests, in addition to accepting large deposits which include only currency.

In another bank in a large center, a special currency department consisting of five tellers is maintained. Currency and coin come to the department from three sources:

1. Receiving and paying tellers, for counting, sorting, and packaging
2. Out-of-town banks and commercial customers by registered mail or express
3. Delivery at the window by armored car transport representatives or by special messengers of customers.

All requests for currency of sizable amounts are filled by this department, whether for local or for out-of-town use. Local deliveries are made at the window to customers' authorized representatives (whose signatures are on file in the cage) and to the representatives of armored car companies also under specific authorization.

Out-of-town shipments are made by mail or express and are insured. Each shipment is dually verified, one teller making up the shipment and the other checking it, and both are present when it is sealed in the bag for shipment.

Exclusive of tellers proving, about $25,000 in coins and $50,000 in currency are handled daily. A regular schedule of charges for the service is in effect, and expenses are added.

Paying a Check—In paying a check presented at the window, the paying teller is governed by two major considerations. If the check is good and the party presenting it is properly identified, it should be paid; non-payment is a reflection on a customer's credit, and may render the bank liable for damages. If the check is not good for any reason or if the party presenting it is not identified to the bank's satisfaction, the check should not be paid; money once paid is difficult to recover, and if it has been paid improperly, the bank will suffer the loss.

In determining whether or not to pay a check, the paying teller is guided by the following conditions:

1. The customer must have a collected balance sufficient to cover the check.
2. The check must not be altered in any way.
3. The signature must be genuine and authorized.
4. The check may not be post-dated or have a "stale" date.
5. There must be no "hold" on the account by reason of attachment, bankruptcy of the maker of the check, or death of the maker.
6. There must be no stop-payment in effect.
7. The party to whom the money is being paid must be the proper party.

Sufficient Collected Balance—The customer must have a sufficient collected balance to pay the check. In the relationship between the customer and the bank, each is held to certain responsibilities and duties. Among them, the customer agrees always to have a balance sufficient to meet all orders drawn by him against the account, and the balance must be in the form of available funds—those actually collected by the bank. If the check presented exceeds the collected funds (but not the total balance), it is said to be *drawn against uncollected funds* and may be returned unpaid for that reason. If a check is paid in *excess of the balance,* the deficiency so created is called an *overdraft.* Overdrafts require special attention and sometimes result in losses; they are disliked by banks not only for these reasons but also because they are in effect unauthorized loans, not drawing interest, and are a violation of the customer's responsibility to provide sufficient funds. Bank examiners scrutinize the overdraft list and criticize any institution if overdrafts are large or if overdrafts of any customer are allowed too frequently. Banks follow the rule that overdrafts will be permitted only in exceptional cases, such as an overdraft on one account where other funds in excess of the amount are controlled by the same party. Some banks penalize overdrafts by making a charge. All banks make their position regarding overdrafts perfectly plain to their customers. So effective has been this control that today overdrafts are few in number and small in amount.

Generally, the paying teller has no option in the matter of payment. If there are sufficient collected funds and all other requirements are satisfactory, the check is paid; otherwise payment is refused. The one exception to this rule is that if the bank is familiar with the outstanding items, the customer may be permitted to draw against uncollected funds, but only with the approval of some designated officer, or officers, of the bank.

Alterations—The check must not be altered in any way. Another responsibility of the bank is that of paying the check only according to the terms established by the maker as to amount, date, and payee. Any change in the check is an alteration of the customer's order, and the bank is presumed to discover the alteration and refuse payment. The most common alteration attempted by criminals is that of increasing the amount of the check, which is called *raising* the check. A check for $10, for example, might be raised to $110 by the addition of a figure and additional writing in the space where the amount is written out.

Changing the name of the payee is a common form of forgery. Usually a criminal takes the precaution of establishing a name among merchants or others and by using this name is able to cash the check of a well known company if the change from the name of the original payee is not discovered.

Even the date may be changed, if for some reason it prevents the cashing of the check. In one case where such a fraud was attempted, a stop-payment had been issued against a pay-check which had been reported as lost. The stop-payment identified the check by date and amount. The person perpetrating the fraud changed the date to a week later and then attempted to cash the check by representing it to be for the current week's wages. In some cases the rule of responsibility for detecting alterations seems unfair to the bank, for many people are careless in writing checks and make alteration easy to accomplish and difficult to detect.

A check should be written in ink, and spaces which are left after the listing of amounts should be filled in by a wavy line. With a little care and attention given to the spacing of amounts so that they fit into position, a customer can assist the bank in protecting his account. There may be instances in which a customer is so lax that the bank may use this negligence as a legal defense; but as a rule the burden of proof rests on the bank.

Banks impress upon their customers the importance of filling out checks in ink, to eliminate, as far as possible, the temptation for alteration. Many banks have also adopted the use of safety paper for checks. This paper is so treated that it shows up attempts to change or alter the writing by the use of chemicals or erasures. While more expensive than ordinary paper, it affords considerable protection.

Banks were among the first organizations to make use of check protectors, which, by stamping the amount desired in ink and at the same time either perforating or roughening the check, make alterations or erasures extremely difficult.

These devices have also been adopted by many business concerns and their use is constantly increasing. However, mechanical devices alone should not be depended upon for absolute protection.

Forgery—The signature must be genuine and authorized. The bank uses the specimen signature of a customer for checking the genuineness of any order issued by him. The authority obtained from each customer also designates those who may *sign on the account*—that is, those whose signatures are authority for the bank in connection with that customer's funds. Both of these responsibilities must be met. In actual practice, unauthorized signatures do not present much of a problem and, if encountered, will usually prove to be a mistake on the part of officers of corporations who erroneously think they have authority to sign.

The responsibility for determining the genuineness of a signature is a very real one, inasmuch as the imitation of true signatures for the purpose of fraud is a widespread activity of criminals. If the bank pays funds upon a *forged* signature, it must stand the loss. Insurance is often carried for the bank's protection against loss of this kind.

The ingenuity of forgers is a constant source of loss to banks, but through the careful training of tellers, the dissemination of information by bankers associations on the activities of known criminals, and the cooperation of banks in the arrest and conviction of forgers, the losses from this source may be decreased.

The study of handwriting is an art, if not a science, and there are many persons who can identify the writing of an individual even when that individual attempts to disguise it. By constant study of signatures, a teller becomes familiar with a large number; he is able to recognize the peculiarities in any signature and becomes so adept that tampering with the hand-

THE RECEIVING FUNCTION AND THE PAYING FUNCTION 165

writing is detected instantly even when the fraud is so well done that the customer himself may be deceived. It occasionally happens that when a signature is questioned by a paying teller and referred to the customer, the customer is obliged to consult his records in order to discover whether the signature is his own or a forgery.

Specimen signatures are filed in each teller's cage for all customers whose signatures he may be called upon to verify. As explained in Chapter III, new specimen signatures are obtained at intervals in order that the teller may have current specimens on file. The teller knows most of the signatures that he is called upon to verify without consulting the signature file. Any signature with which he is not familiar is compared with the specimen, and if he is not satisfied that it is unquestionably genuine, he makes further inquiry, often by verifying the issuance of the check with the maker.

Stale or Post-Dated Check—The check may not be post-dated or have a stale date. The holder of a check is obligated to present it for payment within a reasonable time. If a check bearing a date three to six months old is presented for payment, it is investigated to see that payment is still the wish of the customer. Often it is not paid until approved by the customer. Each bank has in effect a time limit beyond which checks are considered *stale;* this limit may be ninety days or six months from the date of issue of the check.

A check dated in the future is not an effective order on the bank and does not become so until the date is reached. Such a check is said to be *post-dated,* and payment must be refused.

Bankruptcy, Death of the Maker, Attachment, and Other Holds—There must be no "hold" on the account by reason of attachment, bankruptcy of the maker of the check, or death of the maker. The relationship between a customer and the bank may be terminated by action of law, as in the case of bankruptcy or attachment, and the bank is stopped by such legal action from recognizing the authority of the customer on the account. In the case of an attachment, the court becomes the sole authority until it releases the attachment.

In individual accounts, the death of the drawer of a check immediately revokes all outstanding checks that have been signed by him. Therefore they are not paid if presented to the bank. State laws vary somewhat in regard to these matters and must be taken into consideration.

Stop-Payment—There must be no stop-payment in effect. Every customer has the right to revoke any check issued by him at any time before it is paid. If he properly notifies the bank of his desire to have an order revoked, the bank is then bound to see that it is not paid. This notification is called a *stop-payment* order (see Figure 14).

To avoid liability by refusing to pay such an item, a bank requires that the order to stop payment be in writing and signed by the customer. Occasionally a telephone request for stop-payment is accepted if the customer is well known and properly identified. When this is the case, a written verification of the stop-payment order must be furnished immediately.

If a bank pays a check after it has received a stop-payment notice, it must collect from the party, or parties, to whom the money has been paid, which is sometimes difficult.

Watching stop-payment orders is not a hard task, for they are not numerous and older ones are checked in connection with stale-dated checks.

An officer or department head is designated to receive stop-payment orders; duplicates are made and sent to the bookkeeping and paying teller departments, where they are kept in a reference file. For further convenience, the paying teller may post an up-to-date list of all stop-payments against accounts in his division.

STOP-PAYMENT REQUEST

....19.......

To X BANK AND TRUST COMPANY
   NEW YORK, N. Y.

Please stop payment on .... No. ....

dated .... for $ .... in

favor of ....

In requesting you to stop payment of this or any other item, the undersigned agrees to hold you harmless for all expenses and costs incurred by you on account of refusing payment of said item and further agrees not to hold you liable on account of payment contrary to this request if same occur through inadvertence, accident, or oversight, or if by reason of such payment other items drawn by the undersigned are returned insufficient.

This request is effective for 30* days, but renewals may be made from time to time.

No stop payment request, renewal, or revocation thereof heretofore or hereafter given shall be valid if oral or unless served at the bank.

Reasons for wishing payment stopped: ....

....

....

Date stopped: .... Hour stopped: ....

....
(Signature of Depositor)

* Insert 30, 60, or 90 days or any period of time desired.

FIGURE 14. STOP-PAYMENT FORM

Identification—The party to whom the money is being paid must be the proper party. A bank is under no obligation to pay a check until and unless it is satisfied with the identification of the indorser and his right to the check. In most instances, checks are presented for payment by customers or others who are well known to the teller. When this is not the case, the party presenting the check may be able to identify himself by means of papers in his possession, but the paying teller must be certain that these papers are *bona fide*. Many companies and organizations supply their representatives with identification cards to assist them in cashing salary checks and expense checks, or else they file with the bank the signatures of employees. In other cases the company or individual guarantees the signature of the indorser.

Sometimes checks drawn on other banks are cashed by the paying teller, usually because of the good standing of the indorser, for there is no way to check the other points before cashing such an order.

Most banks have definite rules to guide the teller. He may be instructed to refer to some designated officer, or officers, matters of identification or requests to cash checks on other banks. The officer indicates his approval by initialing the check and adding some code notation. In many banks the tellers' cages are so near the officers' quarters that no extra precautions are needed to prevent forgery of these approvals by evildoers. In banks where the tellers are not in the line of vision of the officers, it is customary for the approving officer to send an item back to the teller's window by a guard or himself to accompany the party whose check has been approved. Sometimes the location of the bank and the nature of the items for which approval is sought determine whether any precautions other than the approval of the check by an officer's initials and a suitable code will be required.

Special Payer—In order that regular customers may be taken care of promptly and efficiently, it is often advisable to set up a cage for a *special payer* who deals only with customers that carry large accounts or with those needing special attention. Such a teller handles payroll requests, large currency deposits, and currency shipments. When shipments of money are made, this teller prepares them and either delivers the shipments at the window to authorized express or money transfer companies or sends them out by express or registered mail.

Unit Teller System—Before considering the organization of the paying teller divisions, the work of the unit teller system should be thoroughly understood, particularly since this arrangement has been found suitable for both large and small banks. In the unit teller system, both paying and receiving are done in the same cage for a certain group of accounts, whether selected alphabetically or by number. At the end of the day the teller usually carries over his remaining cash, reporting the amount only to the proof department; from the records of this department the auditor, in combination with the head teller, obtains a proof of all cash.

Under the unit system the teller becomes familiar with the accounts in the group assigned to him, and where the depositing and the cashing of checks by customers are fairly regular, the work can be done more efficiently by such a teller. Customers or their representatives often have deposits to make and checks to cash at the same time, and it is an advantage to have both of these operations handled by one teller rather than by two tellers at different cages.

Paying Teller Organization—Paying teller divisions are set up, and these divisions have arrangements similar to those of the receiving teller divisions as to the alphabetical handling of accounts, the unit system of paying and receiving on a group of accounts, and the system of using two or three paying cages to take care of all accounts.

Department Operations—A description of the paying teller division of a large bank will illustrate the set-up. In this bank the vault cash is under the joint custody of the auditing department and the head paying teller. The working cash is subject to the head paying teller's control. Any changes made in the vault cash must be reported to the cashier by the auditing department.

There are six paying teller cages, and each handles an alphabetical group of accounts—A to C, D to G, and so forth. At the beginning of each day, the head paying teller, from the working fund, charges out to each cage the cash that is to be used for the purpose of paying checks. At the end of the day, all cash is turned in to the head paying teller. (In many banks the tellers carry forward their own cash from day to day, turning over to the head teller only excess amounts.) During the day, if necessary, he makes additional charges to the paying tellers. The cash returned at the end of the day, plus checks cashed, is balanced against the cash charged to each paying teller's cage in the morning and during the day.

Proving Currency—In this bank, as in many large banks, there is a separate currency cage or department. Each morning this department counts, sorts, packages, and proves all the currency that has been checked into the head paying teller's custody the night before from the paying teller cages and other cages or departments. The currency cage also has charge of the shipments of currency to customers. These currency shipments are assembled by one teller and proved by another; they are packaged and sealed in the presence of both tellers and are then sent out by registered mail or express.

The currency cage handles all other special requests from customers, including regular payrolls. Special deposits consisting almost entirely of cash, such as those of a local bus company, are received by this cage.

Equipment—Each paying teller's cage is provided with special drawers divided into compartments for the storage of the various denominations of currency. It is also supplied with a coin changer and with coins in rolls of standard size. Packaged cash is kept in racks, divided into equal amounts of the same denomination.

In each cage is posted a list of all stop-payments in effect against the accounts handled by that cage. Duplicate signatures in the form of photograph copies of the original signature cards are kept in visible record cabinets.

Communication with the bookkeeping department to verify balances, holds, and so on is made by means of a pneumatic tube system. Requests are written by the paying teller on a special memorandum slip and are sent through the tube to the bookkeeping department. The ledgers are consulted and the correct information is entered on the slip, which is then returned to the paying teller by the pneumatic tube. By the use of this system, the paying teller can take care of other customers at the window while awaiting verification of previous requests. (Later in the chapter other methods of communication, such as telautographs and intercommunicating telephones, will be explained.)

Other Departments—Counter change for other departments (such as coupon, collection, loan and discount) is provided by the head paying teller. Each morning the requirements of each of these departments are charged out to them, and each evening their cash is balanced and returned to the head paying teller. Thus there is a complete count and verification of all working funds every day, and a complete balancing of the cash of every department with the head paying teller.

Paying Teller Division in a Moderate Sized Bank—In a moderate sized bank it is not necessary to have a separate currency cage, since the work of proving currency is done by the paying tellers, sometimes with the assistance of the receiving tellers at quiet times during the day. Payrolls are made up by the paying tellers for customers in their division. Shipments of currency and special requests are handled by the head paying teller and his assistant. In other ways the operations of such a division are similar to those of the large bank already described. The head paying teller is custodian of the cash; he charges currency out to the paying tellers and to the other departments each morning and charges it in and balances it each night.

Paying Teller Division in a Small Bank—This division consists of one cage with two tellers assigned to it. They handle all payroll and other currency requests and shipments, cash all checks, sometimes pay savings withdrawals, issue cashier's checks and drafts, and prove all currency. In a larger bank, each paying teller balances his work, and a recapitulation is taken for the total paying teller division proof. In a small bank, however, the balancing of the work is the total proof not only of paying teller activities but also of cashier's checks and drafts, both issued and paid, since they are included in the proof sheet.

Certification—In many business transactions, the obligation of a bank is required instead of the obligation of the customer. In bids for construction work, for example, a small percentage of the total bid must be deposited to insure good faith, this pledge being in the form of a bank obligation. In transactions between security houses, the payments for securities are generally made by bank obligations.

These obligations are usually in the form of cashier's checks, which are orders of the bank on itself, or bank drafts, which are orders on one of the bank's correspondents. A bank obligation may likewise be created by the *certification* of a check.

While banks are not required to do so, they are usually willing to certify customers' checks as a courtesy to their customers. Certification is accomplished by stamping across the face of the check an acceptance that is worded similarly to the following:

CERTIFIED

PAYABLE ONLY AS ORIGINALLY DRAWN
AND WHEN PROPERLY INDORSED

NAME OF BANK

Authorized Signature

The certification statement is signed by the cashier or other designated bank officer. *In accepting or certifying a check, the bank guarantees the "goodness" of the check and agrees to pay the amount to a holder in due course.* The check then becomes an obligation of the bank; the funds are charged against the customer's account immediately and are transferred to the "certified check" account on the general books of the bank. The check is paid as far as the customer is concerned. It is charged to his account, and he has no further control over it. For example, it is impossible for him to stop payment on it.

Certification is made by the paying teller, who follows the same procedure as when he pays a check except that identification of the party presenting it is not necessary at this time. Banking law prohibits the certification of a check when the customer's balance is insufficient, and tellers are most particular on this point. Banking laws also regulate certification in some states (Pennsylvania, for example) by requiring that the bank obtain the customer's permission or that of his agent before making certification.

In localities where the use of certified checks is extensive, the number and amount outstanding often reach substantial proportions, and the service rendered the customer by certification is an important one.

Special Tellers—We have seen that in many banks it is customary to use special tellers to handle payroll requests, large currency deposits, and shipments of currency. The advantage of routing such requests to a special teller is that the regular cages are not delayed in their ordinary work by requests that require extra time to handle. Special problems arise out of the activities of chain stores, filling stations, and similar organizations, where the receipts of each unit or branch must be accounted for separately from the others. The receipts from several filling stations belonging to the same company may be deposited separately. In order to handle such deposits most effectively, the bank arranges to have them made at a special window, and the proving of the deposits and crediting to the parent company's account is done by this special cage.

Chain stores often make arrangements with bonded transportation companies to pick up the receipts from the branches and deposit them in the bank. These armored car companies may make all deposits at the special cage in order that the work may be more economically and effectively handled and with a minimum of inconvenience to other customers.

The special cage can be used to advantage by banks of all sizes and in all locations, either as a permanent method or as a temporary expedient. In a certain community of 10,000 population in the East, the main problem of a special service nature is the cashing of payroll checks of the principal business in the community. The payroll checks are presented on Saturday evening in large numbers. To meet this situation, one paying teller becomes a special teller during this period and devotes his entire time to the cashing of these checks, thus making it possible for the regular customers to be served without delay at the windows of the other tellers.

Segregation of special requests and designation and training of tellers for the work will solve the problem that arises when unusual or extensive special services must be given.

Applying the Safeguards—The duties involved in the paying of a check may appear to be a constant burden on the teller, but in actual practice they are performed rapidly and easily. The teller, selected for his training and experience, is accustomed to consider his responsibilities in the light of his knowledge of the customer or of the account involved. Most requests for cashing checks are from customers who are well known to him, others are from persons properly identified, and so only a relatively few requests require judgment.

The paying teller is aided in his duties by the bank's policies and its established operating procedure. The strict attitude of a bank toward accounts near the borderline of sufficient and not sufficient funds, the careful selection of business through the new account procedure, the close cooperation between the bookkeeping department and the paying teller, the assistance of the counter officers in approving or disapproving requests, all combine to make the number of checks the paying teller must investigate thoroughly few in proportion to the total handled. In some banks all checks drawn on other banks are paid by a special paying teller. This practice eliminates from the regular teller all checks except those on his own bank drawn against accounts in his section.

The Qualifications of a Paying Teller—It is obvious, without further comment, that the paying teller must be a man of unquestioned integrity and honesty, since he is required to handle large sums of currency. He should possess a natural aptitude for the work. Some persons are exceptionally well fitted for the work of paying; others seem to be temperamentally disqualified. The selection of those best suited for the tasks is a responsibility of the personnel manager.

A primary qualification of a paying teller is accuracy, since mistakes in his work are difficult to correct. Speed also is essential, for often there are rush periods to be met.

Another qualification is the ability to detect alterations or forgeries. It is difficult to explain the methods by which paying tellers detect such frauds. Some of their ability is the result of experience; some of it seems to be due to a natural instinct to observe and detect variations at a glance.

Not only must the paying teller be thoroughly familiar with the mechanics of his position, but he must realize, through a knowledge of the principles involved, just what the consequences of his mistakes or omissions may be.

Add one more qualification, courtesy, and the sum total is an efficient, well rounded individual.

How effective the paying teller can be in his work, how rapidly and readily the required tests can be applied in actual practice, is shown in the two examples which follow.

Out of fifty checks presented at the paying teller's window in a bank recently, forty-three were presented by people who came to the window regularly and frequently. The teller knew these accounts so well that an examination of the checks was all that was necessary. One request required reference to the stop-payment file, since the drawer of the check had stop-payments out against several checks which had been lost. Two checks were those of customers whose checks were seldom presented at the window, and the balances of these accounts were checked by the teller with the bookkeeping department. Two requests required identification of the party, which was readily accomplished. Two more were referred to a counter officer for identification and approval of the indorser.

By actual count in another institution, the best trained and most experienced paying teller paid 141 checks the day of the count, an ordinary day as far as volume was concerned. Only one of the accounts involved was checked for sufficient balance, two checks required identification, one was referred for stop-payment and one for signature, none were referred to counter officers, and the rest were cashed without reference.

THE RECEIVING FUNCTION AND THE PAYING FUNCTION 177

Forms and Equipment—Few forms are necessary in the paying teller department. The paying teller's proof is the most important, and either combined with it or on a separate sheet is the memorandum of checks cashed, called the *scratcher*.

AMOUNT	INDORSER	KIND OF ITEM
Teller		Date

FIGURE 15. SCRATCHER FORM

In receiving teller operations, the indorsement of the checks and the deposit slip may be used to trace any item either while it is in the bank or after it has been forwarded for payment. In the paying teller department some record must be made on the checks cashed to identify the teller who cashed them, and for his information there must be a readily available record of the transaction which is complete enough for him to identify the circumstances of the transaction. (See Figure 15.)

The identification of the teller who paid the check is made simply by the use of a rubber stamp with the symbol or number which has been assigned to him or his cage. Upon the scratcher sheet kept for his own information he may list the amounts, makers, and indorsers of the checks cashed by him.

A machine which is particularly adaptable for the recording of a complete description of the items cashed is the recordak, which is really a moving picture machine into which checks are placed and photographed. The film then becomes the record and can be projected when desired, thus eliminating the need for cage scratchers and often for teller identification.

Communication between the paying teller and the bookkeeping department is maintained in several ways. Where space permits, the bookkeeping department may be located in the rear of the receiving and paying cages. When the tellers need to verify the amounts of balances or to obtain other information, they note their request on a slip, which is picked up immediately by a messenger or bookkeeper and returned in a few moments with the correct information. Pneumatic tube systems and intercommunicating telephones are used when the departments are located at a distance from each other. The pneumatic tube system has already been explained.

In one bank in which the intercommunicating telephone system is used, there is a telephone at each bookkeeping section. When the teller desires information which a particular section can give, he calls that section and states his request, and the bookkeeper calls the teller back when the information is ready.

Another useful device is the telautograph. The teller writes the information desired on a broad tape in a machine which instantly duplicates this notation on the tape in a machine in the bookkeeping department. The bookkeeper writes the answer on his machine, and it is duplicated on the teller's machine. By the use of these machines, it is possible for the information to be obtained with only slight interruption of either the teller's or the bookkeeper's work.

In a San Francisco bank, five telautographs are used in the bookkeeping department, one in front of each section consisting of three or four bookkeepers. Any teller can communicate with any one of the fifteen or twenty bookkeepers. When a message is being sent, a red light flashes on the telautograph in the section from which information is desired, and a buzzer signals the particular bookkeeper so that no other bookkeeper need stop his work. Each day the tapes upon which the messages have been written are dated and filed for reference.

In using the telautograph or other written forms of communication, it is advisable, for the protection of tellers and bookkeepers alike, that each request for information and the answer be initialed by the persons requesting and imparting the information.

The use of communicating systems of various kinds and their arrangement is an operating problem in each bank. A system which is readily adaptable in one bank may not be so useful in another. Therefore each bank uses those systems that experience has shown are most satisfactory.

Questions Based on Chapter IV

1. What two operations are performed simultaneously by the batch proof system?
2. How can the need for a distribution department be determined?
3. State the four main duties of the mail department.
4. What type of work does the mail teller do?
5. What are the two main duties of the paying teller department?
6. What tests are applied by the paying teller in determining whether or not to pay a check?
7. What is meant by stop-payment? Who can require it?

8. Who is responsible for detecting alteration or forgery?
9. What is the effect of a post-date on a check?
10. Explain what is meant by the term uncollected funds. What are overdrafts?

Questions for Outside Investigation

1. What type of paying teller system is used in the commercial department of your bank?
2. What are the duties of the mail division of your bank?
3. Is the batch or block system used in your bank? If so, what name is used for the department that operates the system?
4. What tellers in your bank handle payroll requests? currency counting and packaging?
5. Who accepts stop-payment orders in your bank?

Assignment

As the cashier of the Institute State Bank, you are confronted with two operating problems. The first is the peak load on the receiving tellers from 10:00 a.m. to 1:00 p.m. each Saturday and from 12:30 p.m. to 2:00 p.m. on week days. You have a teller who can be used for the additional work and an extra receiving window available. You also have a competent machine operator in the bookkeeping department who can run a modified batch system, which you do not now operate.

Your other problem is that of cashing payroll checks for a large manufacturing company, an excellent customer of the bank. The peak load in this work comes from 1:15 p.m. to 2:30 p.m. on Saturdays, and to a smaller degree from 12:00 noon to 1:00 p.m. on Mondays.

There is only one extra cage, so if it is used for receiving teller work alone, there will be no facility for a special paying cage. What would be your solution—a special paying teller, a modified batch system, an extra receiving teller, or some combination of these?

Write your conclusions and the reasons for them briefly, not exceeding 200 words.

CHAPTER V

THE CLEARING PRINCIPLE. ANALYSIS OF ACCOUNTS

The Purposes of This Chapter:
1. To explain the clearing principle.
2. To review the constructive influence of clearing house associations.
3. To explain the duties and operations of the clearings department.
4. To discuss the purpose of analysis of accounts and to describe the methods used.

THE clearing principle may be defined, broadly, as *the offsetting of counterclaims and liquidation of balances.* This process is applied to claims other than checks, but in banking the term *clearings* is understood to mean the daily exchange of checks between local banks and the settlement of net balances in one amount. Thus the characteristic feature of the bank clearing operation is the exchange of checks between local banks at a set time each day and the payment or collection of the balance in one sum.

No better examples of the variations in banking terminology could be found than the terms that are used to describe the principle of exchange and settlement. The local application of the principle is termed *clearings;* the nationwide application of exchange and settlement is called *transits;* and the application of the clearing principle in foreign trade is given the distinguishing name of *balance of trade.* These terms, as used in commercial banking, should be clearly understood, for they denote precisely some operation or series of operations and are always used in that particular sense.

An excellent way to determine the utility of a method or arrangement is either to dispense with it and observe the effect or else to imagine that no such arrangement exists and see what other procedure might be used, and with what results.

Therefore, in order to determine just how important the clearing arrangement is to banks, let us suppose that no such arrangement exists and that banks have to use other ways and means of collecting checks drawn on local banks.

An individual who holds a check drawn on a local bank other than the one in which he carries an account may collect it in either one of two ways. First, he may present it in person at the paying teller window in the bank on which it is drawn, identify himself, and cash the check. As we observed in the study of the paying teller division, this practice is not followed extensively; in fact, most of the persons presenting checks at the paying teller window are customers of the bank.

If the individual uses the other method, he will have his own bank collect the check on his behalf; therefore, he either cashes the check at his bank or (more frequently) deposits it. The bank, in turn, presents it and receives payment if the check is good. If no clearing arrangement exists, the bank must present the item at the paying teller division of the bank on which it is drawn, just as the customer himself might have done.

Consider what a task it would be to present the thousands of local items deposited by customers. Even if the items drawn on each of the other banks were consolidated and presentment made in batches, the result inevitably would be the constant use of a large messenger force, many trips a day, and hundreds of adjustments of balances, verifications, payments, and refusals. Contrast that cumbersome, costly, and generally unsatisfactory procedure with the daily clearing operations between banks in thousands of cities and towns in all parts of the world, by means of which the items on each other are presented *at one time, at one place,* and are paid for *in one total.* It would be hard to estimate just how cumbersome and costly the collection of checks entirely by messenger would be, but some idea of the cost may be obtained by comparing the cost of presenting a collection draft by messenger with the cost of presenting a check through the clearings. An analysis of these operations by the most accurate method of cost accounting determined the cost of collection by messenger to be twenty-five cents, while the cost of presenting a check through the clearings was found to be not over one cent for each item.

The objectives of a clearing arrangement are threefold: (1) to dispense with the expensive and cumbersome process of presentation by messenger, (2) to reduce to a single settlement the many interbank settlements that would be required under the messenger system, and (3) to reduce cash payments by using other forms of payment that are equally acceptable and much more convenient.

In order to accomplish these objectives, certain regulations and agreements are necessary:
1. Agreement as to the time and place of clearing
2. Agreement as to the kinds of items that will be accepted
3. Provision for the correction of errors
4. Arrangements for the return of dishonored items
5. A method of settling balances.

The voluntary associations formed by banks for the purpose of exchanging checks drawn on each other and of settling the balances arising out of that exchange are called *clearing house associations*.

Clearing House Associations—*Clearing house associations, then, are formed primarily to facilitate the exchange of checks between banks and the settlement of balances arising out of that exchange.* Since such an association is entirely voluntary, the rules adopted by its members comprise its only source of authority. These rules are enforced by a series of fines imposed for violations, and the maximum penalty is expulsion from the association. This is effective enough, for the advantages of membership in the association are so substantial, in the saving of both time and money, and the prestige attached to membership is so well recognized that no bank will forfeit the connection for light and trivial reasons.

The rules and regulations of a clearing house association are set forth in its by-laws, which are expanded or revised from time to time as occasion demands. The executive work is carried on by association officers elected by the member banks. In small associations, the banks contribute management without cost to the associations, and also provide the necessary clerical help. In large associations, salaried executive managers and other employees are needed, in addition to the regular officers, because of the large volume of business and the many other activities of the association.

Nearly every city in the world has a clearing organization, generally known as a clearing house association. In a recent edition of the Rand McNally Bankers Directory, 350 clearing house associations were listed as operating in the United States alone.

The Operation of Clearing—To illustrate the principle of clearing, let us consider the situation in a southern city in which there are six banks. One of the customers of the First National Bank is the local electric light and power company. Checks deposited by the light company in the First National Bank are drawn on all six banks, since the customers of the company are customers of the several banks.

Without a clearing house arrangement, the First National Bank would have to send the checks to the other banks by messengers. On presenting the checks, the messengers would receive payment in cash if the checks were good. Many trips would be necessary each day, and after each trip new balances would have to be made. All the other banks would have to send messengers to the First National Bank to collect checks deposited by their customers. The result would be a steady stream of messengers going to and from each bank. So many messengers would be needed and so frequent would be the settlements that the banks would be engaged in the work of collection and settlement from the opening until the close of business each day.

The clearing house arrangement greatly simplifies all this. The six banks meet each day at the place agreed upon and make the exchanges. As the exchanges are made, the manager of the clearing house association determines the net result for each bank and informs it whether a balance is due from the other banks or whether it is required to pay a debit. In one simple operation the complicated procedure of collecting by messengers is eliminated. With only one clearing a day, the internal work of the bank is expedited. Once the clearing is over and the settlement made, that division of the work is out of the way. Under the old system it continued from the opening of the bank in the morning until its closing hour in the afternoon.

How effectively exchange and settlement are accomplished may be seen from the figures made public by clearing house associations. During the year 1938, for example, the Chicago Clearing House Association had clearings totaling $14,561,-389,212.38. The settlement balances were $1,508,321,625.20. Not a single cent of these settlements was made in cash; all payments were effected through clearing house settlement accounts maintained with the Federal Reserve Bank of Chicago.

The information contained in Figure 16 is the result of the operation of a clearing house in a city with five banks, all members of the association. In this instance, the exchange takes place at eleven o'clock each morning in the directors' room of the Citizens State Bank. The manager of the clearing house association is an assistant cashier of the First State Bank in that city. He acts in this capacity for one year, as an incident to his position with the First State Bank. One of the clerks of his bank assists him. By annual rotation, each bank provides the manager and clerk without expense to the association.

Each bank has two representatives: a *clearing messenger,* who makes the actual exchanges, and a *settlement clerk,* who keeps a record of the exchanges both for and from the other banks.

Shortly before eleven o'clock, representatives of the five banks arrive at the designated clearing place, bringing the packages of checks which are to be exchanged with the other banks. As each clearing messenger enters, he gives the manager the total of the items being exchanged by his bank with the other banks (this is the total of the items listed under the column headed "Debit C.H." on the individual bank's sheet, as shown in Figure 16).

When the signal is given by the manager at eleven o'clock, the settlement clerk remains at the desk provided for his bank, while the clearing messenger distributes the checks to the banks upon which they are drawn. Thus, each bank receives the checks drawn on it in exchange for the checks drawn on the other banks.

As each batch of checks is received, the total is noted on the individual bank's sheet in a column headed "Credit C.H.," as shown in Figure 16. As soon as these credits are entered and totaled, a memorandum is sent to the clearing house manager showing the total of checks brought to the clearing house, the total of checks received from other banks at the clearing house, and the difference. These figures are then entered in the proper columns on the clearing house proof (see Figure 16) by the clearing house manager; they serve to verify the total clearings and also make up the clearing settlement total.

As soon as the clearing house proof sheet is completed, the figures are "called back" to the individual banks. If the figures balance, that fact is announced; if they do not balance, the

THE CLEARING PRINCIPLE. ANALYSIS OF ACCOUNTS 187

Individual Bank Sheets

Debit C. H.	First National Bank	Credit C. H.	Debit C. H.	First State Bank	Credit C. H.
$ 1,026.33	First State	$ 2,014.10	$ 2,014.10	First National ...	$1,026.33
5,631.01	Jones Trust	5,716.30	5,965.50	Jones Trust	6,210.02
1,262.12	F. & M. State ...	498.17	410.05	F. & M. State ...	320.20
3,246.09	Exchange National	3,162.12	2,102.10	Exchange National	2,116.11
$11,165.55		$11,390.69	$10,491.75		$9,672.66

Debit C. H.	Jones Trust Company	Credit C. H.	Debit C. H.	Farmers & Merchants State Bank	Credit C. H.
$ 5,716.30	First National ...$	5,631.01	$ 498.17	First National ...	$1,262.12
6,210.02	First State	5,965.50	320.20	First State	410.05
110.90	F. & M. State ...	205.40	205.40	Jones Trust	110.90
1,042.10	Exchange National	962.43	1,072.62	Exchange National	627.03
$13,079.32		$12,764.34	$2,096.39		$2,410.10

Debit C. H.	Exchange National Bank	Credit C. H.
$3,162,12	First National ...	$3,246.09
2,116.11	First State	2,102.10
962.43	Jones Trust	1,042.10
627.03	F. & M. State ...	1,072.62
$6,867.69		$7,462.91

Clearing House Proof

Bank	Balance Due to Clearing House	Bank Dr.	Bank Cr.	Balance Due to Banks
First National Bank	$ 225.14	$11,390.69	$11,165.55	
First State Bank		9,672.66	10,491.75	$ 819.09
Jones Trust Company ...		12,764.34	13,079.32	314.98
Exchange National Bank ..	595.22	7,462.91	6,867.69	
Farmers & Merchants State Bank	313.71	2,410.10	2,096.39	
	$1,134.07	$43,700.70	$43,700.70	$1,134.07

The total, $43,700.70, is the *clearings* figure, or total exchanges, which is used for comparative purposes to indicate business activity. The totals presented by the clearing messengers on arrival are entered in the Bank Credit column. After the exchanges have been made, the totals received from other banks, as reported to the clearing house manager by the various banks, are entered in the Bank Debit column, and this column total serves to prove the Bank Credit total. In like manner, the two columns Balance Due to Banks and Balance Due to Clearing House must balance, since they represent the net settlement made as a result of the clearings.

In this clearing house proof, it will be noted, the clearings are *for* the First State Bank and the Jones Trust Company and *against* the First National Bank, the Exchange National Bank, and the Farmers & Merchants State Bank.

Figure 16. Individual Bank Sheet and Clearing House Proof

clearing house manager states the amount of the difference, and each settlement clerk checks over his figures until the error is located and corrected.

Banks with debit balances are required to pay over to the clearing house manager at an agreed hour the amount they owe. Payments are often made by drafts drawn on the Federal Reserve bank or branch in a nearby center. The receipts are then distributed by the clearing house manager to the banks with credit balances. Formerly, settlement was usually made in cash but this practice is now uncommon.

The operation of the moderate sized clearing house association which has been described is characteristic of the clearing operation which takes place every business day in hundreds of cities and towns in the United States.

In the larger cities it is necessary to maintain a permanent force and to have a space specially equipped to facilitate the exchanges. In such cities there is generally an oval or circular counter placed in the center of the room used for the exchanges, with divisions assigned to the various banks. The settlement clerk takes his position at his designated station, and the exchanges are made by the clearing messenger, who delivers the packages by making the circuit of this counter. So well organized are these large clearing house associations that frequently all exchanges are made, the figures balanced, and each bank informed of its net debit or credit within fifteen or twenty minutes after the actual start of the operation.

Settlement may be made in various ways—through a clearing house settlement account maintained with one of the local banks, through accounts maintained in a neighboring large center, or (as in Chicago) through balances maintained with the Federal Reserve bank.

A method of settlement that merits comment is the *wire clearing balance*. Through the facilities of the Federal Reserve

System, many clearing house associations wire (in code) to the Federal Reserve bank of their district the debit and credit balances of the members of their association as soon as the exchanges have been made and balanced. The balances are then debited or credited, as the case may be, to the reserve accounts which these banks carry in the Federal Reserve bank. Thus the clearings settlement is made by the adjustment of balances on the books of the Federal Reserve bank, and the individual banks simply make bookkeeping entries to conform to these settlements.

Maintenance of Clearing House Associations—The revenue necessary to establish and to maintain a clearing house association comes from three sources: (1) membership fees, (2) current assessments on members, and (3) fines imposed for violations of rules.

1. Membership fees. The membership fee is usually a fixed sum, such as $100 or $1,000, which each regular member contributes. In cities where the initial fee for membership is large, an affiliated membership is also provided for smaller banks that desire to receive the benefits of membership but for whom the regular fee is too great an expense. An affiliated member is required to subscribe to the rules and regulations of the association and to pay the penalties imposed for violation. It may enter the clearing transaction either directly or through the deposit of its checks with a regular member. If the second practice is followed, the regular member incorporates the checks of the affiliated member in its own consolidated total and accepts as part of its debits from other members the checks drawn on the affiliate.

2. Current assessments on members. A clearing house generally prepares a budget for a period in advance, and in this budget estimates are made of the various costs of operation. The major expenditures, such as salaries, rent, and current

costs, can be fairly accurately estimated. While some variation in the other expenses may be expected, the net result will not be far from the estimate. After the budget has been adopted, the amount required is prorated among the members upon an equitable basis, such as the volume of clearings for the preceding period. The revenue thus obtained is the major source of income for the association.

Assessments are made at regular intervals—annually, semi-annually, or monthly. The Louisville, Kentucky association (which, incidentally, has been in continuous operation since November 24, 1875) provides in section 4 of its regulations: "The expenses of the Association shall be assessed monthly upon the several members of the Association from time to time in an equitable manner as determined by a majority vote of the members present at a regular meeting of the Association."

The Chicago Clearing House Association provides in section 18 of its rules: "The expenses of the Clearing House shall be borne and paid as follows: Each member shall be assessed annually Two Thousand Dollars ($2,000.00), and the balance necessary after that pro rata according to their daily average of the exchanges sent to the Clearing House for the months of October, November, and December, immediately preceding."

3. Fines imposed for violation of rules. Fines are imposed for many reasons—late arrival at clearing, errors, boisterous conduct on the part of messengers, and others. This is, of course, a minor source of income.

Other Clearing House Association Activities—While the primary purpose of a clearing house is to facilitate the exchange of checks, it is only natural that the habit of cooperation formed in solving the mutual problems of the exchange of checks should lead the members to use the association for other purposes beneficial to the local banking situation. In large clearing house associations a trained staff is used to examine the condition of member banks. These examinations are particularly helpful since a knowledge of local conditions by the examining staff, obtained through constant work in a limited geographical area, results in reports of outstanding merit. In many cases in the past, concerted action on the part of clearing house member banks has prevented disaster by making possible the consolidation of weak institutions with strong ones with the publicly announced support of the entire association. Naturally, the condition of any bank requiring such action would be revealed by the *clearing house examination*.

With the increasing complexity of problems common to banks, *the clearing house association has become the vehicle for establishing local rules to solve those problems.* Service charges, banking hours, interest on deposits, trust fees, exchange charges, and the procedures in providing other facilities are the subjects of study by the association; and the standard procedures adopted as a result of such study all tend to improve the banking facilities for customers and to increase profits of the member banks. Innumerable examples of local banking problems that have been solved in a constructive way through the medium of the clearing house association could be cited.

In discussing the importance of local clearing arrangements, the application of the clearing principle in wider areas through the collection of checks payable in other cities and towns must not be forgotten. The most important and far reaching application of the clearing principle is that made by the Federal Reserve System, which acts as a nationwide clearing house. The application of the principle in these wider areas is a *transit* matter and therefore will be considered in the discussion of the transit department.

The Clearing House Department—This department should *not be confused* with the clearing house association. The *clearing house,* or *clearings, department* is the division of the bank that is charged with the duty of preparing items for exchange at the clearing house association and of distributing to the bookkeeping department the checks drawn on its own institution which have been received from the other banks. For purposes of operation, this department is frequently divided into two sections: the *out-clearings* and the *in-clearings*.

Out-Clearings—The *out-clearings section* prepares the checks for exchange at the clearing house. The checks come to this section from several divisions or departments in the bank. Many of them come from the receiving teller, by reason of deposits made by customers; from the mail division come checks received in deposits by mail; the collection department turns over checks received in payment of items handled; checks cashed by the paying tellers and items from various other departments and cages are also turned over to the out-clearings section. From the time the section starts work until the deadline for the clearings, checks from these various sources pass to the out-clearings section in a steady stream. On the receipt of checks from any teller or department, a balance is drawn, and the checks are then re-sorted in racks, which have separate compartments for each bank in the clearing house association. This process continues until shortly before the time set for the items to be in the clearing house association for exchange; the *deadline* is generally twenty or thirty minutes before that hour.

After the checks are sorted, each package is totaled, and the total is entered on the sheet for the settlement clerk. In "running up" the checks in these packages, an adding machine with a carbon tape is used; one list is attached to the package to be exchanged, while the other is kept by the out-clearings section for reference in case of error. All this work must be completed a few minutes before the clearing time, and when the messengers have left for the clearing house association, the operation of out-clearings is completed for a time.

The need for speed in preparing the checks for exchange is so urgent that a special machine for sorting and listing the checks is now in use in the larger banks. This machine is equipped with a drum divided into twenty-four compartments. When a check is to be listed, the operator enters the amount by the adding machine keyboard, presses a selector key corresponding to the sorting desired, and puts the check into a slot. The automatic sorter puts the check in the proper compartment; the listing is entered on an individual tape at the back of the machine and on the master tape at the same time. The total clearings figures also are automatically listed on the master tape. When the sorting is completed, the operator removes the checks from the compartment and attaches the individual list. After the bank's indorsement or receipt stamp is affixed, the checks are ready for the clearings. The machine contains devices for preventing missorts, for notifying the operator when any compartment is filled to capacity, and for signaling when the tape is running low.

In the recording of items for the clearings, the simplest of all bank records is made, the so-called *straight list,* which is merely a list of the amounts of the checks and their total. This is all that is necessary in the clearings operations, because comparison with the tape list in case of error in an item or of its return unpaid will be sufficient to identify the item in question. Since all clearings items are disposed of each day either by payment or by their return, only temporary records are needed; therefore the records of the clearing house department are the simplest of all departmental records.

Another type of machine developed in recent years and used extensively is the motion picture machine, adapted to bank use. This machine automatically photographs each check as it goes through the mechanism, and the film is used for *identification* purposes. While used to some extent in clearings operations, this device is more widely used in transit and bookkeeping operations, and it will be mentioned again in connection with the explanation of those operations in later chapters.

Operation of the Out-Clearings Department—In small banks there is no division into out-clearings and in-clearings departments, since a small force, often only one or two persons, can handle both out- and in-clearings. In one small bank, which is typical of others, the same clerk handles out-clearings, in-clearings, and transit work. Each morning this individual "runs up" the day's exchanges with the other banks, takes the checks to the clearing house for exchange, and receives the items drawn on his own bank. He sorts and charges these items to the various bookkeepers, and upon the completion of this task he starts on the transit letters to correspondent banks.

In a moderate sized bank the clearings are usually handled by three clerks, who work on out-clearings until 11:00 a.m. and in-clearings from 12:00 noon until 1:30 p.m. After that they assist in the work of the other departments.

In large metropolitan banks the volume of items is so large that separate out-clearings and in-clearings departments are maintained. In one large bank the out-clearings department has a force of seventy-five clerks. On ordinary days these clerks handle from 150,000 to 175,000 items a day. On extra heavy days, such as after a holiday, the number of items handled may run as high as 300,000, or at the rate of 2,000 to 4,000 items a day for each person.

The clearings day extends from noon of one day to 10:30 of the next (the clearing hour), for after the regular morning clearings, the department is kept busy assembling the work for the next day. Most of the items received after the morning deadline for the clearings come from the receiving tellers, the in-mail division, and special tellers, although some are received from the other departments.

The items are first balanced and reconciled with the figures of the departments from which they are received; they are then sorted according to the banks with which the exchanges are to be made, listed, and again balanced. These batches are then ready to be sent to the clearing house association for exchange on the following day.

In-Clearings—When the messenger returns from the clearing house association with the checks drawn on his bank, the *in-clearings* section balances and then re-sorts them, charging the checks to the various bookkeepers. Any errors that are found, such as the receipt of a check not drawn on the bank, are corrected immediately. At the conclusion of the charging out to the bookkeepers, there are no totals either for or against in-clearings.

When this work is completed, the department as a whole may devote its time to out-clearings—balancing, sorting, and packaging the checks coming from the various departments, so that on the next day the staff may be free to start work immediately on the items received through the mail and from the various departments during the course of the morning. In metropolitan centers these out-clearings are often sent to (traded with) the other banks in the afternoon and in this case the amounts are included in the next morning's total.

Here again, the organization of the department depends upon the volume of work to be handled. In some banks the same clerk, or clerks, that handle out-clearings also attend to in-clearings. In other banks the volume is so large that separate departments or divisions are maintained.

In the metropolitan bank previously referred to in the operation of the out-clearings department, the in-clearings division has a force of eighty-six clerks, who handle the items in batches, ranging from 100 to 200 batches each day, or approximately the same volume as that of the out-clearings. After proving the batches received from the clearing house association, the items are sorted into eight groups for the bookkeeping department. They are then charged to the bookkeeping sections, a special charge being made to the country bank for drafts of correspondent bank accounts and a special charge to the general books for certified checks and cashier's checks which are obligations of the bank.

The in-clearings division also handles the checks drawn on the bank which are received from the Federal Reserve bank. These checks are obtained directly from the Federal Reserve bank and not through the clearing house exchange.

At the end of each business day the in-clearings department balances and no items are held over.

Forms and Equipment—No special forms are needed for either the in-clearings or the out-clearings department work. The only special forms needed in the exchange and settlement of items are those used by the clearing house teller.

The equipment of the clearings department is simple. It consists almost entirely of sorting racks and adding machines. While the special machines mentioned earlier in the chapter are used in some banks, standard adding machines are more commonly installed, since they are entirely adequate for moderate volume and more flexible in use.

Some of the members of the department are trained to become proficient in both sorting and listing and can be shifted in their work as occasion demands. There are times when sorting is heavy and other times, particularly just before the clearing hour, when listing and proving are heavy.

The routine of the clearings department is outlined in Figure 17, which shows the flow of items from departments

THE CLEARING PRINCIPLE. ANALYSIS OF ACCOUNTS 197

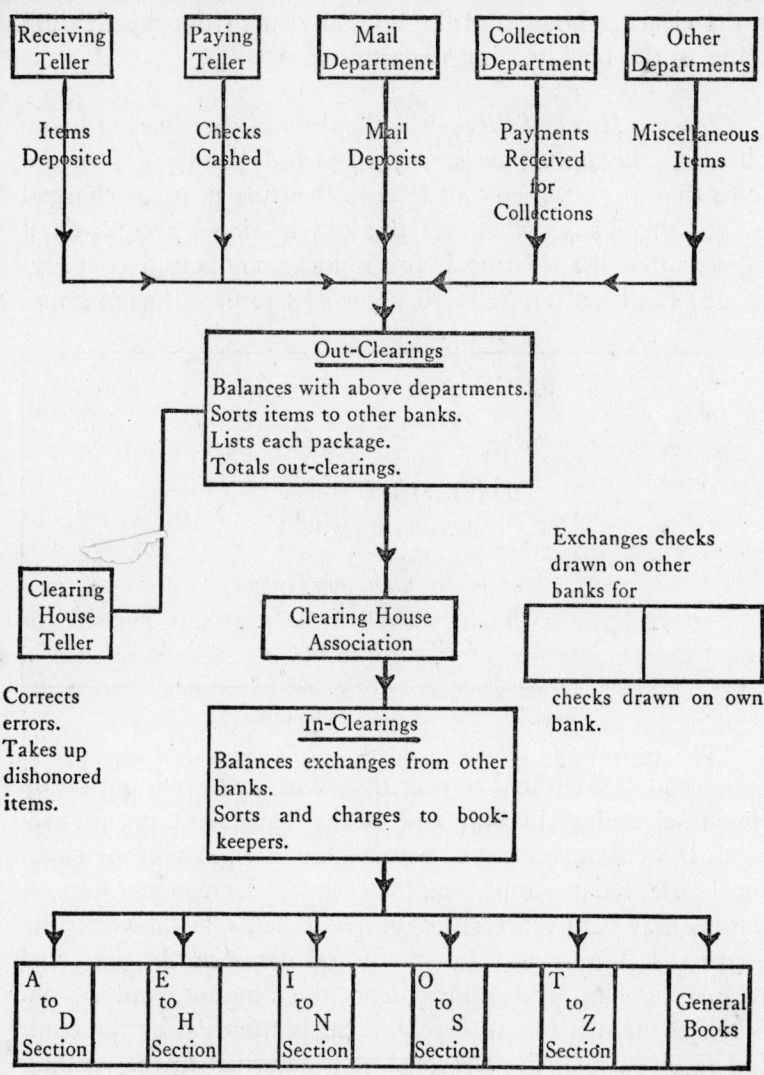

FIGURE 17. CLEARINGS DEPARTMENT OPERATION

to the clearing house and the flow of items from the clearing house to the bookkeeping department.

Clearing House Teller—It is the duty of the clearing house teller to take up (that is, pay for) and handle dishonored items that are returned and to correct errors in items charged to the other banks whenever this can be done. Frequently it happens that the clearing house indorsement stamp (see Figure 18) has been omitted. All items sent to the clearing house

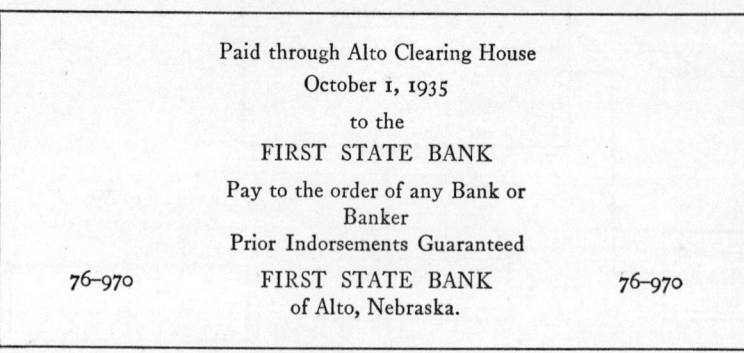

FIGURE 18. CLEARING HOUSE INDORSEMENT

association are required to bear this stamp, which is put on by the out-clearings division and is the equivalent of indorsement. If a check is returned because of this omission, the clearing house teller simply supplies the indorsement. Various reasons may be given for the return of items, as shown in the *return slip,* Figure 19. Many returned items can be corrected by guaranteeing the indorsement, the amount, and so on. When an item is found to require such attention by the bank that received it in the clearings, it is returned to the sending bank by messenger, presented at the clearing house teller's window, and either corrected immediately or left on receipt to be picked up later by the messenger.

THE CLEARING PRINCIPLE. ANALYSIS OF ACCOUNTS 199

Items that are not paid are called *dishonored items* and are returned to the sending bank by messenger, with a slip attached showing the reason for non-payment. These items are *taken up* by the clearing house teller, who accepts them and has a check issued to the returning bank in payment or pays cash if the amount is small.

In regulating the return of dishonored items, it is customary to have a time limit (generally in the afternoon shortly after the close of banking hours) before which an item must be returned if it is to be taken up; after that time has passed,

Returned by FIRST STATE BANK, ALTO Reason for return (x) below	
Indorsement	Payment Stopped
Receipt Unsigned	Signature Incomplete
Guaranty Alteration	Uncollected Funds
Guaranty Amount	Not Sufficient Funds

FIGURE 19. RETURN SLIP (SHORT FORM)

the sending bank is not required to take back the item. Such a regulation is necessary because many out-of-town checks are subject to special instructions, such as "wire payment" or "wire non-payment." If they are dishonored, they must be returned in ample time for the presenting bank to follow the instructions; hence the receiving bank must be in a position to assume payment if checks are not returned by the hour set.

If the hour for the return of dishonored items is fixed at 2:15, a bank to which a dishonored item is to be returned may, as a matter of courtesy, extend the time limit when there is reason to expect payment of the item if held longer. Let us suppose that the Second National Bank has sent to the clearings a check drawn on the Fourth State Bank and that the latter bank finds that the customer's balance is insufficient. Ordinarily, the check would be returned with a notation "insufficient funds." The Fourth State Bank, knowing its customer, believes that the item will be made good by a deposit as soon as the customer is aware of the deficiency in his account. Therefore, the Fourth State Bank asks the Second National Bank for *time,* meaning an extension of the return deadline for a quarter of an hour or half an hour, in the meantime endeavoring to obtain a deposit from the customer.

This courtesy observed between banks is primarily for the customer's benefit, for it is his desire to have the item paid. By waiving the deadline upon occasion, it is often possible to receive payment rather than have the item dishonored and returned.

Where the volume of clearings is so large that the handling of return items requires too much time and messenger service, arrangements are made for the acceptance of dishonored items by each bank; a record is kept and settlement for the items is included in the next day's clearings. For example, the First National Bank returns to the Second State Bank items totaling $4,528.17. Instead of paying for the items immediately, the Second State Bank issues a clearing house credit to the First National Bank, which includes that credit among its other items cleared and settled the next day. In other cases a time is set for the exchange of return items—a *clearing of returns.* This is in effect a smaller scale clearing, the difference being that only return items are handled and settlement for them is made through the regular clearings the following day.

General Operations—In handling both out-clearings and in-clearings, extensive use is made of the batch or block method of proving charges. For example, the amounts received by the out-clearings division from the various departments must balance with the totals of exchanges sent to other banks.

All items that go to the clearing house association must bear the indorsement of the sending bank; such indorsement serves to identify the source of the item and to guarantee prior indorsements (see Figure 18). The indorsement is made by a hand stamp or (particularly in large banks) by an indorsing machine.

The clearings department is organized with two main factors in mind: the *volume of clearings it has to handle* and *the rate at which deposits are received just before the clearing hour*. If the deposits are fairly steady from the opening of the bank until the clearings deadline, a somewhat different organization may be effectively used than if the rate of deposits just before the deadline is accelerated.

Large items deposited just before clearing time should be included, and so, instead of going through the ordinary sorting and proving routine, they are routed directly to a designated individual in the department, who includes them in the proper totals just before the messengers leave for the daily exchange.

Clearing Operations—In a large clearings department, two sections, the out-clearings and the in-clearings, are necessary to handle the volume of items, particularly where the bank has many correspondents and other customers outside the city who send deposits by mail in substantial volume.

In a smaller community, where there are three or four banks, for example, all members of the clearings department handle both out- and in-clearings; they handle the out-clearings up to the time for exchange, the in-clearings immediately after the exchange, and then work on either of the two as the occasion demands.

In still smaller institutions, the receiving and paying tellers run up the clearings, sort and charge them, and do all the work of preparing for the exchange. A messenger or settlement clerk then makes the actual trade at the clearing house association. This clerk, upon returning with the in-clearings, is assisted by the tellers in the work of charging and sorting to the bookkeepers. Thus no separate clearings department is used. In some banks the bookkeeping department acts as the in-clearings department.

Analysis of Accounts—The services of a bank are numerous and extensive, and the cost of providing them amounts to a substantial sum. If the owners of a bank are to attain their objective (*profit* obtained by *conservative performance of banking functions*), these services must be rendered at a profit. Profit may result from the use of deposits in loans and investments or from the collection of fees from customers for the performance of other services (or both).

In the earlier days of American banking, ample opportunities for profit presented themselves through the use of deposits in loans and investments. In recent years, because of changed conditions, it has become necessary to supplement these sources of income by direct charges or fees for other services rendered. There were many factors that helped bring about this change, the chief of which are outlined briefly in the following paragraphs.

Reference was made in Chapter I to the limited activity and scope of banking services in earlier times. The number of checks used in the early days of banking in this country was but a small fraction of the number used today. Limited trade areas resulted in localized banking, and few transactions involved the collection of checks drawn on banks in distant cities. Local merchants received a substantial part of their payments in currency, and other payments were made almost entirely by *local checks*. In those days, too, there were many channels for the employment of funds in earning assets, and interest rates were higher than they are now.

As the number of services increased and as banking transactions increased in both activity and volume, the expenses of banks increased correspondingly. For a time this increase was somewhat offset by the wide variety of sources for loans and investments and the continuance of interest rates at fairly high levels; but continued increasing activity and widening of services, together with decreasing channels for the employment of bank funds and declining interest rates, brought the matter of *cost of services* to the point where its control became a major factor in the successful operation of a bank.

This problem was partially solved by more effective bank operations, but even increased efficiency has not been sufficient to counteract the effect of decreased income from earning assets and increased volume and activity in banking transactions. So today, in order to receive adequate compensation for services rendered, banks find it necessary to collect fees directly from customers in the form of what are termed *analysis* or *service charges*. The first step in this procedure is the calculation, as nearly as possible, of the expense involved in performing each type of transaction. This analysis is called *cost finding*.

Cost Finding—Cost finding is a broad subject; it includes policies of bank management and administrative problems and actions, in addition to those bearing upon account analysis. Since management policies and administrative problems are dealt with in Banking III, only a brief outline of these factors will be given at this point, chiefly for the purpose of more clearly explaining the reasons for the analysis of accounts and the procedure established.

Expenses may be divided into two classes, *operating* and *overhead*. Although there are variations in this classification, expenses directly incurred by a department are generally considered operating expenses, while overhead expenses are those that apply to the bank as a whole. Such expenses as executive management, taxes, and cost of investments are regarded as applying to the entire bank and so are considered an *over-all charge*. There may be considerable variation in the allocation of overhead expenses to departments or to item charges or to account charges; at best the allocation can be only an estimate.

In the determination of overhead cost, a segregation of the general costs is first made by deciding which are actually general and which are specific department costs. In the next step, allocation of overhead cost to departments, many methods are used. By one method the overhead is simply divided by the deposits to determine the average cost per thousand dollars of deposits. Another method calls for the valuation of the space used by a department, the proportion of telephone service used, and so on; these expense items are then included in the amount chargeable to the department. Other methods are more detailed; in general, the method used by any bank will depend largely upon the extent of its activities and the advantages to be gained by a more or less exact system of cost finding.

Operating cost figures may be obtained more readily and applied more scientifically. To illustrate the procedure, let us take the bookkeeping department. The cost of equipment per year (figured on the basis of replacement and depreciation), stationery, supplies, wages, and salaries can be accurately determined, for these expenses all apply to the one department.

Once the operating cost of the department has been determined, it is a simple matter to divide that cost by the number of items handled and thus determine the average cost per item. This cost can be directly applied in analysis work. If the department is large and its work subdivided, a further breakdown of the cost of operations can very easily be made if desired.

Generally, the duty of figuring costs and allocating them is assigned to a particular individual—sometimes more than one. In a small bank the cashier is often assigned to this task. In larger banks the auditing, or comptroller's, division or the analysis, or planning, division does the work.

Service Charges and Analysis Methods—The object of analysis and service charges is to obtain fair and reasonable compensation for services rendered. While there are various methods by which these charges may be established and calculated, the three principal methods are:

1. The *flat,* or estimated, charge
2. The *metered* service, or graduated, charge
3. The *analyzed,* or calculated, charge.

As in the case of many other bank operations, different names are used to describe these methods, or combinations of them; *single standard, measured service charges,* and *activity charges* are among the many terms used. But whatever the name may be, the method will be found to be one of the three listed, or a combination of them.

The *flat,* or estimated, basis was the first method generally used and often is the initial one where a bank employs several methods. By means of cost finding, a bank may discover that accounts below a certain average monthly balance are carried at a cost which exceeds the income derived from the use of the funds. The bank therefore decides to make a flat service charge on these accounts. It may set $300 as the minimum balance required and make a charge on all accounts with average balances below that figure; or it may set up a graduated schedule of rates, the rate for any account depending on how much below this minimum figure its balance averages for the month. Under this system, an average balance below $300 but above $200 may be charged 50 cents each month, one below $200 but more than $100 may carry a monthly charge of $1, and an average balance below $100 may be charged $1.50 a month.

The flat charge has certain merits. If the general activity of accounts is low and the use made of the bank's facilities is fairly uniform among customers, the charge may be a reasonably fair one and have the advantage of requiring only a limited amount of examination of the accounts each month to determine the charge. Such a basis, however, is unsatisfactory when there are more than moderate variations in the activity of customers' accounts, or when the extent to which use is made of the bank's facilities by its customers varies. These variations often occur so frequently that the flat basis proves to be inadequate; hence many banks have discarded it for the measured, or *metered*, service charge.

The metered service charge goes one step further than the flat charge, for in addition to the charge based upon the size of the account, a partial activity charge is made. Metered service charges are most commonly applied by allowing a maximum activity per unit of balance and making pro rata charges for activity in excess of the allowance. The activity applies only to checks issued by the customer and does not take into account the cost of operations in connection with deposits, transits, collections, and so on. The following is a typical schedule of metered service charges:

Average Daily Balance	Maintenance Charge	Checks Permitted Each Month	Additional Checks Each
$200 to $300	$0.50	One check for each $10 average balance	5¢
$100 to $200	$1.00	One check for each $10 average balance	5¢
Under $100	$1.50	One check for each $10 average balance	5¢

To use a simple illustration, let us consider two accounts with a $250 average daily balance, one with thirty-five checks issued during the month and the other with fifteen. Under the flat charge basis, both accounts would be charged the same, although the cost to the bank in each case would differ since one account is more than twice as active in checks issued as the other. With a flat charge of 50 cents for average balances from $200 to $300, each customer would be charged the same amount, 50 cents.

Under the *metered* service plan, the first customer would be charged the maintenance fee of 50 cents and an additional fee at the rate of 5 cents for each check issued over the number allowed for each $10 of average balance. With an average balance of $250, therefore, he would be entitled to twenty-five checks without charge, leaving ten to be charged for at the rate of 5 cents. This activity charge plus the maintenance charge of 50 cents would bring the total charge to $1. Since the second customer, who also would be entitled to twenty-five checks, issued only fifteen, he would not be subject to the activity charge, his total charge representing only the maintenance fee of 50 cents.

The Analysis Method—Both the flat charge basis and the metered service basis result in estimated profit and loss statements of the accounts. The analysis basis is used to determine the actual profit or loss on each account by taking into consideration all the factors that apply to that account. For example, let us consider the account analysis form (Figure 20), which is widely used, and from it observe the steps taken and the reasons for them.

In account analysis four series of calculations are necessary. First of all, the bank must find out what portion of each account is available for use in earning assets—that is, the total funds that can be employed in loans, investments, and the like.

Therefore, the object of the first calculation is to ascertain the average daily balance of the account for the period under analysis; this is a relatively simple matter. As we have already learned, banks make up a duplicate record for each account, called the *customer's statement*. Upon it are listed all deposits, all checks paid, and the balance for each day. The daily balances are listed on the right-hand portion of the statement, and this section is divided by perforations from the remainder of the statement. When a statement is prepared for delivery to a customer, the balance column is torn off, and the information is used for the purpose of ascertaining the average daily balance. The *average daily balance* is computed simply by totaling the balances at the end of each day and dividing by the number of days involved.

The next calculation, as the account analysis form shows, relates to *average daily uncollected funds*. The average daily balance is simply the amount to the credit of the customer. Some of it may represent items deposited (cash items for which credit has been given) but still in the process of collection. If the bank in which this analysis is being made is located in Chicago and a check for $1,000 drawn on a New York bank is deposited today, the customer's balance will be increased by $1,000 today, *even though it will be two days before the check reaches New York, is presented through the clearings, and paid*. So for two days, while the $1,000 is included in the customer's daily balance, the amount is in the process of collection, and the bank has not received payment. This situation is true of all checks deposited that are not drawn on the bank itself. Such amounts are called the *uncollected,* or *float,* balances. Obviously, funds not yet collected cannot be employed in loans and investments and so must be deducted from the average daily balance to find the amount collected.

Float will be considered in more detail in the discussion of the transit department in the following chapter. At this point,

THE CLEARING PRINCIPLE. ANALYSIS OF ACCOUNTS

it is necessary merely to understand what float is, and also to know that the length of time required to collect a check drawn upon some bank other than the one in which it is deposited has been estimated and included in tables, which are called *availability schedules*. These schedules show the number of days needed to collect checks drawn upon banks in other major cities, and in all states.

There are two ways of figuring float for analysis purposes. One is to carry the amount uncollected in each daily analysis figure until by the schedule of availability it should be collected. For example, a $1,000 item that requires four days for collection could be set up on the work sheet as an uncollected amount for four days; but since analysis is based upon the *average* balance, float, and collected funds combined, the second method is more commonly used. This method simply considers the $1,000 item requiring four days to collect as the equivalent of $4,000 for one day—as it is from a float calculation standpoint—and all items are reduced to a one-day basis. For example, the float on three items $1,200, $500, and $2,200, with respective availabilities of 2, 3, and 4 days, would be computed as follows:

$1,200 for 2 days equivalent to........$2,400 for one day
$ 500 for 3 days equivalent to........ 1,500 for one day
$2,200 for 4 days equivalent to........ 8,800 for one day
                                                 $12,700

Thus, instead of carrying each amount forward for the number of days, the total is used, and the average is found by dividing this total by the number of days in the analysis period. This method, of course, can be used only for analysis purposes, because actual uncollected amounts and not averages must be used in such cases as paying the check (discussed in Chapter IV).

One more step must be taken before the net loanable, or usable, balance is determined. Banking laws require certain sums to be set aside as reserves. In the case of Federal Reserve members, these reserves must be in the form of balance at the Federal Reserve bank, and they are not available for loaning and investment purposes. Therefore, the amount required for reserves and also the amount of cash needed to be kept on hand for cashing checks, making up payrolls, and the like must be taken into consideration in arriving at the net loanable balance. The analysis reserve percentage of 18% (shown in Figure 20) is based on these two factors; by deducting this percentage figure from the net available balance, the *net loanable balance* is obtained. This represents the amount of each account that may be used in earning assets.

Income—The next series of calculations deal with the income received from the use of net loanable funds, *together with* any income received directly from the customer. The estimated income from the use of net loanable funds is calculated by multiplying the *net loanable balance* by the *average interest earned* by the bank (considering the interest received in relation to the collected portion of each customer's deposit). Then *exchange* is added. In some localities a charge called *exchange* is made for checks drawn on banks in other cities, the charge taking into account the expenses of collection. Exchange charges are collected from the customer either at the time each check subject to exchange is deposited or at the end of the month for all checks that have been deposited. Since exchange charges constitute a direct income from the customer for services rendered, they are properly included as income in the analysis. Exchange charges collected are therefore an offset to the analysis cost of handling the items. Any other income is then added; such income may include special fees for currency services, collection department fees, and other

Account Analysis

Month of ——————— 19__

Average Daily Balance			
Less Average Daily Uncollected Funds			
Net Available Balance			
Less 25% Cash Reserve			
Net Loanable Balance			
INCOME			
Interest on Loanable Funds @ 2½%			
Exchange Charged			
Miscellaneous Income			
Total Income			
EXPENSE			
Transit Items @ 2¢ per item			
Clearing Items @ 1½¢ per item			
Checks on Us @ 3¢ per item			
Deposit Tickets @ 6¢ per ticket			
Currency Deposited @ 30¢ per M			
Investment Cost $ per M			
Miscellaneous (itemize)			
Total Expense			

Total Income			
Total Expense			
Desired Profit $\frac{1}{12}$ of 1% of Required Collected Balance			
Profit or Loss			

REMARKS

FIGURE 20. ACCOUNT ANALYSIS FORM

charges. The total of interest earned on loanable funds, exchange received, and miscellaneous income is the income for the account.

Expenses are next calculated. The expense for each item handled or each transaction completed is established by the cost-finding method. To determine the expenses for the account, the number of items or transactions handled is multiplied by the respective *unit* costs. Thus, in the analysis form we observe that the cost of handling transit items is 2 cents each, clearings $1\frac{1}{2}$ cents each, and so on. The information as to the number of items (called *item count*) or transactions comes from various sources. The number of "checks on us" and the number of deposits will show on the ledger sheet in the bookkeeping department; the amount of cash deposited will show on the deposit tickets, which also show the number of clearings and transit checks deposited. In gathering this information, sometimes each department or teller provides the analysis information from his own department; in other banks a separate analysis department gathers all the information.

These cost calculations and the charges imposed as a result of them must be computed as carefully as possible. If care is not taken, the analysis will not be fair to the customer or to the bank and will thus defeat the very purpose for which analysis is established. The basis of analysis should be compensation to which the bank is justly entitled, and the favorable reception of service or analysis charges by bank customers is primarily due to the fairness and justness of those charges.

We are now ready to prepare a *recap* of the analysis form to see whether or not the account has been profitable. Total income less total expense (taking into account the profit the bank believes it is entitled to for the service) will show the profit or loss.

Because of the differences in results obtained by means of the flat charge, the metered service charge, and the analysis method, a combination of the metered service charge and analysis method is often used. In accounts where the principal activity is the result of checks drawn, the metered service basis is very effective. In other accounts where the activity is greater and more varied, such as corporate and other business accounts, the analysis method is used. By such combinations the time and expense involved in analysis are not applied to accounts where such a procedure is unnecessary, but analysis is used for accounts when such a method is really the only one that provides a complete picture of the account.

Summary—At the risk of repeating what has already been discussed regarding the objects and methods of analysis of accounts or of service charges, attention is again called to the fact that much of the success of these charges, from the standpoint of both profit to the bank and satisfaction on the customer's part, depends upon a careful study of the situation in each bank, the establishment of standard charges, and definite provision for explaining to customers the fairness of those charges.

The ideal situation is the complete analysis of all accounts regardless of their size and activity, for by this method each account receives the same consideration. Many banks have hesitated to install complete analysis because of the additional cost which they felt would be incurred, but with modern methods and improved systems it is possible to accomplish a complete analysis of all accounts at a lower cost than the analysis of part of the accounts required only a few years ago.

One of the Chicago banks completely re-equipped its bookkeeping department with the latest machines, which included certain features that made it possible for the statement clerk to enter on a section of the statement sheet most of the figures for analysis purposes. The remaining figures were obtained from various sources. After a full year of trial, the bank discovered that the same analysis force which analyzed 1,800 accounts with the old equipment could make a 100% analysis of 10,000 accounts with the new equipment. This bank also found that it cost no more to handle the bookkeeping and account analysis for 10,000 accounts under the new system than it had cost to handle 1,800 accounts under the old routine.

Not only does this 100% analysis of accounts provide the complete information which was formerly lacking, but the service charges or analysis charges have been materially increased. From the standpoint of the bank's customers, additional good will has been created by the fact that every account is subject to the same degree of analysis, and customers therefore feel that the charges which are imposed are carefully obtained and are unquestionably fair and just. (Figure 20 is a reproduction of the form used by this bank.)

Operation of the Analysis Department—The first step in analysis work is the assembling of the figures on the activity of each account to be analyzed. Next, these figures must be compiled on a daily basis during the month. Third, the figures are reduced to a daily *average* basis. Finally, the analysis is completed, the profit or loss ascertained, and the necessary *charge tickets* (debits to accounts for services rendered) are made out and charged against the accounts.

In performing these tasks, the work may be done by a separate analysis department or by an analysis department augmented by the facilities of other departments. The following illustrations of analysis work in three banks have been selected because they illustrate these various methods of procedure. In two of these banks an analysis department does the major portion of the work. In the third bank a skeleton analysis department is all that is necessary because of the division of the work among other departments.

In the first bank, activity figures (number of clearings,

"us" checks, and transit checks) are compiled by the receiving tellers for the deposits that have a small number of items. This information is noted on the deposit slips. The figures for deposits with more numerous items are compiled by the proof department. The deposit slips are then sent to the analysis department, and the figures are transferred to an *analysis work sheet.* Currency figures (amounts of currency deposited) are indicated on the deposit tickets either by the receiving tellers or by a special teller for deposits consisting largely of cash.

An analysis work sheet is headed with the name of each account, using an addressograph plate for this purpose, and the month is stamped just below. At the left of the sheet there is a column with figures from 1 to 31, corresponding to the days of the month. The next five columns are used for listing the number of deposits, clearings items, transit items, currency, and float totals; the seventh column is used for the average daily balance. All this information is posted from the bookkeeping department ledgers.

On the twenty-fifth of each month, the figures from the work sheet are consolidated and entered on the account analysis sheet. Other information, such as interest earned on loanable funds, is obtained and entered. The analysis is figured from the twenty-sixth of one month to the twenty-fifth of the next, so that charges may go through on the current month.

Charge slips are made out in duplicate upon the completion of the analysis. One copy is used as a debit to the account, the other for department records. After this is done, the department enters the analysis figures for the month on the *account analysis record,* which is a record of the analysis results, month by month, for the entire year.

In the second bank, all analysis work is done by the analysis department, which assembles the activity figures, float, and so on, directly from the deposit tickets. The analysis of the figures, the charges, and the make-up of the permanent analysis record are handled the same way as in the first bank.

In the third bank, a skeleton analysis force is used. The figures on number of transit items and clearings items are assembled by the distribution department. The bookkeeping department uses machines which are equipped for entering the analysis figures, in addition to the regular entries, on the ledger sheets and statements. This bank has a special statement form, perforated in the center. One half is used for the statement and the other half as an analysis work sheet. The figures obtained from the distribution department are entered by the statement clerk, as well as the number of "us" checks and deposits from the regular bookkeeping department.

At the end of each month, the analysis stubs are torn from the statement and sent to the analysis department. On the back of each stub is a printed recapitulation form for the calculation of the analysis, similar to the account analysis sheet illustrated in Figure 20. An extra force of calculating machine operators is employed for two days at this time in order to complete all analyses. The charge slips are also made out by these operators. After the charges have gone through, the figures are entered on the account analysis record by receiving tellers during the first hour or so each morning when the window work is light. By thus using the facilities of other departments and tellers—distribution, bookkeeping, receiving tellers, and special calculators—the analysis department has been reduced to three members in contrast to the regular force of twelve used prior to the distribution of the duties.

Inaugurating and Explaining Service Charges—In any discussion of service charges, the maintenance of amicable customer relations must be considered. Many bankers have feared that charges, even though justified, would be resented by customers and that ill will and loss of business would result. This apprehension has proved to be much exaggerated. While it is true that some business is usually lost when service charges are inaugurated, it is also true that the business lost is almost entirely that which has been unprofitable and is therefore well lost. Customers as a rule do not object when a reasonable and scientific system of charges is established and properly explained to them.

Experience has proved repeatedly that a well planned, carefully studied, and ably presented plan of reasonable charges will be well received and will become a steady source of income without appreciably creating ill will. The practice of a certain bank is given here to illustrate a successful procedure.

In this bank emphasis is placed upon *three angles of the service charge problem.* The first is *uniformity*—the use of the same basis of charges to all customers. This fact, in itself, when clearly explained, makes the individual customer feel that the charges are *fair and reasonable* because they are *uniform and not discriminating*. This uniformity is emphasized by using printed service and analysis charge rates, which are given to each customer and are explained by representatives of the bank whenever possible.

The second angle is that *the customer,* by *his own regulation of his account,* can determine what charges, if any, will be made. By the maintenance of balances in excess of the averages subject to charge and by the control of checks issued and of transactions made, the customer can absolutely control the cost to him of banking services.

Suppose, for example, that the overhead on maintenance cost for a given bank is 50 cents a month for each account and that the gross income from earning assets in the same bank is at the rate of 3%. In order to earn the 50 cents a month, a loanable balance of $200 would be necessary, and a book balance of $250 might, after allowance for reserves and uncollected funds, provide the necessary loanable balance. In fact, many banks establish a schedule of average balances, checks permitted, and the like, and the customer can readily see what he must do to avoid the service charge. Accounts which are completely analyzed can be regulated by the customer equally well. By noting the loss to the bank, as shown by the analysis, and by determining the added collected balance that will provide sufficient earnings to compensate for the loss, the customer can maintain balances which will eliminate analysis charges. Banks assist their customers in calculating the additional balances thus required; this is constructive work that brings additional income to banks and creates satisfaction among customers.

The third angle is that of *customer contact*. Every question on analysis and service charges is referred to one of the bank's staff selected for the work. This arrangement insures complete and correct understanding on the part of customers since their questions are answered by trained and well informed representatives of the bank. Supplementing this direct contact, a copy of every analysis resulting in a charge is forwarded to the customer. As a result of well planned and well executed customer contacts, misunderstandings resulting from lack of information or from misinformation are minimized.

One more comment should be made. From the bank's standpoint, to analyze *every* account may not be possible under existing conditions. Training and experience on the part of those who compile the final analysis figures enable them, without difficulty, to separate the unquestionably profitable accounts from the doubtful or unprofitable ones, and only the doubtful and unprofitable groups are then analyzed.

Bankers are always interested in profit figures, or at least they should be. In concluding this explanation of the purposes and methods of analysis, a survey made in 1934 by the Mid-Continent Banker [1] of St. Louis, Missouri will serve to illus-

---

[1] The Dollar Value of Service Charges, Mid-Continent Banker, November 1934, p 4, St. Louis

trate, in dollars and cents, just what analysis and service charges mean to a representative group of banks. The survey embraced a study of 103 banks in the states of Missouri, Kansas, Illinois, Arkansas, Oklahoma, Indiana, Tennessee, Kentucky, Louisiana, Mississippi, and Texas.

The study revealed that these banks had an average capital of $205,000, average deposits of $2,330,000, an average gross income of $95,000 a year, and an average total income of $8,600 from all service charges in the same year.

The study also revealed that the average bank received 9.05% of its average income from service charges, representing 4.19% on the average capital stock.

A practice that results in an average income of 4.19% on the average capital stock of 103 banks can well be said to be a successful and profitable part of commercial banking.

Pay-As-You-Go Accounts—One of the later developments in bank service charges is the adoption of a system, or systems, known as the "pay-as-you-go" accounts. While there is some variation in the manner in which the systems are handled, their chief characteristic is that the depositor is not required to carry a stated minimum balance (or at most a small balance), and the common objective of the various plans is to make a limited checking system available to people who are not able to maintain the balances usually required in checking accounts and who cannot afford to pay the usual service charges.

In order to accomplish this objective, it is customary to impose a charge of 5 cents for each check issued and, in many cases, a similar charge for each deposit made. This charge is imposed in two ways—either by posting it to the account every time an item is presented or a deposit made or by charging the customer 5 cents for each check when the blank checks are furnished him.

A special committee of the Bank Management Commission of the American Bankers Association [2] has made a study of these plans, and its findings are of interest not only to banks that contemplate introducing the pay-as-you-go plan but to those that have already adopted it. The results of this study showed that approximately half the banks using the plan imposed the charges by posting them to the books at the time the checks or deposits were received; the other half used the device of selling checks or checkbooks to their pay-as-you-go customers. Some of the significant favorable comments received from the banks reporting in the survey were:

"The revenue from this type of account is important and desirable, particularly if we are able to handle this increased volume without having to add additional machines or personnel and at the same time not impair the service rendered to our regular commercial depositors."

"A greater number of people in any given community are 'exposed' to the influence of the bank and are made aware of the other banking facilities offered, such as foreign remittance, safe deposit box facilities, etc. . . ."

"It helps a bank to retain those of its personal checking accounts who wish to close because of 'service charge' and 'minimum balance requirement' policies."

"It opens up an entirely new field of prospective depositors for the bank. In the majority of cases, these people never would have had a checking account."

"The appeal is to an entirely new field, new customers. Works hand in hand with the small loan departments, and, with volume, is profitable."

"The advantages in a 'pay-as-you-go' checking account service are that it builds good-will and provides a means for

---

[2] Pay-As-You-Go Checking Accounts (Commercial Bank Management Booklet No. 18); Bank Management Commission, American Bankers Association, New York, 1937, pp. 4, 5, and 24

using excess capacity. If the plan is set up properly (as we believe ours is) there should be a substantial profit."

It follows that the plan also has features that may become objectionable unless properly guarded against. Some of those listed by the commission were:

"Many of the reporting banks are laying themselves open to serious losses and embarrassment, because, in their effort to acquire 'volume' (which is essential if pay-as-you-go service is to be profitable), they have adopted the unwise, and dangerous, course of requiring no references from, or investigation of, prospective pay-as-you-go depositors. . . . The efficiency, cleverness and organization of present-day forgery rings make more than a perfunctory investigation of new depositors necessary if serious losses are to be avoided. . . .

"Far too many banks lack a real knowledge of their costs which is so essential to the proper and successful conduct of their business. . . . It is obvious, therefore, that in considering the statements made by many of these banks to the effect that their pay-as-you-go service is profitable, due allowance must be made for their lack of knowledge of their costs."

"The widespread adoption of the pay-as-you-go idea will tend to accentuate the dormant account problem. . . .

"There is apparently no uniformity of policy with respect to the rendering of statements and cancelled vouchers to pay-as-you-go depositors; or with respect to the extent to which such depositors are privileged to avail themselves of the services of the banks."

It is evident that this new banking service has distinct constructive good will and profit possibilities. The problem of the individual bank is to adapt the system to its own situation.

Cost Figures as an Index to Departmental Efficiency—It often happens that information obtained for one purpose can be effectively used in other ways. Cost figures, for example, are used for purposes other than analysis.

In using the cost figures to determine the comparative efficiency of a particular department in two institutions, a uniform basis of duties must first be established. One bank may divide certain duties between two or three departments, or it may have a type of business that must be handled by certain systems, or the peak loads of the two banks may vary.

Suppose that a comparison of the cost of handling an over-the-counter deposit is to be made between the receiving teller departments of two banks. In one bank the tellers receive, prove, and charge items directly to the transit, clearings, and bookkeeping departments. In the other bank, the proving and charging are done by a proof clerk or proof department. Obviously, a comparison of receiving teller costs in the handling of deposits would be unfair, for a comparison of all costs connected with the receipt of deposits must be made. In one bank this involves one department; in the other, two departments are involved. If one bank is able to handle a substantial proportion of transits by the *piece* system—that is, by using the total of a batch received from a customer and passing it on without re-running the separate items—while another bank cannot do this effectively because of the nature of its accounts, the *cost per item* will vary greatly unless due weight is given to the difference in the type of work of the two departments.

Here are the analysis figures of seven metropolitan banks.

Cost per Item or Transaction

Bank	Checks on Us	Clearings Checks	Transit Checks	Deposit Tickets	Currency Handled per M
A	.03	.01	.02	.07	.25
B	.025	.01	.02	.06	.25
C	.03	.01	.02	.07	.25
D	.03	.01	.02	.07	.25
E	.03	.01	.02	.06	.25
F	.03	.01	.02	.07	.50
G	.03	.01	.02	.07	.30

In view of such uniformity, if bank H found its costs of checks on us to be $.05, for example, it would seem to indicate that the efficiency was considerably out of line. Investigation and study of such a discrepancy might result in changes in methods, systems, and personnel in order to bring about more uniform costs, increased effectiveness, and increased profits.

Questions Based on Chapter V

1. What regulations or agreements are necessary to exchange checks and settle balances satisfactorily?
2. In what ways are funds obtained for the maintenance of clearing house association operations?
3. What agreements and regulations, in addition to those relating to the exchange of checks, are often adopted by clearing house associations?
4. What are the divisions of the clearings department? What are the principal duties of each division?
5. By what authority do clearing house associations exist?
6. What is the characteristic of clearings department records as compared with the records of other commercial departments?
7. What are the purposes of analysis of accounts?
8. State the principal methods by which these purposes are accomplished.
9. Why are combinations of these methods sometimes used instead of a single method to apply to all accounts in the same bank?
10. Do you consider the application of analysis a relatively important operation? Why?

Questions for Outside Investigation

1. What other regulations besides those used in connection with the exchange of checks have been adopted by your local clearing house association?

224 THE CLEARING PRINCIPLE. ANALYSIS OF ACCOUNTS

2. Is the clearings department of your bank divided into out-clearings and in-clearings sections? or is the work done by all members of the department?
3. At what time does the exchange take place in your local clearing house association?
4. Does your bank have a separate analysis department? or is the analysis work done by members of other departments?
5. What method is used by your bank in making service charges? or what combination of methods?

Assignment

From the following information, construct the individual bank sheets, the clearing house settlement, and the settlement accounts.

The Clearing House Association of Erewhon consists of four banks. On February 24 these banks brought the totals for exchange, as noted.

The First National Bank brought checks drawn on the

Security State	$1,017.05
Merchants Trust	2,810.15
Erewhon National	1,198.17

The Merchants Trust Company brought checks drawn on the

First National	$2,815.16
Security State	1,531.10
Erewhon National	905.40

The Security State Bank brought checks drawn on the

First National	$ 926.31
Merchants Trust	3,105.04
Erewhon National	791.14

The Erewhon National Bank brought checks drawn on the

First National	$1,006.12
Security State	743.18
Merchants Trust	404.07

CHAPTER VI

THE TRANSIT DEPARTMENT

The Purposes of This Chapter:
1. To explain the function of the transit department and to contrast its methods with those of the clearings department.
2. To investigate the methods of collecting checks on distant points.
3. To show the means and devices for the transfer of funds by wire.

THE clearing principle is the same in transit work as in clearings. The difference in application of the principle is that the clearings department collects cash items in the local area, while the transit department collects items outside the clearing area. Rules and customs in the collection of cash items have been developed by the banks and are so standardized that they are now practically uniform in all parts of the country. The Federal Reserve banks have definite rules governing their handling of items, and since by far the greater number of check collections in transit work are effected by means of the facilities of the Federal Reserve System, a uniform set of rules is automatically established. These rules are published in convenient pamphlet form by each Federal Reserve bank, and copies are sent to the member banks in the district.

While the *principle of the exchange of checks and settlement of balances* is the same whether the exchange is national or local, the *mechanics* of operation in these two areas *are quite different*. Why the mechanics are necessarily different may be most easily understood by a study of the contrasts in the nature of the items handled by and their method of treatment in the clearings and transit departments.

All items handled by the clearings department through the clearing house are disposed of daily, for they are either paid immediately or returned unpaid. Settlements are therefore made daily for *all* items handled by the clearings department.

Since unpaid checks are returned the same day, the records of the clearings department do not need to contain more than the barest identification of the items. In fact, simply the amount of each item included in a list of items going to the clearing house is sufficient.

The items handled by the transit department, on the other hand, are disposed of only after varying lapses of time. Some will be paid (or unpaid) in one day, others in two, three, four days, and so on. Even in a collection schedule arranged by days, consideration must be given to variations due to Sundays and holidays; some items may require two *business* days instead of two *calendar* days for collection.

Time schedules of collection (the length of time required for the collection of an item at the point of presentation) are reasonably accurate estimates based upon experience, but they are necessarily dependent on other factors, such as interruptions by storms or any accidents that delay the mails. For items of small amounts, a delay is of little moment, but with larger amounts, $500 and over, uncertainty of payment is a matter of importance. Ordinarily, a schedule of collection may be relied upon, but when severe storms delay the mails, the delay must be taken into account. In the early part of February blizzards are often so severe that collections which ordinarily take only two days may still be en route after seven days. In February also widespread floods which completely demoralize transit routines are not uncommon.

In local clearings an unpaid check is returned the same day; hence the clearings department has available on the check itself all the information that is needed to complete the return of the item to the customer—in others words, the amount, the name of the bank upon which the check is drawn, the name of the maker, and the name of the indorser. Therefore, it is not necessary to keep a detailed record of the information in any other manner.

In the transit department the situation is altogether different. An item may be reported unpaid by telegraph, and action may be taken while it is still in the mail on the way back. It is the practice of Federal Reserve banks to wire non-payment of items of $500 and over. In order that the collecting bank may show which item is unpaid, a system of symbols is used to indicate the banks upon which items are drawn, the amounts, and the indorsers' names. The transit department records which are used for reference purposes are simply duplicates of the descriptions and instructions that accompany the checks sent out for collection.

In transit operations, settlements also are more involved. In local clearings payment for all exchanges in one day is received in one sum. In transit settlements payments come through three main channels, as will be noted in detail later. The fact that some of the checks sent out on any day will be paid in one day, others in two days, and so on, requires that a staggered record be kept so that only the funds due to be collected on a particular day will be considered as collected funds for that day. Clearings settlements are made immediately and in one payment, while transit settlements are deferred and are made in many payments.

There is another fundamental difference between the mechanics of transit and clearing operations. All clearings checks go through the same channel—the clearing house association. Transit checks may go through four possible channels—the Federal Reserve bank of the district in which the bank is located, other Federal Reserve banks and branches, correspondent banks, and non-correspondent banks.

Thus it is evident that the problem presented by transit operations is quite different from that of clearings. Although locally and nationally the same *principle* is followed in the exchange of checks and settlement of balances, the *operations* of nationwide clearings are much more involved than those of local clearings.

Factors of Transit Collection—Prior to the formation of the Federal Reserve System, arrangements for the exchange of checks and settlement were made entirely between the individual banks. An Albany, New York bank, for example, made special arrangements with the banks in Tonawanda and North Tonawanda, New York. Even though these communities were located near Buffalo, New York, an exchange rule was in effect on items coming from Buffalo. The banks in Buffalo therefore sent items payable in Tonawanda and North Tonawanda across the state to Albany, for the Albany banks, which were not subject to the local exchange rule, could effect collections at lower cost. Thus items payable in nearby centers went across the state and back again before presentation. Such extremely artificial and unnecessarily circuitous routing was a common feature of transit work before the inauguration of the Federal Reserve System.

After the panic of 1907, the National Monetary Commission was appointed to study the needs and requirements of the banking system of the country. After a careful study, it reported, among other things, that the system used for collecting checks on out-of-town banks at that time was objectionable from several standpoints. The length of time taken to collect an item was much too long, the cost was excessive, and the roundabout manner of collecting was unsatisfactory. The system by its very nature required so long a time for collection that checks totaling large amounts were always in the mail, final payment was delayed beyond reason, and the funds in transit were of no use to either the banks or their customers for long periods of time.

The modern transit department has the responsibility of

collecting items as promptly, efficiently, safely, and economically as possible. The *volume* of items handled by the bank, the *kinds* of customers, the *parts of the country* upon which the deposited items are drawn, and many other factors determine what constitute proper transit facilities for each institution. To effect prompt collection, transit departments follow the *most direct routing consistent with the volume of items*. There may be variations in this direct routing made necessary by other factors. For example, it would be inefficient and costly to send a transit letter with two or three items through a separate source when with perhaps a slightly longer collection period they could be consolidated with 200 other items routed through some other channel. The *three factors of cost, volume, and time* are taken into consideration in establishing each collection arrangement, and the best results from the standpoint of prompt, efficient, and economical conversion of items into collected and therefore usable balances are accordingly obtained.

Transit Collection through the Federal Reserve System— A list of the facilities available to members of the Federal Reserve System was given in Chapter I. One of these facilities, direct use of the Federal Reserve check collection system, is concerned with transit collections. This nationwide system of exchanging checks and settling balances is of primary importance to all member banks. Thousands of banks use this facility daily. It provides an extensive, economical, and convenient way of collecting checks for large and small banks alike. An idea of the importance of the Federal Reserve check collection system may be gained from a consideration of the volume of business handled, the number of banks involved in this nationwide collection system, and the proportion of collections effected through the Federal Reserve System in contrast to other channels.

In Chapter I it was pointed out that on December 31, 1938 [1] member banks held about 70% of the banking resources of the United States, that a total of 6,338 banks were members of the Federal Reserve System, and that these banks are located in all parts of the United States. The member banks, the twelve Federal Reserve banks and their branches, and the non-member banks which by agreement join in the par collection system (there were 5,635 non-member banks on the par list on December 31, 1938) together constitute a network of interbank relations that provides the most extensive transit collection facilities in the world.

The Federal Reserve check collection system is not the only collection agency employed by member banks, for the majority of banks make some use of correspondent banks. Some member banks, however, particularly the smaller banks, rely almost entirely upon the Federal Reserve System for the collection of items.

The larger banks in metropolitan centers are likely to make extensive use of correspondent banks in the principal cities of the country, or to use the customers of their correspondent banks in connection with transit activities, but these metropolitan banks also depend to a great extent upon the Federal Reserve facilities. In a recent inquiry of ten metropolitan banks, two reported that approximately 65% of their items were sent through the Federal Reserve check collection system, six estimated that 70% to 75% went through Federal Reserve channels, one bank's estimate was 80%, and the tenth bank's estimate was 90%.

The rules governing collection through the Federal Reserve System, compiled in bulletin form, are sent to all member banks and to those non-members that are on the par collection list. A typical bulletin on the collection of cash items

---

[1] Twenty-Fifth Annual Report of the Board of Governors of the Federal Reserve System Covering Operations for the Year 1938, p. 33

THE TRANSIT DEPARTMENT 231

contains the following sections setting forth the rules and pertinent information:
1. Items which will be accepted as cash items
2. Terms and conditions of collection
3. Special provisions regarding government checks and warrants
4. Preparation of cash letters by sending banks
5. Indorsements
6. Uniform instructions
7. Telegraphic costs
8. Time schedules and availability of credits
9. Instructions for paying and collecting banks
10. Direct sending of cash items to other Federal Reserve banks
11. Method of handling items
12. How member banks may maintain balances.

These rules, which are definite and complete, enable any member bank to adjust its collection routine to conform to Federal Reserve practices and thus know just how and when the items will be available in collected funds for loans, etc.

In the handling of transits, batches are charged through as one total when the checks in those batches are all drawn on the same point. A member bank may sort items on Philadelphia, for example, into one batch and attach a memorandum showing the total of that batch. In handling the items, the Federal Reserve bank simply takes the total of the batch and sorts it through. Batches of two or more items are called "pieces" and are so listed in the Federal Reserve figures.

An idea of the extent of collection through the Federal Reserve System may be obtained from the figures contained in the Annual Report of the Board of Governors of the Federal Reserve System for the year 1938.[2] This re-

---
[2] Twenty-Fifth Annual Report of the Board of Governors of the Federal Reserve System Covering Operations for the Year 1938, p. 53

port shows that the number of checks handled by the transit departments of the Federal Reserve banks and branches during 1938 was 1,098,115,000 and that the total amount of these checks was $232,090,217,000.

The figures also give an approximate comparison of the use of money and the use of checks. The figures for currency and coin handled by the system for the year 1938, listed in the paying teller department study, are: currency received and counted, $8,883,728,000; coin received and counted, $271,128,000. The total currency and coin of $9,154,856,000, as compared with the figure for checks of $232,090,217,000 shows that approximately 3.9% of the volume handled consisted of currency and coin. (A comparison of these activities for the years 1934 through 1938 is shown in Table VI of the Appendix.)

A brief description of the transit department of one of the Federal Reserve banks will illustrate the operation of the Federal Reserve collection system.

Incoming checks are sorted to eighty sections. Each section re-sorts the items, prepares the transit letters, and sends out the checks for collection. A different colored sheet is used for each state in the district. Each section balances the total of the day's work and reports to the main transit department.

During the first six months of 1937 this Federal Reserve bank handled 62,430,219 pieces totaling $13,078,076,004. Estimating the separate checks handled for this period on the basis that the number of checks would exceed the number of pieces by approximately 50,000 a month, the total checks handled during the six months approximated 362,430,200.

Transit Collection Channels—As already indicated, there are four main channels through which the transit department collects items: (1) through the Federal Reserve bank of its own district, (2) through other Federal Reserve banks and branches (this is done by sending the items direct to these other banks and branches and is called *direct sendings*), (3) through correspondent banks, and (4) by direct collection from the bank upon which an item is drawn. (When a special service is rendered by routing an item directly to the drawee bank instead of through Federal Reserve or correspondent channels, an exchange charge is usually made.)

Federal Reserve Par Collection—One of the charges levied in the earlier methods of collecting checks was an *exchange charge* to cover the cost of postage and extra handling and other costs incident to the collection of items received through the mail—costs not involved in the payment of checks presented at the paying teller's window. This charge was deducted from the face amount of the check, and the balance remitted. If, for example, the exchange charge was 25 cents on a check for $100, the net amount remitted to the bank sending the item was $99.75. The determination of exchange charges was an arbitrary matter with the individual bank, and in many cases the charges far exceeded the reasonable expenses incurred for postage, handling, and maintaining accounts in reserve cities for the purpose of settling balances.

In 1916 the Federal Reserve System adopted a method of collection without charge for all its members and for any nonmembers that cared to qualify and join in the arrangement. This is called the *par collection system;* it provides that a check drawn on any member bank (or other bank participating in the plan) and presented through a Federal Reserve bank must be paid at the face amount, without any deduction for postage, handling, or other costs—in other words, without an *exchange charge*. The result of this arrangement is that the banks cooperate in par collection, and each has exactly the same privileges as the other member and participating banks. In effect, the Federal Reserve bank of each district has as correspondents the other eleven Federal Reserve banks, their branches, their member banks, and non-member participants in par collection.

Correspondent Bank Relations—Banks find it desirable to carry balances with banks in other cities for various reasons—because of the requests of their customers for drafts payable in those financial centers or because of the volume of collection items sent to a particular city or territory or for other reasons. Correspondent bank relationships are usually built up over a long period of time and result in the establishment of many reciprocal services beyond the purely mechanical collection of items. Credit information, investment assistance, operating information, and many other valuable services are exchanged by the banks daily. When the Federal Reserve System was inaugurated, it was believed by many that correspondent bank relationships would decrease because of the requirement that all member banks carry their reserves with the Federal Reserve bank of their district instead of with qualified correspondent banks as theretofore. This has proved not to be the case, however; correspondent bank relationships have continued to expand and to become increasingly valuable to banks and bankers.

There are two ways in which settlement for collections by a correspondent bank may be handled: (1) The correspondent bank may credit the account of the sending bank with the amount of the collection; or (2) the sending bank may deduct from the correspondent bank's balance with it, after sufficient time has elapsed for presentation and payment, the amount of the items sent for collection.

Aside from collection through the Federal Reserve System, the relative importance of collection through correspondent channels and by direct sending to the banks upon which the items are drawn, varies greatly among banks. One factor in this variation is essentially a matter of policy; another, a matter of necessity. Many banks in the eastern part of the United States find it sufficient to supplement the facilities of the Federal Reserve System with a moderate number of correspondent points. This is particularly true in the districts where all, or nearly all, banks are upon a *par* basis. (One large metropolitan bank in the East, for example, uses approximately eighty correspondents for transit collection.) Most of these arrangements are *reciprocal;* the large bank carries accounts with these correspondents, which in turn carry accounts with the large bank. By agreement as to the time when the respective accounts will be finally credited with the items received, the transit work is effectively and economically accomplished. In this case it will be noted especially that there is no *charging of accounts,* but *credit each way* is given as required.

In territories where there are a large number of no par points or where it is customary to send a bank its own items, the procedure is quite different. In one western bank, for example, there are many *charge* accounts, and smaller banks maintain balances with this metropolitan bank. The items are forwarded to them by the metropolitan bank, and the total is deducted from the accounts of the smaller banks. Collection in this particular territory requires numerous direct sendings to banks upon which the items are drawn. The direct collections, or *remittance* points, are more numerous than the *charge* points, and both are more numerous than the *reciprocal* points. In fact, out of an average of 1,005 transit letters sent each day, 709 are remittance letters; and of these, 232 are sent to banks that do not maintain accounts with the sending bank. Charge accounts total 196, while reciprocal accounts number only 29. The rest of the sendings are to the Federal Reserve banks and branches (37 in all) and to local country points under special arrangements.

On the Pacific coast, one branch banking institution uses

the Federal Reserve System for practically all items except those drawn on branches. Policies, conditions, volume of items, number of correspondent bank accounts—all these are factors which must be considered in determining which of the methods listed will be used most, and in what manner.

Uncollected Funds, or Float—As we have already seen, in the interval between the time the customer deposits a check and the time it is actually collected, the funds it represents are not available to the bank for reserve or earning asset purposes, nor are they available to the customer for current use, although the customer's account is increased by the amount of the check at the time of the deposit. That portion of every customer's account which is represented by checks deposited but not collected is the *uncollected balance in his account* and is called *uncollected funds,* or *float.*

Obviously, the bank must know what portion of every account is still uncollected, because uncollected funds cannot be used for reserve or earning asset purposes or be paid out to the customer until they become collected funds. Float is calculated in various ways, depending upon the total of uncollected funds and the number of accounts affected.

A Federal Reserve bank carries a reserve account, for each member and a deferred account which is shared by all the members in the district. When a cash letter is received from a member, the amount of checks which cannot be paid that day is credited to the deferred account. The acknowledgment states on what dates the various amounts of proceeds will be available. Copies of the acknowledgment—filed under dates, and by names of member banks—are used as ticklers. On the day the Federal Reserve bank receives payment for checks, the member banks' respective reserve accounts are credited and the common deferred account is debited.

Commercial banks cannot employ this system effectively

except possibly for their correspondent bank accounts. While all member banks make more or less constant use of the Federal Reserve check collection system, many commercial accounts have infrequent and small amounts of uncollected funds; hence it is impracticable to employ the dual system in use at the Federal Reserve banks. Such a duplication of accounts would make the additional accounting a burden.

Since float is a result of transit activities, the transit department often has the duty of figuring float for all accounts in the bank. Frequent reference to the records of the transit department is made by the bookkeeping department in marking outstanding amounts, since the transit department records constitute the complete bank records of all outstanding cash items.

The Transit Letter—When items are sent out for collection, full instructions for the collecting bank must accompany them. A description of each item also must be included for identification purposes. The form used for instructions and identifications is called the *transit letter* (see Figure 21). The instructions are included in the printed portion of the form. Columns for listing the amounts, the names of the banks upon which the items are drawn, and the names of the depositors of the items are arranged to conform to the equipment used in preparing the letter. Where special instructions must be added to the regular ones, or included as exceptions, the individual check is stamped or else a slip containing the special instructions is attached to the check. How this is done will be explained later in the text.

When the transit letter alone is used, a complete description of the items is included in the one record. Many banks now use the recordak for transit purposes. By sending a film record of the items, they are relieved of the necessity of making the transit letter a complete description.

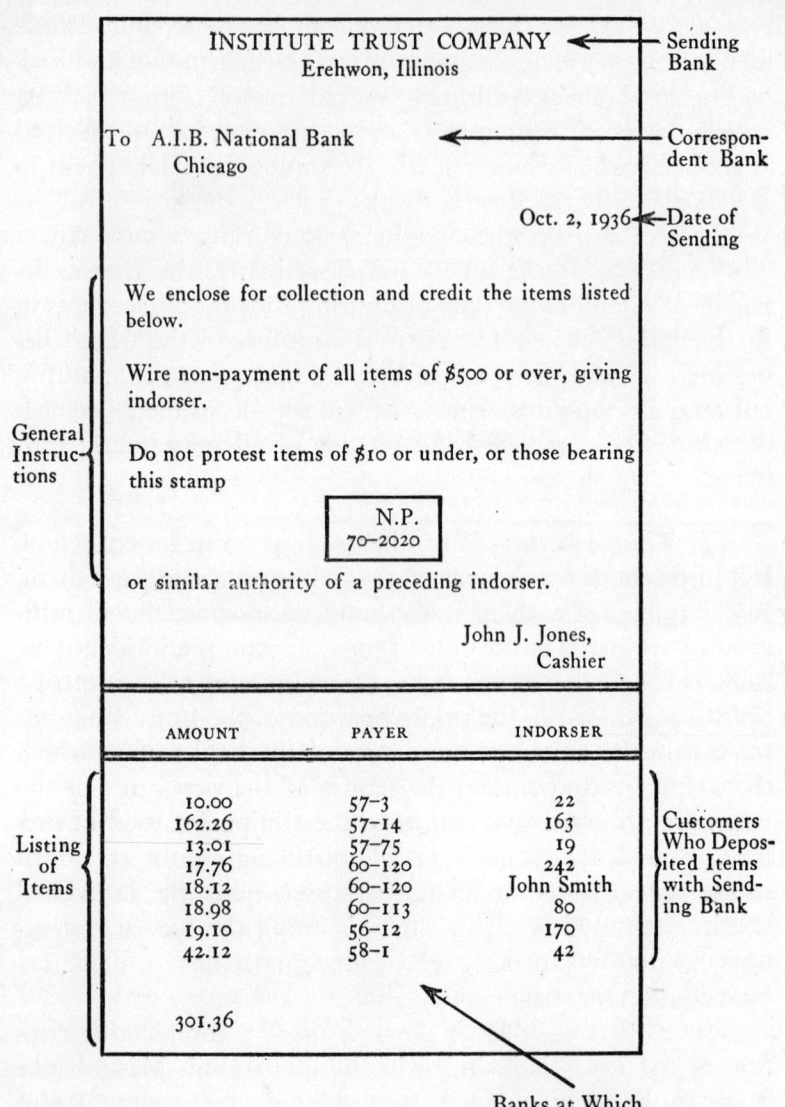

FIGURE 21. TRANSIT LETTER

National Numerical System—Before adding machines were commonly used in banking, all transit letters were written by hand. The amount of an item, the full name of the bank upon which it was drawn, and the full name of the indorser were written on the form, and copies were made on a hand press. When the adding machine was introduced, some time saving was possible by the use of the machine for amounts and totals; but the description still had to be recorded in ink by hand or on the typewriter.

As time went on, the practice of using a number identification of each bank upon which an item was drawn gradually developed, and both the amount and the number of the drawee bank could then be listed on the adding machine in the same operation. Thus the use of a code number instead of the full name of the drawee bank resulted in considerable saving of time and expense. To simplify the procedure of identification, the American Bankers Association, through its Clearing House Section (now the Bank Management Commission), worked out the details of a plan for numbering all banks in the country so that each would have a distinctive identification which could be used in place of the full name and location of the bank. The system is known as the *national numerical system,* or the *numerical transit system.*

Under the National Bank Act, certain large cities were designated as *reserve cities,* and the banks in these cities were *authorized depositaries* for *reserve funds* of banks located in smaller communities. The American Bankers Association assigned a number to each of these reserve cities, numbering New York City 1 and other cities, in the order of size and importance at that time, up to 49. The states were numbered from 50 up. Each bank was given a number, and the numbers of all banks in the country were listed in a numerical code book. For identification purposes, the number designating a city is followed by a hyphen and then the number assigned to the bank. Thus, in the designation 2-4, the prefix 2 at once identifies the bank as a Chicago bank, and the name of the bank can be found by reference to the numerical code book.

These numerical identifications have proved convenient and effective in the preparation of transit letters. As a matter of routine, a bank today has its transit number printed directly below the name of the bank on all forms in external use, including checks. In addition to the transit number, some banks indicate the Federal Reserve district in which they are located, by placing the number of the district below a line drawn under the bank's transit number. This additional numbering is an aid to rapid sorting.

When a new bank is organized, it obtains a transit number from Rand McNally & Company, which is authorized by the American Bankers Association to maintain the records of outstanding transit numbers, to assign numbers to new banks, and to publish periodically a *key book* which lists all banks in the United States and their transit numbers.

Availability Schedule—As we have seen, from the time a check is deposited until it has had time to be presented for payment at its destination, it is not *available* for banking uses. In order to know when, in the average course of business, a particular check has had time to reach its destination and be paid, schedules showing the average length of time required to reach various collection points are established. These *schedules of availability* (already referred to) are prepared for all states and major cities by each Federal Reserve bank. The following will illustrate how the time schedules are arranged.

Time Schedule of the Federal Reserve Bank of St. Louis, Missouri
Immediate—St. Louis
One day after receipt (actual)—Little Rock, North Little Rock, Chi-

cago, Kansas City (Kansas), Louisville, Kansas City (Missouri), Omaha, Cincinnati, Cleveland, Memphis

Two days after receipt (actual)—Birmingham, Denver, Jacksonville, Atlanta, New Orleans, Baltimore, Boston, Detroit, Minneapolis, Saint Paul, Buffalo, New York City, Charlotte, Oklahoma City, Philadelphia, Pittsburgh, Nashville, Dallas, El Paso, Houston, San Antonio, Richmond; (business) Illinois,* Missouri *

Three days after receipt (actual)—Los Angeles, Helena, Portland, Salt Lake City; (business) Arkansas,* Kansas,* Indiana, Iowa, Kentucky,* Nebraska,* Ohio,* Tennessee *

Four days after receipt (actual)—San Francisco, Seattle, Spokane; (business) Alabama,* Connecticut, Delaware, District of Columbia, Florida,* Georgia,* Louisiana,* Maine, Maryland,* Massachusetts,* Michigan,* Mississippi, New Hampshire, New Jersey, New York,* North Carolina,* Oklahoma,* Pennsylvania,* Rhode Island, South Carolina, Vermont, Virginia,* West Virginia, Wisconsin

Five days after receipt (business)—Colorado,* New Mexico, Texas,* Wyoming

Six days after receipt (business)—Arizona, California,* Idaho, Montana,* Nevada, North Dakota, Oregon,* South Dakota, Utah,* Washington.*

Special Instructions—The foregoing schedule of availability is based on the *average* and may be considerably upset by delay in the mails occasioned by floods, blizzards, and the like. Important items, therefore, are subject to special instructions, in addition to the regular instructions contained in the transit letter form, and these special instructions are attached to the items concerned. Special instructions may be used to meet many situations. For example, in the transit letter shown in Figure 21, "wire non-payment" is limited to items of $500 and over. If any item under $500 is to be subject to a wire of non-payment, that fact must be individually noted, which is done by attaching to the check a slip with some such notation as *"wire non-payment," "wire payment,"* or *"wire payment or non-payment."* When the check has been presented, the bank

---
* Except banks in cities listed in this schedule.

then knows immediately whether or not it has been paid and can advise its customer accordingly. A similar slip can be used for *"protest"* or *"no protest,"* although it is more common to use a rubber-stamp notation to that effect on the item itself.

Tracing—If a report on a transit letter is not received within the usual time, either by an advice of payment of the items listed in that letter or by reports on individual checks according to instructions, a *tracer* is sent out. The tracer merely calls to the attention of the bank to which the letter was sent the fact that a report has not been received. If the items in the letter have been received, presented, and paid or returned, and the original advice of payment has apparently been lost, a duplicate advice is sent. If, on receipt of the tracer, the bank finds that the transit letter has not been received, it notifies the sending bank immediately so that steps may be taken to locate the missing letter and items or to secure duplicates.

Exchange Charges—There are in effect in some localities so-called *exchange charges,* which are charges made by banks in those localities to their customers to cover (or partially cover) the cost of collecting items. These are not to be confused with the exchange charges previously mentioned, which applied to items received through the mail. Originally, these so-called exchange charges were estimated costs. The present tendency is to substitute cost analysis figures for exchange charges, but in cities where exchange charges still prevail, due allowance in the analysis of accounts is made for them, as noted in the preceding chapter.

In some banks the receiving and paying tellers figure and collect exchange; in others this work is done by the transit department.

Exchange charge schedules are generally enforced by local clearing house association regulations.

No Par Points—While by far the greater portion of the daily transit items, both in number and amount, can be handled through the Federal Reserve System on a par collection basis or through correspondent banks on a similar basis, there are a number of smaller state banks in the country that are not members of the Federal Reserve System and that do not consent to the par collection arrangement. The collection of no par items is always a problem to the transit department, particularly because of the increased cost involved through exchange deductions. Therefore, a bank which does not use the par collection facilities usually makes arrangements with a bank in a large city in the territory to handle its collections upon a uniform basis of cost to the sending bank. In the northwest territory between Minneapolis and the coast, for example, there are a large number of no par points, and the banks in Minneapolis and Saint Paul, over a period of time, have built up an excellent system of collecting no par items in that territory on a lower cost basis than is available to banks generally.

Not only are no par items collected at less cost under these arrangements, but they are collected more rapidly than is possible by direct collection in other parts of the country. Suppose that a bank in St. Louis makes arrangements with a bank in Minneapolis to handle all its no par items in the territory west of Minneapolis almost to the Pacific coast. The no par items are sent in a separate transit letter to the Minneapolis bank, which makes the collection and advises the St. Louis bank. The various exchange charges are paid by the Minneapolis bank, which in turn charges the St. Louis bank a flat rate per $1,000 of no par items collected, ranging from $2.50 a thousand (the minimum charge established by the clearing house association in Minneapolis and Saint Paul) upward. The cost of collecting no par items depends upon many factors, one of which is the use by the Minneapolis bank of the St. Louis bank for the collections of its no par items in the St. Louis territory.

The checks upon no par points must be collected through correspondent banks since the Federal Reserve banks will not accept them. As already stated, no par collection is much more of a problem in some parts of the country than in others. The Annual Report of the Board of Governors of the Federal Reserve System Covering Operations for the Year 1938 states: "As will be seen from the table, all of the banks in the Boston, New York, and Philadelphia districts and all but two banks in the Cleveland district, were on the Federal Reserve par list at the end of 1938. At the end of the year the distribution of the number of non-par banks by States was as follows: Minnesota 410, Georgia 254, Mississippi 175, Tennessee 169, Nebraska 163, North Carolina 163, Wisconsin 161, Alabama 130, Arkansas 129, North Dakota 125, South Carolina 121, Iowa 108, Texas 105, Missouri 105, Louisiana 104, South Dakota 92, Florida 84, Virginia 45, and twelve other States 117." [3]

The par and no par situations by districts are as follows:

INTERDISTRICT COLLECTION SYSTEM

Federal Reserve district	Member banks		Nonmember banks, other than mutual savings banks			
	Dec. 31, 1938	Dec. 31, 1937	On par list		Not on par list	
			Dec. 31, 1938	Dec. 31, 1937	Dec. 31, 1938	Dec. 31, 1937
United States	6,338	6,341	5,635	r 5,800	2,760	r 2,776
Boston	356	357	169	169	...	...
New York	772	776	288	r 290	...	...
Philadelphia	655	655	258	263	...	...
Cleveland	624	622	617	624	2	2
Richmond	406	405	314	r 321	335	r 343
Atlanta	320	324	90	94	690	683
Chicago	787	769	1,515	1,568	218	220
St. Louis	391	392	727	762	437	436
Minneapolis	461	469	156	171	710	722
Kansas City	734	733	964	985	178	177
Dallas	544	547	283	288	161	161
San Francisco	288	292	254	265	29	32

r Revised.

Reference to the Federal Reserve districts shown on page 26, and to these figures will give the student an idea of the parts of the country in which no par collection is a problem.

---

[3] Twenty-Fifth Annual Report of the Board of Governors of the Federal Reserve System Covering Operations for the Year 1938, p. 34.

THE TRANSIT DEPARTMENT

Settlement—There are four ways in which settlement is made for checks collected by the transit department. These methods will be described briefly.

1. Payment by credit to the bank's balance with the Federal Reserve bank of its district. All items sent through the Federal Reserve banks and branches are handled on the basis of the schedules of availability of the Federal Reserve banks. When items are received by the Federal Reserve bank of the district in which a member bank is located, or advices of sendings to other Federal Reserve banks and branches are received, the funds are transferred to the collected, or reserve, account of availability and are carried in a deferred, or transit, account. When sufficient time has elapsed for payment of the items, the funds are transferred to the collected, or reserve, account of the member bank. Therefore, all items sent through the Federal Reserve bank and branches of the district in which a bank is located or through other Federal Reserve banks and branches will ultimately result in a credit to the reserve account of the member or participating bank in its own Federal Reserve bank.

2. Payment by credit to the sending bank's balance carried at a correspondent bank when checks are sent to that bank for collection instead of to the Federal Reserve bank.

3. Payment by deducting the amounts of the items from the correspondent bank's account with the sending bank when sufficient time has elapsed for the collection of the items.

4. Remittance by the collecting bank. In such cases the sending bank requests payment of the items by drafts drawn on banks in the larger cities.

In settlements through the Federal Reserve System, the rules require a division of the items according to the time, or availability, schedule. As the time schedule of the Federal Reserve Bank of St. Louis (shown earlier in the chapter) indicates, calendar days and business days are designated.

Forms are provided for the convenience of banks in listing the item totals according to the cities or localities upon which the items are drawn, each list containing points with the same availability—one-day calendar points, two-day business points, and so on. These lists are sent to the Federal Reserve bank of the district in order that it may transfer the amounts in collection from the deferred, or transit, account to the reserve, or collected, account as they are collected according to the schedule of availability. These lists are also used by the transit department in order to make up the daily record of collected funds.

In transit letters to correspondent banks, similar arrangements are made covering the availability of funds. Credit to the sending bank's account or debit by the sending bank of the collecting bank's balance is made according to these arrangements.

Interdistrict Settlement Fund—An exchange of checks, either through a local clearing house association or through a national clearings arrangement, requires a method for prompt and uniform settlement of the balances arising out of the exchange. When the Federal Reserve System was established, the member banks, by means of the credits to their accounts in the Federal Reserve banks, were provided a uniform method of settling their balances. There still remained, however, the matter of settlement among the *several Federal Reserve banks.*

To effect this settlement, a store of gold, owned by the Federal Reserve banks, was placed in the vaults of the Treasury of the United States in Washington and was subject to control by the Federal Reserve Board (now the Board of Governors of the Federal Reserve System). The fund was originally called the *gold settlement fund,* but as a result of the regulation of gold by legislation, the fund is now carried in terms of gold certificates without reference to their actual value in terms of gold bullion; hence the name of the fund has been changed to the *interdistrict settlement fund*.

At the end of each business day, each Federal Reserve bank wires to the board at Washington its position with regard to the other eleven Federal Reserve banks. This is done in the same manner that each individual bank in a clearing house association reports its position to the clearing house manager. The board makes a daily settlement for the entire system, crediting or debiting each Federal Reserve bank as necessary and transferring proportionate ownership of the interdistrict settlement fund as a result. In this way settlement is made for all checks collected through the Federal Reserve banks all over the country on a daily basis in one settlement operation, thus eliminating other inconvenient and expensive procedures, such as the shipment of coins or currency to effect payment.

Preparing the Transit Letter—In order to identify the transit items properly, both in the letter to the collecting bank and also for the records of the transit department, the amount of the check, the name of the bank upon which it is drawn, and the name of the indorser are shown for each item. The amount is easily listed, and the bank upon which an item is drawn is readily identified by use of the transit number; thus the *indorser identification* is the only requirement that presents a problem. By the use of symbols for the identification of indorsers, the work of the transit department is greatly simplified in this connection.

Originally, the name of the indorser was written in full on the transit letter, and transit billing machines, which are combination typewriter-adding machines, continue to provide for this. Banks with a small number of transit items may still use this method, since the time saved in using some other device may be too slight to be important. In most banks the full name of the indorser is still used occasionally, as devices for identification of the indorsement do not apply in every instance. In large banks, however, the volume of transit items is so substantial that indorser identification codes or systems effect a substantial economy when used in place of the full written method.

Several methods of indorser identification are widely used. Two or more are often used in the same bank, one identification code being used for a particular class of items or for the department from which they come to the transit department, another code or codes being used in other cages or departments. By this means an inside identification of the departmental source of an item is immediately established.

Different methods of indorser identification are shown in Figure 21. These are typical of modern procedure and practice.

Indorser Identification Systems—One way to identify indorsers by code is to assign numbers to customer accounts and to include the identifying number on the indorsement stamp issued to each customer. Identifications of this kind are listed for the convenience of interested departments. Such a number eliminates the necessity of having the name typewritten, is just as accurate, and is much more convenient and economical.

This method is sometimes combined with the full written one; numbers are assigned to customers who deposit a large volume of transit items, and the name of the customer is typewritten in cases where transit items are seldom deposited. This method is illustrated in Figure 21.

Another form of identification used by banks is the *alphabetic code* for identifying unnumbered indorsers. This code simply substitutes a number for each letter of the alphabet, the numbers representing the initials of the depositor. For example, in the illustration of the transit letter (Figure 21), instead of the typewritten name of John Smith, a number might be used, such as 1019, the first two figures (10) being the code for "J" and the second two (19) the code for "S."

Still another means of identification is the *batch number method*. As charges are made to the transit department from the proof, or distribution, department, the number of the batch or block in which the items were proved and charged is carried on as the indorser identification.

In one of the leading banks in a southern city, a numbering machine system is used for identification. Starting with number one each day, a deposit ticket and all items with it are given the same number, and identification of each indorser is thus made positive.

An interesting use of a combination of systems, with internal department identification, is that of one bank in which the customers are assigned numbers if their transit items are frequent and in volume, other customers of the commercial department being identified by alphabetic code. When a photographic system is employed, the use of numbers to identify transit items is greatly simplified, since the photographic records provide detailed identification.

Transit items received from the savings department are identified by a department number, and items received in mail deposits are treated similarly. This method makes it possible for any item to be referred to the department from which it came.

In simplifying transit identification and description of items, some banks have arrangements with their correspondents to accept a straight list of the transits instead of a list with the usual identifications. This method can be used to advantage in some cases, but care must be taken to adapt it to the particular situation in which it will be effective. The Federal Reserve banks will not accept straight list transits, but require the identification of all items.

Experience has shown that the use of indorser codes in-

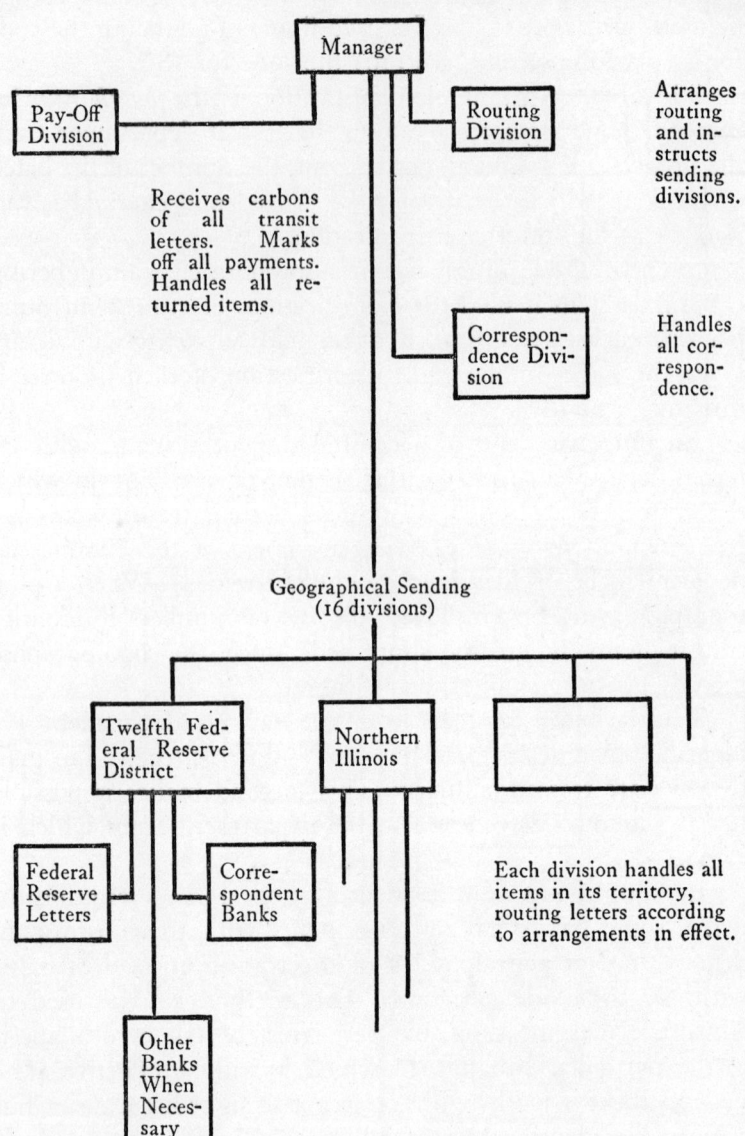

Figure 22. Transit Department Organization of a Large Metropolitan Bank

THE TRANSIT DEPARTMENT

Transit Block and Sort

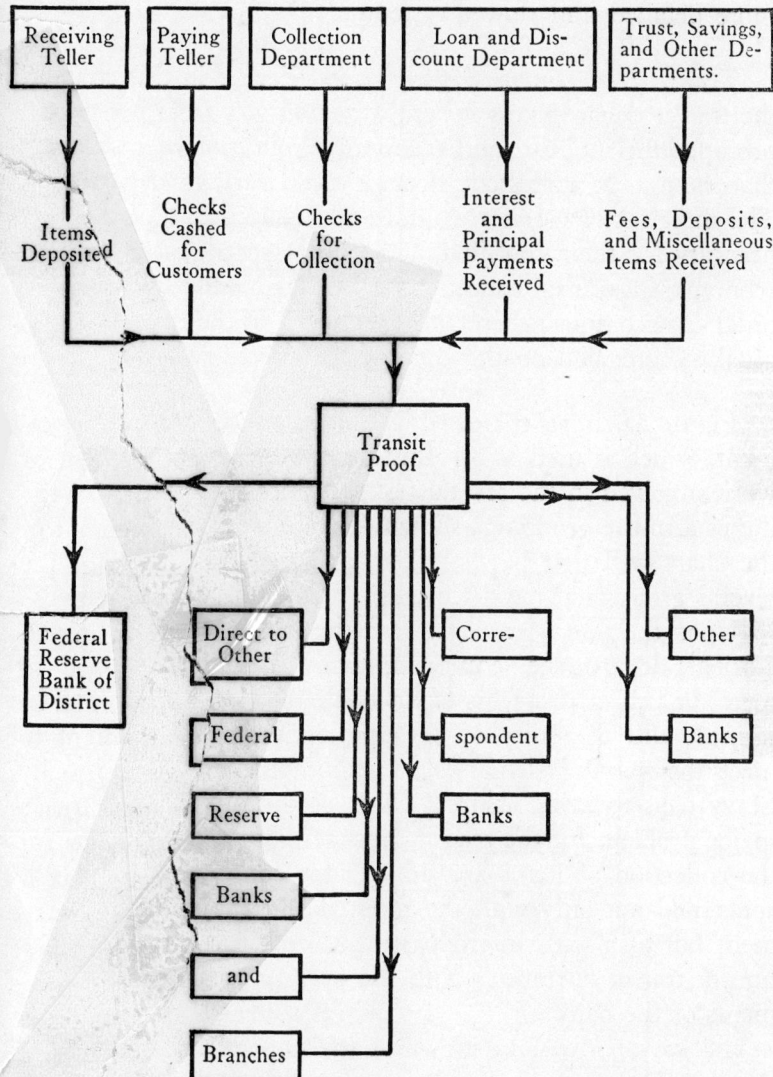

FIGURE 22. TRANSIT DEPARTMENT ORGANIZATION OF A LARGE METROPOLITAN BANK

creases the speed of preparing transit letters and results in greater accuracy in identification than is possible with the more detailed and slower systems.

Transit Department Organization—Earlier in this chapter, the transit department's general function was described as the prompt, efficient, safe, and economical collection of cash items that cannot be collected through the clearings department. The three factors of cost, volume, and collection time and the necessity for their coordination to effect speed, accuracy, and economy in transit collections have also been discussed. In order to accomplish these aims, the work of the department is usually segregated on the basis of the necessary tasks.

Figure 22 shows the organization of a large transit department, which is used as an illustration because the amount of work involved in the several tasks justifies the division of the duties into the groupings shown. The general arrangement of the chart will first be described, and then the work of the several groups will be discussed.

Upon the *transit manager* rests the duty of maintaining an efficient department, equipped, manned, and organized to meet the transit problems of his bank. The personnel must be trained, and flexibility of both personnel and equipment to meet the varying demands at peak hours or on unusually heavy days must be assured. Costs of operations constitute a major problem for the transit manager, and arrangements for the collection of items are subjects for constant study. He is concerned not only with the internal efficiency of his department but also with interdepartmental efficiency—the correlation of transit operations with the operations of other departments of the bank.

The *pay-off* division, shown at the upper left-hand side of the chart, keeps the records of outstanding and paid items. It also prepares the daily record of settlements made (according to the schedule of availability) and balances with the general bookkeeper.

At the upper right-hand side of the chart is shown the *routing* division, which studies collection routes and arranges those routes to meet the problems of the department most effectively.

Just below the routing division is shown the *correspondence* division, which handles the large volume of correspondence and follows up pending matters.

This transit department provides for sixteen *sending* divisions. In these divisions are the *sorters,* who divide the checks according to the manner and the routes by which they are to be collected, and the *billers,* who actually prepare the transit letters. Many of the workers are trained to be both billers and sorters and thus are used in whichever part of the work happens to be heaviest.

All these duties must be performed by the transit department, whether it be large or small. Often smaller banks will discover that through neglect of the principles of transit collection, they are not obtaining the most efficient and economical results, and it is in problems of this kind that they find the transit managers of their city correspondents of practical assistance.

The portion of Figure 22 headed *transit block and sort* shows the flow of items and the redistribution after the items reach the sending division.

Transit Department Operations—Items coming to the transit department are charged and proved by use of the block system. In the department under consideration (Figure 22), the charge and proof is made by the central proof department. The items are immediately recharged to the geographical sending divisions after the first sort is made.

Sending Divisions—Each of the sixteen sending divisions collects items in a geographical area assigned to it. For example, one division collects all items payable in the Twelfth Federal Reserve District, consisting of the states of California, Oregon, Washington, Idaho, Nevada, Utah, and that part of Arizona included in the Twelfth Federal Reserve District. The Federal Reserve Bank of San Francisco has branches located in Los Angeles, Salt Lake City, Portland, Seattle, and Spokane; hence the division sends Federal Reserve transit letters to these six points.

Correspondent banks in the principal cities in the territory are also used. The routing to these correspondents is arranged to obtain the most prompt and economical results in the collection of items drawn on banks in the vicinity of the correspondent banks or in other territories quickly reached by well arranged transportation routes and schedules. Correspondent banks are of course used for the collection of no par items in the territory. The routing is determined by the routing division and is revised frequently in order that maximum efficiency may be maintained at all times.

Where Federal Reserve banks are used for transit collections, the procedure described in connection with the use of Federal Reserve check collection facilities is followed. Collections are listed according to the schedule of availability, and collection advices are mailed to the Federal Reserve bank of the district in which the sending bank is located (for all direct sendings to other Federal Reserve banks and branches), in order that credit to the bank's reserve account may be made when the funds are considered available.

After the items have been sent out for collection, the file copies of all transit letters are referred to the pay-off division for further action. Upon completion of the day's work the sending divisions have no records to carry over and no outstanding items to account for.

Pay-off Division—The pay-off division keeps an up-to-date and accurate record of all items paid, returned unpaid, or still outstanding (in the process of collection). In the case of a returned unpaid item, a notice is sent to the customer by messenger or by mail, and a duplicate of the notice is turned over to the bookkeeping department for use in deducting the amount of the item from the customer's account. Current information on transit items is centralized in the pay-off division, which receives all wire notices of payment or non-payment. By reference to the records of this division at any time, full information on the status of current transit collections can be obtained.

Correspondence Division—While routine payments and returns are primarily the work of the pay-off division, many occasions arise when special and continued attention must be given to items or transit letters, and this requires special correspondence and follow-up work. The tracing of unreported letters or items, claims due to closed banks, delayed payments, and similar matters makes it necessary to give some items individual attention. This is the duty of the correspondence division, which receives from the pay-off division all matters requiring special attention.

Since the sending divisions are operated on a daily basis, they are responsible only for items that are in preparation for collection. The pay-off division then carries the records for a short period, usually ten days or two weeks. Thereafter all items still *open* are transferred to the correspondence division for further action.

Routing Division—So many variables enter into the prompt and economical collection of items by a department such as this one (which handles an average of 90,000 to 100,000 items daily) that a division, called the *routing* division, devotes its time exclusively to reviewing routing arrangements, constantly revising and readjusting them to better advantage. The routing division establishes all transit collection arrangements, designates the banks to be used, and schedules outgoing mail (in order to make connections that will effect saving of time). It is often possible to reduce the collection period at a distant point by a full day simply by an earlier mailing of the transit letters to this point—for example, by sending the mail to the post office by messenger to meet a post office deadline. Connections will then be assured. In such cases, definite instructions are issued by the routing division as to the *closing* time for certain points, and mail for those points must be ready for the pick-up by messenger at the stated time. The sending divisions handle "specials" either by making up such letters before any others or by assigning a member of the staff to handle them. The arrangement adopted depends upon the amount and number of specials scheduled.

Smaller Transit Departments—In small banks the transit problem is comparatively simple. If the items handled amount to twenty or thirty a day, a single letter to a correspondent bank is all that is necessary. The correspondent bank sorts, routes, and follows the items and sends back an advice of payment or non-payment.

In somewhat larger institutions, where the volume runs to 300 or 400 items a day, several transit letters are sent to correspondent banks or to Federal Reserve banks. In a department handling this volume no subdivision of the work is necessary; the entire staff sorts, lists, and traces items and handles payment advices and returns under the direction of an officer of the bank. The more important matters and correspondence are referred to this officer. Segregating its work into a few groups of states, the bank depends on its correspondents for further sorting and routing.

Many banks in the large centers have an arrangement whereby their smaller correspondent banks may route items through them as far as possible. For example, if a small bank has fifty items drawn on the San Francisco region, it prepares a transit letter to the Federal Reserve Bank of San Francisco and sends this letter to its city correspondent bank, which does no re-sorting but simply passes the letter on to the Federal Reserve Bank of San Francisco. In such cases, the form of transit letter of the city correspondent is used.

Equipment and Personnel—In a small transit department the work is often performed by individuals from other departments after they have finished their regular work. Even the equipment used is often that required in other operations and adapted to transit work by means of devices which can be added to standard equipment and by forms developed for transit use.

In addition to the combination typewriter-adding machine, the photographic machine is often useful in transit work. The checks are fed into this machine, rapidly photographed, and thus completely recorded. The film, when developed, provides a full description of every item. When reference to a transit item is required, the film furnishes complete and uncontradictable information. Furthermore, it has the advantage of speed of recording, simplification of operation, and elimination of more bulky records. The duplicate of the film is sent to the collecting bank as a transit letter.

In order to meet the requirements of peak periods in large transit departments, flexibility of personnel is imperative. The sending division is an excellent example of this. Ordinarily the regular sorters can handle the distribution of the items into the sorting racks without difficulty, and the machine operators, or billers, can easily handle the preparation of transit letters. At times, however, when the sorting is heavy, machine operators assist in this work; and when the work of sorting falls off, some of the sorters help run up the transit letters. In each of the sending divisions the work is so adjusted by the exchange of duties that a steady operation results.

So diversified are the requirements of individual banks that to acquire a complete understanding of transit work, a separate study would have to be made of each institution. A bank located in a community of 10,000 population, with deposits of $1,000,000, may have a moderate volume of transits. In another locality of the same size, a bank with about the same deposit total may have among its customers a local manufacturing enterprise that sells its products widely, and so the transit department must be organized on a more comprehensive scale.

Many banks in larger centers find it advisable to run two shifts in the transit department, the nature and extent of this extra facility depending upon the territory in which the large volume of items is to be collected, the total volume, train and other transportation schedules, customer requirements, and other factors.

So constantly are collection channels and time factors changing that review and revision of routings and methods must be made frequently if speed and efficiency in collections are to be maintained.

Transit Operations and Earnings—While the transit department receives no fees or other income direct from the customers of the bank and may be regarded as a non-income-producing department from an accounting standpoint, it is obvious that a well operated department will directly increase income, while a poorly operated department will decrease profits. Using the same personnel and equipment, a well organized transit department can handle a larger volume of items than can a less efficiently operated department. Efficiency reduces the per item cost and so enables the bank to make a profit on accounts that otherwise might show a loss. A trained and flexible personnel makes it possible for the bank to take advantage of early or special mailings, with a resultant decrease in the float. Any reduction in the time necessary to collect items converts the float (funds that are not usable) into collected funds available for reserves, loans, investments, and other earning asset uses.

Special study of the prevailing mail-routing schedules is well worth while. Because of the limitations set by railroad lines and train connections, better time is made in many cases by using a circuitous route than by using the shorter direct route. To take only one of many examples, items going from a certain eastern city to another 150 miles distant are a longer time in the mails when they are sent directly than when they are routed through a third city 237 miles distant from the first. In a well regulated transit department one member will devote the requisite attention to mail routing and mail timing, and by the judicious use of both will decrease the time required for collection.

Commercial enterprises, faced with the problem of collecting checks in other parts of the country, often decide to become customers of a particular bank because of the advantages offered by the transit department of that bank, and concerns that are already customers are increasingly satisfied with the services of a bank that provides effective transit collections. Systems which are mutually advantageous are often devised for chain store customers and others with national collection problems. The reduction of direct or indirect costs to the customer creates good will, and the additional funds available increase the bank's profits. Efficient and low-cost transit operations may be a basis upon which to solicit substantial balances from concerns that otherwise have no reason to prefer one bank to another.

Group Clearance—The Federal Reserve Bank of New York and the Federal Reserve Bank of Philadelphia have in recent years applied the clearing principle to an increasing degree through what is known as the *group clearance plan*. Under this plan, items drawn on banks within counties or trade areas in the district are sent direct to the banks upon which they are drawn, instead of to the Federal Reserve bank or other correspondent for collection as formerly. A list of the sendings is sent to the Federal Reserve bank of the district, which is authorized to debit the balance of the bank to which the items are sent the day after they are forwarded and to credit the sending bank's account. The old method often required two, three, or four days for the collection of checks at many points actually not far distant from the sending bank; the direct sending under the group clearance plan often effects a time saving of two or more days.

Each day the Federal Reserve bank sends to every participating bank a notice of the debits and credits made during that business day. Banks that are not members of the Federal Reserve System can obtain the privileges of the group clearance plan by maintaining balances with the Federal Reserve bank for settlement purposes and by agreeing to the other rules of the Federal Reserve System governing the operation of the plan.

The group clearance plan presents substantial advantages to the smaller banks in hastening presentation and availability. In one instance, which is typical of many, a bank sends all items or totals above $1,000 direct to the clearance member. In a single day it is able to effect collection over a wide territory as a result of the increased speed of presentation and availability provided by the group clearance plan. Banks which have a fairly large number of transit items can make effective use of direct sendings under the group clearance plan and thus extend their transit activities.

Wire Transfer—The various channels through which deposits are received were listed in Chapter III, and attention was directed to the facilities for the transfer of funds by telegraph, particularly the services provided by the Federal Reserve System to member banks in this connection. In addition to the Federal Reserve wire transfer system, the services of commercial telegraph companies are used extensively, and between large centers some banks have their own private wire connections. Debits and credits to customer accounts, then, may be handled through these three channels—the *Federal Reserve wire transfer system, commercial wires,* and *private wires.* Between small banks and their city correspondents, between commercial banks and Federal Reserve banks, between large commercial customers and banks, these wire transfers of funds are constantly being effected. The transfer is inexpensive and affords great convenience in providing funds immediately.

Federal Reserve Wire Service—The Federal Reserve banks operate a *leased wire system,* a network of telegraph facilities which are rented from the commercial companies on an annual basis. This network of leased wires connects every Federal Reserve bank with every other Federal Reserve bank and branch and with the Board of Governors of the Federal Reserve System at Washington.

Member banks that wish to create balances or pay funds in other parts of the country without delay may do so through this wire transfer service without cost if the amounts transferred are in even, or round, amounts (multiples of $100) and for the benefit of a member bank. If the funds transferred are in odd amounts or for some designated customer of a bank, the regular telegraph charge is made. These transfers are made to and from the member bank's reserve account and are reflected in the daily settlement of the Federal Reserve System through the interdistrict settlement fund.

In addition to the use of the Federal Reserve leased wire system on behalf of the member banks, extensive use is made of it by the Federal Reserve banks themselves for the many interbank messages and transactions that arise. Much of this use arises in connection with the activities of the system as the fiscal agent of the United States Government.

The wire transfer facilities are also used in tracing transit letters and collection sendings. For example, the widespread storms prevailing in the early part of 1936 so delayed the mails that the Federal Reserve banks traced thousands of delayed letters by wire.

Transfers of funds or other messages to banks outside the leased wire system are handled through the commercial companies on a cost basis to the member bank requesting the service.

Code Books—Wherever extensive use is made of telegraph facilities, code words are used for two impelling reasons: first, to make the message more brief and, second, to insure correct transmittal of instructions. Various codes are in use but the code developed by the American Bankers Association is used most frequently. Code books which contain a key to the code words are printed and made available to the banks. Many large banks have their own codes which they use when wiring their correspondents.

To illustrate how much a message can be shortened by the use of code, let us take the following example of a common banking message. "We credit your account $10,000, proceeds of your collection number 675." In code, the message would read something like this: "Adamt abent corsair dent." (The words used in this illustration are not actual code words.) By the use of a code, the words in the message have been reduced from nine to four.

Code books are placed in the custody of an officer of the

bank or of the senior man in the wire transfer division and are carefully guarded so that they may not fall into the hands of unscrupulous persons. Each night the code books should be placed in the vaults.

In order to be certain that the bank to which a wire is addressed has and uses a code book, the list of all American banks that use the A.B.A. code is consulted. If the bank to which the message is going does not use a code, the message is sent *open*—that is, in ordinary language.

Operation of a Wire Transfer Division—Unless the volume of wires is substantial, the work of wire transfers will be handled by an individual in part time. Frequently an officer of the bank, perhaps an assistant cashier, will do this, coding outgoing messages and decoding incoming ones. A carbon copy of each message sent is filed in a permanent file.

In banks where the volume of telegraph messages justifies a wire transfer division, one member of the division will be charged with the duty of coding outgoing messages and another member with the duty of decoding incoming messages. Debits or credits to accounts will be made by the manager of the division, and a copy of the debits or credits will be attached to the telegram of authorization.

In some banks telegrams are sent by messenger to the commercial telegraph company for transmission. In other banks a telegraph operator is installed in the wire transfer department; all messages to the bank are relayed from the local telegraph office direct to him, and all outgoing messages are transmitted by him to the local telegraph office.

For volume work, a machine that combines the sending or receiving of a message with the printing of the message has been devised and is widely used. This machine is similar in appearance to a typewriter. Incoming messages are automatically printed on tapes, which are rapidly cut and pasted on the regular telegraph form by the operator. The ease of operation of these machines and the immediate reproduction of the message in printed form are of great convenience. In one of the Federal Reserve banks, for example, several of these machines are used in the wire transfer division. All work is divided into territorial groups, and each operator handles all messages to and from banks in the territory assigned to her.

Care must be taken to verify the coding and decoding of messages, for large sums are frequently involved in wire transfers. In the Federal Reserve wire transfer division referred to, a daily record of all messages sent to and received from the various points is kept. At the end of the day, the count of these messages is verified by checking the total involved with each Federal Reserve bank or branch from which wires were received and by checking the commercial messages with the local offices of the telegraph companies, to be certain that every message has been received correctly.

Questions Based on Chapter VI

1. What are the main factors to be considered in transit collection?
2. What is the extent of the Federal Reserve check collection facilities?
3. Name the four channels for transit collections.
4. Briefly describe the par collection system.
5. What is the purpose of a transit letter? What is meant by float?
6. What is the national numerical system? What is an availability schedule?
7. What are no par points? Through what channel are items drawn on these points usually collected? Why?
8. Discuss the chief methods used for customer or indorser identification.
9. How do the records of the transit department differ from those of the clearings department? Why?
10. What channels are used in the transfer of funds by wire?

Questions for Outside Investigation

1. In your bank, are most of the transit collections made through the Federal Reserve banks or through correspondent banks? to what extent?
2. What is the transit number of your bank?
3. What is the approximate daily volume of transit items handled by your bank?
4. What method or methods of indorser identification are used by your bank?
5. Is the transit letter form used by your bank similar to the one illustrated or considerably different? If it is different, wherein does the difference lie?

Assignment

Last Friday, the Institute Trust Company of Erehwon, Illinois, numerical transit number 70-2020, forwarded a transit letter to its Boston, Massachusetts correspondent, the Jones Trust Company. The general instructions on this letter were: "Collect and credit the items listed on the letter. Wire non-payment of all items over $500. Do not protest items under $15 or those marked N. P. 70-2020 or showing a similar authority of a preceding indorser." The cashier of the Institute Trust Company is Harold R. Smith. The checks listed in this letter are as follows:

$10 on the Beveral National Bank, Beverly, Massachusetts, deposited by Hayes and Hayes, whose indorsement number is 743.

$2,046.10 on the First National Bank, Boston, deposited by Arthur Mann, indorsement number 81.

$719.43 on the Waltham National Bank, Waltham, Massachusetts, deposited by Sam Oman, indorsement number 42.

$1,864.34 on the First National Bank, Concord, New Hampshire, deposited by John Jones.

$846.31 on the Second National Bank, Nashua, New Hampshire, deposited by Oscar Anders, indorsement number 73.

$992.42 on the Bar Harbor Banking & Trust Company, Bar Harbor, Maine, deposited by Smith and Smith, indorsement number 116.

$27.10 on the First National Bank & Trust Company, Bridgeport, Connecticut, deposited by J. V. Wansor.

$185.06 on the Hartford National Bank and Trust Company, Hartford, Connecticut, deposited by Star Insurance Company, indorsement number 91.

$72.04 on the National Bank of Commerce, New London, Connecticut, deposited by Northeastern and Southwestern Railway, indorsement number 545.

$81.91 on the Merchants National Bank, Burlington, Vermont, deposited by James J. Junius.

$142.04 on the Montpelier National Bank, Montpelier, Vermont, deposited by Main Hardware Company, indorsement number 27.

$889.89 on the Merchants National Bank, Bangor, Maine, deposited by Stom and Adams, indorsement number 167.

$404.04 on the New Hampshire National Bank, Portsmouth, New Hampshire, deposited by R. B. Deman, indorsement number 710.

From this information, prepare a transit letter, giving instructions and listing and describing the items as in an actual transit letter.

After this is done, again list the items, and opposite each item place the number of days the item would be outstanding if it were sent through the Federal Reserve bank of your district.

CHAPTER VII

THE COLLECTION DEPARTMENT. THE SAVINGS DEPARTMENT. THE SAFE DEPOSIT COMPANY

The Purposes of This Chapter:
1. To explain the methods of handling collection items and the operations of the collection department.
2. To describe the duties and operations of the savings department.
3. To explain the purpose of the safe deposit company and to show how its operations are performed.

THE characteristics of cash items and of collection items were described and contrasted in Chapter III, and it was there explained why collection operations differ essentially from those relating to cash items.

To review: Cash items are due on demand, they have no documents or papers attached, they are subject to simple and uniform instructions and can therefore be handled in batches; hence operating systems and methods for cash items can be based upon a large volume per person. Thus, in receiving teller department work, and to a greater degree in distribution, clearings, and transit work, a large number of items are handled per person, and mass production methods are applied. The cost for each cash item handled is only a fraction of the cost for handling a collection item, which demands *individual attention*.

The records required for cash items are much simpler than those required for collection items. In the clearings department the only record kept is a tape list (by banks) of the amounts of the checks sent to the clearing house; in the transit department a transit letter with its code devices is used; in the distribution department identification is made by amounts and deposit customers. The handling of collection items, in contrast, requires entirely different methods and systems, and the forms are more numerous and detailed.

The basic operating difference may be summed up by the statement that *cash items* are handled *in batches* (even to passing on as a single total a batch of items drawn on the same point), while *collection items* require *individual attention* and *cannot* be handled in batches.

Another difference between the operation of the collection department and other commercial departments is that relating to accounting. In other departments, verification of department totals is made automatically through interdepartment balancing. For example, checks deposited are first balanced between the customer and the bank, then between the receiving teller and the clearings, transit, and bookkeeping departments. Verification is part of the transaction itself, obtained by balancing the total of deposits with the total of cash and checks received. The instant a deposit enters into the receiving department total, it becomes a *part of the assets of the bank and must be accounted for.*

In the collection department, on the other hand, after the balance between the customer and the bank is made and a receipt is issued for the items left for collection, these items *do not go through any other department* but are sent *direct* to correspondent banks or other collection agents. Except where advances are made against them, collection items are not credited until they are *actually paid;* they do not appear as bank assets during the collection period and are charged nowhere except in the records of the department or in supplementary records kept for audit purposes. (The problem of auditing collection department work will be discussed in connection with the subject of auditing in a later chapter.) Throughout the study of the operations of the collection department, the difference in the balancing of collection work should be kept in mind since it accounts for the fact that many of the records of this department are not found in other departments.

Duties of the Collection Department—The collection department is charged with the duty of collecting items (not drawn on the bank itself) *that cannot be reached through the clearings and transit departments.* Collection items which are not credited until payment is actually received by the bank constitute the principal items handled. The collection department also handles "cash collections," items for which immediate credit is given but which require special handling by the collection department; in addition, it collects *coupons* and *bonds* which require special attention because they are payable to bearer.

The collection department must be so organized as to be able to handle promptly, safely, and economically all items that come to it. The department must be particularly certain that full instructions accompany all items sent out or received, in order that errors which might prove costly may be avoided. It may be regarded as a first principle of collection procedure to obtain *full* and *complete* instructions regarding each and every collection item, whether that item is received from a customer at the window or through the mail, and whether it is to be collected locally or in some other town or city. Instructions for handling can come only from the customer. The item itself contains some information, such as the amount, the due date, the name of the maker, and the place of payment. In addition, the customer must give special instructions, such as those relating to the delivery of documents, the collection of interest in case of delayed payment, telegraphic advice, and whether credit is to be made to the customer's account or a cashier's check is desired in payment.

For cash items a customer gives instructions simply by depositing the items subject to the rules of the bank. It is understood that if any variation from the regular and routine instructions is desired by the customer, he must inform the bank just what he wishes. In collection work, in contrast, while general rules and regulations prevail, the treatment that may be desired for items of the same type varies so widely that definite instructions must be furnished with each item presented for collection.

Most of the collections received by mail come from other banks, and full instructions are given in the accompanying letters. The collection department issues a receipt immediately for each item entered for collection. For over-the-counter collections, the teller often uses a receipt form instead of entering the amount and his initial in the collection section of the passbook. On this receipt form (written in triplicate) the teller describes the collection and lists the *instructions*. The original of the form is given to the customer as a receipt; one copy serves as the collection department record and the other as the auditing department record. These receipt forms are numbered consecutively, and they must all be accounted for.

Many banks enclose an *acknowledgment* receipt form with collections sent to other banks, particularly with *those which are not collectable the same day*. This form is stamped and initialed by some member of the collection department of the bank receiving it and is mailed back. It serves not only as a receipt but, equally important, as notice that the item is in due process of collection.

Kinds of Collection Items—The principal kinds of collections handled by the department are as follows:
1. Drafts
    a. To be paid upon presentation
    b. To be paid after a designated time
    c. To be paid upon the arrival of goods

d. With bills of lading attached, to be surrendered upon payment of the drafts
e. With bills of lading attached, to be surrendered upon acceptance of the drafts
f. With warehouse receipts attached, to be surrendered upon payment of the drafts
g. With warehouse receipts attached, to be surrendered upon acceptance of the drafts
h. With other documents attached, to be surrendered upon payment or acceptance of the drafts; and with securities attached, to be delivered upon payment
2. Acceptances
   a. To be paid
3. Notes
   a. To be paid
4. Real estate contracts
   a. To be executed
   b. To be paid
5. Stock certificates
   a. To be transferred
   b. To be delivered against payment
   c. To be deposited with protective committees
6. Bonds and coupons
   a. To be paid
   b. To be delivered against payment
   c. To be deposited with protective committees
7. Mortgages
   a. To be executed
   b. To be paid
8. Miscellaneous documents under escrow agreements
   a. To be delivered against receipt
   b. To be delivered against execution of agreements and so on.

From this list it may be readily seen that collection items

vary greatly and are subject to instructions ranging from the simple to the complex. It is this latitude of collection facilities that makes the department so valuable to customers, for through its operations many transactions are executed for customers safely and promptly and at moderate cost.

Departmental Divisions—While the work of the department can usually be conducted without subdivision of duties, and is so conducted in moderate sized banks, a large volume of items is handled more efficiently by separating the work into three main divisions, termed the country collection, the city collection, and the coupon divisions. Sometimes the city collection division is designated as the note teller, or the section of the city collection division that handles notes and acceptances is so designated.

The *country collection* division collects items payable outside the local area—that is, outside the area which can be easily reached by messenger service through the city collection division. In country collections, extensive use is made of correspondent bank facilities, and a variety of reciprocal arrangements exists between a bank and its correspondents. The Federal Reserve System maintains a non-cash collection service, which is used extensively in addition to correspondent channels. Some smaller banks use the Federal Reserve facilities for all country collection work. When a bank that is not a correspondent is used for collection purposes, payment for the items is requested in funds payable in the sending bank's city, or payable in some other large center if the collecting bank does not maintain balances in the sending bank's city.

The *city collection* division handles collection items payable locally (within a radius that can be easily reached by messenger service). Most of these items are due and payable on demand (such as sight drafts) or are to be accepted on presentation. Others, such as time drafts, notes, and acceptances which are due within a few days, are entered for collection in advance of the due dates in order that the division may have ample time to send out the usual notices to the makers, drawees, or acceptors. Both those immediately due and those due within a short time are called *regular* collections.

In addition to regular collections, there are those that consist of a series of collections to be made at regular intervals (generally monthly) for a period of a year or more. These continuing collections, frequently real estate contracts or similar items, are called *file collections*.

It is the duty of the *coupon* division to collect all coupons and bonds regardless of whether they are payable locally or in some other part of the country.

Country Collection Division—After a receipt for a collection item has been issued to the customer and full and complete instructions have been received, the country collection division proceeds to prepare a record of the item. A form which is widely used for this work is the *fanfold* or *multiple* form, so arranged that with the entry of the information on one form, from two to six carbon copies are made, thus giving a complete set of records for use in connection with the collection both in and out of the department. The entries on the form are verified as soon as the collection has been recorded. Since the information is identical on all forms, verification of one form verifies all.

As may be seen from the detailed description which follows, these forms are devised to cover all the steps required in the process of collection from the initial recording of the item to final payment.

The first copy of this form serves as the *letter of transmittal*. It contains such information as the following: the name of the party to whom the item is to be presented, the kind of item, the maturity date, a notation of the documents attached, the amount of the item, the name of the bank through which the collection is being sent, special instructions, and the name of the customer who left the item for collection. Each collection has an identifying number, which is used in correspondence and in telegraphic communication, if necessary. The number is also useful in the audit procedure of the bank, since each collection can be checked by this means. The letter of transmittal is attached to the item sent for collection.

The second copy of the form is used as a *credit memorandum* after the item is paid and serves the same purpose as a deposit ticket.

The third copy is used as an *advice of credit;* it is sent to the customer at the time the proceeds of the collection are credited to his account.

The fourth copy is the *debit* form, which is used to charge the correspondent bank's account upon notice that payment has been received by it. This is the usual arrangement where the bank to which an item is sent carries an account with the sending bank.

The fifth form is the *permanent file* record; it is a complete record of the item from the time it enters the department until it is disposed of by payment or return.

A sixth form is often used as an *audit* form and is sent to the audit department for verification purposes.

An additional form may be used as a *tracer* if a prompt report on the disposition of the collection is not received.

There are many modifications in the number and use of forms, depending upon the problems of the individual bank, the nature of its collection arrangements, the extent of the collection department's activities, and the kinds of collection items handled.

A typical collection department operation is shown in Figure 23. In this illustration the use of five of the forms described is indicated.

COLLECTIONS, SAVINGS, AND SAFE DEPOSIT

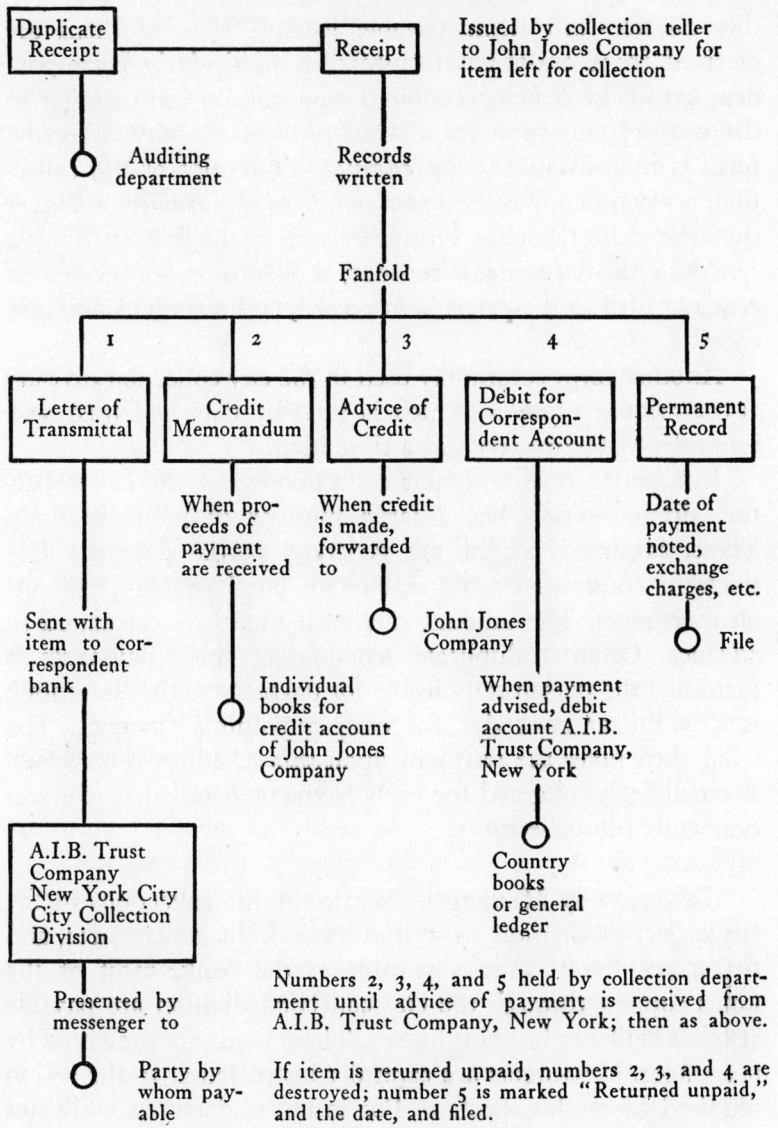

Figure 23. Collection Operation

City Collection Division—The city collection division handles all *non-cash* items payable locally. Most of them are received from out-of-town customers, particularly correspondent banks. Each item is entered on a fanfold form similar to the country collection form. One copy of the city collection form is used as an *acknowledgment* or receipt of the collection, a second copy is used as a *notice to the drawee or maker* that the collection has been received, a third is used as a *credit* to the customer's account, a fourth as an *advice of credit,* a fifth as the *permanent* record, and a sixth as an *audit* copy.

Another form commonly used in the city collection division is the *maturity tickler,* which is filed by date and used as a reminder of the due date of a time item.

In addition to the regular collection items, the city collection division often has a large number of *file* collections. These, as already noted, are generally partial payment contracts in connection with real estate purchases or payments on mortgages. The amount due each month is calculated in advance. Often a duplicate schedule of these payments is furnished the person responsible for payment so that he knows exactly the amount due for each remaining payment. The teller then notes the payment upon this schedule as a receipt. A small fee is charged for each payment handled in connection with file collections.

Collection by Messenger—While the file collections in the city collection division, as well as some drafts, acceptances, and notes, are almost always payable at the bank, most of the items coming through the city collection division are payable at other banks or business houses. These items are presented by messenger. Messengers are carefully instructed as to the action required for each collection. For instance, documents are not left without payment or other action required by the attached draft, except in cases where the bank is willing to assume the responsibility for leaving such documents on receipt.

The position of the collection department may be readily appreciated by again recalling the essential difference between cash and collection items. While cash items are credited immediately to the account of the customer, it is understood (and so stated in the rules and regulations to which the customer agrees) that the credit is subject to *final* payment. Collection items, however, are not credited at the time they are left with the bank; when they are credited, it is understood that the items have been paid, and the customer is entitled to regard the payments as final. Therefore, the collection department must be certain that it does not report or credit any payment until final payment has been received.

Technically, in accepting payment in any form other than cash, the collection department assumes responsibility for the final payment of the check or other instrument received. In actual practice, therefore, only cash or certified checks are accepted, unless the credit standing of the payer is unquestioned. This requirement is stated on the notice sent to the payer of the item.

In certain cases, where the party upon whom an item is drawn is either a customer of the bank in good standing or a firm or individual known to be of unquestioned responsibility, the bank will accept in payment checks that are not certified, knowing that the risk is negligible.

If an uncertified check is to be accepted in payment or an item is to be left on receipt, definite instructions regarding variations from the general rule are always given to the messenger. He should never make an exception on his own responsibility.

By giving definite instructions to the messengers, the collection department is assured of correct handling of all items and greatly aids proper presentation. The collection department often assists the messenger force by informing the paying or accepting party by telephone that an item will be presented by messenger. This courtesy enables the party to consult his records and have the check drawn (in case of payment) before the arrival of the messenger, or to refuse action on the item immediately. Thus the party to whom the item is to be presented is accommodated by advance notice, and the messenger work is made more effective by the elimination of delays that might otherwise occur.

Coupon Collection Division—It is customary to credit bond and coupon payments only when the proceeds are actually received, except in the case of government bonds, some municipal bonds, and a few others where there is no question of prompt payment. The *coupon* division handles bonds and coupons for collection for the various departments of the bank, in addition to those handled for customers. At some periods, when the number of bonds and coupons maturing is large, the division will be extremely busy; at such times the coupon division is often assisted by other members of the collection department or by employees from other departments. When the work of the coupon division is light, the members of this division assist in the work of the other collection divisions. Departments (such as the trust department) which have a large amount of coupons and bonds to be collected assist the coupon division by sorting and listing the coupons and bonds in advance of the forwarding dates. The coupon division then simply verifies the amounts, enters the items in the records, and forwards them for payment. Customers of the bank who make constant use of this division are also encouraged to cooperate by sorting and listing their items.

A simplified form is used for the records of the coupon division, since the instructions applying to bonds and coupons forwarded for collection are standardized. A coupon envelope is used to hold the coupons or is attached to the bonds (see Figure 24). In the collection of these items, the coupon division often uses correspondents other than those regularly used by the country collection division, taking advantage of particularly good facilities.

```
No.................

Item.................................        Payable at.................

...................due...........@............ $............

...................due...........@............ $............

...................due...........@............ $............

Remarks..........................Total.......$............

        INSTITUTE STATE BANK
              Atlanta, Georgia
     Please Report Non-Payment Immediately
```

FIGURE 24. COUPON ENVELOPE

Collection Department Operations—In some banks the volume of collections is so small that the work is performed by a teller in addition to his regular assignment. Suitable forms and records are used, and the collection routine follows much the same procedure as that described. In such banks items are usually sent to the city correspondent for collection or credit, or they are routed through the non-cash collection division of the Federal Reserve bank or branch.

In somewhat larger banks a full-time collection teller is employed. He handles country, city, and coupon collections; and in some cases he also handles the issuing of certificates of deposit, cashier's checks, and bank drafts.

In large banks the work is divided into country, city, and coupon divisions (as already described), with subdivisions if necessary.

The statistics of one large bank may be of interest since they show the extent of collection operations and the difference between the volume of cash items and the volume of items handled by the collection department.

The transit department of this bank employed 81 persons and handled on an average from 84,431 to 112,613 items daily, or a daily average total *per person* of from 1,042 items on light days to 1,390 on heavy days.

The country and city collection divisions of the same bank had a total of 31 employees; their daily averages of items handled were as follows:

    77 city notes
     8 miscellaneous transactions
    29 security payment and delivery transactions
  108 city and country security drafts
  418 other out of-town collections

or a total of 640 items. This was at the rate of approximately 20 collections per person daily.

In the coupon collection division of the bank there were 26 regular employees, with the addition of 20 special employees for two hours a day at rush periods three or four days each month. In point of time the extra help was about the equivalent of five full-time persons; so for purposes of comparison, it may be assumed that the force was 31 employees, instead of 26 regular and 20 part time.

This division handled an average of 37,445 transactions a month, or 1,337 a day, representing about 43 transactions per person daily.

These figures show clearly the difference between handling cash items and collection items from an operating point of view. The average number of items handled per person each day in the transit department is many times the average handled in the collection department.

While the work of the department in most cases can be done by using the forms described and the methods and systems outlined, occasionally there are collections which require instructions of so extensive or unusual a nature that it is necessary to supplement the forms with special letters of instruction, written by the department manager or by an officer of the bank.

Collection Charges—The fees and charges for collections vary with the kinds of transactions handled, and many banks list their charges in bank directories in order to attract collection business. Security drafts are charged at rates based on the par value plus expenses, such as postage and insurance. Other transactions are handled at rates agreed upon, or flat rates. Real estate file collections, for example, are charged at the rate of 35 cents for each contract and 10 cents for each payment in many instances.

When the scope and efficiency of the services of the collection department and the ease with which customers can expedite their business are taken into consideration, it is little wonder that the fees charged are regarded as moderate and that frequent use is made of the collection department facilities by all kinds of customers.

Federal Reserve Collection Service—The *non-cash collection service* offered by the Federal Reserve banks operates in a manner similar to the collection department of the large commercial bank. The multiple form, maturity ticklers, tracers, acknowledgments, and advices of credit are used, as in commercial banks. There is one difference, however, that should be noted.

There is a *par arrangement* in Federal Reserve *non-cash collection work,* banks voluntarily agreeing to remit at par for collection items and in return receiving a similar service from other banks participating in the arrangement. Although preference is of course given to par points, collections are also sent to banks which do not enter into the arrangement but which make reasonable charges.

While non-cash collection service is not as extensive as the par collection of checks, it is nevertheless a major facility, as the figures of the Federal Reserve System show. Exclusive of the collection of United States Government coupons, the total number of non-cash items, or pieces, handled in the year 1938 was 6,389,000, representing a total of $5,321,443,000.[1]

Collection Department Balance—Each day, as payments are received, the collection department credits the balances of the customers or departments from which the items were entered for collection, deducting collection and exchange charges. The charges deducted are credited to the proper accounts on the general books of the bank. In addition to accounting for these payments, the collection department at the end of the day accounts only for the cash charged to it by the head paying teller, and the day's business is completed with no balance due to or from any other department.

It is important, therefore, in the operations of the department that a balance be drawn within the department and that all transactions be readily audited. In departments where large amounts of collection items are outstanding at all times, the only way to verify them is by audit procedure since they are not reflected on the bank's books during the period of collection. This may be done in a number of ways—by requiring more than one member of the department to handle each item, by the use of numbered forms as a running audit, and by fre-

---

[1] See Table VI, Appendix.

quent verifications to determine that the items are properly handled and accounted for.

Savings Banks and Savings Departments

The Nature of Savings Institutions—Savings banks are organized to receive thrift deposits from people of moderate means, particularly salaried persons and wage earners. These deposits are received on a time basis and interest is paid for their use. The bank profits by the investment of a large portion of these deposits in mortgages and bonds of excellent rating. The difference between the income from the investments and the cost of operating the department, including interest paid, is the principal source of profit for savings banks, as such banks do not provide other major banking facilities. The savings department of a commercial bank is organized for the same purpose as the individual savings bank although, with some exceptions (in Massachusetts, for example), the investment of the funds available through savings deposits is included in the general investments of the bank.

In the eastern part of the United States there are a large number of these strictly savings banks, institutions that provide facilities for savings but do not engage in commercial banking or trust banking. In Chapter I, under the subject of mutual savings banks, the extent of savings institutions was shown by the fact that in 1936 they had over ten billions of deposits and over fourteen million customers. They form a substantial part of the banking structure in the United States, and when deposits and customers of the savings departments of commercial banks are added, the importance of savings is still more obvious.

Outside of New England and adjacent areas, savings facilities are provided to a large extent by the savings departments of commercial banks. The kinds of accounts in these departments and their methods of operation are similar to those of strictly savings institutions. In fact, the savings department of a commercial bank is often operated almost as an individual banking unit from the standpoint of teller and other operating procedures, although, as before noted, the investment of the funds is commonly a part of the general investment activities of the bank.

Characteristics of Savings Accounts—*The ideal savings account is characterized by its inactivity in withdrawals and its gradual but steady increase by the making of regular deposits.* Persons of thrifty habits maintain savings deposits as reserves in anticipation of possible future needs or as a means of building up a fund to meet specific future obligations—insurance premiums, mortgage payments, and the like. Since savings banks are designed to provide facilities for persons of moderate means, the maximum total allowed in any account is often limited to $2,500 or $5,000. The bank desires many accounts of true savings character rather than a smaller number of accounts of larger amounts that may not be thrift accounts. Recent national banking legislation and regulation provide for a strict definition of thrift accounts in order to limit the use of savings privileges to those who are actually savings customers. These limitations are discussed further under "types of accounts" later in this chapter.

A comparison of the operations of the savings department of a certain bank with those of the commercial department in the same bank affords an interesting study. The commercial deposits in this bank total $4,150,000 (in round figures), the savings deposits, $2,450,000. The number of commercial accounts is 3,380, with an average balance of $1,228 per account. The number of savings accounts is 13,583, with an average balance of $174 per account (this does not include the school savings accounts which constitute a minor portion and are handled in a special way, different from the regular savings routine).

The commercial customers make an average of 533 deposits a day, or at the rate of one deposit for each six accounts. The savings customers make an average of 135 deposits a day, or at the rate of one deposit for each 100 accounts.

On an average, 2,430 checks are paid against commercial accounts by the bookkeeping department each day, 990 of which are received in deposits and 1,440 through the clearings exchange. The debits to the savings accounts average 105 daily. With the exception of an occasional withdrawal received through the collection department, all savings withdrawals are made at the windows. In the commercial department, the average of debits *per account each day* is between *one* and *two*, while in the savings department the average is *one* for each *128* accounts.

Translating these figures into operations, the commercial department of this bank has three receiving tellers, two paying tellers, a distribution department of three persons, and six employees in the bookkeeping department, all of whom handle deposits and checks. The savings department has a total force of four to handle deposits, withdrawals, and bookkeeping for the entire department.

From this comparison, it can be seen that the problem of operating a savings department is very different from that of operating a commercial department and that savings accounts with their infrequent transactions lend themselves to methods quite different from those governing commercial accounts with their great activity. The systems used in savings departments are designed to apply to relatively inactive accounts, and overactivity in even a small proportion of the accounts presents a disturbing problem. With overactivity, they cease to be true savings accounts and become commercial accounts in reality (if not in name).

Overactivity also increases the expense of handling. The activity of a few accounts may seriously interfere with the service to other savings customers. As almost every savings transaction is cared for at the window, a teller must handle it, in contrast to commercial items which frequently come through other channels, such as in-clearings; therefore the per item cost for transactions handled by the tellers is greater in the savings department than in other departments.

Correction of Overactive Accounts—Various methods are used to eliminate overactive accounts. Interviews with customers, suggested transfer of balances to the commercial department, and elimination of interest paid are among the methods used to place and maintain savings business on a proper basis.

The use of the personal interview to eliminate overactive accounts and to improve the business of the department has been fairly successful. In one instance service charges on commercial accounts in the locality had resulted in a substantial increase in the number of savings accounts, which were in reality commercial accounts used for current purposes and active in deposits and withdrawals. As a result, the service to other savings customers was impaired and peak loads in the department increased, with a corresponding increase in personnel. In short, expenses increased rapidly and profits declined.

It was decided to try the interview method in an attempt to correct the overactivity of those accounts that were interfering with the efficient operation of the department. The average activity of all active savings accounts (as distinguished from the dormant accounts) was .25 withdrawals each month per account, or at the rate of one withdrawal per account each four months. The number of overactive accounts was 1,285. It was decided that the first time each of these customers made a deposit or a withdrawal after the segregation of the accounts

COLLECTIONS, SAVINGS, AND SAFE DEPOSIT

had been made, he was to be interviewed by the manager or assistant manager of the department.

In the interview the overactivity was discussed, the reasons for the interview explained, and ways and means of improving the account suggested. After making the situation perfectly clear to the customer, the bank representative requested him to improve his account (to make it a true savings account) or else to transfer his balance to the commercial department. A record of each interview was made for the 1,285 customers interviewed; after an experience of four months these accounts were reviewed and the following results tabulated.

Monthly withdrawal activity per account

First month after interview	1.46
Second month after interview	1.31
Third month after interview	1.14
Fourth month after interview	1.10

Even this steady improvement does not give the full picture of accomplishment. A more encouraging picture is presented by a classification of the accounts at the end of four months, which was as follows:

	Number	Per Cent
No withdrawals since interview	94	7.3
Not more than one withdrawal in any month	246	19.1
More than one withdrawal in some months	343	26.7
Account still too active	310	24.1
Account closed	292	22.8
	1,285	100.0

While by number the accounts closed constituted 22.8%, by amount they represented less than 9% of the total of over-active accounts. Every account that closed had been unprofitable to the bank.

Considering that all the accounts selected for interview and analysis were unsatisfactory at the start and were unprofitable to the bank, the result of the interview method was very good: 26.4% of the accounts were changed from *overactive* and *unprofitable* to *inactive* and *profitable;* 26.7% were greatly improved but were still somewhat too active, about breaking even in profit; and 24.1% were still too active.

Savings departments often have rules governing overactivity, and if any account exceeds the activity permitted, the customer is requested to transfer the account to the commercial department.

Another device to discourage overactivity of accounts, and at the same time to increase balances, is to place a limitation on the interest paid. This is done either by eliminating interest payments on overactive accounts or by paying interest only when it exceeds a minimum amount (such as $1), or both. A few banks have also adopted service charges for savings accounts.

The Passbook—The use of the passbook as a complete record for the commercial department customer (a use now of less importance than formerly) was discussed in Chapter III. While the activity of commercial accounts has to a large extent resulted in the elimination of the passbook for this purpose, in the savings department the passbook is still a duplicate record of the ledger account and constitutes the customer's record of his transactions and balances. The nature of savings accounts and the methods of operation make the use of the passbook a satisfactory procedure. Because of the relative inactivity of savings accounts, one passbook will be sufficient for these entries for several years. The passbook must be presented when each transaction is made, since all deposits and withdrawals are recorded in the passbook.

The average savings deposit consists largely of cash, and

COLLECTIONS, SAVINGS, AND SAFE DEPOSIT 289

only a few checks (if any) are deposited at one time. This makes the proving of the deposit and the entering of the new balance a task that can be rapidly and easily performed. A

IN ACCOUNT WITH...NO.....................				
DATE	WITHDRAWAL	DEPOSIT	BALANCE

It is agreed that the depositor accepts this passbook and makes all deposits subject to the by-laws of the bank applicable to savings deposits.

INSTITUTE STATE BANK

FIGURE 25. SAVINGS PASSBOOK

recent survey of several savings departments showed the average number of checks deposited to be approximately *two* for each *three deposits*.

Since each deposit or withdrawal and the new balance are figured and entered at the time of the transaction, the only entry that remains to be made is the interest credit (which will be explained later in the text).

A savings passbook is illustrated in Figure 25. The rules and regulations pertaining to savings accounts are included in the first page or two of the book, just as the rules and regulations for commercial accounts are printed in the commercial passbook. The entries made in the savings passbook take the place of both the passbook and the customer's statement in the commercial department; receipts for deposits are given, withdrawals recorded, and balances calculated, all in the one savings passbook, as may be seen from the illustration.

Types of Accounts—The services of a savings bank or savings department are designed to appeal to the thrifty person who wishes to build up an inactive reserve account. Therefore, corporation and other business accounts are not accepted even if they are time accounts, but they are referred to the certificate of deposit division in the commercial department. In fact, the regulations of the Federal Reserve System prohibit the acceptance of corporation and other business accounts in the savings department, regarding such accounts as outside the "thrift" classification. Savings accounts, then, are primarily individual accounts limited to those who may be considered as using the accounts for actual thrift purposes. Guardianship and trustee accounts are subjected to careful scrutiny before they are accepted by savings institutions.

"Time deposits, open account" represent another type of time account and should be considered in connection with savings and certificates of deposit. These time deposits, open account are discussed in Chapter VIII.

Individual accounts are those of one, two, or several persons—the individual account, the joint account, and the survivorship account. Limiting deposits in maximum amount and in activity, a savings bank or savings department has as its goal a large number of moderate sized inactive and steadily growing accounts, and much help is given to individuals striving to build such accounts.

One type of savings account that is not found in the commercial department is the *coupon account*.

The Coupon (or Club) Account—*The coupon (or club) account is designed to assist the individual by establishing a regular plan of depositing fixed sums at regular intervals.* This plan continues for varying periods, the most common being fifty weeks. At the end of the time the total saved is paid to the customer, with or without interest, according to the policy of the bank.

The object of the coupon account is to enable the depositor to build up a fund over a period of a few months to meet extraordinary or unusual expenses that are likely to occur at the end of the time. Many banks find that these accounts result in regular and satisfactory savings accounts of a more permanent nature, as the customer develops thrift habits, finds that a regular schedule of thrift is less difficult than he thought, and so learns to be a true savings customer.

Coupon accounts are handled somewhat differently from regular accounts; no withdrawals are permitted and the addition of fixed deposits makes it possible to figure the balance at various times in advance. Passbooks are not used; instead, a coupon book is issued with pages corresponding to the scheduled payments. As payments are made, two coupons corresponding to the payment are stamped by the teller. One remains in the book as the customer's receipt; the other is torn out and used as a credit memorandum. Another method frequently used is a punch card system, by means of which the bank keeps a record of the account and the customer a duplicate; both cards are punched whenever the customer makes a deposit.

Christmas savings clubs, vacation clubs, and the like are names commonly given to coupon accounts. Mortgage principal or interest payments, insurance premiums, taxes, and many other annual bills that represent substantial outlays to a person of moderate income may be anticipated by using this system.

Savings Department Records—The use and importance of the passbook have already been explained. The specimen signature cards used in the savings department are similar to those used in the commercial department. Since savings customers almost without exception are individuals, the card is also used as authority for the account, and information desired by the bank is entered on the back of it; thus the card often takes the place of the new account sheet used in the commercial department. The savings customers should always be identified positively; therefore, if needed, specimen signature identification slips such as those used in the commercial department may be required.

The savings deposit slip is usually somewhat smaller than the one used in the commercial department, because of the fact that the average savings deposit consists of cash and seldom more than one or two checks. The number of the account, as well as the name of the customer, is entered on each deposit slip, and the records are sorted numerically rather than alphabetically. On some savings deposit slips space is provided for entering the new balance of the account as a result of the deposit or withdrawal, to be verified as the transaction is posted on the ledger.

In place of the checks that are handled in the commercial department, a receipt form, signed by the customer, stating that he has received the funds from the savings department, is used for withdrawals. This is not a draft; it is non-negotiable and therefore cannot be used by others. If for any reason the customer wishes to make a withdrawal without coming into the bank, a regular form of draft is used and the passbook attached. About the only case where this procedure is likely to be followed is for transfers to other banks. It is rarely used for payments to third parties other than banks, since the regulations governing Federal Reserve and Federal Deposit Insurance Corporation members do not permit a direct withdrawal to be made to a third party unless that party is an agent of the savings customer.

In addition to the number of the account and the new balance resulting from the withdrawal, space is provided on some withdrawal forms for the initials of the teller or clerk who verifies the signature on the withdrawal, pays out the funds, or enters the transaction on the books of the department.

The bookkeeping or ledger records of savings accounts are kept either on sheets, one for each account in the department, or on cards. The transactions are posted by pen and ink or by use of a bookkeeping machine. Where the number of accounts in the department is not large, the ledgers may be alphabetically arranged; more frequently, and particularly where there are many accounts, the accounts are numbered and the ledgers arranged numerically.

Savings Receiving and Paying Teller Systems—In the commercial department of the bank, the alphabetical, general cage, and unit teller systems are most commonly used. In the savings department two systems are generally employed, one combining features of the general and unit systems and the other combining features of the numerical and unit systems. They might well be called, respectively, the unit-general system and the unit-numerical system.

The unit-general system is found to be satisfactory for a moderate number of savings accounts. The small number of items included in the average savings deposit makes it easy for the teller to do both paying and receiving without delay, and the moderate number of relatively inactive accounts makes it possible for all savings transactions to be handled by one teller or one cage.

The unit-numerical system is used in larger departments. Each teller handles a group of consecutively numbered accounts, both paying and receiving, such as accounts numbered from 50,001 to 100,000.

In both receiving and paying transactions, the savings teller must have ready access to the bookkeeping division of the department, for in some departments the passbook is balanced each time a transaction is made. The bookkeeping division is located adjacent to the cages, and often each bookkeeping unit is placed directly behind the cage handling its numbered accounts.

The problems of savings department tellers are somewhat different from those of commercial tellers. In the savings department the verification of deposit totals is a simple matter and is most frequently done by the teller himself. The sorting and charging of checks to other departments is also a simple procedure, since the volume of clearings, "us" checks, and transit items is proportionately small. A receiving teller's proof is used for balancing with the other departments. Currency must be counted and verified, just as in commercial department work, but the amounts are not large and the task is easy. Indorsements must be examined and the items looked over to be sure they are cash items, but this check-up is rapidly done since the items are few in number.

Only in large savings departments or savings banks is the block system ever used, for batch proof is of benefit only when the volume of items is very large.

From the viewpoint of the paying teller, the principal task in savings work is the verification of signatures on withdrawals or on checks that are cashed. In the commercial department the paying tellers encounter the signatures of customers in their groups so frequently that many signatures soon become well known to them. The reverse is true in the savings department; so seldom does the savings teller see the signatures of customers that he can become familiar with only a small number of them. It is a general practice of savings departments to have the signature verified (by comparison with the specimen signature on file) *each time a withdrawal is made.*

Stale dates and post dates are no problem at all in the savings department. Since withdrawal requests ordinarily are filled out at the bank and cashed immediately, forgery and alteration are not so likely to be encountered as in the commercial department, where checks may go through many hands between the time they are issued and the time they are paid.

When a savings teller is called upon to cash a check for a savings customer, he usually checks the balance in the customer's account to see that it exceeds the amount of the check presented and at the same time verifies the indorsement of the customer by reference to the signature card. He then places on the ledger card of the account a notation of the amount of the check that has been cashed and the time it will take for the check to be collected, thus insuring that the funds in the account will not be paid out until the check has been collected. The savings account number and a stamp indicating the teller who cashed the check are placed on the back of the check, so that if it is returned unpaid, it can be referred to the proper savings division immediately.

Many banks have adopted the policy of requiring a customer first to deposit an item presented for cashing and then to make a withdrawal of the amount in the usual way. This method is preferable to cashing an item because it eliminates possible legal complications. There are many court decisions to the effect that deducting a returned item from the balance in an account is legal only *if the item was actually deposited.*

Banks do not charge for this check-cashing service unless it is used too frequently or is used by customers who maintain small balances. In cities where exchange charges prevail, charges on transits are assessed by the teller on the same basis as in the commercial department.

Cashier's Checks and Bank Drafts—Many savings customers do not have any other bank accounts; therefore when they find it convenient or necessary to pay a bill by check, they purchase a cashier's check or a bank draft. The methods used in handling requests for cashier's checks and drafts vary. If the number of requests is not too large, the cashier's check and draft division of the bank's commercial department is used. If the number of requests increases in volume, a separate cashier's check and draft division of the savings department may be established.

The charges for this service vary. A flat charge of five cents or ten cents for each check issued may be made, or the charge may depend on the amount of the check or the size of the customer's account.

An analysis of the cashier's service by one bank over a period of a year revealed that the proportion of cashier's checks issued by the savings department to the number of withdrawals made during the same period was approximately one-third. Another bank found the proportion of cashier's checks and drafts issued to savings customers to be one-half the number of withdrawals. A third bank found them to be one-fourth. In all these banks charges were made for the service in order partially to pay the cost of the facilities.

Savings Department Bookkeeping—In the bookkeeping division of the savings department, each bookkeeper can handle a large number of accounts, since only a small percentage of the accounts will have transactions on any one day. The figures of the savings department in a southern bank are typical. This department has 6,768 accounts. The average daily activity is 90 withdrawals and 102 deposits, which means that on the average 192 out of 6,768 accounts will be affected daily, assuming that each deposit or each withdrawal is for a different account. Reference to the discussion earlier in the chapter under "characteristics of savings accounts" will illustrate the point further. There the daily rate of deposits in the commercial department was given as 1 to each 6 accounts and the daily rate in the savings department of the same bank as 1 to each 100 accounts; in other words, about one-twentieth as many accounts were affected in the savings department as in the commercial department each day.

This difference in the number of accounts handled makes possible the use of different ledger records in the savings department. In using either the ledger sheet with pen and ink posting or the ledger card or sheet with machine posting, one of two general methods is followed in savings bookkeeping. One method provides for the posting of both the passbook and the ledger at the time the transaction is made; the other provides for the posting of the ledger at a later time, even at the close of the day. The first method will be described and illustrated shortly.

In savings department bookkeeping the problem of uncollected funds is slight; the ledger card is simply marked or tagged when necessary to indicate this and other "holds." Stop-payments are almost unknown, for the customer's passbook or signed withdrawal slip is seldom in another's hands, the only exception to the rule being in the case of a lost passbook.

Lost Passbooks—Because of the general rule that the savings passbook must be presented with each deposit or withdrawal, if the passbook is lost the customer must sign a statement to that effect and provide an indemnity bond to protect the bank in the event the book reappears and a demand is made for funds by means of a draft or other order of the customer in the hands of the party presenting the passbook.

When a passbook is reported lost and the indemnity arranged, the ledger card of the account is immediately marked, and no payments may be made until the matter is adjusted. A period of time is allowed for the passbook to turn up, if temporarily misplaced. If the book has not appeared after this lapse of time, a new passbook is issued. This is done by closing the old account and transferring the funds to a new account with a new number; thus a very definite stop is placed against the withdrawal of funds by the use of the old passbook.

Savings Department Organization and Operation—To illustrate savings department organization and operation, the savings department of a large city bank is taken as an example. Accounts are handled by numbers under the unit teller system, both paying and receiving being done by the same teller at the window designated for the group of accounts assigned to him, such as 251,000 to 300,000.

When the customer presents his passbook, deposit slip, and items at the window, the ledger card is removed from the file. (This card is similar to the one illustrated in Figure 26.) The passbook is placed in position on one side of the posting machine, the ledger card on the other; the entry is then made on the keyboard and the machine operated, simultaneously printing the transaction and the resultant balance on both the passbook and the ledger card. At the same time the machine records the transaction on an inside tape which is locked in a compartment. This tape record is used by the auditing department to check transactions and also by the savings department for daily balancing purposes. (In another

TITLE OF ACCOUNT			
Number			
DATE	WITHDRAWAL	DEPOSIT	BALANCE
INSTITUTE STATE BANK			

FIGURE 26. SAVINGS LEDGER CARD

bank, while the passbook and ledger card are both posted at the time the transaction occurs, each is posted independently, one serving to check the other.)

For withdrawals, the customer presents the passbook and a signed withdrawal slip to the teller. The signature is verified from the specimen on the ledger card, the passbook and card are then posted, as in the deposit work, and the withdrawal cashed.

In this bank the ledger cards are kept in the cage during the day for convenience in posting. In another bank which uses the same posting equipment, the ledger cards are located directly behind the cage, and the verification of signatures is made by the bookkeepers.

Paying Signatures—In some savings organizations, there is a separate *withdrawal* division, where the passbook and withdrawal slip are presented, the signature verified, and the customer then sent to the teller for the posting of the passbook and payment of the withdrawal. Sometimes the withdrawal division does the posting as well as the verification, and payment only is made by the teller. Under another method the withdrawal division verifies the balance, and the teller checks the signature when the passbook and withdrawal slip are presented at his window.

Occasionally a transaction which is unusual may be referred to an authorized department officer for decision.

Interest—Interest is calculated and paid on the accounts periodically, often semiannually—January 1 and July 1, for example. Interest periods are unusually busy times for savings banks or savings departments, for directly following the date for crediting interest a large number of customers present their passbooks to have the interest entered.

The amount of interest is calculated by the use of tables designed for this work and is then entered on the ledger card. From the ledger card it is posted in the passbook. In both interest calculation periods and interest payment periods, extra help may be needed in the department. Often a special counter force is used for a few days during interest periods, and all interest entries are made at the counter to relieve the regular tellers of this detail and enable them to wait on customers for the usual deposit and withdrawal transactions.

There are two kinds of interest; one is called *simple* interest, the other, *compound*. With simple interest, the principal amount (the sum upon which the interest is calculated and paid) and the interest are accounted for separately. For example, in accounting for simple interest at 2% on $100 for one year, the interest would be $2, and the two sums would be set up and treated separately: principal, $100; interest, $2. Even if the $2 interest were left on deposit, the next year the calculation would be made the same way, assuming no changes in the principal amount by either deposit or withdrawal in the meantime.

When compound interest is used, the interest is added to the principal and a new principal amount is created. The interest on $100 at 2% for one year, amounting to $2, would be added to the $100 principal, and the new principal would be $102, upon which the interest for the next year would be $2.04.

Although most banking transactions involving interest calculations are on the basis of simple interest, in savings departments compound interest is the rule.

Members of the Federal Reserve System and of the Federal Deposit Insurance Corporation are subject to regulation of the maximum interest which may be paid on time accounts. Since savings accounts constitute the greater portion of accounts in the time deposit class, this regulation applies particularly to their operation.

Methods Used in Calculating Interest—Interest may be calculated in various ways; some are the result of bank policies, others the result of mechanical methods adopted. For example, some banks calculate interest only on balances that have had no withdrawals during the interest period; others make allowance for the variations and compute interest on the undisturbed balance.

In the mechanics employed there are similar variations. Convenient tables may be used, or interest may be figured mathematically by the teller, or calculating machines may be used. Often a force outside the department figures the interest and enters the results on the ledger sheets.

Where savings accounts are in the main inactive, some banks calculate interest at the beginning of an interest period and then carry it along each time there is a posted increase or decrease, as the case may be. Thus on a balance shown in the account at any time, the interest calculation is based on the amount which would be credited to that account at the next interest period provided there is no further activity in the account. It is really a form of calculation of accrued interest in advance, but it serves the purpose of eliminating a tremendous amount of calculation and figuring at the close of an interest period.

Other Services of the Savings Department—The officers and employees of the savings department have many opportunities to assist customers by referring them to other departments of the bank for facilities needed or desired, thus helping increase the business and the profits of the bank. Many savings customers have little knowledge of financial transactions; they do not know where to go for services that are well known to business men, and so they depend upon their only banking connection, the savings department, for advice and counsel.

The savings department, through its officers and employees, can be of very direct assistance in promoting thrift by helping customers to plan their expenditures, to budget their income, and to adopt a definite and workable thrift plan. The promotion of thrift habits in school children through school savings plans is a fairly common practice of savings departments. Although these ventures are likely to cost more than the income received from the use of the funds deposited, nevertheless the efforts are considered well worth while from a public relations standpoint.

THE SAFE DEPOSIT COMPANY

Purpose of the Safe Deposit Company—A safe deposit company is operated for the purpose of providing facilities for the protection of the valuables of its customers. It is a special kind of warehouse for the storage of personal property. In this capacity, a safe deposit company is subject to the general standard required of a warehouseman; namely, that the customer's property be accorded protection at least equal to that afforded the company's own property.

A safe deposit institution frequently is a separate company, although in many cases it is a department of the bank. Safe deposit activities are so closely affiliated with banking facilities, however, that state and national laws recognize the natural connection and permit banks to own substantial amounts of stock in safe deposit companies. In addition to the safe deposit companies that are affiliated with banks, there are many that have no such connection and operate solely for safe deposit purposes.

In addition to the individual safes provided, safe deposit companies or departments provide storage facilities for articles of bulk. These storage facilities, in many cases, are the source of substantial revenue.

In the years preceding and during the 1929-1933 depression, many independent safe deposit companies came into existence as a result of two conditions. During these years there were many bank consolidations, and often two or three institutions were combined in the quarters of one. Where safe deposit companies had been established in banking quarters that were no longer to be used, the business and equipment were frequently sold to new companies, formed to conduct a safe deposit business only. Then too, safe deposit facilities originally operated by banks that failed were often purchased by companies formed for the purpose of conducting a safe deposit business, and the service to the community was continued as a profitable venture.

Sometimes in cities the owners of a large office building will organize a safe deposit company and establish it in the building, as a service to the tenants of the building and others nearby. The object, of course, is to obtain revenue and profit.

The majority of safe deposit companies, however, are connected with banks and are usually located on the bank's premises; thus they are patronized by the bank's customers and sometimes constitute a source of income to the stockholders.

Responsibilities of Safe Deposit Companies—The responsibilities of the safe deposit company may be summed up in the single word *protection*. The company's part of the contract is to provide this, and nothing is left undone in a well regulated safe deposit company to insure the utmost protection of the property of its customers.

Vault equipment, alarms, and guards are all part of the physical protection against robbery. Identification, access methods, and verification of entries are part of the protection against fraud. Both kinds of protection are equally essential.

It is customary under present routine to have the keys for an unused safe deposit box sealed, the envelope containing them being identified only after the prospective renter has selected a box. A set screw is then released which discloses the number corresponding with the number on the sealed envelope containing the keys. These keys are receipted for by the renter of the box. As a result of this procedure, it is not possible for a safe deposit department attendant to have access to the keys to a safe deposit box before it is rented.

The customer also has his obligations. He must give the necessary information and authority to the company. By promptly reporting lost keys and by following the routine of access carefully, he does his part in assisting the company to protect his valuables.

Equipment—The essential equipment of a safe deposit company consists of a vault, or vaults, with the usual time locks, alarms, and other safety devices. Within this vault are rows of individual safes, arranged in tiers and numbered. Inside each safe is a metal container in which the contents are stored. These individual safe compartments, or boxes, are equipped with two locks; one can be unlocked by a master key in the hands of a representative of the company, the other can be unlocked only by a key in the customer's possession. Therefore, a representative of the company *alone* cannot unlock the safe, and the customer *alone* cannot unlock the safe; both keys must be used simultaneously. In this way the customer is assured that the contents of his safe are absolutely inviolable, and the company is assured that the safe cannot be opened unless proper access authority has been received.

Properly operated safe deposit companies invariably use this method or a slight modification of it; *in no instance* does the company have any arrangement of keys that will permit any one connected with it to enter a box. In fact, when a box must be opened because the customer's keys are lost, or for non-payment of rent, or on court order, it is necessary to *drill the locks*. This is done only in the presence of reliable witnesses in order that there may be no question regarding the contents of the box. If anything is found in the box, the contents are packaged and sealed in the presence of these witnesses, and the package is placed in safety until called for by the owner of the box or otherwise legally disposed of.

In addition to these double-lock safe compartments, some safe deposit vaults have individual combination safes. The combination of the safe is reset for each succeeding customer, and the new combination is known only to that customer.

Identification—Safe deposit companies are extremely careful to obtain positive identification of persons who represent themselves to be prospective customers. Moreover, since many customers visit the vaults only infrequently, their identification must be verified each time access to the safe deposit box is requested.

The contract between the company and the renter of a safe deposit box contains a statement of the rules and regulations agreed to and of the rental; in addition, the form provides for complete authority and identification. Those who are to have access to the box must file specimen signatures on the contract form and on the signature cards and also furnish the customary information regarding address, business connections, telephone, and other information that may be used for identification purposes, such as the date of birth, physical description of the renter, complexion, height, and weight. Special means of identification which may be used consist of the fingerprints of the customer and unusual personal information, such as the maiden name of the customer's mother, the middle name of the father, or other family names or connections that are not likely to be known to unauthorized persons. A code word known only to the company and to the customer is also frequently used.

In smaller departments or companies where most customers are well known, access by signature on the access slip is all that is necessary, and from the access slip a record is made of the visit to the box.

Kinds of Accounts—The safe deposit company has the same kinds of customers as the commercial department and obtains its authority for the different kinds in the same way that authority is obtained for commercial accounts. Individual, survivorship, corporation, partnership, and trustee arrangements will all be found in a safe deposit company.

Access Procedure—When a customer wishes to obtain access to his safe, he fills out a request slip and presents it to the person in charge of the identification records and signature cards. The signatures are compared and a further verification made if necessary. If the identification is satisfactory, the request slip is stamped with the *time* and *date,* initialed by the custodian to indicate satisfactory identification, and then presented by the customer at the grilled door of the vault. The customer enters the vault, and an attendant uses his pass key in conjunction with that of the customer to open the safe. The request is then filed as the company record of the customer's access to the box.

The owner of a box may arrange to permit access by a deputy to whom he has given authority. Although the deputyship ceases immediately on the death of the owner, it is always possible for either the deputy or some member of the family who is in possession of the keys to visit the box with a representative of the safe deposit company or department in order that an examination of the contents of the box may be made to ascertain whether or not it contains burial instructions and also to obtain a copy of the will if one has been drawn.

Separate rooms are provided for the use of customers in which they may examine the contents of their boxes in privacy and safety. A record is kept of the use of each room so that if anything is found after a customer has left the room, it can be readily identified as his property. It is customary for an attendant to search the room immediately after a customer has finished using it, to see that nothing has accidentally been left behind.

When the customer has examined the contents of his box, he returns it to the safe, and the attendant, using the two keys, locks the safe. Even when the safe is open and the contents are in the customer's hands, his key should be always in his possession.

Operation of a Safe Deposit Company—The following description of the operation of a specific safe deposit company illustrates the general procedure that is used.

This company has 4,678 safes, or safe deposit boxes, ranging from small ones (about 6″ by 3″ by 15″) which are rented for $4 a year to large safes which rent for $20 a year. The average rental price is about $6. At the time of this survey, 4,121 of the boxes were rented, with a gross income of $24,726 a year.

The contract signed by the customer contains approximately the information already mentioned. All authority forms, such as resolutions of corporations, are attached to the contract, which is filed under the customer's name and cross-indexed by box number in a card file.

When the contract is made, two keys are issued to the renter of the box, for which a deposit of $1 is required. This deposit is returned upon the expiration of the lease if full payment for the term has been made and the keys are returned. A payment receipt, written on a register machine, contains the name of the customer, the address, the box number, the date of rental, the amount of rental paid, and the key deposit. This receipt is prepared in triplicate; the original is given to the customer as his receipt, the first copy is filed in the company's records, and the second is filed for audit purposes.

In this company all the rentals have been adjusted to fall due on January 1 of each year, so that a maturity or rental due record is not necessary. In other companies, a simple card form is used for rental due dates, and the cards are filed in the order of the due dates.

An entrance, or access, ticket must be signed by a customer in the presence of the vault custodian. The signature is verified by him from the signature card file, which is kept in a truck cabinet directly behind him. This cabinet is placed in the vaults at night.

After verification of the signature and the use of any other identification, the custodian stamps the date and time by means of a time-recording machine, initials the slip, and hands it back to the customer as authority to enter the vault.

The customer hands the slip to the vault attendant, who unlocks the safe, using the customer's key and his master key, and returns the customer's key to him. When the customer replaces the box, the attendant locks the safe, again using both keys. The customer's key is returned to him, and the entry slip is filed.

In the safe deposit company, as in the commercial department of the bank, there may arise circumstances that will revoke the authority of the tenant. Death of the tenant, bankruptcy, attachment or other court orders, including inheritance tax law requirements, all must be carefully watched for and access to the box withheld pending receipt of proper authority.

Whenever such *holds* occur, the contract and signature card are immediately tagged with the information, so that the custodian will not permit access to the box. In addition, by the use of colored buttons or pins inserted in the lock of the safe itself, the attendant is notified of the situation. In the safe deposit company described, red buttons are used to denote unpaid rent due, black buttons for deceased tenants, green for legal proceedings, and white for mail returned.

Ten days in advance of the rental due date a notice is mailed to the customer, and a return envelope is enclosed for his convenience in making payment. If this notice is unanswered, a second notice is sent ten days after the due date, followed by a third notice one month after the due date. If these are not answered, a final notice is sent, requesting the keys and stating that the box will be drilled if the keys are not returned immediately.

When drilling is necessary for unpaid rent or lost keys or on court order, the opening of the safe is done in the presence of the vault manager, an officer of the bank, and two other witnesses. The contents, if any, are packaged and sealed in the presence of these witnesses and the customer's name and safe number are placed on the package, which is then put in a special safe, subject to the control of two vault company officers jointly.

The cost of drilling and replacing the locks is by the contract billed to the renter, and the key deposit is applied on this cost.

Use of Safe Deposit Facilities—The customers of a bank find the use of a safe deposit company located in the bank building a convenient and inexpensive service. Valuable personal property is thus kept safe from fire and burglary hazards; and stocks, bonds, mortgages, and similar properties are so located that they can be readily taken to the bank for coupon collection and other purposes.

In some safe deposit companies a separate room in the vault is used for the storage of articles of larger bulk—trunks, chests, and so on.

Questions Based on Chapter VII

1. What are the duties of the collection department? Through what divisions are they generally exercised?
2. In handling collection items, why is it necessary to adopt methods different from those used in handling cash items?
3. For what purposes are the various parts of the multiple form used in the country collection division? in the city collection division?
4. From the standpoint of bank accounting, what is the nature of the difference between the collection department and other departments?
5. To what type of customer does the savings department appeal?
6. What are the characteristic differences between savings accounts and commercial accounts?
7. To what extent do these differences affect operations?
8. To what extent does the use of the passbook in the savings department differ from its use in the commercial department?
9. What is the purpose of the safe deposit company?
10. What two kinds of protection are afforded by such a company? How are they generally accomplished?

Questions for Outside Investigation

1. Is there a separate collection department in your bank? If so, does it have divisions similar to those mentioned in the text?
2. Does the department in your bank use a multiple form? If so, for what purposes are the various parts used?
3. If there is a savings department in your bank, how do the savings deposits compare with the commercial deposits in total amount?
4. Is the alphabetical or numerical arrangement of ledger accounts used? What teller system is used?
5. If there is a safe deposit company located on the bank's premises, is it owned by the bank? How large is it? That is, how many boxes does the vault contain? Is the procedure similar to that described in the text?

Assignment

1. Arthur R. Glade, a customer of the Institute State Bank, Chicago, Illinois, enters for collection on August 25, 1939 a trade acceptance dated May 18, 1939, due August 31, 1939, in the amount of $1,026.42. The acceptor is Smith and Brand, Inc., and the item is payable at the Blank National Bank, New Orleans, Louisiana. The New Orleans correspondent of the Institute State Bank is the Jones Trust Company. The Jones Trust Company carries a balance with the Institute State Bank.

The acceptance is subject to protest, and the proceeds are to be credited to the account of Arthur R. Glade. The item is paid, and the proceeds (after exchange charges of $1.50 are deducted) are advised under date of August 31, the advice being received the next day by the Institute State Bank.

Prepare facsimile collection forms, following the form used by your bank, and trace the transaction on a diagram such as that shown in Figure 23.

Be sure that the collection is completely described, that full instructions are given, and that you make clear all the steps, amounts, and so on from the time the collection is entered until final payment is received by the customer.

2. On March 23, 1939 the Institute State Bank receives for collection from the Jones Trust Company of New Orleans a sight draft for $450.50 drawn on the R.D.C. Company, 300 Bankers Building, Chicago, Illinois. The proceeds are to be credited to the Jones Trust Company's account.

Make a simple diagram showing the route of the draft (which is paid upon presentation) from the time it is received by the Institute State Bank to final payment and advice to the Jones Trust Company.

Note. Do *not* make facsimile collection forms for this assignment.

CHAPTER VIII

BANK ACCOUNTING AND AUDITING

The Purposes of This Chapter:
1. To explain the nature and scope of the accounting system.
2. To outline the function of the general books.
3. To describe the operation of the individual books.
4. To review the principles of audit procedure.

A BANK is essentially a huge accounting machine, transferring the ownership of money and credit and keeping a record of such transfers. Practically every person in a bank engages in some form of record making. Some give all their time to it, some very little; but every one contributes in some way to the mass of record. Although such a mass gives the appearance of complexity, bank bookkeeping and accounting are nevertheless relatively simple, since banks deal with but one commodity, money.

Banking laws, both national and state, require that banks submit sworn statements of assets and liabilities upon notice from supervisory authority. The accounting processes of every bank must therefore be adequate to provide an accurate and complete statement of condition daily.

Bank bookkeeping must also provide a method for accounting for all items and transactions during the time of handling. For example, in the collection of a check, a complete record is maintained during the period between the time the check is deposited or cashed and the time it is paid or returned. These records are also used as the means of balancing the work between departments. But accounting does not cease with the completion of a transaction; a record must be kept in permanent form. Many occasions arise when it is necessary for the bank's records to be produced—upon the request of customers or by legal demand in court action, for example. From the standpoint of the bank, these permanent records afford definite protection, evidence that a past transaction has been correctly handled.

Accurate bank records are invaluable in settling disputes that may arise long after transactions have been completed. For example, a few of the loans made by a bank are not paid when due for one reason or another. Some are merely slow and will be paid later. Others are classed as *doubtful*— that is, not likely to be collected in full. Still others are regarded as losses and are *charged off*—that is, reduced to nothing in the valuation of the bank's assets. Obviously, these charge-offs must be carefully followed up so that no opportunity will be overlooked to recover some of the loss at a later date. In order to accomplish this, the accounting method is designed to bring such cases to the attention of designated members of the staff at suitable times.

Notes are negotiable instruments and are subject to the statute of limitations. This statute provides that unless legal action is taken by the holder of an instrument within the period of limitation (from four to twenty years, depending on the state laws), the courts will not intervene to enforce recovery. Proper accounting records enable the bank to know when action must be taken within the limitation period, and in some cases they furnish the sole proof that appropriate action was taken at the proper time.

In recent years the use of budgetary control, cost accounting, and account analysis has increased, and accounting processes are organized to provide the necessary data without undue increase of accounting machinery.

The four objectives of bank accounting may be summarized as follows:

1. The preparation of the daily statement of condition

2. The identification and recording of items in the process of collection (or other handling)

3. The establishment of a record of past transactions for use when it is necessary for action to be taken with respect to items no longer in the possession of the bank

4. The facilitation of budgetary control, cost accounting, and account analysis.

Extent of Bank Accounting—Bank accounting is involved in every transaction made by every department or division, beginning with the original entry of the transaction in the departmental records and continuing until the effect of the transaction is reflected in the statement of condition of the bank—either in the assets or in the liabilities. Memoranda, straight lists, receipt forms, and records of all kinds, temporary or permanent, are part of the accounting records of the bank.

Consider the deposit of a check drawn on a bank in another city. The first accounting entry is that of the receiving teller. From the teller the item goes through the batch, or central proof, department and is included in that department's total to the transit department; it is again included in the transit proof and the transit letter; and finally it is reflected in the "due from Federal Reserve banks" or "due from banks and bankers" total on the general books. Another record of this item (the credit) goes from the central proof to the bookkeeping department and finally is credited to the individual account. Certain corporate records—stock ledger, transfer book, minute book, and the like—are maintained by the bank for its own use; others are kept for the customer transactions effected through the bank.

Kinds of Records—Three kinds of records are commonly used in bank accounting. The first is the *memorandum record*.

This record is purely temporary and is used in balancing operations within and between departments; it consists of machine listings, batch proofs, and the like. While it is convenient and saves time when made, it is supplanted by more permanent records in other departments or within the department at a later time. Many of the memorandum records are not needed after the day's work is completed and are discarded. At the most, memorandum records are kept only for a short time.

Another record is the *temporary* record, used for a few days or weeks and then supplanted by other records. Many temporary records are simply copies or duplicates of more permanent records. The customer's statement of his account, which is a copy of the bookkeeping ledger, is kept as a temporary record and is then given to the customer with his canceled checks. Duplicates of transit letters are used until the items listed in them are disposed of, either by payment and credit or by non-payment and return. The temporary records are filed for a short time in case reference to them is necessary and are then destroyed.

The *permanent* records are the ledgers and, in some cases, the journals. File copies of collections, loan and discount journals and ledgers, bookkeeping department ledgers, and general books (journals, ledgers, and subsidiary records) constitute the permanent records and are preserved for a certain number of years, depending on bank policies and on the statute of limitations and other local laws. Operating divisions establish schedules governing the length of time various records will be kept, for if a schedule is not followed, obsolete and unnecessary records will be stored and will constitute an unnecessary burden and expense.

While most bank records are in the conventional form of typed, written, or machine-posted paper tapes or sheets, the records made by the photographic device (previously explained) deserve special comment. Their advantage lies in the completeness of the records made and the small space required to store the films. When storage space is limited or a matter of considerable expense, film records may solve the problem.

Double Entry Bookkeeping—In banking the *double entry* system of accounting is used. This is the application of the theory that every transaction affects two or more accounts and that the total result of the accounts affected must be equal in amount as far as debits and credits are concerned. For example, in making a loan for $1,000, the accounting procedure would show an increase in assets of $1,000 under Loans and Discounts. In the liabilities section, two accounts would be affected: (1) Deposits, through the credit of the proceeds of the loan to the customer's account, and (2) Interest Collected but Not Earned (or unearned discount). The total of the additions to these two accounts would equal $1,000. Here one account in the assets is increased by exactly the same amount as two accounts combined in the liabilities.

The use of the double entry system of accounting, with resultant equal amounts of debits and credits for each transaction, enables frequent balances to be made within and between departments. This facilitates proof of the accurate recording of all transactions.

General Books—In bank accounting, records are entered in two ways. The first is by recording transactions *as they occur,* or in chronological order. Such a record is called a *journal* and is known as the *book of original entry*. The second method is by classification; the resulting record is called the *ledger,* or *book of final entry*.

Various kinds of journals and ledgers are used by the several departments, depending upon the need for departmental records of a permanent nature. While ordinarily entries are actually made first in the journal and then in the ledger, departments using multiple forms may write both in the same operation.

Bank accounting is a constant process of consolidation of transactions into group totals. The ultimate object of these consolidations is to summarize the day's work, to adjust the assets and liabilities of the bank by the changes, and as a result to construct a correct statement of the bank's condition at the end of each day. The general books contain the consolidated records in final form, and from them the daily statement of condition is prepared.

To illustrate this consolidation procedure, let us consider the case of the savings department referred to in Chapter VII. The total daily deposits averaged 135; the withdrawals averaged 105. The figures to the general books would be departmental totals, and so 240 transactions would result in one debit, one credit, and one *net change* in the balance of the account Time Deposits, Savings on the general books.

Operation of General Books—General books are characterized by relatively few accounts and by the permanency of the records. While machine bookkeeping is widely used for the general books, many banks still prefer to use the permanently bound journals and ledgers and have the posting done in pen and ink.

The majority of the entries for the general books come from departments and divisions as totals and are not entered in detail on the general books; some, however, are routed directly to the general books and are detailed and totaled there. These are transactions that affect the bank as a whole, and for which there is little or no need for departmental recording. Cashier's checks, certified checks, expenses, and the like are examples of such transactions. The subsidiary records which are used for these transactions are handled by the general ledger bookkeeping department. This direct routing of cashier's checks and certified checks is shown in the clearings department operation chart, Figure 17, Chapter V.

All postings to the general books are made first in the journal and then to the proper ledger accounts. In a small institution a single bound book will be sufficient for the journal and another one for the ledger. In banks of moderate size both journal and ledger are divided into sections, each consisting of a partial journal or ledger. For details, subsidiary journals or ledgers are used. In such cases, the final results are posted to a single journal or ledger and carried in one total; Deposits, Individuals is an example of such a summarizing account.

In large banks the work of keeping the general books is so extensive that members of the staff are assigned individual accounts, one making all entries and balances for "deposits," another for "expense," and so on.

As might be expected, some accounts on the general books are active; many entries are made, and balances are affected daily. Cash and Due from Banks, Deposits, and Loans and Discounts are typical of such accounts. Others have few entries, made at infrequent intervals; Capital Stock and Surplus are typical of these inactive accounts.

The general bookkeeper must "pay" the certified checks and cashier's checks, a procedure which is not at all difficult since he has a record of all checks issued. Upon occasion, if the accounts of other banks are kept on the general books rather than on the ledgers of the bookkeeping department, he must "pay" them also. Inquiries regarding general book accounts are few and normally come only from officers of the bank.

An enumeration of the accounts on the general books, the transactions, the departments represented, and the general practices will be included in the last chapter of this text in the explanation of the statement of condition.

In a certain medium sized bank one journal is used, and the items are posted as totals as they come from the departments. A division of the accounts is made in three ledgers.

The distribution department recapitulates and proves the tellers' totals and reports the results to the general books. Individual debits and credits, clearings, and transits also are totaled and proved by the distribution department. Cashier's checks and certified checks are totaled and proved by the general bookkeepers.

The bookkeepers report at 8 a.m. First, they post to the respective ledgers the items remaining from the work of the preceding day and strike a balance. A report is next prepared for the cashier, showing total deposits, cash and due from banks, savings deposit total, and cashier's and certified checks outstanding. This work must be completed by 8:45 a.m. A daily balance sheet is then made up and submitted to the president of the bank by 9:45 a.m.

Between this time and the receipt of department totals in the afternoon, the items requiring detailed entry are handled (expense checks, cashier's checks, certified checks, and so on). The department totals begin to come through at about 2:45 p.m.; final figures are in by 4:30 p.m. on ordinary days and by 5:15 p.m. on heavy days.

The number of accounts carried on the general books varies from time to time, as new accounts are set up or as accounts already on the books are consolidated or removed. In this bank the number of accounts at any time is usually between 140 and 150. (Other banks of the same size may have from 50 to 55 accounts, depending on the detail of classification.)

The number of entries varies from approximately 225 on ordinary days to 300 on busy days. (Here again, other banks of comparable size may have only 40 or 50.) Accrued interest and other accruals are entered at various times—some daily, others monthly or quarterly, and still others at varying intervals.

Individual Books—The bookkeeping department, so called, is actually a *division of general books*. The general books, as we have seen, contain the division and classification of the assets and liabilities of the bank. The largest total among the liabilities is the obligation to customers by reason of deposits of funds. Ordinarily the number of these accounts is so great that it is impracticable to carry them as separate accounts on the general books, and subsidiary ledgers are opened in which only the deposit balances of customers appear. The sum of all the balances on any one of these ledgers, or possibly a group of them, will appear as one total on the general ledger. Time deposits are listed under Certificates of Deposit or Savings Accounts or Time Deposits, Open Account. Demand deposits are listed under Commercial Deposits, Public and Private. In the past the rare exception of a commercial account under a time agreement (generally in the form of a letter) was the single exception to the demand basis of all accounts carried on the records of the bookkeeping department. Since regulations have been issued limiting time accounts in savings deposits, more Time Deposits, Open Account are being established.

In the general books, in addition to the time-demand designations, there are usually subsidiary control accounts for the demand deposits, these subsidiary subtotals corresponding to bookkeeping department sections or ledgers. Thus, the total balances on the A-Ce section of the bookkeeping section or ledger, for example, is carried on the general books as Individual Ledgers—A-Ce. Whether or not such a subdivision is made depends on the arrangement prevailing in each bank. In many banks the entire bookkeeping department total is carried as a single item on the general books. In others a division is made to facilitate the work on general books and the balancing of the bookkeeping department with them. It may be said that the purpose of subdivision is to limit, as much as possible, the number of entries on the general ledger to those actually necessary to disclose the condition of the bank.

Bookkeeping Department Responsibilities—The bookkeeping department has four chief responsibilities, and the methods and systems by which they are met will be considered in detail in this chapter. These four main duties are:

1. Maintaining complete, accurate, and current records on all commercial accounts
2. Assuming responsibility for the payment or non-payment of all checks drawn by customers except those presented at the tellers' windows
3. Providing information on accounts at the request of authorized parties
4. Rendering statements of account to customers monthly or at intervals agreed upon.

The responsibility for maintaining the records falls upon the *bookkeeper*. He must carefully, accurately, and currently maintain the ledger records assigned to him. Other records, such as listing large balances weekly, compiling lists of overdrafts, and the like may also be assigned to him, although sometimes they are handled by other members of the department.

From systems in which the bookkeeper is entirely responsible for paying checks drawn against the accounts to systems in which others assume the responsibility, the variation is extensive. In some banks the signatures are verified by other members of the department, and the stop-payments, uncollected funds, and insufficient balances are checked by the bookkeeper. In other banks the paying tellers verify signatures; in still others special *signature payers* are used.

In some banks the bookkeeper is directly responsible for providing information on accounts; in others, all information must be given by a person who specializes in this work.

The preparation of statements for customers is the duty of the *statement clerk*. Delivery of these statements and the paid checks to customers is often done by the mail division, by the receiving tellers, or by others specifically designated.

While the responsibilities of the bookkeeping department are identical in the small, the medium sized, and the large bank, varying circumstances determine the best division of these responsibilities among the members of the department. As will be seen in the discussion at a later point, the bookkeeping department often assumes additional duties, such as the compiling of analysis figures. On the other hand, the department often depends upon other persons or departments for assistance in such matters as the *paying* of signatures on checks coming through clearings. This may be done by the paying tellers, for example. The nature of the business of any bank requires systems and methods particularly adapted to its needs.

The Ledgers—Before the advent of the adding machine and its subsequent improvements for bookkeeping work, the bank's ledgers were books with ruled sheets upon which all entries were made in pen and ink. The most popular of the pen and ink ledger forms was the Boston ledger, which is still used in a few banks.

The Boston ledger was a bound book, with each page ruled vertically into sections for the six business days of the week. Horizontal rulings divided the page into sections for the several accounts carried on the page. The vertical rulings for each day provided columns for deposits, checks, and old and new balances. The horizontal rulings provided space for the listing of the entries for each customer. At the side of the page were written the names of the accounts. Each page was balanced by totaling the columnar balances and recapitulating the figures. The entire ledger was balanced by combining the page totals.

As bookkeeping machines were developed, looseleaf ledger records were introduced. In these records a separate sheet is kept for each account, which is posted and calculated mechanically. All entries are identified as to character and listed under the current date, deposits are added, checks are deducted, and the new balance is entered in a column at the right-hand side of the page. There is a technique to machine operation that is necessary for efficient work, and accuracy in listing is of course essential.

There were two principal reasons for the change from the use of the Boston ledger to machine methods: One was the increasing volume of transactions, requiring a larger number of entries to be made by each bookkeeper (a requirement which was met by the rapidity of machine operation); the other was the fact that in the face of an increasing demand for competent bookkeepers, it became increasingly difficult to obtain those who were rapid, accurate in posting and calculating, and also good penmen.

The Statements—For many years prior to the complete use of machine operation for both ledgers and statements, many banks used the Boston ledger in conjunction with machine-posted statements. In recent years the statement form has come to be used almost exclusively, a part of the sheet serving as an analysis record, and the data is posted by the statement clerks. Another method of preparing statements is by the use of a carbonized ledger sheet, the copy being detached and used as the customer's statement. Still another method is by the use of a photographing machine. The ledgers are photographed and the resultant picture used as the bank record, or the ledger sheets are retained and enlargements of the photographs of these ledger sheets are used as statements.

The object of all these devices and methods is to provide a neat, accurate, and complete record of the transactions of each customer for his information.

Balancing Ledgers and Statements—In addition to the balancing between the bookkeeping and other departments and the verification of totals forwarded to the general books (discussed elsewhere), there is the necessity of proving the ledger record. The usual method is to compare the balance with the statement record for each account, primarily for the purpose of detecting any inaccuracies in posting, such as the posting of the debit or credit to the wrong account on either the ledger or the statement sheet.

In the Boston ledger-machine statement system, it was, and still is, common practice to *call* the statements. Each morning the statement balances are *called* to the bookkeeper, who verifies their agreement with the ledger balances. In case of discrepancy, the debits and credits are checked to discover the error. Posting to the wrong account and incorrect listing of the items are the errors most commonly made. This same procedure is now frequently used for the machine-posted ledgers and statements.

In the study of the paying teller department, emphasis was placed on the careful writing of checks by customers in order that the bank might more readily protect their accounts from fraud. Carelessness in writing checks is also an annoyance to the bookkeeping department, for illegible writing of the amount numerically often leads to incorrect posting. Checks written so that the amount is likely to be misread are called *blind* checks.

In posting ledgers and statements, a method called *parallel posting* is used, which is simply the posting of checks and deposits in the same order by both bookkeeper and statement clerk. This method facilitates the rapid correction of errors. On some machines, separate tapes list all entries and are used for balancing purposes. On others, a journal sheet is used. This sheet is placed back of the ledger sheet, and all entries are recorded on it by a carbon impression. The journal sheet is then used for comparative and balance purposes. A system of balancing by using old balances, debits, credits, and new balances is used in place of the individual call-back (noted elsewhere in the text) for single posting verification.

Duties of Bookkeepers and Statement Clerks—The bookkeeper should make a study of the accounts on his ledger. His familiarity with the kinds of transactions, the time and composition of deposits, and the like will greatly assist him in his work. For example, an account that deposits a large number of transit items and therefore has a substantial amount of uncollected funds on the books requires a different method of handling from an account of similar size that has few transit items in its deposits. Most accounts rarely have stop-payments in effect, but a few have them frequently. Fluctuations in balances of a major degree, either increases or decreases, may have a significant aspect. Often the bookkeeper is required to report such changes; but even if he is not, he should realize that major changes are of practical interest to the officers of the bank and should be alert to report information disclosed by the transactions passing before his eyes. The bookkeeper must also keep a record of uncollected funds. This may be obtained from the deposit slips, the distribution department, or the transit department (or all three). His ledger must be in clear, neat, and current condition and in balance at all times. The information he gives at the request of authorized persons must be correct and current.

The primary duty of the statement clerk is to compile the

record which is prepared for the customer and to verify it with the ledger account. Statement clerks also assist in special work. For example, the posting of checks to a large railroad account may be done by a statement clerk, and verification of his work made by some other member of the department. This greatly assists the bookkeeper when volume is great. A payroll account, for example, is very active at times, with a large number of checks paid against it directly following pay day, but after this rush period it is inactive for days.

In many banks, statement clerks cancel and file the checks, file the deposit tickets, prepare special reports, and perform other special tasks.

It often happens that the same persons act as bookkeepers and statement clerks, posting one ledger and *running* the statements of another. When this is done, the individual performs both the bookkeeping and statement duties here outlined.

Paying the Checks—In Chapter IV the seven facts to be ascertained in deciding whether or not to pay a check were set forth, and the reasons for those safeguards and the methods of arriving at decisions were discussed in detail. That portion of Chapter IV should be reviewed in considering the work of the bookkeeping department in the matter of the paying of checks.

Of the seven matters to be investigated, the indorsement is the least difficult for the bookkeeping department. Most checks come to the bookkeeping department from the in-clearings and the receiving tellers. All checks from in-clearings are indorsed with the clearing house indorsement (see Figure 18, Chapter V) by the bank that brought them to the clearing house association. If the bank indorsement is missing or the prior indorsement is incorrect or incomplete, the check is returned to the clearing house teller of the bank in question, with a request that the indorsement be made.

The checks received from the receiving teller are indorsed by the depositor and verified by the receiving teller in the manner explained in Chapter III. Here again, the bookkeeping department simply sees that the indorsement is on the check. Other departments that send items to the bookkeeping department, including the paying tellers, are responsible for checking the indorsements.

Technically, the acceptance in a deposit of a check drawn on the bank itself constitutes payment, and the check cannot be returned subsequently for forgery, insufficient funds, or similar cause. However, it is customary for a bank, by a specific agreement with the depositor (usually printed with the other rules in the passbook), to reserve the right to pass on the "goodness" of a check after it is deposited.

Other duties in connection with the paying of a check are grouped according to the method best suited to the department. Since each bookkeeper has a complete list of stop-payments and other holds and knows the amount of uncollected funds and total balances at all times, the duties pertaining to these matters are commonly assigned to him. Determination of the genuineness and authorization of signatures, alterations, post-dates, and stale dates are assigned to the bookkeeper, to other members of the department, or to members of other departments—the paying tellers, for example. Even if the bookkeeper is not primarily responsible for these details, his attention to them is frequently rewarded by the discovery of a discrepancy of importance. The statement clerk also can discover errors by watching the items carefully as they are posted on the statement.

Additional Duties of the Bookkeeping Department—In addition to the duties listed earlier in the chapter, other duties are frequently assigned to the bookkeeping department either because under existing methods they properly belong there or because they can best be accomplished by that department. Among these duties are the following:

1. Responsibility for notice of stop-payment to other departments and tellers
2. Partial or complete compilation of analysis charges, exchange charges, and the like
3. Preparation of reports on balances, new and closed accounts, signature and resolution changes.

These additional duties will be discussed at a later point in the text.

Stop-Payments and Holds—One of the most important matters in connection with payments is the notification of every interested department or individual immediately upon receipt of a stop-payment order or a hold. Otherwise, checks may be paid after the stop-payment or hold is in effect, causing the bank to suffer a loss. As already stated, banks generally designate some member, or members, of the staff to accept all stop-payments and holds and place upon them the responsibility for notifying interested departments and individuals. They also send out the notices when stop-payments or holds are released. The bookkeeping department is often assigned these tasks.

Stop-payments or holds may be classed as follows:

1. Stop-payments issued by customers
2. Court orders (garnishments, receivership or trustee notifications, estate matters, and others)
3. Internal holds, including those for uncollected funds and amounts marked for specific purposes.

Whenever a stop-payment or hold falling in one of the first two categories is received, copies of the order are made up and sent to the departments and tellers. The initial of the teller or department manager on a memorandum is an acknowledgment of the notice.

Providing Information on Accounts—By means of communicating systems between the bookkeeping department and other departments and tellers, full and complete information is rapidly given whenever desired. Inquiries by individuals in person or over the telephone involve identification so that no information will be given to unauthorized persons.

Efforts to get information are not uncommon. For example, persons who contemplate legal action against a customer sometimes endeavor to find out his balance, as a preliminary to obtaining a court order against the account. Others may wish information for fraudulent purposes. Each customer feels, and rightly so, that his balance and transactions with the bank are matters of concern only to himself and to the bank and that information regarding his account should be given only under unquestionably proper circumstances. Most frequently, however, a request for information comes from a customer who simply wants to know his balance, or whether certain checks issued have been paid. Such requests may be made in person, by telephone, by letter, or through the customer's representative.

If the request is made by letter, the customer's signature can be verified, when necessary, to prove the authenticity of the inquiry. In nearly all cases where a request is made personally, the customer is known to the bank representative. If he is not so known, he can be readily identified. If a request is received by telephone, many banks make it a practice to take the request and then call back with the information. To avoid being tricked, the bank representative who takes the call should verify the telephone number to be certain that the return call is actually going to the customer.

The problem of giving out information varies greatly among banks. Some receive almost no inquiries except those of a routine nature, while others are constantly besieged with inquiries that call for verification. In smaller banks the number of inquiries handled each day requires little time; in large banks one person (or more than one) may spend most of his time each day answering inquiries. Such an individual is often called the *customers auditor* or by some other name indicative of the nature of his work. In addition to purely informational duties, he may correct errors and explain transactions or rules to inquiring customers.

Division of Ledgers—The division of accounts in both teller and bookkeeping departments is based upon the number of accounts and the volume of business, which frequently are quite different for the receiving or paying teller and for the bookkeeper. To illustrate: In one bank where the alphabetical teller system is used, the first receiving teller handles accounts from A to D inclusive, but the first ledger carries accounts from A to Co because of the fact that among the accounts in this group are those of several large corporations which deposit almost entirely by mail, so that large numbers of checks come to the bookkeeping department through the in-clearings division.

The ledgers are known as the *individual books*. Sometimes the accounts of other banks are kept in separate ledgers, called *due to bank ledgers,* or *country books*. Whenever there are enough accounts of banks to justify a segregation, these separate ledgers are used; otherwise the bank accounts are carried on the *general books*. There are various reasons why accounts of other banks are carried in separate ledgers. The activities of correspondent bank accounts are fairly uniform in nature, daily statements are often required, deposits are received by mail or by wire transfer, and the accounts are verified monthly (this operation is called *reconciling*). The operating work is therefore somewhat different from that required for other types of accounts, and segregation is advantageous.

Another division of accounts is often made by means of an

inactive, or *dormant,* ledger. In the course of time some accounts cease to be active for one reason or another. The customer may have moved away, leaving a small balance that he either did not know he had or simply neglected to transfer. Then too, customers sometimes maintain a balance for some specific purpose which has not yet become apparent, such as to cover a check which is never presented.

Inactive or dormant accounts are separated from the active accounts for two reasons. First, they constitute an unnecessary burden for both bookkeeper and statement clerk; second, large dormant accounts offer a temptation for the perpetration of fraud, either by those inside the bank or by outsiders who may know of the existence of such accounts. Since the customer often neglects to verify his balance, it is difficult for the bank to know that the account is in order. The most effective way to handle such accounts, therefore, is to keep them in a special ledger and have all transactions scrutinized and passed upon by both the department manager and the auditor of the bank. A separate control account for the "inactives" is kept by the head bookkeeper, who prepares the report for the general ledger bookkeeping department. In some banks a separate control is kept on the general books.

Most state laws govern the disposition of inactive accounts after several years have elapsed and these accounts have apparently been abandoned by their owners. In some states, when prescribed attempts to locate the owners of unclaimed accounts have proved unsuccessful, the state may take possession of certain of them. In other states, a dormant account must be held subject to the owner's demand for an indefinite time. The student of banking should familiarize himself with the regulations applying in the state in which his bank is located.

Checks of Large Amounts—Checks over a certain amount are referred to the department manager for additional verification of the signature and other details. They are also reported (either verbally or in memorandum lists) to the officers of the bank for their information. Other reports commonly prepared by the department are weekly balances on the large accounts, new and closed accounts (with pertinent comments), daily reports on unsatisfactory accounts, and the like.

Filing and Statement Duties—Most customer statements are rendered and the paid checks returned monthly; in the meantime the checks are filed in the bank. Before filing, the checks are *canceled*—that is, marked to show that they have been paid. The most common way to cancel a check is to use a machine that perforates the date and the notation "Paid" on the check. In some banks the checks are filed in drawers in the filing division; in others they are filed in drawers in the bookkeeper's or statement clerk's desk. Deposit tickets and credits are kept in special files.

At the end of the month, verification of the number of checks (or debits) to each account is made by counting the entries on the statement sheet and the actual canceled checks. This work is done by the bookkeeping division, assisted by tellers and others, since the prompt delivery of statements and canceled checks is desirable.

Delivery of the statement is made in person to the customer (or his authorized representative) at the bank or by mail or by messenger. In delivery at the bank, the receiving teller of the division at which the customer makes his deposits may have the statement in his cage, or delivery may be made at the bookkeeping department. Where the number justifies it, a temporary statement delivery division is used, with a force to expedite deliveries. A receipt card is used for deliveries in person, with spaces for the customer to sign each month. The same form of card is used when delivery is made by messenger. Messenger delivery is sometimes used for special reasons or for large accounts if they so desire. The customer assumes the responsibility for statements that are mailed, and the bank is held blameless if a statement is lost en route or falls into the hands of an unauthorized person after it leaves the bank.

The neglect of customers to call for their statements is a common cause of annoyance to the bank, thus requiring that the statements be held in the files. For this reason and for reasons of economy, many banks encourage the delivery of statements by mail. The circumstances of each bank will determine the most effective and economical method to follow. In a recent survey of twenty banks, the proportion of statements mailed and called for varied widely. The maximum percentage of statements mailed was reported to be 91%, the minimum 11%.

It will be noted in the illustration of the new account sheet (Figure 8, Chapter III) that the bank obtains instructions from each new customer with respect to whether his statements are to be mailed or called for. It is usual to ask the customer to verify the statement within ten days; to encourage prompt verification, the statement bears a notation that it will be considered correct unless the bank is notified to the contrary within ten days.

Overdrafts—In the discussion of the paying teller duties (Chapter IV) under the heading *sufficient collected balance* the attitude of banks toward overdrafts and the reason for that attitude were explained. The responsibility for preventing overdrafts falls primarily upon the bookkeeping department. The paying tellers, and other tellers and departments as well, depend upon the bookkeeping department for information as to the amount of the balance in an account.

In connection with overdrafts, the bookkeeping department is subject to the same regulations as the paying tellers; namely, that overdrafts will not be allowed without the specific approval of a designated officer, or in some cases without the approval of the manager of the bookkeeping department. In an earlier chapter it was pointed out that the matter of overdrafts is directly related to the proper selection of accounts.

An effective safeguard against overdrafts is the rapid and steady flow of both credits and checks from the receiving tellers either directly or through the distribution department. There must also be ready access to the deposits in the proving process if necessary. Another factor of major importance is the maintenance of current balances during the day by the bookkeepers. The third safeguard is the prompt report by the teller or department that is called upon to accept a check in payment of an obligation or to cash it.

Efficient organization of receiving teller or distribution facilities will make the first safeguard effective; current and accurate posting by bookkeepers will take care of the second; and these, together with prompt inquiry by tellers and departments in doubtful cases, will suffice for the third safeguard.

The bookkeeper, of course, cannot be striking balances constantly, and indeed this is not necessary in a well ordered bank since few accounts will be subject to overdrafts. Banks are prone to close an account that is constantly drawing against uncollected funds or endeavoring to overdraw, because such an account is always a source of additional expense and work.

All accounts are balanced after the close of business each day; thus the bookkeeper starts work the next morning with the exact balance for each account. Deposits received before the clearings deadline are entered and the "us" checks are posted in the morning. A balance may then be drawn so that the work up to that point can be disregarded from a balance standpoint later on. After the in-clearings are received, another balance is drawn. At the end of the day's work the final balance is made.

Organization of the Bookkeeping Department—Figure 27 is a chart of the organization of the bookkeeping department of a large bank, used to illustrate the division of responsibilities. The *manager* is accountable for the smooth and efficient operation of the department with regard to both intradepartment activities and its relations with other departments and with customers. At the left of the chart is shown the *customers auditor,* who handles requests for balances, explains entries or charges, corrects errors, and otherwise deals with the public. On the opposite side of the chart is shown the *stop-payment* division, which accepts stop-payments, notifies bookkeepers, tellers, and departments of stop-payments, and maintains the stop-payment file. Below this division on the chart is the *filing and canceling* division, which cancels and files paid checks and files deposit tickets. Across from this division appears the *statement* division, which is charged with the duty of verifying and delivering statements to customers. At the bottom of the chart are shown the *bookkeeping* sections, including the individual books and the country books.

These duties are variously assigned, as may be seen in the following discussion of the operations of typical bookkeeping departments.

Operation of the Bookkeeping Department—Figure 28 indicates the operations of the bookkeeping department—the flow of items to the department, the sources, and the routing within the department.

There are variations in the manner in which *charges* are made to the bookkeeping department. Each department, division, or teller unit may charge the items to the bookkeeping department as a whole and balance that way; or charges may be made to ledger sections or to individual ledgers. A combination of these two methods is frequently used, divisions having a large number of items charging them by sections

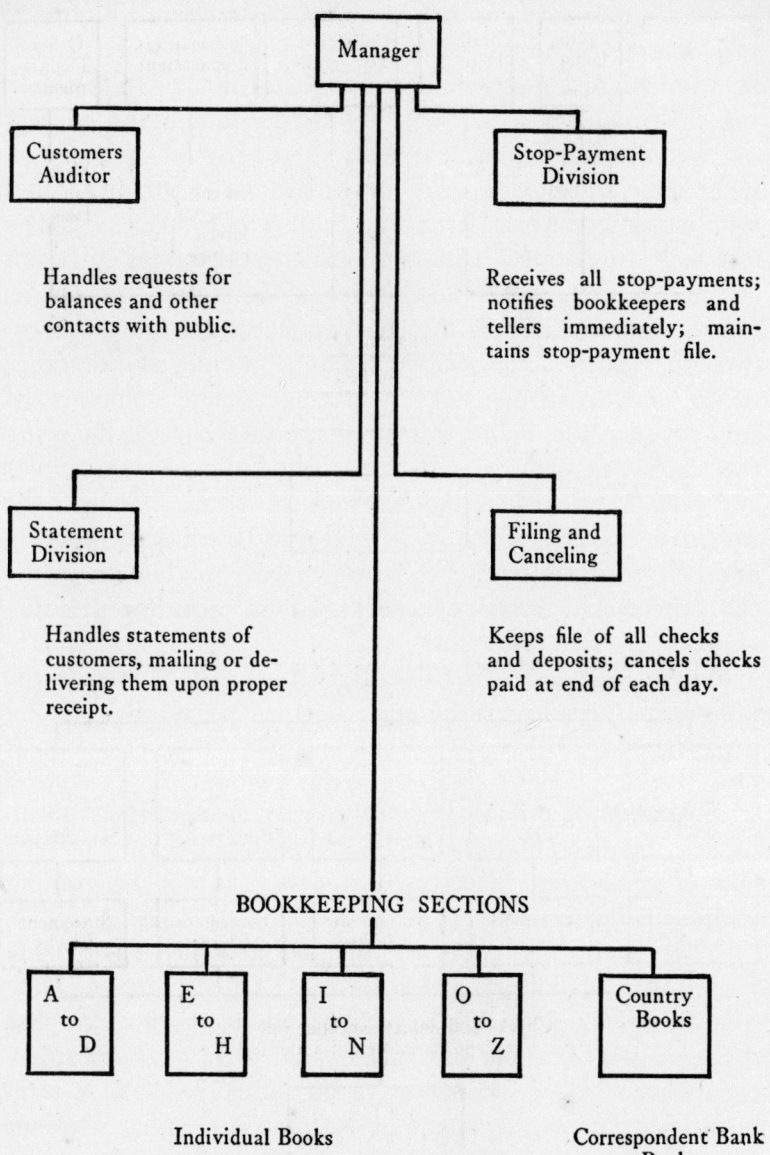

FIGURE 27. BOOKKEEPING DEPARTMENT ORGANIZATION

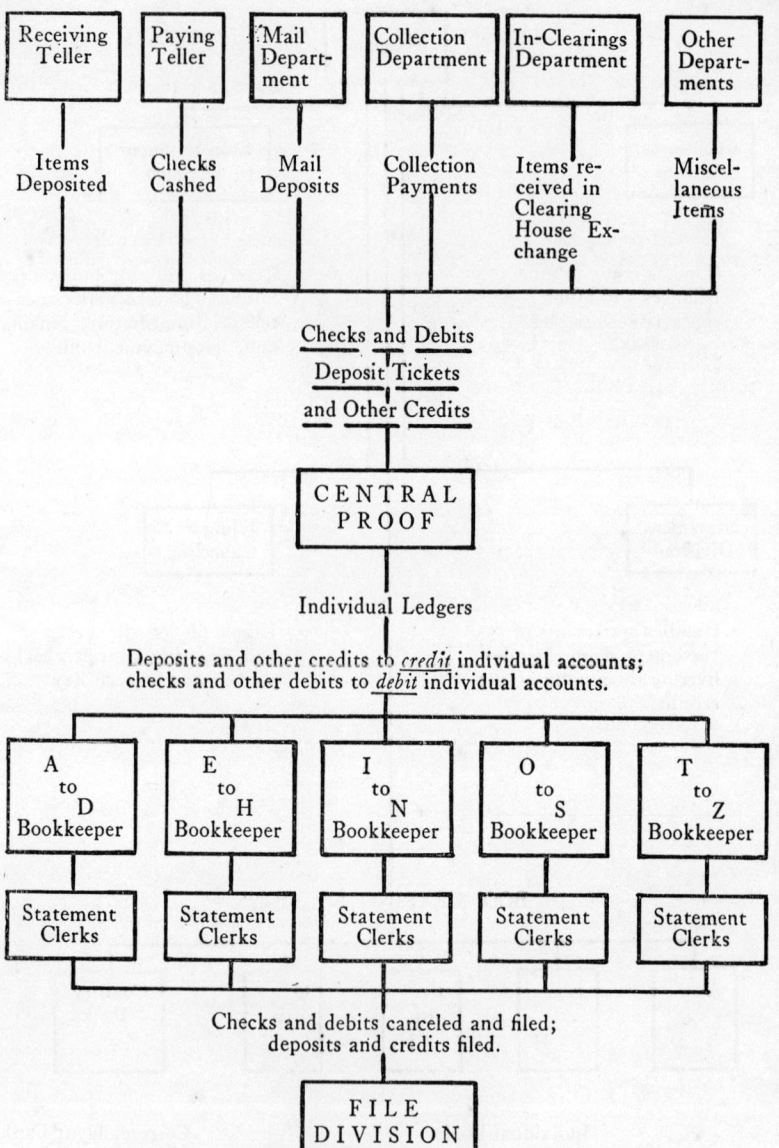

FIGURE 28. BOOKKEEPING DEPARTMENT OPERATION

Time	Operation
8:30 to 9:00 A.M.	Post counter debits and credits to statement.
9:00 to 9:20 A.M.	File checks.
9:20 to 10:15 A.M.	Pay clearings for signatures, dates, amounts, indorsements, and sort.
10:15 to 11:30 A.M.	Post clearings to ledgers.
11:30 to 12:30	Lunch.
12:30 to 2:00 P.M.	Post clearings to statement.
2:00 to 4:00 P.M.	Post counter debits and credits to ledgers.

FIGURE 29. TIME SCHEDULE OF OPERATIONS—BOOKKEEPING DEPARTMENT

or ledgers (in-clearings, receiving teller, mail teller, and paying teller), the others (collection, loan and discount, and so on) making the charges to the department. In the operations chart (Figure 28) all charges come through central proof and are then charged directly to ledger units.

Figure 5, Chapter II, shows a time schedule of operations for several departments. To illustrate its application to the bookkeeping department, a time schedule of operations for that department in a middle western bank is illustrated in Figure 29. Starting at 8:30 a.m., the statement clerks post the counter debits and credits of the previous afternoon. (The ledger, of course, was posted and balanced after the close of business the day before.) At 9:00 o'clock the checks are filed, this work taking about twenty minutes. From 9:20 to 10:15 clearings are verified for payment and are sorted. From 10:15 to 11:30 these clearings are posted on the ledger, and a balance is made. At 12:30 p.m. the clearings are posted on the statement, and from 2:00 to 4:00 p.m. the counter debits and credits are posted to the ledger.

As may be seen, this bank uses the bookkeeper-statement clerk system, the same person acting as bookkeeper for one ledger and as statement clerk for another group of accounts.

Operation of the Bookkeeping Department of a Small Bank—There are two operators in this department, each acting as both bookkeeper and statement clerk. Their first duty in the morning is to run and balance the mail deposits, charging them to the tellers. Clearings are then run and balanced. This work continues until about 11:45, when the bookkeepers have their lunch hour. In order that some one may be in the department to answer inquiries during this time, a relief clerk, whose regular work is clearings and transit, is on duty from 11:45 a.m. until 12:45 p.m.

After lunch the bookkeepers start verifying, sorting, and

posting the counter items. All checks under $500 are paid for signature, stop-payment, and so on by the bookkeepers; checks of $500 and over are referred to the assistant cashier of the bank, who acts as department manager.

Machine posting is used. Ledger sheets and statements are called each morning. A run and balance of the ledgers is made weekly in addition to the regular daily balance.

Each morning, either before or just after clearings are posted, the bookkeepers cancel the checks of the previous day and file them. Statements are delivered to customers by the receiving teller for personal deliveries, and those mailed are handled by the clerk who does the general mail work. Only about 3% are mailed. The verification and preparation of statements and checks at the end of the month for delivery is done by the receiving and paying tellers.

Stop-payments are handled by the assistant cashier, and any customer contacts are also referred to him.

This bank has 1,244 commercial accounts, 652 on the first ledger and 592 on the second.

Bookkeeping Department Operations of a Medium Sized Bank—The bookkeeping department of this bank consists of a manager and five bookkeepers. The total commercial deposits of the bank are $3,461,029, and the number of accounts is 3,182. There are five ledger divisions; thus the average number of accounts per ledger is 636. A survey of items handled over a period of a year showed that each bookkeeper handled an average of 876 checks and 192 deposits a day. The bookkeepers are also statement clerks, each running one ledger and the statement set of another. In the weekly balance verification of the ledgers, each bookkeeper verifies a ledger other than his own and the one for which he runs the statements.

Items are charged to the bookkeeping department from the distribution and in-clearings departments by ledgers. The bookkeeper then *pays* the items, including signatures. Items of $500 and over are referred to the manager for verification. All items of $2,000 and over are listed daily and referred to the cashier. The listing includes the amount, the maker's name, and the payee's name.

The counter work is charged in three batches, the first in the morning, the second at 1:30 p.m., and the third directly after banking hours. In addition, there is the in-clearings batch. All clearings items that are to be returned are held until 1:00 p.m. to provide opportunity for correction of the situation demanding the return. All uncorrected items must be returned by the 1:30 deadline. N.S.F. (not sufficient funds) items deposited by customers are held and checked against credits in the second batch of charges at 1:30 p.m. If the N.S.F. still exists, these items are entered upon a "return item sheet" by each bookkeeper; the items are stamped N.S.F. and are sent with the sheets to the manager for the return of the items to the depositors. If the N.S.F. items came from another bank, they are returned to that bank by the *return teller*. The return item sheets are then referred to the cashier, who in turn, in the officers' meeting the following morning, reads the amounts, the makers' names, average balances, and the balances in the accounts the previous day.

In this bookkeeping department the number of deposits (or credits), the number of checks drawn, and the balance at the end of the day are entered on the analysis sheets. Other analysis figures are entered by the distribution and transit divisions.

Department Operations of a Large Bank—In the metropolitan bank taken as an example, the bookkeeping department work is divided into (1) management and supervision, (2) stop-payment division, and (3) bookkeeping and statement work.

BANK ACCOUNTING AND AUDITING

While Figure 28 is not a chart of this bank, reference to it will assist greatly in observing how the responsibilities are fulfilled. The ledgers are 35 in number, 33 for commercial accounts and 2 for correspondent bank accounts—country books. The number of accounts per book averages 591. Machine posting, parallel method, with accumulating tape recording is used. The ledgers are divided into sections, eight for commercial accounts and one for country books. Each section is under the direction of a supervisor, who verifies the signatures on the checks, the remainder of the paying check-up being done by the individual bookkeepers. The supervisor answers inquiries on balances from tellers and departments (a pneumatic tube system is used for this purpose). The supervisor also answers outside inquiries received by telephone. Counter inquiries are handled by the assistant manager, who in turn depends upon the supervisor for information on any account in his section.

One member of the department is assigned the responsibility for accepting stop-payments and notifying interested parties. Signature changes are routed by the manager to the supervisors. Each supervisor has on file in his desk a complete set of signature cards for accounts in his section.

The canceling and filing of checks is done by the statement clerks, who maintain files in their desks. Deposit tickets are sent to the general file, where special cabinets are used for filing them.

Referring to the bookkeeping organization chart (Figure 27), it will be seen that the responsibilities of the manager, stop-payment division, customers auditor, and statement division have been provided for.

Charges to each bookkeeping section come through the distribution department direct to the supervisor. He then balances the charges between his section and the distribution department, verifies the signatures, and sorts the checks to the individual ledgers. Any checks that are charged to his section in error (missorts) are charged back for proper routing.

Some idea of the volume of work in the bookkeeping department of a large bank may be gained from the daily averages of this department. Over a period of a year, checks received from in-clearings averaged 21,602 daily, and counter checks (paid by paying tellers or received in deposits) averaged 4,623 daily—a total of 26,225 checks, or debits, a day. Credits, or deposits (including mail deposits), averaged 3,635 daily.

In this department the usual reports on returned items, new and closed accounts, large checks drawn, and the like are prepared by the supervisors and are consolidated into a departmental report by the manager.

In all these banks used as examples, machine posting of statements is used. Attention is again called to the photographic method of recording. In the bookkeeping department the photograph is either used as the customer's statement or retained as a ledger record. The duplicate posting of statements by means of carbon copies should also be included as a common machine-posting method.

The Auditing Department—One of the principal objectives of internal control is the protection of the property of both the customers and the bank against loss by carelessness or misuse. The protective devices mentioned in the study of the paying teller division (Chapter IV) are a part of the general plan of protection. The methods and systems used in the various departments of the bank are designed quite as much from the safety angle as from the standpoint of accuracy and economy. Insurance against loss is an important part of banking policy (and as such is more fully treated in the study of bank management problems in Banking III).

No system of protection is complete unless it includes

auditing activities that are constructive and effective. The nature of auditing is such that it is best accomplished by having an individual or a department devote its time and effort to the ends desired—an individual or a department responsible to the board of directors and with access to all records. The *auditor,* or auditing department, should be responsible to the board of directors directly, or through the examination committee (as shown in the internal control chart, Figure 4, Chapter II), or through the chairman of the board, or through the president of the bank.

In the following outline of the duties of the auditor, the principles brought out apply equally to the small, the medium sized, and the large bank. The methods followed are also very similar in all banks, even though the auditing work may require only a part of the time of some officer in a small bank, the full time of an auditor in a moderate sized institution, and an entire auditing department in a metropolitan bank.

Auditing Duties—The major duties of the auditor are (1) the verification of the assets and liabilities, (2) the establishment and maintenance of effective controls, and (3) the preparation of reports and recommendations to the board of directors.

In addition to these major duties, others commonly assigned to the department, or auditor, are the preparation of income tax reports, the supervision of expense, the accrual and allocation of income, the preparation of reports to governmental bodies, the reconcilement of "due from banks" balances, the obtaining of statistical information for use in operations, and the receipt of legal notices involving the bank.

Auditing Methods—In fulfilling these duties, two general methods are depended upon. The first is the examination of departments or transactions. This is known as the *spot* audit.

The auditor, without previous notice, takes charge of all records, verifies and balances the department work, investigates systems and activities, and includes his findings in a comprehensive report on the department. The second method requires a daily record of transactions for audit purposes, the maintenance of control accounts, and the use of interdepartment balances to verify the work. This is called the *continuous* audit. An example of this method was given in the discussion of the savings department (Chapter VII), where it was explained that in one type of machine a master tape in a locked compartment under the control of the auditing department records all transactions. This tape, used in conjunction with the balancing figures of the savings department, provides an independent proof of the department's work for the day. Another device is the use of numbered records, such as the multiple form previously described.

The *basic principle* of modern auditing procedure is the *prevention* of carelessness and misuse of the property of the customers and the bank. Continuous audit methods are very effective and, when supplemented by frequent use of the spot audit, contribute admirably to safety.

An understanding of the principles of accounting and the special application of these principles to auditing and other work of the bank requires a thorough study covering several courses of the Institute. In this study of bank operations, the subject can be treated only briefly and incompletely; thus in the following examples of auditing departments only the most general idea of the application of accounting principles can be expected.

Auditing Organization and Operation Illustrations—In a small bank the amount of auditing work does not require the entire time of one person. The assistant cashier also acts as auditor. Reports to governmental bodies, income tax returns,

BANK ACCOUNTING AND AUDITING

and miscellaneous reports are prepared by him. Extensive use is made of numbered forms, and audits are made of various transactions from time to time. The control accounts are few but adequate, and with this officer devoting only part time to audit work, the bank still has adequate audit protection.

In a medium sized bank, the entire time of the auditor and two assistants is required. It is the duty of the department to maintain and supervise an adequate accounting system, to coordinate the auditing of assets, liabilities, income, and expense, and to provide all figures for budgetary planning and expense control.

Examinations are made on an annual, a semiannual, a quarterly, and a monthly basis. One examination is annual, sixteen are semiannual, seven are quarterly, and fifty-three are monthly—a total of seventy-seven different examinations.

Other duties common to auditing departments are also assumed by this department. In addition, the purchasing of supplies is assigned to the department, since the volume does not warrant a separate purchasing agent. This latter practice obviously leaves an open end, which requires an audit of purchasing and payments by an officer of the bank.

The third illustration is that of a large metropolitan bank. The personnel of the department consists of seventy-eight workers—the auditor, eight senior audit clerks, sixty-two junior audit clerks, three stenographers, two typists, one calculating machine operator, and one file clerk. The auditor is directly responsible to the chairman of the board of directors. The work is divided into eight sections, each under the supervision of a senior audit clerk. Each section establishes and maintains the controls and makes periodic audits of the departments and divisions assigned to it. These audit reports and others are prepared according to a regular program.

Any operating matters requiring attention which come to the notice of the auditors during their departmental examinations are included in a separate report to the comptroller, who is directly in charge of operations.

Questions Based on Chapter VIII

1. State the principal objects of bank accounting.
2. How extensive is bank accounting?
3. What types of records are used?
4. What position does the general books division occupy with regard to bank accounting?
5. What are the major duties of a bank auditor?
6. What two general methods of procedure are used in audit work?
7. Mention the four main duties of the bookkeeping department.
8. What responsibilities are commonly assigned to the bookkeeper? to the statement clerk?
9. From what department do most of the checks come to the bookkeeping department?
10. What are the classifications of stop-payments or holds on accounts?

Questions for Outside Investigation

1. What kind of record is chiefly used in the department in which you are located?
2. What person or persons are responsible for auditing duties?
3. How many individual ledgers are there in your bookkeeping department? Do the bookkeepers *pay* signatures? Do they *pay* stop-payments?
4. What method of balancing ledgers and statements is used in your bank? Is parallel posting used?
5. What analysis work is done by your bookkeeping department? What proportion of statements are mailed? Who verifies and prepares the statements for delivery?

Assignment

Using the bookkeeping organization chart (Figure 27) as a basis, describe briefly how these operations are performed in the bookkeeping department of your bank.

Prepare a bookkeeping department operations chart for your bank, showing the flow of debits and credits from the various departments to the bookkeeping department, the division of ledgers, whether or not charges are made through central proof, and whether the charges are made to the bookkeeping department as a whole, to sections, or to individual ledgers.

List, *but do not chart,* a time schedule of operations for the bookkeeping department of your bank along the lines of that illustrated in this chapter.

CHAPTER IX

THE LOANING FUNCTION

The Purposes of This Chapter:
1. To show the importance of the loaning function.
2. To explain the kinds of loans and define the main classes of security.
3. To discuss the duties and organization of the loaning staff.
4. To outline the duties of the credit department and illustrate credit department organization and operation.

ONE of the principal functions of a commercial bank is that of making loans. By the exercise of this function, the bank assists its customers in the operation of their business enterprises and at the same time receives an income through the employment of deposits. In fact, interest on loans is the *largest source of income* for commercial banks. There are laws, rules, and policies that determine the proper field for bank loans; the most important of these determining factors are:
 1. The limitations imposed by law
 2. The obligations of a bank to its customers in the way of deposit liability
 3. Prevailing business conditions or trends in business
 4. The policies established by the bank's board of directors.

As mentioned in Chapter II, banking laws place certain limitations on the loaning activities of banks. The most common limitation is the maximum proportion to capital and surplus that may be loaned to any one borrower. The national banking laws limit the amount to 10% of the bank's capital and surplus; the state laws vary on this point. The maximum amount that may be loaned to any one borrower is called the *legal limit*.

Other national laws, which apply to all banks and brokers,

regulate the proportion to market value that can be loaned on stocks and bonds when the funds borrowed are to be used in speculation.

The sections of the Federal Reserve Act providing for the rediscount of eligible paper for member banks by the Federal Reserve banks place another restraint upon the lending activities of banks. Member banks, in turn, limit the amount of non-eligible loans they will make. While the Banking Act of 1935 made provision for advances by Federal Reserve banks upon other than eligible paper under circumstances to be determined by the reserve banks, this in itself is a direct regulation.

In the performance of the loaning function, commercial banks not only must comply with the laws and regulations established but must establish conservative policies for their own protection and must conduct their loaning activities well within the range of available funds.

Most of the deposits in a commercial bank are due and payable upon the demand of depositors; therefore the general field of bank loans is properly regarded as that of short term advances. The majority of commercial bank loans are made to mature within a period of from 60 to 120 days. For a few specific purposes it is sometimes advisable to grant loans on a demand basis, in order that there may be no question of the bank's ability to meet the demands of its depositors. The policy, or policies, that are best suited to this requirement are major considerations for bank management and are discussed in the Institute course Banking III.

As a result of the constant change in business conditions, the trend in the fields of commercial activity have an important bearing on the lending activities of banks, both large and small. A thorough knowledge of the principles of economics and of money and banking is extremely valuable to the banker in viewing the problems of his own institution. Contacts with customers, knowledge of the fields of business in which substantial amounts are loaned, and careful study of trends and conditions are all necessary and important aids in the successful performance of the loaning function.

The board of directors, as the governing body of the bank, must determine the field of loaning activity and through its committees make certain that the established policies are followed. In addition to outlining the general types of loans considered most suitable for the bank, the board of directors generally passes upon the larger loans. As conditions change, the board must be prompt to adjust the loaning policies of the bank to meet new situations.

The object of both external controls and internal controls is to insure the employment of the bank's funds at a profit to the bank, without undue risk of loss and without tying them up indefinitely in slow assets. Therefore, the two principal considerations governing bank loans are *safety of principal and liquidity*. To these might be added a third, *income received*, although this feature is considered only after safety and liquidity are definitely established. The rate of interest is determined by the relative safety and liquidity of the loan, subject, as all interest rates are, to the demand and supply of money and credit.

Safety of Principal—A loan is an advance of money or credit upon the promise of repayment by the borrower. From this definition it follows that no advance will be made unless the bank is convinced that the borrower *can* and *will* repay the amount borrowed. All loans involve risk, and in spite of every precaution cases are certain to arise where the full amount is not repaid and the bank must suffer loss. The following illustration shows how a small loss eats up the income earned by a much larger amount.

A bank loaned $100,000 at 4% for ninety days. The loan was paid at maturity, the money was reloaned, and this process continued for a year. By the end of the year the money, which had been fully repaid, had earned approximately $4,000 interest. When the expenses of loaning were deducted from this gross income of $4,000, the remaining amount represented the bank's profit on the risk of actually $400,000.

At the same time the $100,000 loan was originally made, another loan for $3,000 was put on the books. The borrower became involved in financial difficulties, and while part of the loan was finally repaid, a sizable balance was not. The loss which the bank sustained was approximately the same amount as the net profit on the $100,000 loan; thus the entire net income from a much greater risk merely offset the loss on the small loan.

The significance of safety of principal is further emphasized by the difference between the gross profit resulting from banking transactions and the gross profit obtained in other fields of business. The gross income from loans (interest received) is much less than the difference between cost and selling price in other fields. Therefore, while some losses from bank loans will inevitably occur, they must represent only a very small proportion of the total loaned.

The methods used to assure the safety of principal will be mentioned in the discussion of the operations of the credit department later in this chapter.

Liquidity of the Loan—Since the commercial bank must consider its loans in relation to its obligations to depositors, the *time of repayment* of a loan is almost as important as the repayment itself. The availability of funds on short notice is called *liquidity*. For the individual bank, liquidity may be obtained in one or more of four ways.

1. The loan may be repaid from the proceeds of the transaction for which the borrowed funds were used or from other resources of the customer. A loan repaid from the pro-

ceeds of the transaction for which the money was borrowed is called a *self-liquidating* loan. The self-liquidating characteristic of a transaction, either complete or partial, or the lack of it is a basic reason for the acceptance or rejection of a proposed loan. The following is an example of such a loan.

The Jones Manufacturing Company wishes to finance a shipment of goods to the Ajax Company. An order bill of lading covering the shipment is attached to a demand draft for the amount of the payment due, and the draft is then used by the Jones Manufacturing Company as the basis for a loan from its bank. The bank loans the Jones Manufacturing Company the amount (or part of the amount) of the draft, using the bill of lading as security. The draft with bill of lading attached is then forwarded by the lending bank to its correspondent bank, which presents the draft to the Ajax Company. The draft is paid, and the proceeds are remitted to the lending bank. The Jones Manufacturing Company's loan is paid with these proceeds and a self-liquidating transaction has been completed.

The self-liquidating feature of loans is recognized by banking laws. In the national banking laws and in the banking laws of many states, the limitations on the total amount that may be loaned to a single borrower *do not apply* to the truly self-liquidating transaction.

2. A bank may maintain the liquidity of its funds by borrowing from the Federal Reserve bank or from a correspondent bank, rediscounting the notes of its customer for this purpose.

One of the privileges of membership in the Federal Reserve System is the use of its rediscount facilities. Loans to member banks ordinarily are limited either to notes secured by government obligations or to commercial paper that meets the requirements of the Federal Reserve bank. Acceptable loans are called *eligible;* others are classed as *non-eligible.*

Eligibility is determined by the laws and regulations governing the rediscount facilities of the Federal Reserve System. Section 13 of the Federal Reserve Act states that eligibility is restricted to notes, drafts, and bills of exchange "arising out of actual commercial transactions; that is, notes, drafts, and bills of exchange issued or drawn for agricultural, industrial, or commercial purposes, or the proceeds of which have been or are to be used for such purposes."

Many otherwise excellent loans are not eligible solely because they do not conform to the laws and regulations establishing eligibility—in most cases because the loans are not made for purposes recognized as suitable by the regulations. However, a loan, after investigation by the credit department and loaning officers of the Federal Reserve bank, may be classed as not acceptable for rediscount because of its credit classification, even though it is eligible as far as form and purpose are concerned.

The Banking Act of 1935 made one important change with respect to the rediscount privilege by permitting a Federal Reserve bank to accept non-eligible paper under circumstances where the loaning officers of the Federal Reserve bank deem the advance necessary to meet an emergency situation.

3. The third way in which the liquidity of loans may be assured, as far as the individual bank is concerned, is through the direct sale of the notes or the security behind them (or both) to another party. This method, however, is less important than the first two.

4. Liquidity may also be obtained by *rotation of loans.* In American banking it is customary for large corporations to maintain lines of credit at several banks. This is entirely different from the procedure followed in England and Canada, where a corporation maintains a line of credit at only one bank. Therefore, in American banking a loan at one bank will often be paid with the proceeds of a loan made at one

of the other banks with which the corporation does business. This payment of one loan through borrowing from another bank or another source (such as in the open market) is called rotation of loans.

Use of Promissory Notes—In Chapter III mention was made of the use of negotiable promissory notes in the loaning activities of a bank. Each loan is represented by a promise to pay in the form of either a negotiable promissory note or a trade or bank acceptance. Since it is important that notes or acceptances be signed or indorsed by authorized parties, the bank must obtain full authority in each case. Authority for borrowing is given in the same way as authority for withdrawals on a customer's account. The resolution form shown in Chapter III contains provision for authorization in connection with borrowing as well as for withdrawals on the account. In order to be certain that the authorization is current and complete, the records are checked frequently.

Kinds of Loans—Notes are classified in various ways—according to type of note, maturity, form of security, and eligibility. By means of daily summaries of the notes in these classes, the executives, directors, and loaning officers are kept informed of how the bank's funds are employed at all times; thus they are able to make new loans in accordance with established policies, to expand or to decrease any type according to the situation, and to see what funds are available for loaning purposes.

Negotiable promissory notes may be *unsecured* or *secured*. If they are secured, they are called *collateral* notes. Unsecured notes are used in loans to companies, partnerships, individuals, and others when an advance is made upon the general credit standing of the borrower.

The use of unsecured notes is the result of business practices that prevail in the United States. Much of our business is conducted on an *open account* basis. When a customer buys goods, for example, no formal and written promise to pay is given; the seller simply enters the transaction as a memorandum on his books. At agreed periods, generally once a month, the seller sends the customer a statement of the amount due, but even then payment may be extended for a considerable period.

In view of this practice, American banks extend credit to many of their customers on the basis of the flow of working capital—that is, from merchandise to accounts receivable to cash. While no specific property is pledged for the loan, it is understood that the property of the borrower is to be relied upon for payment, and a definite agreement is made by the borrower that the protection thus afforded the unsecured advance will not be impaired by use of the property for purposes detrimental to the bank's loan. In making such advances, banks carefully investigate the position of the proposed borrower and consider the accounts receivable, inventory, cash, and similar property as indirectly protecting the loan.

The *secured,* or *collateral,* note is used when specific property is pledged to secure the payment of the loan. This security is in addition to the requirements and responsibilities contained in the promissory note itself, for while the bank has certain collateral which by agreement it may use (through sale) for payment of the loan, this fact does not in any way decrease the responsibility and liability of the maker of the note to pay it whether or not the collateral is sufficient. The collateral note form should carry the power of rehypothecation, so that the note may be used by the bank in that fashion if desired.

The agreement regarding the use of the collateral is a part of the note form in most cases, although a separate collateral pledge form may be used. The bank is given wide powers in the matter of disposing of the collateral, as many contingencies arise that make this necessary. If the bank did not have such powers, it might be in the position of having collateral which it could not use for the purpose intended. In practice, banks use every effort to notify the customer when the collateral is insufficient, in order that the customer may correct the situation and so make the sale of the collateral unnecessary. These notifications are made by telephone, by mail, by wire, or by any other means at the bank's command.

In connection with secured, or collateral, loans, the Federal Reserve margin regulations are of the greatest importance. By virtue of national security legislation, regulations are imposed upon security markets and security dealers, and provision is made for the regulation of bank collateral loans through the Federal Reserve System. In loans exceeding $1,000 secured by stocks or bonds, a division is made between loans made for the purpose of purchasing or *carrying* stocks or bonds and loans made for other purposes. The margin required for loans in which the proceeds are to be used for the purchase or carrying of securities is much greater than for other types of loans. It is a responsibility of the bank to find out the purpose of the loan and to require the margin specified by the regulations. Many banks require a letter from the borrower in case the funds are not to be used for stock or bond matters, and in some cases the letter states definitely the purposes for which the funds are to be used.

To illustrate this differentiation in the case of loans secured by stocks and bonds, let us consider the application of Arthur Glade, the sole owner of a haberdashery shop, for a loan of $3,000 for ninety days, the loan to be secured by stocks listed on the New York Stock Exchange. It is apparent that the purpose of the loan may be either one of two things: to *purchase more stocks* or to *buy inventory* for the business.

At the present time a member bank could loan only 45%

of the market value of the securities if additional stocks were to be purchased, but it could loan up to 70%, or whatever it deemed proper, if the funds were to be used for inventory purposes.

Other Sureties—In addition to the use of securities as collateral, a note is often strengthened by having a party other than the maker also assume responsibility for payment. The other party, or parties, may indorse the note and thus assume the liability of an indorser, or the party may sign a separate agreement assuming liability called a *guaranty*.

While the terms *guaranty* and *surety* are often used interchangeably, the legal difference between them should be noted. Technically, a guaranty requires that the creditor (the bank) must exhaust all claims against the debtor (the borrower) before the guarantor may be held responsible. A surety provides that the creditor may proceed at once against the indorser (as a surety) to protect his interests. So while banks sometimes refer to these additional pledges as guaranties or continuing guaranties, they are really sureties and provide immediate recourse to the party, or parties, thus pledging themselves. A guaranty or surety of a corporation is valid only when it can be shown that there is a direct benefit to the corporation.

Where other parties lend their credit in these various ways, the notes so indorsed are termed *accommodation paper,* although presumably the indorser would not agree to the use of his credit unless the transaction were directly or indirectly advantageous to him. Notes for which two or more parties assume liability are often called *indorsed* paper; and paper on which the indorsements represent actual parties to the transaction is known as *two-name* paper, *three-name* paper, and so on, depending on the number of parties assuming liability for payment.

Demand and Time Loans—Loans are also classified on the basis of their maturity—that is, when they are due. Some notes are payable immediately upon the request of the bank; these are called *demand* notes. Other notes, called *time* notes, run for definite periods of time, some due thirty days after the date they are made, some sixty days, some ninety days, and so on. The advances for which these notes are given are called *demand loans* and *time loans,* respectively.

Because of the obligations of a commercial bank in the way of deposit liability and the necessity for liquidity, most loans are due within four months (or less) from the date they are made. Those that run for longer periods are subject to special arrangements.

Obviously, demand loans are repayable on request, in fact as well as in name; therefore they are checked from time to time to see that they are such as to admit of immediate repayment. The tests applied are (1) the nature of the transaction for which the loan is made and (2) the collateral, if any, supporting the loan. If the transaction is to be completed immediately, or if the collateral can be readily sold, or if the borrower has other funds with which to pay immediately, then the loan is truly demand. The following illustrations of typical demand loans will show how the tests are applied.

The Martin Construction Company, customers in good credit standing of the Institute State Bank, are bidding on the construction of a school building. The school board requires as evidence of good faith that each bid submitted be accompanied by a certified check equal to 5% of the estimated cost of the work. This check is to be returned immediately to unsuccessful bidders, and within a few days to the successful one upon acceptance of the work and compliance with the terms. The Institute State Bank therefore grants the request of the construction company and makes a demand loan, the proceeds to be used for the bidder's check.

If the Martin Construction Company is not the low bidder, the check will be returned immediately and the loan paid. If the company is the successful bidder and the terms are met by the company, the check will be returned and the loan paid.

There are some cases, such as the one just cited, where local advances are properly made on a demand basis; but apart from these matters of judgment, the fact that local loans are linked with good will and deposits makes the use of the demand form questionable, for a demand to pay may be resented by the customer. From the standpoint of bank management, the review of demand loans presents a problem, for as long as interest is paid and margins are maintained, these loans are likely to be lost sight of unless some special procedure is arranged for their review. For this reason time loans with the regular review before renewal are preferable. In practice, it may be said that the only demand loans of any great volume are those made to brokers or security dealers in New York and Chicago, with a much smaller volume in other large centers. These demand loans are known as *call loans*.

A *call loan* is an advance made to security houses on the pledge of readily salable securities. Call loans are paid the same day demand is made provided the demand is made by a certain time. The collateral may be sold if the loans are not paid, but this step is seldom found necessary. The experience of banks with call loans during the depression was excellent; thus in times of stress this type of demand loan demonstrated its true worth. Not the least of the factors in its favor is the truly *demand nature* of the loan.

The following illustration shows the use of time loans. The Barton Clothing Company, retail clothing merchants, need a loan in August to complete their purchases of fall and winter clothing. This stock of clothing will be sold during October and November, and payment will be made by most buyers early in December. The company borrows $5,000 from its bank, buys the clothing, sells it, bills its customers, and collects the payments. These funds are then used to repay the loan.

Collateral—The test of collateral is its value in terms of *ready liquidation*. The following kinds of collateral meet this test and constitute the chief source of collateral acceptable by banks:

1. Stocks and bonds listed and traded on recognized exchanges
2. Unlisted stocks and bonds actively bought and sold by brokers and others
3. Negotiable warehouse receipts covering staple commodities
4. Order bills of lading covering staple commodities
5. Trade acceptances
6. Life insurance policies (cash surrender value or collateral protection)
7. Instalment contracts or chattel mortgages of standard, readily salable personal property.

Stocks—A *stock certificate* represents ownership of the assets of a corporation in proportion to the amount of stock held by the shareholder. In the past there were two general classes of stock—*preferred* and *common*. The preferred was entitled to dividends before the common and was also entitled to share in the distribution of the assets ahead of the common stock in the event of liquidation.

Common stock generally carries with it control of the corporation through the election of directors. The holders of this kind of stock are entitled to all earnings declared as dividends over and above the requirements for the preferred stock. The dividend on preferred stock is usually fixed, while the dividend on common stock varies with earnings.

The distinction between the two kinds of stock has been greatly altered in the past few years in view of the fact that stock with characteristics of both preferred and common is now issued. The differing degrees of preference as to assets and dividends have so complicated the position of the stockholder in many cases that he may be said to be a proportionate owner of the corporation subject to the privileges of the other stock issues of the company.

Bonds—*A bond is a written obligation under seal* by which the *obligor* (the borrower) is *bound to pay* to the owner of the bond the amount of money designated. A bond represents the *rights of a creditor* and thus is actually a long term loan by the bondholder to the corporation, whereas stock represents ownership.

Attached to each bond is a series of *coupons,* which are *promises to pay interest.* Sometimes, instead of bonds with coupons attached for the interest payment, the bondholder receives a *registered* bond. When a bond is registered, it is issued in the name of the owner, and interest is paid to him by check. Bonds may be registered as to the principal amount only or as to both principal and interest.

Stock Exchanges—While the liquidity of collateral notes may be assured in other ways, it depends primarily upon the ability of the bank to sell the collateral readily if need be. Markets for stocks and bonds are provided through the facilities of *stock exchanges,* and since many collateral loans are secured by stocks and bonds, the facilities of stock exchanges are widely used by banks.

A stock exchange is an organization of individuals engaged in the business of buying and selling securities. Permanent quarters, equipped with facilities for efficient and economical execution of transactions, are established. The part of the quarters devoted to the actual buying and selling is known as the *floor* of the exchange, and the various locations on the floor where specific stocks and bonds are bought and sold are called *trading posts*.

Numerous rules are adopted by stock exchanges, but in general they cover the regulation of sales, the settlement of amounts due, the requirements for the acceptance of issues to be traded, and the principles governing business conduct for members. A uniform list of charges, or commissions, is established, and these fees are charged by members to non-members who wish to make use of the facilities of the exchange. The commissions charged by members constitute the main source of income for firms in the business of buying and selling securities.

When an issue of stock (or bonds) is accepted for trading on the exchange, it is said to be listed. The advantage of a listed security from the standpoint of the owner or of the bank that accepts it as collateral is that a buyer or a seller at a fair price is more likely to be found through stock exchange facilities than in any other way.

Many issues are bought and sold (*traded*) in substantial amounts each day; these are termed *active* issues. Those less frequently traded are known as *inactive* issues. Obviously, active issues can be more readily marketed than inactive, but even for inactive issues buyers and sellers can usually be found at stated prices. An offer to buy is called the *bid* price, while an offer to sell is the *asked* price.

Many issues of stocks and bonds (particularly municipal bonds) are not listed on any of the recognized exchanges but are bought and sold by those interested. The market for these *unlisted* issues is created by the bids and asks between commission houses and investment dealers in this country. This market is known as the *unlisted,* or *over-the-counter,* market, and many issues are traded in substantial volume daily with prices in narrow ranges and sales or purchases immediately executed.

Since the objective of a bank is to have only collateral which is readily salable, it is of considerable importance to have as collateral either listed (and preferably active) issues or active unlisted securities.

Warehouse Receipts—A *warehouse receipt* is an agreement between the warehouseman and the party storing goods with him, covering the storage and the responsibility of the parties in connection with the transaction. Warehouse receipts are of two kinds, *non-negotiable* and *negotiable*. The non-negotiable form is merely a receipt for the goods stored, a contract for the storage, and an agreement to deliver the goods to the party that stored them. A negotiable warehouse receipt is not only a receipt and a contract for storage but is also an agreement by the warehouseman to deliver the goods only upon the order of the party storing them and the return of the warehouse receipt properly indorsed.

By indorsement of the negotiable receipt, the party storing the goods can transfer control of the goods to another; thus the control of the goods rests with the owner of the warehouse receipt, whoever he may be. The negotiable form is acceptable as collateral (if it covers staple commodities in proper warehouses), for the goods can be obtained by the bank and sold if necessary.

A large volume of loans secured by negotiable warehouse receipts, covering such staples as cotton, sugar, wheat, corn, and so on, are made by banks in all parts of the country. For example, during the canning season advances are made on canned staple vegetables in order to assist the canner during the peak of his operations. These advances are in the form of loans secured by negotiable warehouse receipts covering cases of the canned goods at market values in excess of the amounts of the loans. As the goods are sold, the bank releases them from the warehouse upon proportionate repayment of the loan.

Bills of Lading—*A bill of lading is a contract between the carrier of goods and the shipper* (for example, between a railroad and a shipper) *for the transportation of the goods to the destination specified* in accordance with the agreement made. It is also a receipt for the goods delivered to the carrier. There are two kinds of bills of lading: the *straight* bill, which is simply a contract for the transportation of goods, and the *order* bill, which, in addition to the contract, contains an agreement on the part of the carrier that the goods will not be delivered except upon proper indorsement and surrender of the order bill of lading. The order bill, like the negotiable warehouse receipt, has the effect of placing the goods under the control of the proper holder of the bill. Accordingly, the order bill is satisfactory collateral if it covers a sufficient amount of staple commodities.

A large proportion of the financing of wheat and other grains is done through the use of order bills of lading covering carload lots of standard grain. A grain elevator company which sells a carload of wheat to a milling company attaches a draft to the bill of lading for the amount to be paid by the purchaser. This draft and bill of lading are taken to the bank, which assists in the financing by advancing funds upon the security of the bill of lading. On presentation of the draft to the purchaser, payment is made, the order bill of lading is delivered, and the advance is thus automatically liquidated.

If for any reason payment is not made, the bank still has control of the grain. Being a readily salable standard commodity, the grain can be sold to some other party, and title can be passed simply by indorsement and delivery of the bill of lading.

As in the case of stock exchanges, there are various grain and commodity exchanges in which large amounts of standard grains and commodities are bought and sold daily. Ready markets are thus provided for corn, wheat, oats, cotton, and many other commodities.

Life Insurance Policies—Life insurance policies may be used as collateral in two ways: as a general protection to the bank as beneficiary of the policy in case of the death of the borrower or, more frequently, by assignment of the cash surrender value of the policy. In the latter case, immediate payment can be obtained by the bank through the exercise of its right under the assignment.

Chattel Mortgages and Instalment Contracts—A *chattel mortgage* is a promise of payment secured by *pledge of personal property* under an agreement by the terms of which certain payments are to be made and the lien against the personal property is to be removed on the completion of these payments. In the event the payments are not made according to agreement, the chattel mortgage provides that the lender of the money may take title to the property under the circumstances specified. The property can then be sold to others to obtain funds for the payment of the obligation.

An *instalment contract* provides much the same sort of security for a loan as a chattel mortgage, the difference being that under an instalment contract ownership of the property remains with the lender until all instalments are paid according to the agreement. If all payments are made, the ownership of the property is transferred to the borrower; but if the terms of the agreement are not fully met, the property may be sold to others to pay the balance due.

These two kinds of obligations are used extensively to finance the sale of a wide variety of personal property—notably automobiles. Instalment purchases generally require a cash payment of a percentage of the cost of the property, often from 20% to 25% of the selling price. This provides a margin between the value of the property and the amount of the loan at the start, and the margin is increased through the monthly payments of the balance due. Payment of the balance within a year by equal monthly instalments is a common arrangement.

State laws vary in regard to chattel mortgages. In some states they are not legal; in others they are legal only if the bank holding the collateral assisted in the financing of the transaction.

A common method of financing sales is through the creation of a *collateral trust*. Under the *indenture* creating the trust, the company agrees to lodge the chattel mortgages or instalment contracts with a *trustee* (generally a bank). Against this collateral, promises to pay, called *collateral trust notes,* are issued and are sold to banks and others.

Companies engaged in the business of financing such sales often borrow from banks on the security of the instalment paper. In this case the chattel mortgages or instalment notes pledged as collateral have a value from 10% to 20% greater than the amount of the loan. In addition to the instalment paper itself, the bank has as security the credit of the finance company and the promises of the individual makers of the instalment or chattel notes, which in turn are secured by the value of the personal property involved.

Indirect and Direct Loans—Loans are also classified as *direct* or *indirect*. Direct loans, or direct lines of credit, are advances made to a customer upon his primary responsibility as maker of the notes. Indirect loans, or lines of credit, refer to advances which include the liability of others as well as that of a customer of the bank. For example, the John Smith

Manufacturing Company has a line of credit of $100,000 on an unsecured basis with the Institute State Bank. In order to borrow, the company executes a note payable to the bank signed by the authorized officers of the company. The transaction is directly between the company and the bank, and there is no obligation on the part of any other party.

If, on the other hand, the John Smith Manufacturing Company indorses a note or trade acceptance that is payable to the company and borrows money from the bank on this note or trade acceptance, the transaction is classified as an indirect advance. The party primarily responsible for the payment of the note or acceptance is the maker or the acceptor, as the case may be. The liability of the John Smith Manufacturing Company is secondary; that is, because of its indorsement the company is liable if the maker or acceptor does not pay.

Another term frequently used is *indorsed paper*. As the name indicates, this is paper indorsed by the borrower, who receives credit thereby. The term *indirect* is also used in connection with guaranties; that is, a contingent liability is created by some one who does not receive the proceeds of the loan but who assumes the responsibility of a guarantor. In the foregoing example the John Smith Manufacturing Company received the proceeds of the trade acceptance. If instead of using a trade acceptance the company had borrowed unsecured and under a guaranty of several individuals, these individuals would be *contingently liable* although they had not, as individuals, received the proceeds of the loan.

Performance of the Loaning Function—Three departments or divisions of the bank are established to perform the operations of loaning. Each of these departments has its own duties to perform which are distinctly different from the duties of the others. The work of all three divisions constitutes the loaning operations of the bank. The performance of the loaning function, therefore, divides logically into the following arrangement of duties:

1. The establishment of loaning policies by the board of directors and the proper application of those policies. In this connection the loan and discount committee assists the officers of the bank.

2. The investigation, assembly, and analysis of credit information and the recording of this information constitute the duties of the credit department.

3. The proper handling of the notes and collateral, their protection, and the maintenance of the discount records are the chief duties assigned to the loan and discount department.

The Loaning Staff—While the policies are established by the board of directors and the board works closely with the loaning officers in the execution of those policies, *the primary responsibility for loans rests upon the loaning officers.* The profitable and successful employment of the bank's funds depends upon their knowledge, appraisal, and judgment of the loan applications.

The loaning officers are the senior and junior officers of the commercial department, the vice presidents, the assistant vice presidents, and the assistant cashiers. Each officer has under his direction a number of accounts with which he is expected to keep in close touch, and he considers and passes upon loan applications made by these customers. In many banks the division of accounts comes about in an informal way, for customers habitually prefer to do business with the officers with whom they are best acquainted. In such cases the loaning officers work directly with the board of directors in applying loan policies to individual applications. The informal division of accounts is most likely to occur in small or moderate sized banks.

In metropolitan banks the volume of loans, the number of

loaning officers necessary to handle them, the diversity of credits that must be considered, and the location of the business of the bank all combine to make necessary a more formal organization of loaning activities. In these large banks, the officers are divided into groups, and from two or three to six or eight senior and junior officers are included in each group. The officers in any one group become familiar with the loans of the other members of the group; thus when any officer is absent, others in the group can handle his loans. Often the group will recommend action to the loan and discount committee or to the board of directors in cases involving bank policy or in the larger credit lines.

Because of the volume of loans and the many kinds of credit requests to be considered, accounts are assigned to groups on the basis of either the geographical location of the business or the type of business of the customer. In the geographical method, the loaning groups are able to follow closely the developments in the territory assigned to them; thus they can more effectively serve the bank and its customers. By concentrating on the territory and by making regular trips and calls, they can become closely acquainted with conditions and factors that affect business in the territory.

The arrangement of assigning accounts by industry or type of business has the advantage that the loaning officers become so familiar with the problems of the industries handled by their group that they are better able to judge the merits of proposed loans because of this specialized knowledge.

Figure 30, which shows the arrangement used by one large bank, is typical of loan grouping. As will be noted in this chart, the executive officers of the bank and the loan and discount committee work between the board of directors and the loaning groups. From two to five vice presidents handle the work in each group, and one of them is designated as vice president in charge. The junior officers of the group (the

372   THE LOANING FUNCTION

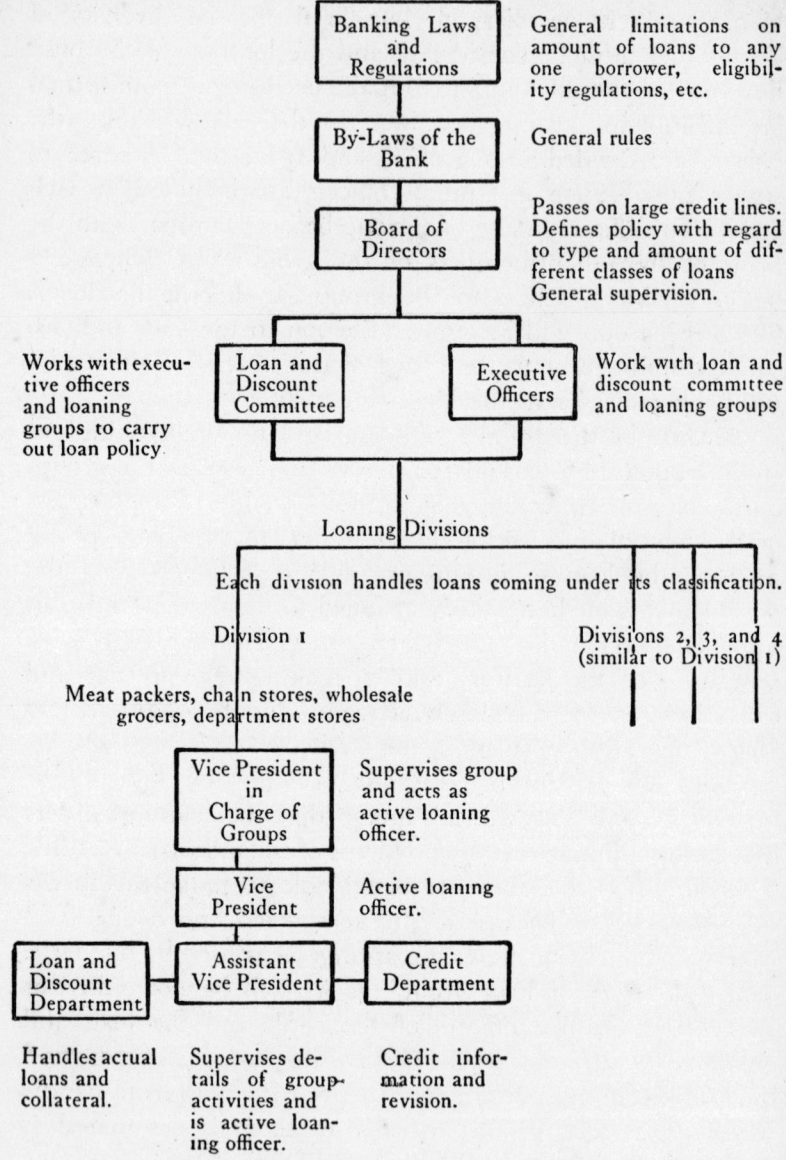

FIGURE 30. ORGANIZATION FOR LOANING OPERATIONS

assistant vice presidents) handle certain loans and supervise the detail work of the group, acting between the group and the credit and loan and discount departments. As a result of the assignment of loans by industry and the mechanics established for the consideration of loans, these groups are able to conduct the loaning activities of the bank promptly, carefully, and profitably.

Proponents of the loaning group arrangement believe that four advantages arise from the consideration of loans by the group.

1. Diversity of opinions by group members, resulting in more complete consideration of the factors affecting the loan.

2. Familiarity with the loan by all members of the group instead of by a single loaning officer.

3. Assumption of responsibility for each loan by the group.

4. Continuity of organization. Temporary absence or death or resignation of one officer does not affect the bank's familiarity with the loan.

In every bank the problem of how best to organize the loaning activities will be somewhat different from that of other banks, even in the same locality. The volume of business, the kind of business, the location of customers, and the experience and training of loaning officers along special lines will all be factors in determining whether, in order to obtain the best results, the accounts should be formally divided into groups, and if so, whether the groups should be established on a geographical or on an industrial basis.

The Credit Department—As already stated, the performance of the loaning function involves three distinct kinds of duties. The first of these, the establishment and application of proper loaning policies, has been discussed. The second group of duties—the investigation, assembly, analysis, and recording of credit information—will now be described.

The credit department performs this second group of duties for the benefit of the loaning officers of the bank and so assists them in determining the proper disposal of loan applications. In addition to assisting the loaning staff, the credit department provides a valuable service to the customers and friends of the bank by commenting upon the credit standing of firms and individuals on request. This courtesy is often a service of great importance to non-borrowing accounts or to other banks, which rely upon the information and analysis for their own decisions. The good will created by this constructive service is directly reflected in increased balances or new accounts and in reciprocal courtesies extended to the bank in connection with investigations for its own use.

From an organization and operating standpoint, the work of the credit department divides logically into three major activities: (1) the assembly of information, (2) the analysis of the facts assembled, and (3) the recording of information in a complete, current, and useful manner.

Obtaining the Information—The credit department uses several well organized sources of information, the chief of which are:

1. The bank's own record of the account
2. Interviews with the customer by loaning officers or other members of the staff
3. Financial statements and audits
4. Information from other banks acquainted with the affairs of the customer and from business concerns with which the customer has had contact
5. General reports prepared by credit agencies
6. General and special information contained in articles or reports in newspapers, magazines, and trade journals.

All this information is classified and assembled in the credit file (as noted under "filing" later in the chapter).

The Bank's Own Records—In most banks a complete statistical record of each customer is kept on sheets or cards known as *loan and balance cards.* This tabulated experience with a customer gives a picture of the manner in which he meets his obligations to the bank, whether they be in the form of a loan or of responsibilities in connection with his account. On these cards are posted the loaning record from the books of the loan and discount department—the amounts of loans made, the security (if any), whether the loans are direct or indirect, whether time or demand, and the record of payment, interest charged, and so on. This loaning record is supplemented by the records of other departments. From the analysis department, for example, comes the record of the average balances collected and uncollected, checks returned, overdrafts paid, items handled, profit or loss, and other miscellaneous information necessary to complete the statistical picture of the account. Thus the information contained in the bank's own records reveals the business attitude of the customer, his regard for his duties, and his value to the bank as a customer.

Interviews—One of the best sources of information is the customer himself. Therefore the loaning officer or credit man interviews the customer and from him ascertains the reasons for the loan request, the use that is to be made of the funds, the current condition of the business, the markets for the company's products, the personnel of the company, and other information applicable to the company's operations, the safety of the funds if advanced, and the probability of their repayment on the due date. As soon as possible after the interview, the officer should dictate a summary for filing in the folder.

Some customers are conservative in their estimates of the profitable use of borrowed funds and of the return of the funds within a short time; others are approximately correct in their appraisal of the profit and time; still others are overoptimistic. A comparison of the statements made in the interview with other comments or with the financial statement of the concern will reveal either consistency or the reverse and open new channels of investigation and new bases of judgment.

If, according to the bank's credit file, a borrower has in the past estimated correctly the profit possibilities of his concern, has borrowed from this bank and repaid the loans, and has honestly stated conditions and probable results in interviews, the loaning officer can be reasonably sure that this borrower will repay a new loan at the time agreed upon.

Financial Statements—In the case of an unsecured loan (discussed earlier in the chapter), reference was made to the dependence of the bank upon certain assets of the company for repayment of the loan, even though those assets were not specifically pledged to secure the obligation. It is important, therefore, that the value of the assets be not decreased, at least to a point where they will not be available for loan repayment purposes.

In order that the bank may ascertain just what these assets are and the amount of them, it asks the borrower for a *financial statement*. This statement represents a complete compilation of the financial condition of the company. The assets and liabilities are listed and classified, showing the relation of the assets to the liabilities, the relation of the company's plant, equipment, inventory, cash, accounts receivable, and so on to sales and to short time obligations, the protection against unforeseen disasters through insurance, the profits earned or the losses sustained for the previous year, and other information bearing on the condition of the company and the trend of its operations.

This statement may be prepared by the company and

certified as correct by authorized representatives, or it may be prepared and certified to by public accountants—individuals or firms in the business of preparing financial statements. In recent years, for income tax requirements and other reasons, an increasing number of firms have found it necessary to have an annual audit made by certified public accountants. When this is done, a copy of the report is given to the bank.

Preliminary to consideration of an application for a loan, it is a recognized procedure of banks to require a financial statement, either an audited copy (if such is available) or a signed statement of the prospective borrower. When an audited statement is not presented, the bank sometimes sends a number of members of its own auditing staff to set up the statements and report to the credit department. Statements are scheduled on comparative forms, and the figures are used chiefly for comparative purposes.

The forms used for these statements include a promise on the part of the customer that he will notify the bank of any major change that may arise adversely affecting the statement.

Customers of the bank who borrow each year or who have lines of credit at their disposal provide the bank with new statements as soon as they are available, or upon request of the credit department or loaning officers. Even if a customer has no loan in contemplation, he realizes that the better informed the bank is regarding his affairs, the better able the credit department will be to answer inquiries from outside sources. Large corporations frequently make it a practice to send statements and other information to many banks with which they have no dealings whatever, simply to assist those banks in answering inquiries that may be received.

Trade and Bank Checkings—As additional information, there is requested a list of banks and other business houses with which the company has dealt in the past, or is now dealing. The extent and nature of the business relationship with these references is stated.

The interchange of credit information between banks and commercial enterprises is a well developed courtesy, and so the credit department is readily able to obtain full information on the experience of other banks and business concerns with the prospective borrower. The credit department makes inquiries of this nature by letter or by personal interviews, and the replies are placed in the credit file. Other banks are requested to state their experience with the subject of inquiry regarding such matters as lines of credit extended, loans made, promptness of repayment, and other information of importance. Trade concerns are asked the amount of business done with the company in question, the arrangements made for payment, and how payments have been met. If desired, these references can again be consulted during the period the loan is outstanding to see whether conditions have changed, as this procedure will give the loaning officer a current basis of appraisal.

Agency Reports—Several companies in the United States engage in the business of preparing credit reports on companies and individuals. These reports are sold to banks and business firms and are extensively used in bank credit work. The business history of the individual or company contained in these reports is probably the most important information from the standpoint of the bank, for that history will include any available information regarding bankruptcies, lawsuits, composition settlements with creditors, and other unfavorable, as well as favorable, facts. The agency reports also contain trade checkings which are valuable. Some agencies specialize in limited fields, while others cover general business.

General Information—A considerable amount of general

information of value is obtained from newspapers and magazines. News items are clipped and filed, and while some of the information may be a duplication of facts obtainable elsewhere, current information is often more readily obtained in this way. Sales figures, large orders, and interim profit figures, often reported in news items, are of direct value in credit work.

Filing—The information regarding loans is filed in the credit department, and custody of the files is an important part of the department's responsibilities. A careful record is kept of all files that are out of the department in order that they may be located without delay when desired. Files can be withdrawn from the department only by authorized persons. The information contained in credit files and the method of filing are fairly uniform among banks. The following description is typical of the average credit file.

This file is of letter size, divided into sections for ready reference. The first section is used for statements. The latest financial statement of the company is bound in with the bank's *comparative statement form,* which is a sheet upon which the various items are entered for a period of years, thus making possible quick comparison of any part of the company's statement with that of the previous year, or years.

The second section of the file contains the interview reported by loaning officers and others.

The third section contains the correspondence with other banks and business firms and corporations relative to the company in question.

The next section contains a file record of the balances and borrowings of the company, with full information on the types of loans, interest rates, length of the loans, and security.

The last section has copies of letters written by the bank in answer to credit inquiries on the company.

Statement Analysis and Credit Management—Both credit management and statement analysis are fields of broad application, and in the curriculum of the American Institute of Banking each requires a full course. In this study of bank organization and operation, therefore, we can merely sketch the problems and methods of credit work.

Without attempting to explain the problems of credit management or the methods of statement analysis, the following examples are given to illustrate the mechanics of credit department organization and operation.

Credit Department of a Moderate Sized Bank—In a moderate sized bank the work is effectively handled by a simple system. A typical example of method follows:

A junior officer of the bank acts as credit manager in addition to his other duties, and all credit work comes under his supervision. Credit investigations and special correspondence are handled by him, while the general correspondence is answered directly by the loaning officers. The credit files in the general filing division are under his supervision. The posting of information, such as the comparative statement forms, is done by the bookkeeping personnel at the direction of the credit manager.

By these simple arrangements, the bank is assured of proper credit department facilities and of centralized responsibility under circumstances that do not justify a separate full-time department.

Credit Department Organization and Operation of a Metropolitan Bank—Figure 31 is a chart illustrating the organization of the credit department of a large eastern bank. This chart shows clearly the division of credit work and the proportion of the department's personnel necessary to perform each phase of the work.

THE LOANING FUNCTION

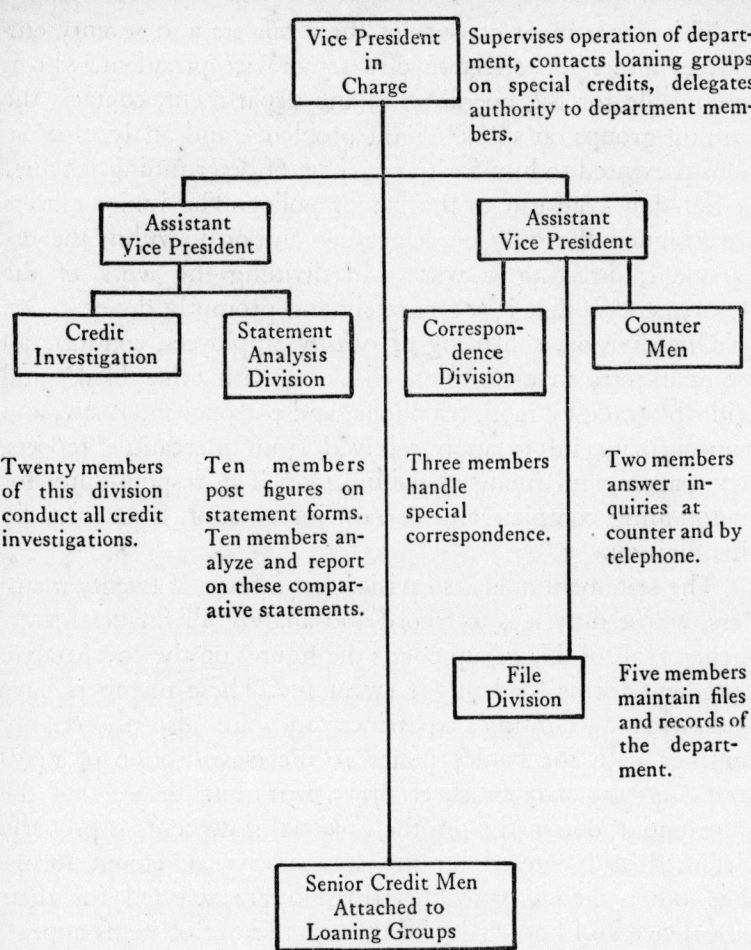

FIGURE 31. CREDIT DEPARTMENT ORGANIZATION

This department consists of three officers and seventy employees under the direction of a senior vice president, who is responsible for the operation of the department, contacts the loaning groups on special credit problems, and analyzes situations presented to him for the purpose of determining whether or not they conform to the bank's policy. The junior officers are assigned the duty of delegating authority within the department, directing activity, and dividing the work of the department so that it is accurately and promptly done.

One division, consisting of twenty employees, conducts all credit inquiry investigations, checking with other banks and with the trade by mail, telephone, and personal interview, and summarizing information received from mercantile reports, newspapers, and financial publications. The responsibility for maintaining complete and current information is assumed by this division.

The statement analysis division has a force of twenty members, whose duty it is to record and analyze all financial statements. Half of this group enters the figures on the comparative statement forms used in the credit file. These members have had wide accounting experience and are also thoroughly familiar with the bank's policy in the classification of items found on the balance sheet. It is their duty to see that the information obtained from the financial statements is properly classified and entered on the comparative statement forms. The other members of this division are selected for their experience and knowledge of the significance of items appearing on the statement; it is their duty to analyze the figures carefully and to prepare reports emphasizing the important features of the financial statements.

Another division of ten is composed of senior men who are attached to the loaning groups of the bank. It is their duty to work with the loaning divisions on correspondence and reports and, as a means of facilitating review, to assemble

THE LOANING FUNCTION

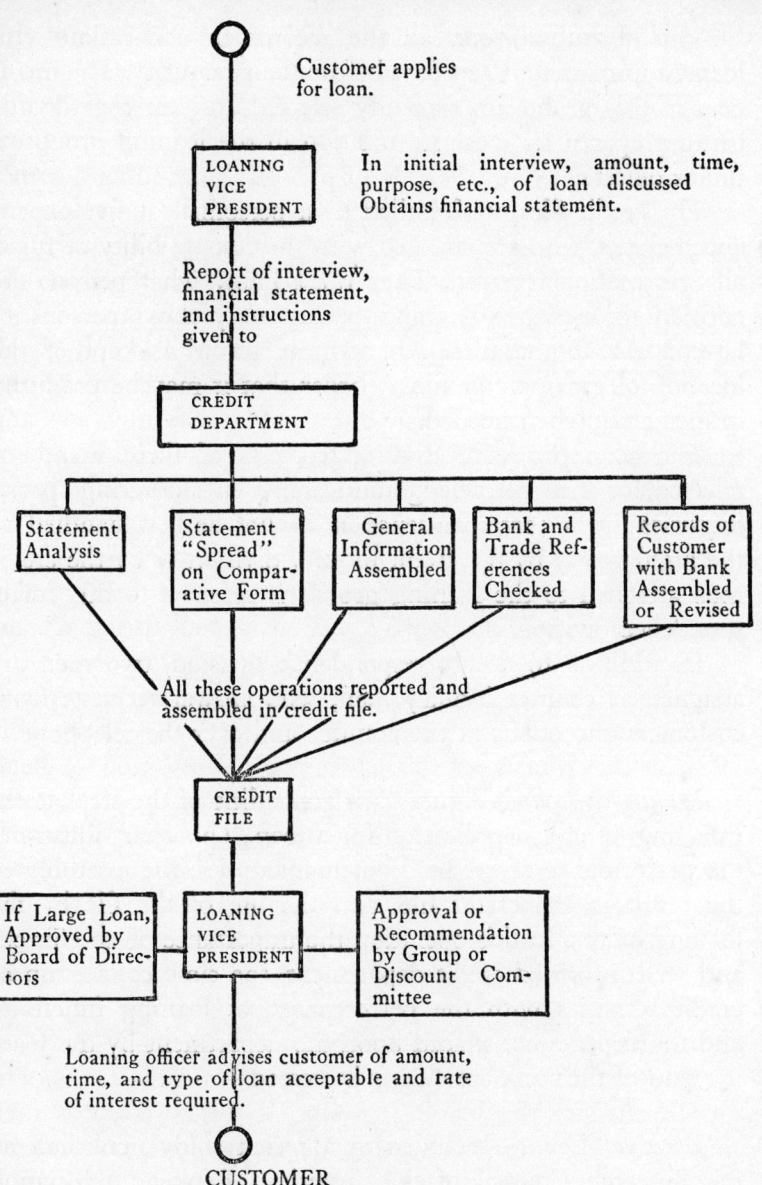

FIGURE 32. PROCESS OF MAKING A LOAN

for each loaning group all the records in connection with loans, approximately ten days before their maturity. The members of this group are carefully selected and are regarded as being prepared for a future position in the loaning groups as junior officers.

The credit files are handled by a personnel of five experienced clerks, who are charged with the responsibility of filing all information received. They must know what persons are entitled to use the files and permit only those persons to have access to the files. An accurate record is kept of the location of every credit file in order that it may be produced immediately when needed.

The correspondence division consists of three members, selected for their knowledge and ability in answering special inquiries. Such correspondence as cannot be best handled in the regular way by the credit inquiry division or by the credit men attached to the loaning groups is referred to this correspondence division.

In addition to the correspondence division, two men are assigned as counter inquiry men, who answer requests from customers and others at the counter and over the telephone.

Making a Loan—Figure 32 is an outline of the steps taken in acting upon an application for a loan. This chart illustrates the performance of credit department duties, the assembly of the result in the credit file, and the use of the file by the loaning officer. In this operation the importance of an efficient and well informed credit department, the close connection of credit activities with the performance of loaning functions, and the dependence placed upon the department by the loaning staff of the bank are clearly indicated.

Personal Loans—Included in a recent study published by the Research Council of the American Bankers Association

(How Banks Lend) is the following result of a survey on personal loans. The information was obtained from questionnaires submitted by a group of banks which represented a cross section of the banking structure in the United States.

"A series of questions was asked as to whether the bank made various types of specialized loans to individuals as distinguished from business loans.

"As to personal loans the returns were as follows:

Banks granting personal loans	83.6%
Banks not granting such loans	11.3%
Banks not answering	5.1%
	100.0%

"Of the banks reporting that they granted personal loans, 68.6% gave information which indicated an average number per bank presently outstanding of 355, and an average size for these loans of $195.

"Loans to aid individuals finance instalment purchases are also extensively granted by the banks. The returns on this item were as follows:

Banks granting instalment purchase loans	62.7%
Banks not granting such loans	28.7%
Banks not answering	8.6%
	100.0%

"Of the banks answering in the affirmative, 71.9% submitted data which indicated an average of 278 of this type of loan per bank outstanding and an average size of $159."

Personal loans often are handled by separate departments established for that purpose. A system which enables the bank to service a large number of loans per person employed in the department is essential if the cost per loan and per unit loaned is to be maintained in reasonable proportions.

The credit analysis of a prospective personal loan follows a standard procedure. The prospective borrower fills out a loan application form which asks for information regarding the employment, position, salary, dependents, property owned, debts, adverse legal actions, and references of the prospective borrower. Co-makers or indorsers provide the bank with similar information on their own situation. From this information and other verifications, the personal loaning officer can determine whether the loan should be made.

The notes used provide for a series of principal and interest payments, with the provision that the entire balance may be declared due if any instalment is defaulted. In other systems, the instalments are credited to a special savings or thrift account, which is pledged as collateral to the loan.

A ledger card is commonly used by banks to record payments and balances still due. The customer is given a "deposit book" or duplicate of the ledger card, and payments and balances still due are entered in it for the information and record of the borrower. When a payment is made, the ledger card and deposit book are often posted simultaneously by a posting machine, thus insuring a correct balance between the customer's and bank's record at all times.

Delinquency notices are sent to borrowers within a very short time of any default. If the borrower does not immediately correct the situation, the co-maker or indorser is notified.

There are many systems and variations with features particularly adaptable to the problems of individual banks.

Generally speaking, personal loan departments are valuable adjuncts to commercial bank services and profits if a sufficient volume of satisfactory loans can be obtained at a reasonable cost and serviced by an economical and efficient system.

For further information on this subject and sample forms, the student is referred to the study entitled Personal Income Loan Department Installation and Operation (Commercial Bank Management Booklet No. 17), issued by the Bank Management Commission of the American Bankers Association.

Questions Based on Chapter IX

1. What is meant by the legal limit? What is meant by eligibility? How is it determined?
2. What two principal considerations govern bank loans?
3. In what ways are loans classified?
4. What are the principal kinds of collateral?
5. What are warehouse receipts? How are they used as collateral?
6. What primary responsibility rests upon the loaning officers?
7. What are the duties of the credit department?
8. What are the principal sources of information used by the credit department?
9. What is the importance of stock and commodity exchanges to the loaning operations of a bank?
10. In what ways may loans be liquidated?

Questions for Outside Investigation

1. How is the loaning staff of your bank organized?
2. Who performs the duties of the credit department?
3. Does your bank have a loan and discount committee of the board of directors?
4. What division of loans is made on the statement of condition of your bank?
5. What is the legal limit for banks chartered by your state?

Assignment

The Institute State Bank, newly organized, requires provision for credit department work. It is your duty as president of the bank to set up an organization for this purpose. The size of the bank does not justify a separate department. In 200 words state the arrangement you would recommend, the division of duties you would make, and just why you would make such a division.

CHAPTER X

THE LOAN AND DISCOUNT DEPARTMENT. THE FOREIGN DEPARTMENT

The Purposes of This Chapter:
1. To explain the duties of the loan and discount department and of the collateral department.
2. To show how these duties are performed.
3. To outline the characteristics of foreign transactions and to illustrate how these transactions are accomplished.

THE third group of duties in connection with the operation of the loaning function relates to the care of notes and collateral and to the maintenance of loaning records. The loan and discount department is organized to perform these duties, and upon the department rests the responsibility not only for the physical protection of the notes and collateral but also for the protection of the rights of the bank through proper presentation of the notes when and where due and through notice to indorsers or guarantors of their liability. In addition, the department is responsible for the protection of the bank's secured position in collateral loans through constant check on the market values of the securities or commodities and calculation of the margin for all secured loans with every change in value.

The duties of the loan and discount department are six in number, as follows:
 1. The safekeeping of paper representing loans
 2. The safekeeping of collateral securing loans
 3. The proper presentation of notes when due
 4. The maintenance of adequate collateral
 5. The calculating and collecting of interest and other charges

6. The maintenance of complete and accurate loan records.

These six duties involve the problem of custody of both notes and collateral, of teller work in connection with all loans, and of accounting and bookkeeping of a permanent and important nature. The personnel of the loan and discount department must be experienced and must have a knowledge of the problems involved, for in every operation of the department the importance of careful handling is emphasized. The personnel is qualified as *discount tellers, custodians,* and *bookkeepers* and in large banks is usually divided into these groups.

The Discount Teller—After the credit department has investigated an application for a loan and the loaning officers have approved it and established the terms—that is, the amount, the time, the interest rate, the amount and type of collateral if any, and indorsements or guaranties—the physical servicing of the loan is completed by the loan and discount department. The approved loan comes to the department direct from the loaning staff with these terms completely described. The duties of the discount teller begin after the actual note has been approved by a loaning officer and sent to the discount department.

Both the initial step and the final step in loan and discount department work are completed by the *discount teller*. His first duty is to see that the note conforms to the instructions of the loaning officer and to the line of credit established, as noted on the department records. For a new loan, this is done simply by checking against the authorization. In renewals, the discount teller may need to look up the record of the previous loan to see that the renewal terms are the same, for often the authorization will indicate that the previous arrangement is to be continued. Obviously, the discount teller must see that the note is properly made out, that indorsements or accompanying papers or collateral are correct and complete. The matter of collateral verification and its importance will be discussed later in this chapter.

When the correctness of the note has been verified, the amount of interest is calculated and the due date noted. This is a purely mechanical process. The discount teller is provided with interest tables; thus he need only refer to the proper schedule to ascertain the exact amount of interest and to a prepared calendar to obtain the due date.

The teller then makes up a *credit ticket,* which is used to credit the customer's account with the proceeds of the loan. A duplicate of this ticket is given to the customer for his own record. If the customer requests a cashier's check or draft instead of credit, the discount teller requisitions it from the draft cage or draft department. The proceeds of a loan presented in person at the window are entered in the customer's passbook. When the memorandum of credit is to be mailed, an advice of credit form is used, similar to that mentioned in connection with the work of the receiving teller. It is usual to give the customer a detailed record of the loan, either separately or on a credit memorandum form.

The discount teller comes in contact with many important customers, and his courteous and careful attention to their transactions creates a good impression. It is necessary that he at all times apply his knowledge of what is required in connection with loans, for incorrect or omitted steps constitute a source of inconvenience and delay and may even result in loss simply because the technical position of the loan is incorrect.

The discount teller is also responsible for accepting payment for loans and for the return of paid notes and collateral released by the payment. He must be certain of the payment received and of the propriety of releasing the collateral. Most notes are paid by charging the account of the customer. In such cases a copy of the debit ticket is given to the customer for his records. Some notes are paid by checks drawn on local banks. A few are paid by checks drawn on banks in other cities. It is a common rule of loan and discount procedure to require that checks drawn on other banks be certified or that a cashier's check or draft of the other bank be used. If a cashier's check, draft, or certified check of another bank is not used for payment, or if the check presented in payment is not drawn on the teller's own bank, the discount teller will refer the check to the loaning officer for approval before returning the note and collateral. While this does not happen frequently, it is nevertheless an important detail to observe.

Calculation of Interest—In calculating interest banks generally use tables based upon a 360-day year. The amount of yearly interest at any rate is divided by 360 and is carried in the table as a day's interest. The interest on any loan is figured according to the actual number of days the note is in effect. If it is a thirty-day note, for example, and the thirtieth day falls on Sunday, under existing laws the note is due and payable the following business day. The thirty-day note then *runs* for thirty-one days, and interest is figured accordingly.

It is customary for banks to *discount* notes—that is, deduct the amount of interest in advance—at the time the loan is made. The interest on a ninety-day note for $10,000 at $4\frac{1}{2}\%$ is $112.50. In discounting the note, the bank deducts this amount from the total loan, crediting the customer with the net amount, $9,887.50. While this procedure gives the bank a slightly higher return than $4\frac{1}{2}\%$, the custom is convenient and is well established.

Interest is money paid for the use of money. Most states provide a maximum rate of interest that can be charged individuals, and any charge above this to individuals is called *usury*—the charging of an illegal rate of interest. The penalties for usury, provided by law, range from forfeiture of the excess interest charged to cancelation of the principal amount.

Custodian Duties—The protection against loss or misuse of the notes, guaranties, collateral, and other valuable papers is the major concern of the loan and discount department. The responsibility for their custody is generally assigned to the manager of the department, who is assisted by a senior clerk, or clerks. All notes are filed in steel cabinets, which are placed in the vaults of the bank each night. Collateral is also filed in vault trucks. Notes and collateral are under the control of the custodian, who may personally supervise their withdrawal from the files. The withdrawal of notes or collateral from the department is permitted only on written receipt by authorized officers. In order to eliminate the need for withdrawal for information purposes, duplicate records are maintained, one for the use of the credit department and one for the loaning officers.

Accounting and Bookkeeping—The purposes of accounting in the loan and discount department are (1) to provide a daily record of the work of the department, (2) to record the liabilities of all borrowers, and (3) to list the due dates of all notes and acceptances.

The daily record of transactions provides the means of balancing the operations of the department with other departments and of reconciling the changes and new position of the department with the position of the previous day. In practice, each transaction is entered in a book of original entry, called the *discount register,* in the order in which it occurs during the day.

All transactions are then classified and entered according to the liabilities of customers in the *liability ledger.*

The necessity for proper presentation of loans at the time

when and the place where they are due requires a third record. This is called the *maturity tickler*.

These three records represent the minimum for accounting and bookkeeping in discount department operations. In small banks the records may consist of just these three, since supplemental or memorandum records are unnecessary. The transactions may be entered in a bound register and thence posted to the liability ledger. A card file usually serves as a maturity tickler. This simple arrangement is adequate for a small volume of loans.

Ordinarily, however, additional records and memoranda are of such practical benefit to the loaning officers and to the department, by providing information without interference with the work on the permanent records, that they are prepared and used extensively. Machine posting and the use of multiple forms in discount department work enable the department to duplicate records and classifications of transactions with little additional time and expense, thus providing exact information for a variety of uses by the credit department and loaning officers.

The records of the loan and discount department are characterized by their completeness and permanency. The protection to both the bank and its customers afforded through records that can be produced at any time has already been emphasized. It is obvious that the records of loans made and paid, of collateral received and returned, of collateral sold and proceeds applied to loan payment, and of proper presentation of notes and acceptances are factual proof which may be relied upon even long after the transactions have been completed. The importance of bank accounting in connection with the recovery of charge-offs was mentioned in a previous chapter. The records of the loan and discount department are even more valuable since they form the basis for proper accounting records of loan activities. Therefore, all loan and discount transactions are completely described, all actions are accounted for, receipts are issued for all collateral entering the department, and acknowledgments are made for all deliveries, in order that an accurate and complete accounting record may be created.

Supplementary Records—Since loans are classified in four ways (direct or indirect, secured or unsecured, time or demand, eligible or non-eligible), memorandum records are generally made for reference purposes. These supplementary records are filed according to their respective classifications, totals of types of loans are made daily, and the information is given to the loaning officers and senior bank executives.

Other supplementary records are used to assist the department in the performance of its duties. In maintaining the collateral margin, copies of the records of secured notes are used. The collateral itself is often classified and listed so that as changes occur in any particular stock, bond, or commodity, the loans affected are immediately shown by this supplementary collateral record, as well as the degree to which they are affected.

The nature and extent of supplementary records are governed by the character and volume of loans, the diversification by types of loans, and the loaning policies and practices. If memorandum records are only occasionally needed, they are assembled as required. A well organized loan and discount department, large or small, is able to supply records in addition to the regular ones as needed. Indeed, the ability of the department to assemble supplemental records is essential in times of rapid change.

The Maturity Tickler—The loan and discount department is responsible for the presentation of all notes and acceptances in its possession when and where due. Most of the notes are due and payable at the bank, and they must be available at the discount windows on the due dates. Notes or trade acceptances that have been discounted by customers are generally payable at other banks, locally or in other cities. The purpose of the maturity tickler is to enable the department to take whatever action is necessary in order to effect prompt and proper presentation.

An effective maturity tickler can be established simply by filing the records of notes by due dates, reviewing notes in advance of the maturity dates, and arranging for their presentation. Where the volume of notes is large, the maturity tickler is frequently divided on the basis of notes payable within the city and those payable in other cities. Such a division facilitates the work by eliminating a review of all notes in order to locate those requiring advance action.

The procedure for collecting out-of-town notes or acceptances is simple. Ten or twelve days before the maturity dates the notes and acceptances are entered in the collection department with full instructions. The collection department presents the items through the usual channels. Notes and acceptances due locally at other banks or offices are presented by messengers, acting for the city collection division.

Operation of Department Accounting and Action—Figure 33 is a chart showing the steps taken in connection with the handling of a loan by the loan and discount department. The posting of the information in the discount register is illustrated by Figure 34, while the posting in the liability ledger and in the maturity tickler is illustrated by Figure 35.

The work of the loan and discount department begins when a customer of the bank presents a note, approved by the loaning officer, at the discount teller's window. The discount teller immediately checks the note and instructions, figures the interest, and credits the account of the customer.

LOAN AND DISCOUNT DEPARTMENT. FOREIGN DEPARTMENT

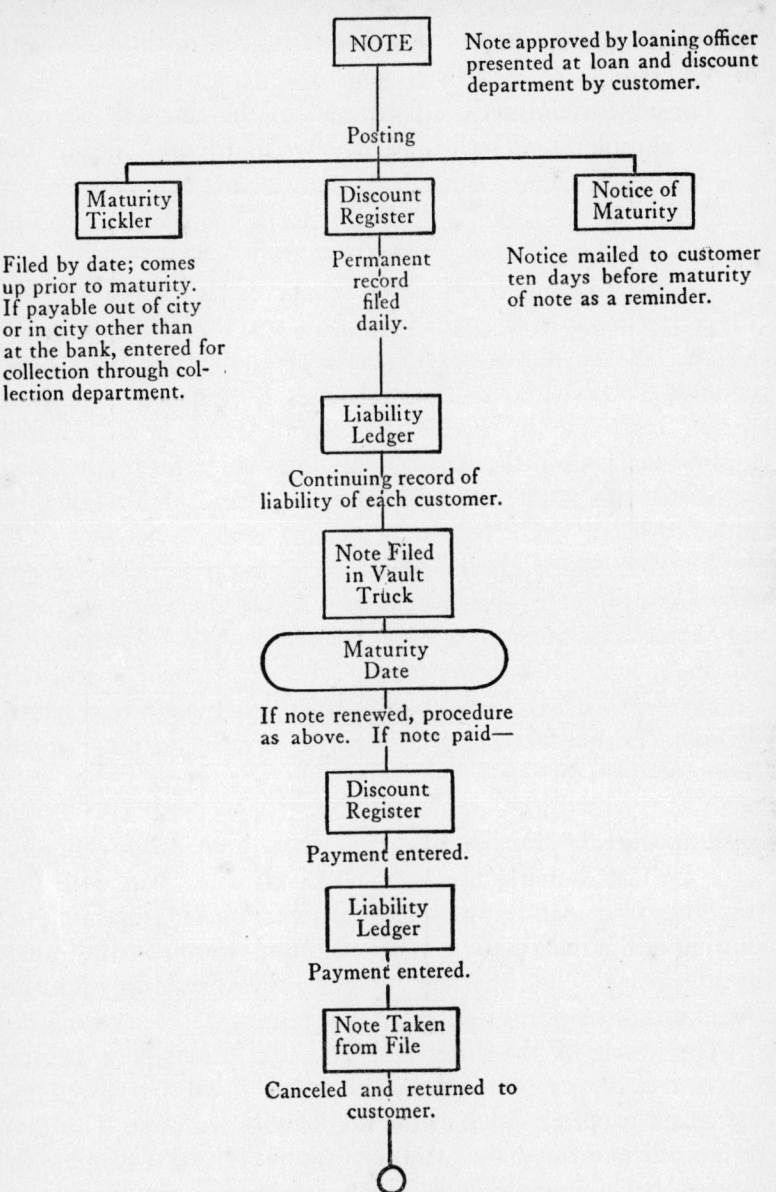

FIGURE 33. DISCOUNT OPERATION

An advice or duplicate of this credit is given to the customer, or the credit is entered in his passbook.

The note is immediately entered in the discount register and is completely described, as shown in Figure 34. The in-

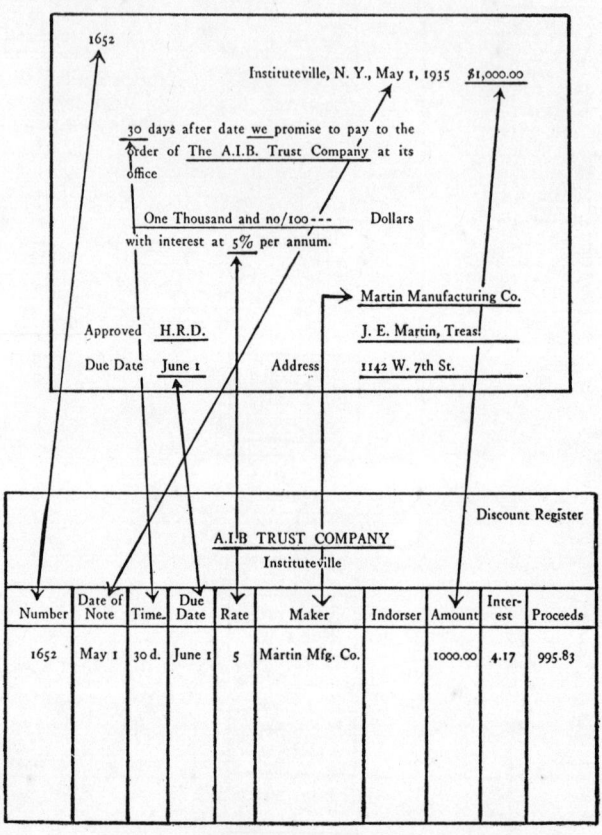

FIGURE 34. POSTING IN THE DISCOUNT REGISTER

formation is then entered in the liability ledger, and other forms are prepared, such as the maturity tickler and the notice which is to be forwarded to the customer ten days in advance of the maturity of the note. This notice is effective in prevent-

LOAN AND DISCOUNT DEPARTMENT. FOREIGN DEPARTMENT

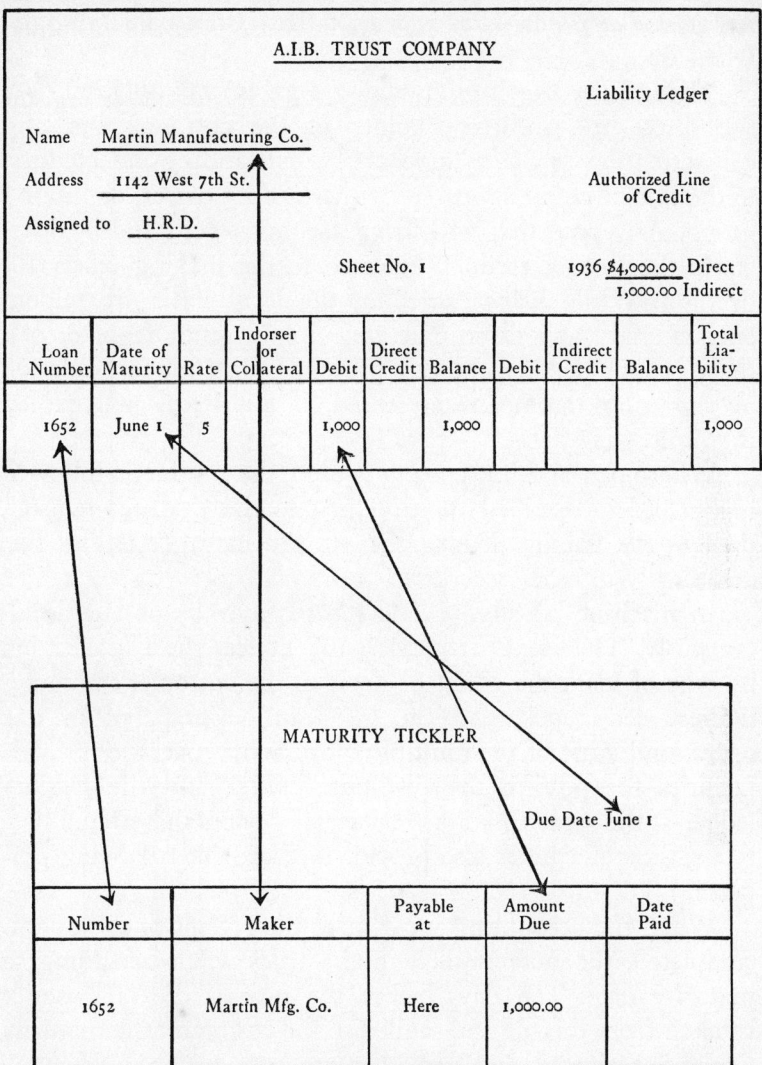

FIGURE 35. POSTING IN THE LIABILITY LEDGER AND IN THE MATURITY TICKLER

ing *past due* paper—that is, a note that is not paid promptly when due.

The liability ledger (shown in Figure 35) not only indicates the direct and indirect liability of the customer but also calls attention to the relation of the outstanding indebtedness to the line of credit approved by the loaning officer, or loaning group. Any note that will bring the borrower's indebtedness above the line of credit is referred to the loaning officer for decision. While loans exceeding the legal limit are seldom encountered (and those that are, usually result from error), the discount department can prevent unintentional violation by reporting that loans presented, if approved, will exceed the limit.

Where pen and ink posting is used, the routine is followed in the order described: posting first to the discount register, then to the liability ledger, then to the maturity tickler file, and finally to other records.

In machine posting, several records may be posted simultaneously. The maturity tickler, the notice, the classification by type of loan, the credit or debit to the customer's account, interest deductions, and the like can be prepared in one operation by use of the multiple form. Some machines provide facilities for posting the discount register and the liability ledger at the same time; and by use of devices that accumulate totals, these machines also provide a record for balancing purposes.

When the accounting incident to the receipt of the note is completed, the note is filed in the truck vault according to maturity date. Ten days before the note is due, the notice is taken from the file and mailed to the customer, the maturity tickler is reviewed, and any other necessary action is taken.

Upon payment of the note, the discount register and the liability ledger are posted. If the note is renewed, the procedure shown at the top of Figure 33 is repeated.

Past-Due Notes—Only a comparatively few notes are not satisfactorily met on the due date. Those that are not paid on time are classed as overdue, or *past-due*. Bankers are most particular regarding prompt attention to loans that are due, and non-payment of a note at maturity, whether through oversight, negligence, or other cause, is a reflection on the borrower's credit standing. So general is this attitude (and correctly so) that banks have reduced past-due loans to a fraction of their total loans. By sending the borrower a notice in advance (which is purely a courtesy and not required by law), the bank eliminates the possibility of neglect through oversight; and by emphasizing the reflection of past-due paper on the customer's credit standing, banks have made it plain that obligations must be met according to agreement. In many clearing house associations, the members make a charge of 25 cents or 50 cents for each day a time loan is permitted to run past due. This practice helps reduce the amount of past-due paper.

From the standpoint of the loan and discount department, past-due paper must be reported immediately so that the loaning officer may take action. A record of past-due notes is kept, and this is one of the first records checked by bank examiners.

It should be realized that there are occasions, though infrequent and exceptional, when notes are past-due through no fault of the borrower. For example, checks mailed in payment may be delayed by storms, or sudden illness of the borrower may account for non-payment of the note when due. Justifiable exceptions are few, however, and past-due notes are accordingly rare in a well regulated bank.

Care of Collateral—While the safeguarding of collateral through physical protection is, of course, a primary responsibility in connection with secured loans, the care of collateral involves also the *protection of the value represented*, by constant observation of market prices in order that suitable steps may be taken to protect the bank's interest if the value declines. The care of collateral requires complete and accurate records, and correct preparation of the necessary accompanying papers is essential for the full protection of both the bank and the customer.

Ordinarily the care of collateral is a duty of the loan and discount department. In many banks, however, the amount of collateral and the detailed work involved in connection with it make it advisable to segregate the duties relating to collateral and to assign this work to a separate division or department. In some large banks the duties pertaining to collateral are still further subdivided, and custody, for example, is assigned to a special division. One large bank separates the custody of collateral from cage operations by placing the collateral under special custodians in a separate vault. Collateral is received by these custodians as soon as it is checked in by the collateral teller, and delivery is made only upon written receipt.

Whether the responsibilities in caring for collateral are fulfilled by the loan and discount department or by a separate collateral department, the steps taken are the same.

Collateral Records—From the standpoint of departmental accounting, collateral records are regarded as supplemental, but from the standpoint of effective use, they are a necessity if any sizable amount of collateral is handled. These records vary in kind and number. It is usual to maintain a register, or journal, in which all securities are recorded as they enter the department. By the use of multiple forms, records for various purposes are written in one operation. In addition to the register, a record is made of all secured loans and the collateral to each. A third record is kept in which the collateral is listed by individual issues.

Suppose that a loan is secured by 100 shares of United

States Steel Corporation common stock, 50 shares of American Telephone and Telegraph Company common stock, and a $1,000 bond of the Pennsylvania Railroad Company due in 1960 and carrying a $4\frac{1}{2}\%$ coupon. In the collateral register these securities would be given a complete description—name, number of shares or part amount of bonds, numbers of stock certificates and bonds, the loan for which they are held as collateral, the amount of the loan, and the due date. The same information would be filed under the name of the loan. Each security would then be listed with others of the same issue, forming a record of the total amount of each kind of security held as collateral to loans.

The collateral register is the balancing record of the division or department, while the loan record provides the information on kinds of secured loans and secured liability of customers. The third record is used in determining the market effect of the individual issues on the loans.

Maintaining the Margin—One of the main duties in connection with collateral loans is that of maintaining the adequacy of the collateral, commonly known as *maintaining the margin*. The margin is the difference between the value of the collateral and the amount of the loan. The desired excess of market value of the collateral over the amount of the loan is called the *required margin*. When this difference is less than the required amount, the loan is said to be *short margined*. When the value of the collateral is less than the amount of the loan, the loan is said to be *short*. Until recent years, the desired margin was entirely a matter of policy with each bank, and banks still continue to have their own margin requirements. However, recent legislation has given to the Board of Governors of the Federal Reserve System the power to determine the margins to be required for loans for speculative purposes, and this legislation must now be considered a part of external control. Regulation U, which has been issued by the board in accordance with the provisions of section 7 of the Securities Exchange Act of 1934, covers the question of margins.

If the proceeds of the loan are to be used for purchasing or carrying securities, the margin required is usually much greater than if the proceeds are to be used for other business purposes. In the latter case, the bank has complete authority, and banks generally find it practicable to have the customer submit a signed statement that the funds are not to be used for speculative purposes—that is, for purchasing or carrying securities. If the loan is especially large, often the customer will state definitely the use to which the proceeds are to be put.

In determining the margin, the collateral division, or department, uses a *margin card,* which provides columns for recording the amount of the loan, the collateral securing it, and the market price and value. Each security in the list is checked for market value, the value of the security is figured, and the total value of the collateral is computed and compared with the amount of the loan. This margin check-up is done at whatever intervals may be necessary to keep the record reasonably current. Sometimes margins are checked every few days; at other times they are checked daily; and in times of declining markets they may be verified several times a day.

If the margin for any loan is insufficient, the matter is referred to the officer who approved the loan, and he requires the borrower to reduce the principal or to provide additional satisfactory collateral.

Verifying Collateral—In the preceding chapter we observed the part that stock and commodity exchanges play in the marketing of collateral. The facilities of these exchanges and also of unlisted, or over-the-counter, transactions are subject to *good delivery* of the collateral.

Good delivery simply means that the stock, bond, or warehouse receipt is in proper shape for the transfer of ownership by completion of the mechanics of transfer. Stock certificates are issued in the name of the owner, and if he wishes to transfer title, he must indorse the certificate in the place provided for this purpose on the reverse side of the certificate. This indorsement must be witnessed in the place provided for the signature of the witness. It is common practice to require a bank or a stock exchange house to guarantee the authenticity of the indorsement.

Bills of lading and warehouse receipts in negotiable form must be properly indorsed for good delivery. They must be complete and must also contain a definite description of the goods covered.

Mortgages and real estate contracts require certain accompanying papers in order to render them salable, and usually they must have insurance coverage against standard risks.

For stocks, good delivery requires indorsement by the holder and verification of his signature. Sometimes a customer does not wish to indorse the certificate, since he expects to have it returned and does not care to have it in negotiable form for fear of loss or theft. Therefore, in place of the indorsement on the certificate, he may give the same consent in the form of a *power of attorney*. This power, signed by the owner of the certificate, authorizes the transfer of the stock and is called a *stock power*.

Coupon bonds are transferable by delivery if all unpaid coupons are attached. If any coupon is missing, transfer of the bonds is not good delivery until the date of payment of the missing coupon.

Registered bonds require the authority of the party in whose name they are registered for effective transfer to another party or for exchange for coupon bonds. This authority, called a *bond power,* is given in the form of a power of attorney, signed by the registered owner of the bonds, authorizing the sale or exchange.

Another important document is called a *hypothecation power*. When a borrower offers collateral which is in the name of some other party, consent to its use must be in written form, which specifically states that the owner agrees to the use of the collateral by the other party.

The collateral teller must verify the correctness of all the documents necessary for the transfer of collateral, and he must ascertain that the collateral itself, both in kind and amount, is satisfactory to the loaning officer. In a bank where the loan and discount department handles collateral, these duties fall to the discount teller.

Collateral Division or Department Operations—Figure 36 shows the steps followed in receiving and returning collateral. When the collateral is presented by the customer, it is first checked to see that it is complete and correct. Any minor flaw in the condition of the security is noted on the receipt issued. For example, if a bond offered as security has had a coupon removed because it is due within the next few days, the collateral is accepted subject to this exception. However, if some more important defect exists, the matter is referred to the loaning officer for decision.

Upon verification of the security, a receipt is issued to the customer. A copy of this receipt is given to the loan and discount department as its record for posting purposes. Where multiple forms are used, one copy is a *receipt form*.

The next step is to figure the margin. Each security is checked for market value, and the total value of the collateral is figured and compared with the desired margin.

The collateral is then filed; the records made are filed in order; and the process of receiving collateral is completed.

Funds received in payment of the loan by the loan and dis-

LOAN AND DISCOUNT DEPARTMENT. FOREIGN DEPARTMENT

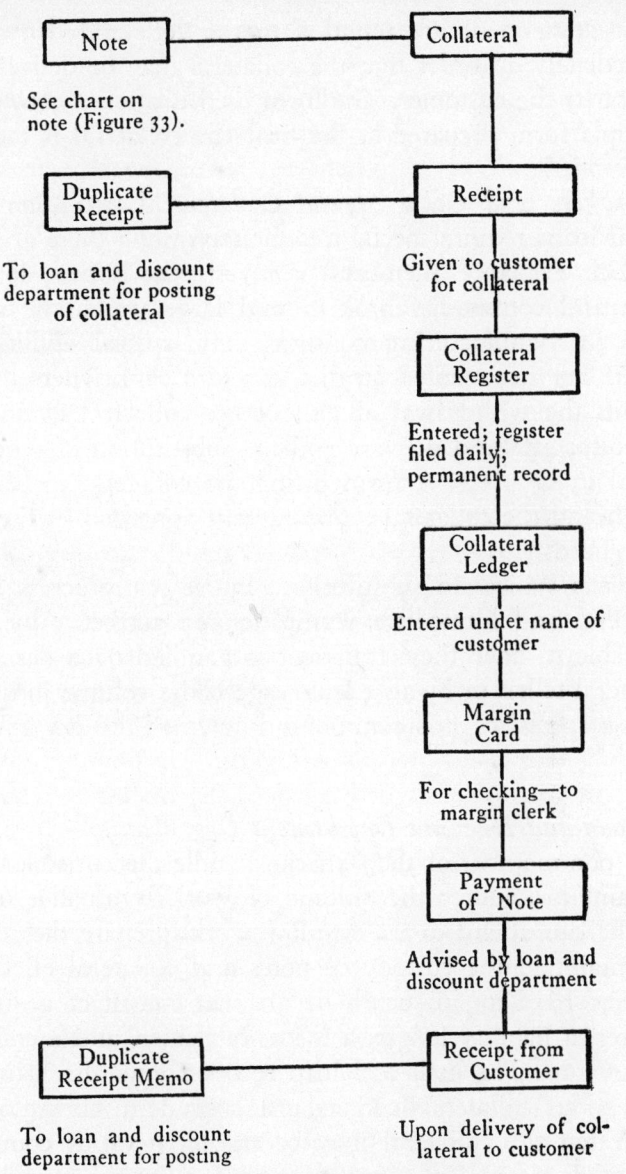

FIGURE 36. COLLATERAL NOTE OPERATIONS

count department are reported to the collateral department immediately, in order that the collateral may be delivered on receipt by the customer. The form used is often a copy of the multiple form prepared at the time the collateral is received.

Brokers' and Other Special Collateral Loans—Some collateral loans require special treatment. Among these are loans to stock exchange members or investment houses, loans to grain and commodity brokers, and large warehouse receipt loans to manufacturing concerns. The special facilities required are necessitated by the *substitution* privilege, which permits the withdrawal of part of the collateral by the customer for sale and delivery and the substitution of other collateral in its place. A form listing the collateral to be withdrawn and the collateral replacing it is approved by the loaning officer.

Loans subject to substitution require ready access to the collateral and immediate verification of market value. It is advisable to have these transactions handled by a designated collateral teller, or by a separate cage if the volume justifies it. Such a special cage is commonly known as the *broker's loan cage*.

Loan and Discount Department Organization—In a small bank one member of the staff can handle the entire loan and discount procedure; the volume of work is usually so light that he can attend to the window work, prepare the records, and maintain the custody of notes and collateral effectively. The records kept in such a department consist of a discount register, a liability ledger, a maturity tickler, and a collateral loan record. The collateral loan record shows the listings of the various collateral held against customers' obligations, in order that the collateral may be priced, margins computed, and other details in connection with collateral attended to.

Any information desired is obtained by direct reference to these records.

In moderate sized banks a division of the work is made. For example, one bank has a force of three, one member acting as discount teller, another handling the bookkeeping for the department, and the third acting as custodian of notes and collateral and assisting in discount teller work. In addition to the regular records, copies of loans are kept for reference purposes by loaning officers.

The discount and collateral department of a certain large metropolitan bank is divided into the teller, bookkeeper, and custodian divisions. This department has a personnel of fifty-five. Under the manager of the department are three assistant managers, each in charge of designated department operations. The bank has a divisional loaning arrangement and so carries its registers and liability ledgers in sections corresponding to the loaning divisions. The collateral is similarly handled according to loaning divisions.

There are nineteen discount or collateral tellers, nine ledger clerks in the loan and discount division, fifteen margin tellers and collateral record clerks, five stenographers and typists, and three general members.

Looseleaf records, machine posting, and multiple forms for collateral receipts, maturity notices, and the like are used.

Character Loans and Small Loans—Mention was made in Chapter I of personal or small loan institutions. The problem of making and servicing small loans is so different from the problem involved in loans to business enterprises that the methods used are quite distinctive.

Briefly, *character loans* (as they are called) have a well established basis for favorable consideration. When carefully made, they have an excellent record of payment and, under applicable operating procedure, a record of consistent profits.

It is obvious that the procedure followed in granting a loan of several thousand dollars cannot be followed for a loan of $200. Loaning officers can pass upon only a limited number of loans in a given amount of time, and for senior loaning officers to devote their time and attention to small loans would be to deprive other borrowers of time and attention required. Credit department routine and loan and discount operations must be adjusted to a more simple and less costly basis for handling these small loans.

There are two general groups of character loans: those secured by the indorsement of two or more parties in addition to the obligation of the maker, which is the largest group, and those secured by pledge of collateral. The majority of borrowers are salary or wage earners, and their income constitutes the principal basis for the extension of credit.

The credit investigation procedure for these loans has become standardized. The application form requests information about the borrower and also about his indorsers or co-makers. Among the facts furnished on this application form are the following: the record of employment of the borrower, his salary, dependents, banking connection, church and lodge affiliations, other income, real estate owned, record of other borrowings, commercial credit record, and purpose of the loan. A somewhat less extensive body of information is obtained regarding the indorsers or co-makers. From an analysis of these facts an appraisal of the application can be readily made. In practice, a standard is usually established, and the prospective borrower is judged by that standard. For example, the proportion of the borrower's income that can be safely loaned, the proper purposes of the loan, and the most effective method of repayment are all quite accurately known through experience, and the credit investigation simply shows whether or not the application conforms to these requirements.

It has been found that character loans should not extend

beyond the period of a year and that monthly, semimonthly, or even weekly payments are best suited to repayment of the loan. In order to eliminate repeated handling through renewal of a loan each time a payment is made, a note form is used for the entire amount, and payments are either indorsed on the note or set aside in a special account until completed. When payments are placed in a special account, a savings account method is used, and indorsements are made either upon the note itself or by detached payment notices. Thus the loan needs little attention unless the agreed payments are not made.

While the gross return on these loans is usually greater than that obtained from other loans because of the customary flat charge for an instalment note, the cost of handling this business must be carefully watched, since the gross income on each loan is small. By establishing a separate division for small loans, by assigning a junior officer to do the credit and loaning work, and by using a separate ledger in the loan and discount department, a commercial bank can eliminate many of the activities, operations, and expenses incident to regular loans.

To illustrate the operation of a small loan department in a commercial bank, the following record of a typical loan is given.

The applicant wishes to borrow $200 for the purpose of paying the balance of general and special property taxes totaling $234.68. He submits an application for the loan to the junior officer in charge of the small loan department, listing as co-makers his employer and a neighbor.

The application is checked within two days, and all references are found to be favorable. The purpose of the loan is satisfactory, and the amount requested is well within the 10% of income limit placed by the bank on small loans, for the applicant has a salary of $225 a month. The applicant is immediately notified that his loan is acceptable, and arrangements are made to have the note signed by him and his co-makers.

The note is for ten months, and repayment is to be made in monthly instalments of $20.

The amount of the loan less the interest at a rate agreed upon is given to the borrower, and he is furnished a special savings account card on which the monthly payments are to be entered. The transaction is recorded on a special ledger and the note filed.

Since the payments are made regularly, no further reference to the loaning officer is necessary, and at maturity the accumulated funds in the special savings account are used to pay the loan.

From an operating standpoint small loans are thus handled economically. A standard and easily made credit checking, a prompt and satisfactory appraisal and approval by the loaning officer, and elimination of repeated review and recording are characteristic of this type of loan. The loan and discount operations occur only twice, once when the loan is made and again when it is paid. No supplementary records are necessary. Through the accumulation of payments in a special savings account, the small loan can be handled more economically than it could by indorsement and handling by the discount department. In short, these loans are considered as a group, handled by standardized methods and at reasonable costs.

The increasing favor of small loan departments in commercial banks is due largely to the record of payment and profit on this type of loan. The service provided is one which is needed and for which a large number of salaried persons and wage earners can qualify.

The Foreign Department

The Field of Foreign Banking Contrasted with Domestic Banking—Within the United States, the purchase and sale of goods and services, the payment of obligations, the investment of surplus funds, and other business transactions involving money payments are all reflected in the operations of banks. Deposits, collection of checks (both locally and nationally), advances of funds in the form of loans, transfers of credit by wire, and other banking facilities and operations are an integral part of business. By means of checks, a widely used and important circulating medium has been created, and this medium is serviced by the various departments of banks, particularly the clearings, bookkeeping, and transit departments.

All these transactions involve a final exchange of orders to pay and the settlement of net balances. Exchanges within the bank are settled by ledger entries; exchanges between local banks are settled through the clearing house association facilities; and exchanges between banks in different cities or different parts of the country are effected through transit settlement methods.

While the principle of exchange and settlement is the same both locally and nationally, the mechanics are different. We have seen that transit operations are more detailed and take longer for completion than clearings; we have also observed that in loan and discount operations the presentation of out-of-town items requires more detail than the presentation of notes payable at the bank itself.

In the field of foreign banking, while the transactions have the same characteristics in principle as domestic banking transactions, the mechanics necessary to accomplish them differ so much from those relating to domestic transactions that a separate department—the foreign department—is organized and operated to handle them.

The exchange of checks and settlement of balances, the advances of credit made to assist in financing trade, the transfer of credit by bank draft, cable, and telegraph, and the presentation of items of a collection nature are handled by the foreign department if they apply to foreign banking. So distinct are the operations of the foreign department that it is operated almost as a separate institution, maintaining its own balances in other banks, handling cash and collection items drawn on other countries in its divisions established for that purpose, making its own loaning arrangements, and handling wire and cable transfers by its own system.

It is obvious that foreign banking, because of its extensiveness, may be considered a separate field of banking study. Therefore, in this course we can do no more than outline the factors that affect foreign transactions and briefly discuss the organization and operation of the foreign department.

The principal activities that give rise to foreign banking transactions are:

1. The importation and exportation of goods and commodities
2. The purchase and sale of securities and the payment of principal, interest, and dividends
3. Payments for services rendered (freight, insurance, and so on)
4. Immigrant remittances and travelers' expenses.

Exchange—The relationship between the value of the currency of one country and the value of the currency of another country is expressed by what is called the *exchange rate,* or rate of exchange. The term exchange rate is not used in domestic banking, since all domestic payments are made in terms of the same currency. Foreign settlements, on the other hand, involve two currencies, and it is therefore necessary to establish the value relationship of the two.

Formerly, the basis of exchange value was the gold coverage, or proportion of gold securing the currencies. Since the World War, this basis has been complicated by the laws of various countries which arbitrarily regulate the flow of gold. Whereas formerly ultimate settlements for international trans-

LOAN AND DISCOUNT DEPARTMENT. FOREIGN DEPARTMENT

actions were made by shipments of gold bullion, settlements are now made by transfers of funds into the desired currency. As might be expected, the operations in foreign exchange transactions require specialized knowledge and experience of a technical nature.

Commercial bankers are interested principally in the facilities provided for exchange, rather than in the mechanics of it. While extensive use of the facilities is made by a large number of banks throughout the United States, foreign exchange departments and foreign exchange bankers are limited to the large banks located in the financial centers.

Foreign Banking Transactions—From the commercial banking viewpoint, foreign banking transactions may be considered in three groups:

1. Transactions involving immediate payment or transfer of funds
2. Transactions providing for future payment or transfer of funds
3. Transactions involving credit arrangements.

In transactions involving immediate payment or transfer of funds, the cable is used extensively. *Cable rates* quote the price of foreign currency for immediate use. Payments are also made by drafts drawn against foreign balances, payable in the currency of the country in which they are drawn.

Future payments or transfers are anticipated by the purchase of exchange to be available at a future date or by the use of drafts drawn against balances.

Credit arrangements are met through the use of *letters of credit* (explained later in this chapter).

Exchange Markets—Exchange is treated as a commodity, and markets or prices for the conversion of dollar funds into the currencies of other countries are available at all times.

Daily rates for the leading currencies are quoted in the financial sections of newspapers, and quotations may be obtained from foreign departments of banks. The following illustration is typical of the use of exchange facilities by customers of commercial banks.

The Mardo Manufacturing Company of Des Moines, Iowa is buying goods in London and wishes to make immediate payment for them in pounds sterling, the British unit of currency. The company requests its bank to arrange for the payment. The bank wires the order to its New York correspondent, which wires back the exchange rate and the total cost for the funds to the Des Moines bank. This rate includes a small profit for the service.

The Mardo Manufacturing Company pays the Des Moines bank, and the Des Moines bank authorizes the New York bank to transfer the funds from its correspondent account. The New York bank buys pounds sterling in London and completes payment on behalf of the Mardo Manufacturing Company.

If the transaction calls for payment at a future time, such as ten days, the rate quoted will be for delivery at the designated time; the transfer will be made from Des Moines to New York and the exchange purchased for delivery in London in ten days.

Future exchange contracts are very important in foreign trade. Just as some domestic transactions call for payment immediately and others in thirty or sixty days or at some other future time, so in foreign transactions the times of payment vary. Let us suppose that payment is to be made by the Mardo Manufacturing Company in sixty days. A future exchange contract is used; this contract provides that some party will supply pounds sterling balances for the Mardo Manufacturing Company on the day required. By entering into the contract, the Mardo Manufacturing Company eliminates from its transaction the *exchange speculation* element, for regardless of the exchange quotation *on the day of delivery of the contract,* the Mardo Manufacturing Company has paid for its pounds sterling according to the *contract price* and so has no interest in the fluctuations of exchange rates during the period or in the price on the day of payment.

Letters of Credit—There are two main classifications of letters of credit: travelers' letters of credit and commercial letters of credit.

A traveler's letter of credit, which is used by persons traveling in other countries, is an agreement by the bank, in the form of a letter, to the effect that the bank will honor drafts drawn in accordance with this agreement up to the total amount of the letter. Drafts drawn under the terms of a letter of credit are called *clean drafts*—that is, drafts without documents attached.

The commercial letter of credit is used for business transactions. This is an agreement between the issuing bank and a foreign bank, or banks, providing for the payment or acceptance of drafts drawn in accordance with the terms of the letter of credit. Generally, *documentary* drafts are used, and the papers and documents which are required to be attached are listed and described in detail in the letter. As each draft is drawn, the amount is deducted from the total by indorsement on the back of the letter, and the balance still available is shown.

Classification of Letters of Credit—Letters of credit are of various kinds, depending on the requirements of the transactions they are to cover.

Irrevocable letters are not subject to cancelation after issuance, while *revocable* letters may be canceled upon proper notice.

Letters of credit are drawn payable in various currencies—dollars, pounds, francs, and so on.

If a single transaction (or a series of transactions) within the amount of the letter is covered, the letter becomes void after completion of the transaction (or transactions). Such a letter is known as a *straight* letter of credit.

If the letter of credit provides for a maximum limit to be outstanding at any time, with like amounts to be made available when the amount has been used, it is called a *revolving* letter of credit. A revolving letter of credit makes available any portion of a credit which has been used and then repaid. In effect, a $25,000 revolving letter of credit is always either partly used or partly unused but is never discharged until the whole credit expires.

Letters of credit are also classified as to purpose (export or import), as to security (clean or documentary drafts), and as to time (whether the drafts are to be paid at sight or after a lapse of time).

Import Use of Commercial Letter of Credit—An illustration of the use of a commercial letter of credit follows.

The Coffee Corporation of Chicago is in the business of roasting and marketing coffee. It arranges by correspondence and cable to purchase a supply of coffee from the Santos Exporting Company in Sao Paulo, Brazil. The price, terms of shipment, and other details are agreed upon.

Each company wants certain assurances: the seller, that payment will be made or provided for in a satisfactory manner upon delivery of the coffee to the buyer's representative in Brazil; the buyer, that the coffee will be of the grade and amount called for and will be delivered at the specified time. By the use of a letter of credit, these requirements will be met completely and without the delay and inconvenience that might otherwise prevail; payment will be made by a bank, an arrangement which is satisfactory to the seller, but that payment will not be made until the delivery has been completed according to the arrangement.

The Coffee Corporation applies to its bank for a letter of credit, stating the amount desired, the purpose of the credit, the currency in which it is to be paid, and the agreements governing the shipment. The application is approved by the loaning officer in the foreign department, since the Coffee Corporation is an excellent customer of the bank. The letter is then drawn up and executed and delivered to the Coffee Corporation.

The Coffee Corporation forwards this letter to the Santos Exporting Company, the seller, which delivers the coffee to a steamer pier in South America and obtains a bill of lading. The bill of lading is then attached to a draft drawn on the bank which issued the letter of credit (the Chicago bank).

Unless the transaction is one of collection only, the seller usually attaches the bill of lading and other documents to the draft drawn on the issuing bank and *sells* this draft to his bank in Brazil, either selling it as a spot transaction at the time of delivery or already having sold the dollar draft for a certain amount in milreis when the transaction was first entered into, in order that he might be protected against exchange fluctuations.

The Sao Paulo bank sends the draft and documents to its New Orleans correspondent, which in turn forwards the draft and documents to the Chicago bank for payment or acceptance.

If the agreement between the Coffee Corporation and the Santos Exporting Company calls for acceptance of the draft instead of payment upon presentation, the Chicago bank accepts the draft and returns it to the New Orleans bank. Instead of sending this *bank acceptance* back to Brazil, to be returned again when due, the New Orleans bank may sell it to an *acceptance house,* whose business it is to buy and sell acceptances (and thus it creates a market for them). The acceptance house deducts from the face of the acceptance a small amount called *discount,* which represents the interest return for the use of the funds. The New Orleans bank may, under instructions from its correspondent in Sao Paulo, hold the acceptance until maturity and then present it to the Chicago bank for payment. In either event, the proceeds of the acceptance are credited to the account of the Sao Paulo bank or are remitted to that bank by its New Orleans correspondent.

To enable the Chicago bank to pay the acceptance on the due date, the Coffee Corporation places the bank in funds a few days prior to the presentment of the acceptance.

In this transaction both buyer and seller have received the services and payments desired, the bank issuing the letter of credit has obtained a fee for the use of its credit in the transaction, and the acceptance house has received a small return for the use of its funds.

Identification—Particularly in the case of the traveler's letter of credit, it is necessary that the holder of the letter be provided with identification, aside from the letter of credit itself, so that he may use it without delay and inconvenience and so that it may not be used by others. Consequently, a *letter of identification* is issued, containing the signature of the holder of the letter. This signature is authenticated by signatures of officers of the issuing bank.

Traveler's Checks—A traveler's check is really a variation of the traveler's letter of credit. Traveler's checks, issued in standard denominations of $20, $50, and so on, are orders by a bank for the payment of funds in convenient amounts. To provide identification for the holder, his signature is written on each check at the time of issue, and he countersigns in the presence of the person cashing the check. In this way identification is provided automatically, by comparison of the second signature with the first.

Traveler's checks are widely used in both domestic and foreign travel, for they are of convenient size, are readily cashed, and yet are protected from unauthorized use by the identification required. They are furnished at moderate cost to the user. In case the checks are lost, payment on them can be stopped by prompt notification to the issuing bank, or to the bank or company on which the checks are drawn.

Other Foreign Department Items—A *banker's bill of exchange,* or *banker's bill,* is an order of one bank upon another. Such orders are used to anticipate future payments or cover foreign balances; they are also used in transactions which take advantage of higher interest rates prevailing in other countries.

Cable transfers are similar to domestic wire transfers, and the exchange rates are quoted in terms of cable transfer. As exchange rates fluctuate, cable transfers of funds are made from credit balances in countries where the balances are in excess of the amount needed to countries where debit balances are prevalent, and the net settlement is thus decreased.

Exchange is also quoted in terms of demand and time rates (thirty, sixty, and ninety days). The facilities provided by these various demand and time quotations were referred to earlier in the chapter under the heading of Exchange Markets.

Foreign Department Organization—Foreign departments are under the direction of a vice president of the bank, or under the direction of a department manager in a moderate sized institution. The work of the department is divided into exchange transactions, collections (both cash items and collection items payable in other countries), credit arrangements, and departmental accounting.

The income of the department results from exchange fees, charges for letters of credit, and commissions on the sale of travelers' checks.

The balances maintained by the department in banks in other countries are limited, ordinarily, to amounts necessary for current use. The value of these balances in terms of dollars varies as exchange rates fluctuate, and in case of large balances which are maintained for a special reason, it is customary to protect the bank against the speculative risk of exchange fluctuations by what is known as *hedging*. Regular brokerage houses make a specialty of buying and selling future contracts —selling against purchases and purchasing against sales at rates which net them a profit. Hedging operations are important activities, but they cannot be discussed in this course because of space limitations.

The accounting procedure of foreign departments must take into consideration the changes in dollar value caused by exchange fluctuations. From the standpoint of bank accounting, the foreign department's balances in other countries must be carried in terms of dollars and so reflected in the daily statement of condition. This means that each foreign balance must be carried on the books of the department in terms of dollars and also in terms of the currencies of the countries in which the balances are located. Frequent adjustments are made, using the prevailing exchange rate to evaluate the foreign balances in terms of dollars.

Foreign Collections—One of the important services of banks is the handling of collections payable in other countries. Because of the fact that these transactions involve exchange and other problems of foreign banking, all collections payable in other countries are handled by the foreign department instead of by the collection department. The strictly collection procedure—that is, credit to the customer when the proceeds are received—is similar to the domestic collection procedure.

In many cases, however, the customer wishes to have the use of the funds before they are actually collected and so an *advance* is made by the bank. This is a *loan secured by the collection* and subject to the usual credit requirements. In a foreign department there are many such advances, and in times of extensive foreign trade the income from the interest on these advances represents a substantial part of the income of the department.

Questions Based on Chapter X

1. State the duties of the loan and discount department.
2. What work is done by the discount teller?
3. How is interest calculated?
4. What are the necessary records of the department?
5. What is meant by direct liability? by indirect liability? How are these shown on the records of the department?
6. What is meant by "maintaining the margin"? How is this done?
7. What is a stock power? a bond power? a hypothecation power?
8. What are the principal activities that give rise to foreign banking transactions?
9. What is meant by the exchange rate? From the commercial banking standpoint, in what three groups may foreign exchange transactions be considered?
10. How does accounting in the foreign department differ from accounting in other departments of the bank?

Questions for Outside Investigation

1. Does your bank have both a collateral department and a loan and discount department? or are these activities combined in one department?

2. How are loans classified on the statement of condition of your bank?
3. Does your bank have a small loan department?
4. Does your bank have a foreign department?
5. Does your bank use multiple forms in the loan and discount department? Does it use looseleaf or bound registers and ledgers?

Assignment

Make up note, register, liability ledger, and maturity tickler forms similar to those illustrated.

I

Fill in the note form from the following information:

The Rhoden Automobile Company discounts a note for $5,000 due ninety days from date. The note is dated November 24, 1936 and is discounted by the A.I.B. Trust Company on November 25. The note is unsecured and is signed by the Rhoden Automobile Company, by F. C. Rhoden, Treasurer. This is an authorized signature of the company for borrowing purposes. Both the company and the bank are located in Instituteville, New York.

The loan is approved by G. R. Fordam, vice president; the interest rate is 4%; the loan number is 1887.

II

The authorized line of credit of the Rhoden Automobile Company is $10,000 direct and $5,000 indirect. On November 24, 1936 none of this line was in use.

With this information and the foregoing, make the entries on the liability ledger, the discount register, and the maturity tickler forms.

III

On December 2, 1936 the Rhoden Automobile Company rediscounts a note of the Alex-Turn Company for $500, dated November 27, 1936, due December 28, 1936, payable at the Third National Bank, Chicago, Illinois. The rate of interest on this note is 5%.

Make the proper entries for this transaction in the discount register and in the liability ledger.

IV

Both notes are paid on the due dates. Make the entries in the discount register and in the liability ledger.

CHAPTER XI

TRUST FUNCTIONS

The Purposes of This Chapter:
1. To explain briefly the services rendered by trust organizations.
2. To discuss some of the methods and systems used in trust organizations.

WHEN an agreement is made for one party to hold the property of another (or others) and to execute instructions in connection with it, the arrangement is called a *trust*. The party selected to execute the terms of the agreement is called the *trustee*. The trust department of a commercial bank is organized and operated to serve as trustee for individuals and corporations and to provide facilities for the execution of a wide range of agreements.

"Trust business is the business of settling estates, administering trusts, administering guardianships, and performing agencies, in all appropriate cases, for individuals, business organizations, municipal and state units of government, and public, educational, social, recreational, and charitable foundations and institutions."[1]

The increasing complexity of the financial problems of individuals and corporations in recent years has emphasized the advantages of trust facilities. For example, there are today income, gift, inheritance, and other taxes, both local and national, that were not in existence a few years ago. To meet the problems arising in connection with these taxes requires a thorough knowledge of their effect on the individual trust and the methods by which the customer can be served best.

---
[1] Trust Business (Trusts I), p. 7; American Institute of Banking, New York, 1934

The qualifications demanded of a trustee are numerous and exacting. The property entrusted to his care must be protected against loss by misappropriation or misuse of any kind, and the integrity of management must be beyond question. The trustee must adhere strictly to the terms of the trust and comply with a multitude of legal regulations. Specialized knowledge, experience, and ability are required in handling the problems that arise. The trustee cannot permit other work to interfere with the execution of the trust. Continuity of the services during the term of the agreement is especially important, for many trusts extend over a long period of years. Accessibility of the trustee at all reasonable times and moderation in expenses incurred and fees charged are likewise important.

Corporate trust organizations—trust companies or trust departments of commercial banks—have distinct advantages over individuals when selection is made upon the basis of these requirements.

The safety of property entrusted and the integrity of trust management are assured in corporate trust organizations by many laws and by a well defined code of practice. Corporate organizations cannot exercise trust powers until they have complied with special legal requirements. A common requirement is that a bank which exercises trust powers must have a larger capitalization than one which does not. In California, for example, commercial banks must have a minimum capitalization of from $50,000 to $300,000, depending upon the population of the city in which the bank is located. These same institutions, if they wish to qualify for trust powers, must have a minimum capitalization of from $150,000 to $500,000, depending upon their location.

It is also common practice to require trust organizations to deposit securities with a designated state officer to insure the fulfilment of trust obligations. In Illinois, a trust organization, *before accepting any trust business,* must deposit with the auditor of public accounts securities in the amount of $50,000; and if the trust organization is located in a city or town of more than 100,000 population, $200,000 must be deposited.

Additional safeguards are established by external control and by internal control and audit, as will be noted in the discussion of operations later in this chapter.

The corporate trustee is conveniently located, accessible at all times during regular business hours, not subject to illness or death as is the individual trustee, equipped to devote the necessary time and attention to each trust without interference from other business, able to employ specialists in the various trust problems, free to use the experience and judgment of several individuals in decisions of importance, and subject to examination by supervising authorities. Because the corporate trustee possesses all these and other advantages, the business of trust companies and trust departments is increasing.

Personal Trusts—From management and operating standpoints, the work of the trust department is divided into two main fields. The facilities applying particularly to the needs of individuals are offered by the *personal trust division;* those applying to corporations are offered by the *corporate trust division.*

The administration of personal trusts by corporate trustees is extensive, and in moderate sized or smaller communities the need for personal trust facilities is so marked that the business of trust departments is predominantly personal trust business. Corporate trusts are limited principally to communities where there are large corporations or business enterprises of considerable size. In this discussion of both personal and corporate trusts, the systems of the larger banks have been used as examples, chiefly because they cover a wide range of trust activities and must be equipped to handle a large volume of business.

The personal trust division is organized to act as:

1. Executor or administrator of estates, conservator of incompetents, and guardian of minors
2. Trustee under wills and life insurance trusts and trustee in living and voluntary trusts
3. Agent, holding real and personal property in escrow or under other agreed arrangements
4. Custodian of securities left by individuals, firms, or corporations.

When an individual designates the person (or persons) who is to carry out the provisions of his will, the one so appointed is called the *executor.*

When an individual dies without leaving a will, his estate is distributed according to the laws of the state in which he was a resident at the time of his death. The person appointed by the court to make this distribution is called the *administrator.*

Estate matters are subject to close regulation by the courts; frequent reports must be made to them and actions of the trustee formally approved by them. Although an individual may serve as executor or administrator, the legal requirements are so exacting and detailed that a trust department is generally better equipped to perform the duties involved.

Under the laws, certain individuals are classed as unable to handle their affairs, either because they have not reached legal age (*minors*) or because they have been adjudged *mentally incompetent.* The court appoints an individual or a corporation to act as *guardian* or *conservator,* as the case may be, and it is the duty of the appointee to hold the property and to administer the affairs of the minor or the incompetent for his benefit. The court requires frequent and detailed accounting and the presentation to it of important matters for approval or disapproval.

Many persons desire that upon their death a part or all of

the net estate be maintained intact for a period of time, that the income be paid to designated *beneficiaries,* and that the principal amount be distributed at later dates. Such purposes are accomplished by a *testamentary trust,* which is a trust created by a will.

The *life insurance trust* is a form of trust that is increasing in popularity. Under this arrangement the proceeds of insurance policies are used to create a trust similar to that established by will.

When individuals make arrangements for a trust department to handle their property while they are still living, in order to relieve them of the expenditure of time and effort in this connection and thus leave them greater freedom for other business matters or for travel or similar activities, such arrangements are called *voluntary,* or *living, trusts.*

Corporate Trusts—The corporate trust division is organized to serve as:

1. Trustee under mortgages, trust deeds, or other indentures
2. Agent and depository for trustees in reorganizations, voting trusts, and similar arrangements
3. Depository under common law trusts
4. Transfer agent and registrar for securities of corporations
5. Fiscal agent in the payment of dividends and interest
6. Trustee in receivership or bankruptcy.

Bonds are issued subject to definite and detailed agreements between the borrower (or issuing corporation) and the owners of the bonds. These detailed agreements are called *trust indentures;* they designate the trustee, specify the kind and amount of bonds to be issued, the method of payment, the rate of interest, and the security to the bond issue (if any specific pledge is made), and set forth numerous other important regulations. The trust department, as trustee, checks carefully to verify that the arrangements are carried out. If the issuing corporation is found to be delinquent, the trust department notifies the bondholders of the delinquency in order that they may take steps to protect their interests. In addition to this service to individual bondholders, the trust department provides the issuing corporation with facilities and equipment that insure accurate, effective, and economical execution of the numerous necessary details. National legislation reciting these duties of corporate trustees is now pending.

If the bonds are simply the obligation of the issuing company and are not secured by specific pledge of collateral, they are called *debentures.*

If the bonds are secured by pledge of real property, they are called *mortgage bonds.*

If the security is personal property, the bonds are called *collateral trust bonds.*

Sinking funds are funds provided by the issuing corporation for the purpose of repayment of the bonds, either as certain of them become due and payable or by payment of a portion in advance of their maturity. The amount of the sinking fund and provisions for its use are included in the terms of the indenture.

Bonds to be retired may be drawn by lot and the numbered bonds thus selected *called* for payment. In other cases, the trustee receives offers for the sale of bonds by bondholders at specified prices and selects for payment those offered at the lowest prices. In still other cases, the trustee is authorized to purchase the bonds in the open market for the purpose of retirement.

Registrar and Transfer Agent Activities—It is essential that no excess amount of stocks or bonds be issued under any authorization and that all matters pertaining to the issuance or exchange of such securities conform to all requirements, legal or otherwise.

As *registrar,* it is the duty of the department to see that stock certificates or bonds are actually a part of the authorized and outstanding issue, to keep an accurate record of the outstanding securities at all times, to cancel those forwarded for exchange, and to issue and authenticate each certificate or bond.

As *transfer agent,* the trust department must be certain that all requirements have been met in the issuance or transfer of the securities.

Whether the trust department acts as registrar or as transfer agent, verification of the duties performed is evidenced by a statement upon each security, signed by an officer of the trust department.

The principal stock exchanges commonly require that the duties of transfer agent and of registrar be performed by corporate trust organizations. The New York Stock Exchange, for example, requires that all securities listed on the exchange have as registrar or as transfer agents banks or trust companies located either in New York City or in Chicago.

Receivership, Bankruptcy, and Reorganization—When a corporation or an individual is unable to meet his financial obligations, it often becomes necessary for the creditors to petition the court to take charge of the affairs of the debtor. The court then appoints an individual or a corporation as *receiver* or *trustee in bankruptcy,* with the duties of conserving the assets, collecting funds due, paying necessary expenses, investigating and approving creditors' claims, and in some cases distributing the assets in proportion to the claims allowed. As representatives of the court, receivers and trustees in bankruptcy must submit frequent reports and obtain approval of actions to be taken. The special laws, both state and national, applying to receivership or bankruptcy and the problems presented require special training and facilities. Trust organizations meet these requirements and therefore are frequently appointed.

Sometimes corporations find it necessary or advisable to *reorganize* their financial structures. This involves readjustment of the stock and bond issues of the corporation and substitution of new securities for old. A common procedure is for a group called a *protective,* or *reorganization, committee* to act on behalf of the stockholders and bondholders. Uniform agreements are drawn up, and the committee obtains its authority by means of written consents supplied by the individual stockholders and bondholders. The securities are then *deposited* with a trustee, in order that concerted action may be taken in accordance with the agreements. The trust department facilities for depositing securities, for transferring ownership, and for issuing new securities are so effective that trust departments are often selected to perform these duties.

Trust Department Characteristics—In the commercial department, items and transactions are identified chiefly by amount. In the clearings department, this is the only identification used other than the assembly of a group of all the checks drawn on another bank. In the transit department, brief descriptions in code form are added to the amounts. The transactions in these and most other commercial departments can therefore be given a uniform treatment.

In the trust department, in contrast, there are both real and personal properties under control—properties of a variety of types, which cannot simply be treated as totals or subjected to a uniform procedure.

In the commercial departments, the contracts between the customers and the bank are *uniform;* items of the same kind are handled subject to the same agreements and regulations for all customers. In the trust department, *individual contracts or arrangements* exist between each customer and the department, and the provisions of one trust are likely to be entirely different from those of another in the same classification.

From the accounting standpoint, the commercial department treats all transactions in terms of amounts, departments balance on that basis, and every customer's transaction is reflected in terms of amount. He may deposit clearings checks or transit items, enter coupons for collection, or make a loan and have the proceeds credited; but all these activities will, without distinction, finally be reflected in terms of amounts.

In the trust department each transaction is handled and accounted for according to type, description, and amount, and even cash balances in an individual trust must be divided into those belonging to the principal and those which are income.

The property held by the trust department is not reflected in the statement of condition of the bank. This prevents the use of interdepartment balances and verification and so requires a system of accounting within the trust department that is complete and independent of other departments.

In short, the trust department is operated almost as a separate institution. Apart from the operating differences that make it necessary to use special equipment, to maintain records quite different from commercial department records, and to use a specially trained personnel, trust administration is so different that policies and controls unlike those in common use in commercial departments must be established.

Major Operating Problems—There are four major operating features to trust department work:
1. Departmental and individual trust accounting
2. Teller duties and cage service
3. Security and document custody
4. Verification and audit control.

Trust Department Records—The three main factors that determine the character and extent of trust department records are:

1. The necessity for the maintenance of records for the department as a whole, without reference to other bank accounting

2. The necessity for complete individual identification and accounting by description and amount for the many properties held in trust

3. The necessity for dividing the property in each individual trust into the *principal amount* (the amount of the trust itself) and the *income* (the earnings of the trust).

The records of the trust department as a whole include (1) the journal, (2) the trust ledger, and (3) the inventory, or asset record.

The *trust journal* is a record of all transactions, completely described and entered in the order of their appearance. This provides a daily record of activities and detailed information for posting to the other records.

The *ledger* shows the department's assets and liabilities, properly classified as to their nature and ownership.

The *inventory* reflects all holdings of the department, divided into the different kinds of real property and personal property. For accounting purposes, each piece of property is given a value. This may be the *par* (face) value, the *appraised* value, or a *nominal* value. Bonds, for example, are frequently carried at par value; real estate, at appraised value; and personal property that is not readily appraised, at a nominal value (ordinarily one dollar). The purpose of assigning values to each piece of property is to facilitate accounting, for balances may be made by amounts as well as by verification of the actual inventory.

Individual Account Records—Each individual account must

contain detailed records of the assets held. The properties, including cash, must also be divided into principal amount and income. Therefore the individual trust records must include:

1. A record of the principal amount, including an itemized list of the investments in both real property and personal property

2. A record of cash income, disbursements, and balance.

It is common practice to provide this information through the maintenance of records for showing:

a. The amount of principal invested in real property and in personal property

b. The principal cash receipts, disbursements, and balance on hand for investment

c. The income account, as noted in (2)

d. An itemized list of the investments of the trust.

At regular intervals—annually, semiannually, quarterly, or even monthly—statements are rendered to those interested in the trust. A duplicate of the ledger record of the account is used for this purpose, and many trust organizations use photographic copies as statements.

Supplementary Records—There are so many kinds of supplementary records that they may be regarded as auxiliary systems of accounting in themselves. In the work of registrar and transfer agent, a detailed account of securities outstanding and transfers made must be maintained. In safekeeping activities, records of securities received, delivered, and still in custody must be maintained. Each trust account has its own documents, receipts, memoranda, correspondence, and other records, all essential and important. The handling of securities, the legal actions, and the agreements made also result in numerous records. While these records will be described in connection with the activities to which they are related, one record deserves special mention at this point, both because of its general importance and because of its widespread application.

The *tickler* records, which are reminders of actions to be taken, are a vital part of trust operations. In the collection department and in the loan and discount department, ticklers are simply reminders of amounts due. In trust work, however, they are reminders of notes due, coupons to be collected, bonds to be presented for payment, mortgage payments to be collected, rents to be collected, taxes to be paid, tax reports to be prepared, court appearances to be made, investments to be considered, income to be disbursed, principal to be paid, statements to be rendered, and other important matters that must receive prompt consideration and action.

It is customary to have separate tickler cards prepared for each type of activity. Often the tickler files are maintained by the division in which the records of the securities or tax accounts or other receipts and payments are kept. Thus, an extensive file of the maturity dates of all bonds and coupons is kept in the security vaults, and several days in advance of the time for action the tickler is referred to the officer in charge of the account or to the division whose duty it is to collect the funds.

These ticklers not only serve as reminders to the individual trust officer; but they also serve to insure the fact that if he is absent because of illness or for any other reason, some one else will know about pending or future necessary actions and see that they are promptly and properly carried out.

Teller Duties and Cage Service—In the trust department, all tellers have occasion to handle securities for a variety of purposes. In transfer or registrar work, securities are left with the bank to be exchanged for securities issued in the names of other parties. In safekeeping, securities are left in custody. In other trust teller cages they are deposited according to reorganization agreements or submitted for payment. In every instance there are important matters to be checked; therefore the trust teller must be selected not only for his integrity and general responsibility but also for his knowledge of the requirements in each case and his reliability in observing that these requirements are fulfilled.

Except in the case of the payment of coupons or bonds, every security received must be accompanied by instructions. Every security must also be properly indorsed (as in the case of stock certificates) or be in good delivery form (as in the case of bonds). In transfer work, the instructions must designate the name of the party to whom a new certificate is to be issued, the number of shares represented by the certificate, and to whom delivery of the new certificate must be made. Each certificate must be indorsed, and the indorsement must agree exactly with the name on the face of the certificate. In order to be certain that the indorsement is bona fide, it is common practice to require a guaranty of that fact by a bank. This guaranty is in the form of a statement stamped upon the back of the certificate, signed by an officer of the guaranteeing bank. A detailed receipt is issued by the trust teller for each security left.

Delivery of securities is made upon receipt by the party to whom they are delivered, and identification of that party as the proper one must be absolute.

When coupons or bonds are to be paid, they must be examined carefully to be certain that they are correct in every respect before payment is made.

When deposits of securities are made under reorganization or other arrangement, they must be accompanied by a *deposit form,* properly executed.

The problem of teller duties and cage service involves the location of cage facilities, careful selection of personnel, arrangements for safe and prompt conveyance of securities to and from the vaults, and the issuance of suitable receipt forms.

Security and Document Custody—In view of the amount of securities that the trust department has in its possession, physical protection against theft (protection by vaults, guards, and alarm systems) is a most important problem. Protection against carelessness or misappropriation must also be assured by protective systems for handling and by frequent audits.

Trust securities are generally placed in vaults used only for the storage of those securities. All the securities belonging to a trust are filed together. Control, both in acceptance of securities in the vault and in delivery from the vault, should be under a *dual* arrangement; that is, at least two persons must verify and approve the receipt or release of securities. Often a member of the trust department and a representative of the bank's auditing department are designated for the dual control.

No securities are delivered, even temporarily, except on proper receipt of the owner or on written authorization, signed and often countersigned by officers or other authorized members of the trust department.

In trust department work there are many original documents that cannot be replaced if lost or destroyed; there are also receipts and other valuable papers that require special protection. All documents, receipts, instructions, and other information relating to a trust account are filed together in the *trust folder* for the particular account. These trust folders are kept in record vaults and are not released even for temporary use except on written requisition signed by an officer or other authorized member of the department. In order to minimize the possibility of loss of original documents, photostat copies of them are often made and used, the originals being left in the vaults.

The *file division* must maintain the trust folders in neat

and complete form; it must release none except on authorization; and it must keep a careful record at all times of the location of each file.

Verification and Audit Control—The problem of verification and audit control in trust department activities is a major one. The transactions are subject to varying instructions; a large number of securities are handled by the department; and every effort is made to insure frequent verification of the transactions performed as well as frequent audit of the securities and other assets.

Without an enumeration in detail of the many devices and methods by which verification and audit control are assured, the following examples will serve to show the general nature of these protections.

As previously explained, an officer of the trust department signs a statement on each certificate that the transfer has been properly made. Before a new certificate is issued, the entire transaction is checked by each department and is initialed by that department; and when the new certificate is presented to the officer for his signature, the old and canceled one is attached. Before signing the new certificate, the officer notes that the amount is correct and checks over both new and old certificates to be certain that they are in order. This verification, which has been preceded by other verifications in the transfer cage and in the transfer records, is the final one.

Extensive verification and audit control should be used in connection with the security vaults. First of all, the trust teller verifies each security and issues a receipt, sending a duplicate receipt to the auditing division. Another copy, initialed by the trust teller, accompanies the security to the vault. There the transaction is verified by dual control, and verification is indicated by the initials of both custodians. In the meanwhile, the audit copy forms a *continuous audit* record. In addition, at frequent intervals the auditing division makes a *spot* audit of the securities.

Safekeeping—One facility of the trust department that merits special mention is that of safekeeping—that is, the custody of securities for customers—and the service rendered in this connection in collecting coupons, bonds, and other securities when due. When such funds are collected, they are either credited to the customer's account in the commercial department or remitted by cashier's check or bank draft, depending on which method is requested. A record of payments received is also forwarded to the customer for his information. The convenience of this service is so marked and the fees charged are so moderate that individuals, corporations, and other banks make extensive use of the safekeeping feature of trust department work.

One of the services offered by Federal Reserve banks without charge is the safekeeping of securities for member banks. How extensively this is used may be seen by the report of the Federal Reserve Bank of Chicago for the year ended December 31, 1935. On that date, inclusive of a limited activity of the investment department of the Federal Reserve Bank, the total of securities held in safekeeping was $1,149,559,215.

The method of operation of the safekeeping division in common use is illustrated by the procedure followed by a middle western bank. In this bank the multiple copy record is used in quadruplicate.

The first of the forms is the *receipt to the customer* for securities left in safekeeping. It is a numbered form, containing a complete description of the securities, the due dates for interest, the full name and address of the customer, instructions for credit or remittance of funds collected, and an agreement to abide by the rules of safekeeping, which are printed on the reverse side of the receipt. When securities are withdrawn, the customer signs and returns this form as a *receipt to the bank for the securities returned.*

The second form is sent to the bookkeeping division for *posting* to the records.

The third form is the *auditor's copy,* which is kept in that division as a continuing verification of the activities of the safekeeping division.

The fourth copy is used both as a *vault record* of securities received and delivered and as a *maturity tickler.*

All securities are filed in a separate vault, subject to dual control by a member of the safekeeping division and a representative of the auditing division. All securities received in the vault are checked in by both custodians. No securities are delivered until the customer's receipt for them is presented.

As a further verification, all receipts issued by the safekeeping division are signed by a trust officer.

Trust Investments and the Investment Division—The problem of investing the funds held by the trust department in the various accounts is an extensive one. Some trusts provide that the funds shall be invested in securities established as suitable by law. All securities purchased for such accounts must be checked to be certain that they conform to legal requirements. Other trusts do not limit investments to those *legal for trust funds;* hence selection is not confined to that list. Nevertheless, conservative policies must be established and strictly followed.

In a commercial bank that maintains a trust department, a committee of the board of directors is often appointed to pass on all trust investments (see Figure 4, Chapter II, internal control chart). Such a committee works closely with the trust officers and with the trust investment division. The trust investment division is charged with the responsibility of assembling and analyzing complete and current information on investments already in the trusts and on proposed new invest-

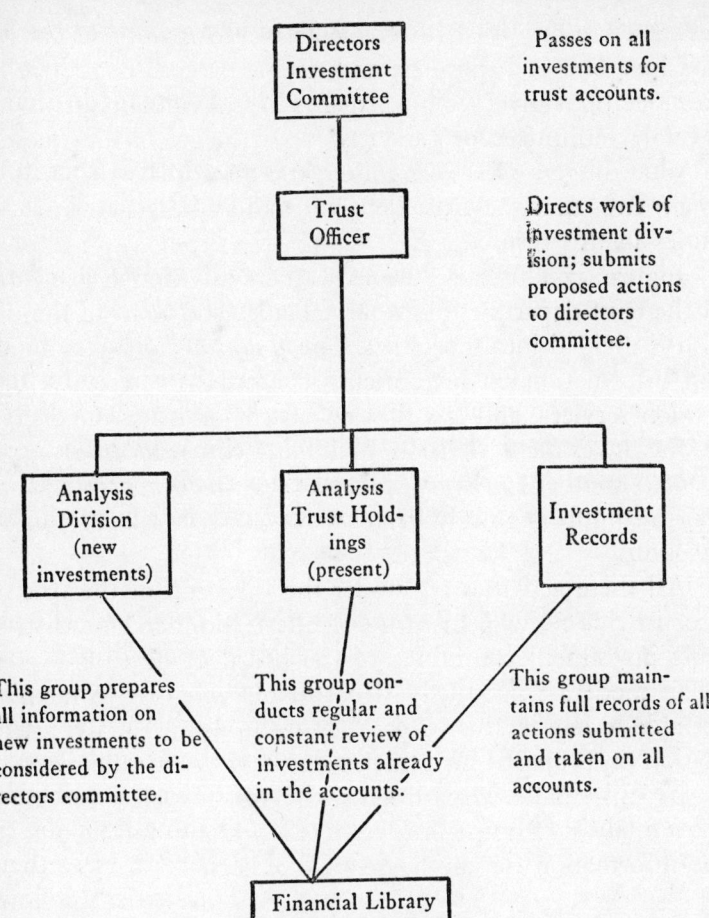

FIGURE 37. INVESTMENT DIVISION ORGANIZATION OF THE TRUST DEPARTMENT

ments. A record of all investments is also maintained by this division. This is a complete and detailed record of the various considerations given to investments in individual trusts by the several committees of the trust department. If the question of "due diligence" is ever raised, these records will be useful in proving that the trust department has fully performed its duties in this respect.

Figure 37 illustrates the investment division organization of the trust department of a large bank. The work of the division is divided into four parts. The *financial library* maintains full information on investments, subscribes to security information services, and has files on all major issues. One group in the investment division maintains the *records of investments,* another *analyzes prospective investments,* and the fourth group regularly *reviews investments* already in the accounts.

All these activities are under the direction of the trust officer in charge, who in turn submits recommendations to the trust investment committee of the board of directors.

In moderate sized trust departments, one or two members are able to handle this work; they assemble and analyze information on proposed investments and review trust holdings.

In still smaller departments, the responsibility for investment analysis falls upon the trust officer alone, and he prepares the information for the board of directors.

Administration and Operation of the Trust Department— The major policies of the trust department are determined by the board of directors. The investment of trust funds is determined by a committee of the board established for that specific purpose. Decisions regarding major policies may be referred to the executive committee of the board of directors, or in the case of a large trust department to a separate trust executive committee.

The chart reproduced in Figure 38 shows a typical trust department organization. Under the direction of the *vice president* in charge there are three main divisions. The personal division, under the direction of the *personal trust officer,* acts as trustee of living trusts, as trustee of life insurance trusts, as custodian of securities of individuals, as escrow agent, and as executor and administrator. The corporate division, under the direction of the *corporate trust officer,* serves as transfer agent, as registrar, as paying agent, as depository, and as trustee in bankruptcy or receivership. The operations division, under the direction of the *operations officer,* performs the duties pertaining to personnel, vault protection, departmental accounting and auditing, filing, cage and other service, and the general supervision of the mechanics of the department.

Organization and Operation of a Moderate Sized Department—The department in question is divided into corporate and personal divisions and has a total of 816 trust accounts. A vice president is in charge of policies and general administration. An assistant vice president has direct charge of activities, including operations. A trust officer is in charge of the corporate division, and another trust officer is in charge of the personal division. The department has a force of nine clerks.

All investment matters are first reviewed by the two trust officers and are then submitted to the trust investment committee, which consists of the vice president of the department and four directors.

All securities are filed in the trust vault under each trust. Securities received by the vault or delivered from the vault must be accepted by joint custodians—a member of the trust department and the auditor of the bank.

Extensive use is made of multiple forms, each set including a form for the auditor and the necessary ticklers. The trust

TRUST FUNCTIONS

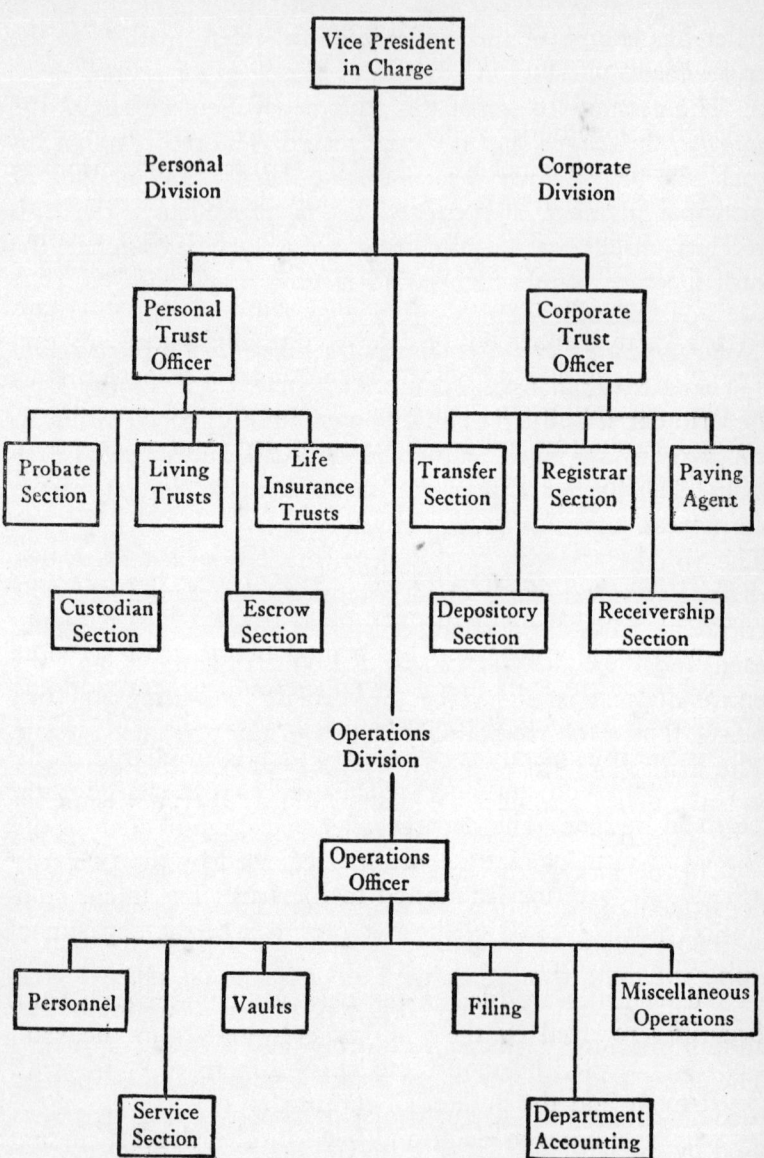

FIGURE 38. TRUST DEPARTMENT ORGANIZATION

teller has charge of the tickler file and refers matters to the trust officers ten days in advance of the dates for action.

The general records of this trust department consist of the *journal,* the *ledger,* and the *asset* record. The records kept for each account include the following details: the amount of principal invested, an itemized list of investments, the cash receipts, disbursements, and balance for each investment, the cash income, disbursements, and income remaining.

Organization and Operation of a Large Trust Department —The general plan of organization of a certain large trust department is similar to that shown in Figure 38, although subdivisions are made within the corporate and personal divisions. The official staff of the department totals 19 and the employees, 425. The total number of active accounts is 5,397. The volume of work in this department is so extensive that division of duties can be made effectively. For example, in the corporate trust division the trusts are divided into sections, each under the direction of an assistant trust officer, and the entire division is under the direction of the corporate trust officer. The same method is followed in the personal division. The work of the investment division is so extensive that individuals specialize, one analyzing industrial issues, another railroad issues, and so on.

The operations division has charge of the vaults, filing, departmental accounting, personnel, and other operations.

The equipment used in connection with the operations is quite different from that used in commercial departments. The trust records require both typewritten description and adding machine facilities for listing and totaling amounts. Therefore, while the ordinary bookkeeping machines may be used in commercial departments, the bookkeeping machines used by the trust department are combination typewriter-adding machines especially devised for trust work.

The problem of the classification of various types of assets is great because of the volume of accounts handled by this department; therefore special record forms are required. These are cards which are perforated in such a way that they can be sorted mechanically by setting the controls on the machine. By mechanical typewriter devices, the machine can be used to reproduce the information on the cards so selected. This device is especially valuable when lists of certain assets are necessary, and it makes possible the accurate, prompt, and complete assembly of information that would otherwise require the attention of a large number of clerks.

Some idea of the scope of activities of this department may be obtained by noting the number of clerks assigned to the various duties. The stock transfer cage has a personnel of 50; the statistical and analysis division has 39; trust bookkeeping, 20; security receiving cage, 7; security delivery cage, 10; and security records, 11. A separate auditing force is maintained by the department. Such matters as the calculation and recording of fees, which in smaller departments are attended to by the personnel assigned to other regular duties, are handled by a special force of 7.

Questions Based on Chapter XI

1. State the advantages of a corporate trustee.
2. What are the principal services provided by the corporate trust division?
3. Differentiate debentures, mortgage bonds, and collateral trust bonds.
4. What is the duty of the department as registrar? as transfer agent?
5. In what major capacities does the department act in the personal trust division?
6. What records pertaining to the trust department as a whole are commonly maintained?

7. What records are generally used for the individual account?
8. What facilities are provided by the safekeeping section?
9. What are the duties of the trust investment division?
10. What are the chief operating problems?

Questions for Outside Investigation

1. Does your bank have a trust department?
2. Is the work of the department such as to require both a corporate division and a personal division?
3. Who is in charge of operations for the department?
4. How does it compare in size—that is, officers and employees—with the commercial department?
5. Are multiple records extensively used in your trust department?

Assignment

Explain briefly (in 200 words or less) why you would select the trust department of a commercial bank in preference to an individual trustee to handle your property, emphasizing the main features desired when property is placed in the hands of another for care and execution of agreements made.

CHAPTER XII

BANK EXAMINATION. THE STATEMENT OF CONDITION

The Purposes of This Chapter:
1. To explain the purposes of bank examination and to outline the methods used.
2. To outline the uses of the statement of condition and to explain the items usually appearing in it.

IN the discussion of external control in Chapter II, the purposes of bank examination were outlined as (1) to verify the solvency of the bank, (2) to ascertain whether any banking laws are being violated, and (3) to discover and correct errors in management or operations which left unchecked might lead to disastrous results.

The examination of banks is provided for by law. State authorities, the Comptroller of the Currency, the Board of Governors of the Federal Reserve System, and the governing body of the Federal Deposit Insurance Corporation all have extensive examining powers and duties. Thus a state member bank is subject to examination by both state and Federal Reserve examiners, but it is subject to examination by Federal Deposit Insurance Corporation authorities only upon written consent of the Board of Governors of the Federal Reserve System. In order to prevent unnecessary duplication of effort, these authorities cooperate in the examination of banks which are subject to more than one authority. In such cases examinations are made jointly or else the examination reports of one authority are forwarded to the others interested, for appraisal and action.

When corrective measures are needed, the suggestion of the supervising authority is generally sufficient to bring immediate

BANK EXAMINATION. STATEMENT OF CONDITION 449

results. If not, the specific powers of the examining authority can be used to enforce compliance.

In addition to the examinations provided by law, many clearing house associations are given the right of examination by voluntary agreement of the members. These clearing house examinations are highly regarded because of the fact that they reflect the knowledge of examiners who are in close touch with local conditions. When an examination reveals unsatisfactory conditions in a member bank, other members of the association can cooperate to remedy the situation. In recent years the reports of clearing house examiners have been extremely valuable in appraising the situations and suggesting the remedies necessary in instances in which weaker clearing members have been consolidated with stronger members.

Within each bank, as we have seen, there is a constant process of examination through auditing procedure. The board of directors is required to make regular examinations and in fulfilling that requirement often employs a firm of certified public accountants to examine the bank and report directly to the board. The outside audit is particularly desirable in the case of smaller banks where the size does not permit extensive auditing features.

In addition to the examinations made for the foregoing purposes, examinations are also required as a basis of admission to membership in the Federal Reserve System and in the Federal Deposit Insurance Corporation. When a bank changes its status from a state to a national institution, or the reverse, by changing its charter, an examination is made to ascertain whether the applying bank is acceptable to the new authority.

The Board of Governors of the Federal Reserve System, in acting upon an application of a state bank for membership in the system, gives special consideration to:

1. The financial history and condition of the applying bank and the general character of its management

2. The adequacy of its capital structure and its future earning prospects

3. The convenience and needs of the community to be served by the bank

4. Whether its corporate powers are consistent with the purposes of the Federal Reserve Act.

Similarly, either state or national authorities examine banks applying for change of charter, to ascertain their conformance to established standards.

Examining Methods—Much the same procedure of examination is used by all supervising authorities. The examiner appears at the bank either just prior to opening time or at the close of the daily banking hours; he takes charge of all records and assumes control of all property for the purpose of examination. He places a seal upon the cash vaults until he has had an opportunity to verify their contents. During the examination, notes and collateral are under his control, and every operation must first be approved by him (in order to keep the examination records complete) before the transaction is finished.

Detailed forms are provided for examination purposes. Specific questions must be answered by the officers and other members of the bank staff. Loans and discounts are reviewed, investments are verified and classified, the minutes of the board of directors are checked to see that the board is passing upon matters that are part of its duties, cash on hand is counted, balances with other banks are verified, demand and time deposits are balanced—in short, a complete and careful verification is made of all the assets and liabilities.

Upon completion of the examination, the examiner forwards his report to the proper authority. There it is analyzed and a copy is sent to the bank's board of directors, together with such comments or suggestions as may seem desirable.

The board must indicate its knowledge of this examination report by a resolution passed at a meeting of the board and recorded in the minutes. Some states (Pennsylvania, for example), and also Federal Reserve bank examiners, require that the response made to the banking department report be signed by all the directors.

The Statement of Condition—The statement of condition is the report of the assets and liabilities of the bank. It is a part of bank control, for both state and national laws require submission of statements of condition to supervising authorities for their information. The requests (known as *calls*) are for statements as of a date just prior to the calls. The Comptroller of the Currency is required by law to issue at least three calls each year for national banks. State laws and regulations vary, some stipulating the number of calls, others leaving that decision to the state authority. Calls are made without previous notice and at varying intervals, in order that no changes may be made by a bank in contemplation of the call. Each bank, upon receiving the call, must submit the statement to the proper authority within a short time, generally not exceeding ten days. The statement must be in the form prescribed and must be sworn to as correct by officers and directors of the bank, and so attested by a notary public.

In addition to submitting the report, the bank usually must publish the report in a paper of general circulation in the vicinity in which the bank is located, for the purpose of informing the public. A copy of this official publication is sent to the supervising authority as proof of compliance with the regulation.

While the statement of condition was initially used for the purpose of informing the supervising authorities and the public, banks have made increasing and beneficial use of it for other purposes. It is common practice to use the statement for advertising purposes, not only by publication in the newspapers but also by dissemination in folder form among customers and prospective customers. These folders may be placed on the counters in the bank, readily accessible to customers; they may be included with the statements mailed or delivered from the bookkeeping department; or they may be mailed out by officers to their customers and friends.

To emphasize the caliber of the men responsible for the bank's management, there is included in this folder a list of the directors and their business connections. The officers are listed, often by departments, in order that customers and others may know whom to consult regarding their banking problems. The facilities of the bank—savings, commercial, and trust departments—are included with a brief statement of the services rendered by each.

Still another use made of the statement of condition is in connection with the daily work of the bank, for the information contained in it can be applied by executive and loaning officers in their daily decisions. Often the statement is read at daily officers' meetings, or copies are made and distributed to the senior officers. Used in conjunction with the other reports to officers—the new and closed accounts, loans made and paid, and the like—it completes the daily picture of the bank.

Preparing the Statement—The daily statement is prepared from the general books. The final figures of the departments and activities are consolidated into the general classifications that appear in the statement. As the figures reflecting the activities of the various departments are reported to general books, they are first entered in the journal and then posted to the ledger, under the proper classifications. From the ledger they are further consolidated and set up on the statement of condition form. To illustrate this operation, let us consider the statement item of Cash and Due from Banks.

First of all, the head paying teller's balance is reported as "vault cash" and "working funds," as noted in the discussion in Chapter IV. These two designations appear on the general books. On the general books also appears the total of transit items in the process of collection—the float. A list of the banks in which balances are kept and the amount of each balance are carried on the general books; or if a "due from banks" ledger is used, the totals are sent to general books. In a separate item are noted the balances at the Federal Reserve bank. These are carried in two divisions, reserve account and deferred (or collection) account. The total of checks in the clearings department for exchange the following day is reported by the clearing house department. Foreign balances are reported by the foreign department. Yet in the statement of condition all these general book accounts may be totaled, with the single item Cash and Due from Banks representing them.

Similarly, the demand deposits reported by bookkeeping sections to general books are consolidated into a single total.

The Assets, or Resources, of the Bank—The assets, or resources, of the bank consist of the cash, securities, and other property owned and the balances or promises due the bank. Cash and Due from Banks is usually the first item appearing on the asset side of the statement. It may be a single item, as already noted, or it may be divided into three or more items—for example, Cash on Hand, Due from Banks and Bankers, and Due from Federal Reserve Bank. When so divided, Cash on Hand represents the vault cash and working funds. Due from Banks and Bankers represents the balances maintained with other banks for transit, collection, and other purposes; it also includes transit items in the process of collection and clearings items on hand for exchange the next business day.

Legal reserves, the amount that must be carried by member banks in the form of collected balances with the Federal Reserve banks of their respective districts, are now subject to variation. The fixed reserves in effect prior to the Banking Act of 1935 may be changed, within limits, by the Board of Governors of the Federal Reserve System at any time they believe such a change is necessary to prevent "injurious credit expansion or contraction." The minimum reserves must not be less than the basic rate, the maximum not more than twice the basic rate.[1]

The basic rate for time deposits is 3%, and so the maximum is 6%. The basic rate for demand deposits for banks located in central reserve cities is 13%, the maximum 26%; for banks located in reserve cities the basic rate is 10%, the maximum 20%; and for banks located outside central reserve and reserve cities the basic rate is 7%, the maximum 14%.

Investments—Following the items of Cash on Hand, Due from Banks and Bankers, and Due from Federal Reserve Bank are the totals of investments. These investments consist of government, municipal, and other bonds. Some investments are long term; that is, the principal amount is not due and payable for several years. Other investments are short term—that is, due within five years or less. The point of determination between so-called short term and long term investments varies, some banks dividing at three years. In preparing the statement, some banks divide the total of bonds into those due in five years or more and those due in less than five years.

In accordance with provisions of the Banking Act of 1935, regulations have been made regarding the investments of member banks. The initial regulation, effective February 15, 1936, provided that all securities purchased for any member bank's account after that date must conform to regulations established, principally with regard to the standing of the bonds and their marketability.

---

[1] See Table II, Appendix.

It is common practice in the statement of condition to carry United States Government obligations as a separate total. This includes government bonds, treasury certificates, and any other bonds guaranteed as to principal and interest by the United States Government, such as the Home Owners' Loan Corporation issues.

While banks invest in government bonds for the purpose of obtaining the highest grade investment, and one readily marketable at all times, government bonds may also be used as security for loans at the Federal Reserve banks, since notes so secured are classed as eligible paper.

A separate classification of investments is often made for municipal bonds, which are the bonds and warrants of states, cities, sanitary districts, school districts, and other governmental subdivisions. The leading municipal issues are highly regarded, and substantial amounts are owned by banks. Municipal bonds are not listed on the stock exchanges but are so widely traded on an over-the-counter basis that market quotations for substantial amounts can always be obtained for the leading issues.

The bonds of railroads, public utilities, and industrial concerns are generally carried in one total, called Other Bonds.

The *book* (or asset) *value* of a security is usually the amount paid for that security and is the value used in preparing the statement of condition. When a bond is purchased at a premium (that is, above its par value), the premium must be charged off if it exceeds the call price of the security or amortized at regular periods if it does not. If the cost of securities is more than the market value, banks frequently establish reserves to reduce the book value to, or below, the market value and in the published statements show this net book value (after deducting reserves) as below actual market value. This is done in order that the actual condition of the bank may be properly shown.

Because of the fact that there are laws requiring additional protection to deposits of governmental bodies by the pledge of securities, it is customary to show the amount of deposits which are secured by assets, and in some cases the record of assets pledged. When the latter procedure is followed, the bonds so pledged are listed as "pledged to secure public funds," and the bonds that are then remaining are listed as "unpledged."

Loans and Discounts—The loans and discounts item is one of the largest assets in the commercial bank. Rarely is it exceeded by any other type of asset, except possibly on occasion by investments. It is also one of the largest earning assets. In the statement, the total may be shown in a single item, Loans and Discounts, or division may be made into the various kinds of loans. Loans and discounts include not only the advances made to bank customers but also commercial paper purchased or call loans made, as explained in Chapters IX and X. A separate classification of call loans is seldom made, although if these loans constitute a substantial proportion of the total loans and discounts, they may be segregated in the statement. Commercial paper may be classified as a separate item if its proportion to the total is large.

In discount department figures, loans and discounts are classified in various ways, as we have seen in the discussion of that department. Member banks find it advisable to maintain a separate control for eligible paper. Separate classifications of this sort are of primary importance to the management in estimating its requirement for secondary reserves. This feature, however, is a subject of study in the Institute course Bank Administration, Banking III.

The common classifications are: Time Loans, Secured; Time Loans, Unsecured; Demand Loans, Secured; and Demand Loans, Unsecured.

Federal Reserve Bank Stock—As noted in the discussion of Federal Reserve banks, Chapter II, all member banks must own stock in the Federal Reserve bank of their district. This stock may be carried as a separate item in the statement under a designation similar to the heading of this paragraph, or it may be included in some other total.

Overdrafts—If there are any overdrafts on the statement date, they must be noted in a separate item in the statement. The amount of overdrafts in a well regulated bank is very small, and frequently there are no overdrafts on the statement date.

Mortgage Loans—Loans secured by mortgages on real property are made in limited volume by commercial banks. Both state and national laws limit the total amount of mortgage loans that may be made by the banks under their jurisdictions. For example, the Banking Act of 1935 provides that for national banks the total amount of mortgage loans must not exceed the paid-in capital stock plus the amount of unimpaired surplus fund of the bank, or must not be in excess of 60% of the amount of the bank's time and savings deposits, whichever is greater.

Limitations are placed on the individual loans as well as on the total amount. In the Banking Act of 1935, the maximum amount of each loan is limited to 50% of the appraised value of the property. Where no reduction is to be made during the life of the loan, the time is limited to five years. If the loan provides for instalment payments that will reduce the principal amount 40% within ten years, the loan can be made for that period and to the extent of 60% of the appraised value of the property.

Exceptions are made for loans already owned and for insured loans provided for under the so-called "housing act."

Banking House—Most banks own the building used for banking purposes and carry it at a conservative valuation on the statement of condition. While adequate premises are essential to the conduct of the bank's business, the amount invested in the building should be moderate in proportion to the capital and surplus. As a matter of policy, banks reduce the book value of the premises by depreciation charges made from current earnings. It is not uncommon for a bank so to reduce the book value of land and bank building over a period of years that the land alone is worth more than the book value of both land and building.

If the item Banking House (or some similar title) does not appear on the statement, the inference is that the banking premises are leased. The bank may lease from a safe deposit company that owns the property, or from a company formed by interested stockholders for the express purpose of owning the building, or from some other landlord. Many banks prefer to lease quarters during the early years of their existence, deferring the building of their own quarters until they are more certain of space requirements.

Furniture and Fixtures—If the banking house is owned by the bank, furniture and fixtures are often included in the general total of Banking Premises and Equipment. If the bank does not own the building, these items are carried on the statement as Furniture and Fixtures, the account including the investment in vaults, cages, machines, and furniture necessary for the business.

Generally speaking, the equipment is valued on the books at a low figure or is even carried at a nominal value. Depreciation is applied to equipment immediately on its purchase and is established at a high enough rate to reduce the book value to a nominal figure long before the equipment is discarded.

Other Real Estate—This item represents real estate other than that in use by the bank for the conduct of its business; most of it consists of real estate which has been obtained as security for loans or other advances that have been unsatisfactory. Every endeavor is made to dispose of such real estate within a short time, and during the time it is owned by the bank it is generally valued below the amount expected to be realized by subsequent sale. State and national laws and regulations provide for the sale of other real estate as soon as reasonably possible.

Other Assets—This classification includes assets that cannot be properly included in the regular items, and its amount is proportionately small. It may include such assets as safe deposit company stock owned by the bank, sums due by reason of liquidation of other real estate, miscellaneous accounts receivable, and the like. The assets included in this classification vary widely among banks, for any group that does not justify a separate classification is made a part of this total.

Liabilities—The liabilities represent the bank's obligations to depositors, to others, and to stockholders. The largest amount of liabilities, and the first to be considered, is that due to depositors. Following this are the liabilities to others, which are not large in proportion to total liabilities. Both deposit liabilities and liabilities to others must be completely satisfied before the obligations to the stockholders are considered.

Deposits—In a commercial bank, the largest item of liability to depositors is the demand deposit liability. The second in size is the item of time deposits, or savings. These may simply be noted on the statement as Demand Deposits and

Time Deposits, respectively, or they may be further detailed. As noted earlier in the text, banks regard their deposit growth primarily in terms of private funds and often show these funds on the statement of condition under the heading Demand Deposits of Individuals and Corporations, making a separate listing of Public Funds. If the public funds consist principally of the deposits of some particular governmental body and amount to a considerable sum, a separate total under a special designation will be carried—for example, United States Government Deposits.

Time deposits are listed simply as Time Deposits (or Savings Deposits) and Certificates of Deposit.

Another designation is Special Deposits. These represent funds not normally carried but temporarily placed with the bank in anticipation of particular and almost immediate use. When, for example, a bond issue that is payable at the bank matures, funds are deposited by the issuing corporation to pay off the bonds. These funds obviously are temporary and special in nature. If large in amount, they are carried separately on the statement; otherwise they are combined under the designation Special Deposits.

Due to Bank and Bankers—We have seen that transit and collection items are cleared and many courtesies and transactions are accomplished by arrangements between commercial banks. To facilitate these arrangements, banks find it advisable to carry balances with other banks, particularly those located in financial and trade centers. Metropolitan banks have as customers many banks located in adjacent territories and in every part of the United States.

In banks where the number of accounts of other banks is not large, these accounts are carried on the general books, and the balances are consolidated in the item Other Deposits on the statement. If the number of accounts of other banks is large, these accounts are carried on the due to banks ledger in the bookkeeping department, and the total is set up on the statement as Due to Banks and Bankers.

Certified Checks, Cashier's Checks, and Bank Drafts—When the bank certifies a check, it assumes the obligation of paying it to a holder in due course. This obligation is often shown in the statement with similar obligations arising from cashier's checks issued by the bank and drafts drawn by the bank on its balances in other banks. A common title used for these items is Cashier's Checks, Drafts, and Certified Checks Outstanding.

Reserves—It is customary for banks to anticipate liabilities that can be calculated or estimated in advance by setting aside funds for these future payments. Such funds are called reserves. Taxes (both local and national), interest on time accounts, operating expenses, and the like are provided for by reserves. These are shown on the statement as Reserves for Taxes, Reserve for Interest, etc. In addition to these specific reserves, it is usual to set aside funds to meet liabilities which cannot be accurately estimated but which may occur, such as losses on loans and investments. These reserves are general or contingent reserves and are so carried on the statement.

Reserves for taxes, interest, and so on are actual liabilities which have accrued, although they may not be payable at the time of accrual. They are included in the liabilities because they represent an accounting of funds set aside to meet specific purposes; they belong neither to the depositors nor to the stockholders, but they are nevertheless liabilities of the bank. Other reserves, such as contingent reserves, are not actual liabilities at the time they are set up, but they are included in the liabilities on the theory that they may become liabilities in the future.

Capital Stock—Until the passage of the Emergency Banking Act of 1933 (March 9, 1933), banks had only one class of stock, and the capital account carried in the liabilities represented funds due stockholders of the bank in proportion to their holdings. This amount, of course, was subject to payment in full of the deposits and liabilities to others.

The Emergency Banking Act of 1933, and later the Banking Act of 1933, provided that the Reconstruction Finance Corporation could supply needed capital funds to banks meeting certain requirements. These funds were advanced in two ways: either by purchase of the notes of the bank by the Reconstruction Finance Corporation or, if state banking laws permitted, by purchase of its preferred stock by the Reconstruction Finance Corporation. This alternative provision applied to state banks, for national banks followed a uniform procedure of issuing preferred stock. The bank's liability for these notes (or debentures, as they are called) or preferred stock was subordinate to its deposit liability and liability to others but superior to its liability on the common stock. A fixed rate of interest or dividend was provided for and the notes or preferred stock made subject to retirement under certain conditions. It should be noted that while the provisions for the sale of preferred stock or debentures were in contemplation of the purchase of these issues by the Reconstruction Finance Corporation, they may be sold to others as well as to the corporation.

These liabilities are shown separately on the statement as Debentures Outstanding and Preferred Capital Stock.

The Common Capital Stock represents ownership of the bank, subject to any debentures or preferred stock outstanding. (This item is usually designated Capital Stock when no preferred stock or debentures are outstanding.) The method of creating common stock and the privileges and responsibilities attached to its ownership have already been discussed.

Surplus—The surplus account represents funds arising through contribution by the stockholders at the time the bank was organized or when the capital was increased or through the accumulation of earnings over and above dividends paid. Funds in the surplus account are regarded as permanently invested in the business, subject only to extraordinary charges; thus surplus provides an additional protection to both depositors and stockholders, since the surplus account can be used for unusual losses without impairing the capital stock. As noted previously, it is mandatory for national banks to set aside at least one-tenth of their earnings in the surplus account until that account equals capital; [2] a similar requirement is provided by most state laws. This is to compensate for the protection formerly afforded by the double liability of stockholders, which has now been eliminated in the national banking system and in many states.

Undivided Profits—The item Undivided Profits represents the earnings of the bank after deductions for dividends. Some indication of the extent of the profitable operations of a bank may be obtained by a comparison of the undivided profits figures over a period of time, after allowance for dividends paid.

When the undivided profits account becomes large in proportion to capital and surplus, the bank usually transfers an amount in even dollars from the undivided profits account to the surplus account.

When the surplus account, in turn, becomes large in proportion to the capital stock, the bank may distribute a portion of it among the stockholders by an increase in capital stock.

Other Liabilities—Like Other Assets, this item represents liabilities that cannot be properly included in any of the regu-

---
[2] National Bank Act, as amended by the Banking Act of 1935, Section 5199

lar classifications; its amount is small in comparison with total liabilities.

Other Items—There follows a list of other items that frequently appear in statements.

1. Interest Earned but Not Collected, an asset, represents interest accrued on various investments and loans—that is, interest that has been earned but either is not yet due or has not yet been collected. Interest on demand notes, for example, is usually collected once a month; hence during the month some part of the interest is earned but not collected. Time notes usually provide for the payment of interest at maturity; in the meantime interest is earned but not yet due.

2. Due from Customers on Account of Acceptances, an asset, represents the amount due the bank from customers because of the liability assumed by the bank in accepting drafts.

3. Unearned Discount, a liability, represents interest collected by the bank at the time the loans were made and adjusted at regular intervals to show the amount still to be earned.

4. Acceptances Executed for Customers, a liability, represents obligations incurred by the bank in accepting drafts drawn under letter of credit arrangements.

5. The item Bills Payable, or Rediscounts, will appear in the liability column of a bank's statement. This item represents the amount borrowed by the bank from the Federal Reserve bank of its district or from a correspondent bank.

Statement Forms—The form in which the statement of condition must be made is established by the laws or regulations of state or national authority. When the statement of condition is used for advertising purposes, various items are often added. For example, the cash, the market value of securities, the market value of secured loans, and the amount of eligible paper may be totaled and compared with the total deposit liability. While it is not possible to give a detailed report of loans, investments are often listed and the book value and market value shown.

The object of these additions is to impress upon customers, and the public as well, the conservative attitude of the bank (as reflected in the careful use of funds entrusted to it) and the conservative valuation of the assets.

Mention has already been made of the elimination of much duplication of effort and information in examinations and statement calls through the cooperation of various authorities. To further this aim, a committee has been formed known as The Permanent Standing Committee on Standardization of Call Reports and Earnings and Dividend Reports. Among those represented on the committee are state supervisors, the Federal Reserve banks, the Federal Deposit Insurance Corporation, the United States Treasury, the National Association of Bank Auditors and Comptrollers, the American Bankers Association, and The Association of Reserve City Bankers.

Conclusion—With the explanation of the statement of condition this text on Bank Organization and Operation is concluded. To serious students of banking, the successful completion of this course is only the initial step toward a thorough and practical knowledge of the banking profession, in the acquirement of which the many carefully prepared courses offered by the American Institute of Banking are invaluable aids. The practical and continued application of banking principles by the student will continue to improve American banking as well as to increase the responsibilities of and the rewards to the individual.

It is not enough to know the principles or the reasons why those principles have become so well established. It is quite as necessary to apply them in daily transactions in a manner that is equally satisfactory to the bank and to customers, for good will on the part of customers is essential to successful banking.

This point of view is appropriately summarized in an advertisement of one of the leading commercial banks, a statement which reflects the attitude of successful banks and bankers.

"Intelligence and competence in dealing with customers does more to establish mutually satisfactory relations than mere politeness."

Questions Based on Chapter XII

1. What are the purposes of bank examinations?
2. What matters are especially considered by the Board of Governors of the Federal Reserve System in connection with the application of a state bank for membership in the system?
3. What is the statement of condition?
4. What regulations apply to the legal reserves of members of the Federal Reserve System?
5. How are investments classified on the statement?
6. How are loans and discounts classified?
7. What other information besides the statement of condition is included in the statement folder? For what purposes is it included?
8. How are deposits ordinarily classified?
9. What are reserve accounts?
10. What does the item Surplus represent? Capital Stock? Undivided Profits?

Questions for Outside Investigation

1. How are loans and discounts shown on the statement of condition of your bank?
2. How are the different kinds of investments shown?
3. What information other than the statement itself is contained in the statement folder of your bank?

BANK EXAMINATION. STATEMENT OF CONDITION

4. What were the dates of the last three calls made upon your bank?
5. By what authorities is your bank subject to examination?

Assignment

The statement of condition of the Institute State Bank, Erewhon, Illinois, on June 30, 1939 contained the items and amounts which follow. From this information construct the statement of condition, supplying the correct amount for Undivided Profits.

Cash and Due from Banks	$294,945.48
United States Government Obligations	527,846.42
Time Deposits	170,350.42
Interest Earned but Not Collected	4,824.17
Reserve for Taxes	3,463.71
Reserve for Interest, etc.	3,101.01
Time Loans	161,747.16
Demand Loans	22,010.22
Interest Collected but Not Earned	1,021.01
Federal Reserve Bank Stock	4,500.00
Capital Stock	100,000.00
Surplus	50,000.00
Other Resources	1,525.00
Banking House	22,800.00
Reserve for Contingencies	10,000.00
Demand Deposits	721,063.10
Other Bonds	52,816.50
Furniture and Fixtures	4,218.16
Undivided Profits	?

APPENDIX

TABLE I

(From Twenty-Fifth Annual Report of the Board of Governors of the Federal Reserve System Covering Operations for the Year 1938, p. 7)

BANKING STRUCTURE OF THE UNITED STATES
June 30, 1938

	Number of banks	Gross deposits [1] (in millions of dollars)	Percent of total Number of banks	Percent of total Deposits
All banks	15,287	59,044	100	100
Insured banks:				
National	5,242	26,763	34	45
State member	1,096	14,546	7	25
Insured nonmember	7,437	7,123	49	12
Noninsured banks	1,512	10,612	10	18

[1] Include interbank deposits.

TABLE II

(From Twenty-Fifth Annual Report of the Board of Governors of the Federal Reserve System Covering Operations for the Year 1938, p. 60)

Member Bank Reserve Requirements
(Percent of deposits)

Classes of deposits and banks	June 21, 1917–Aug. 15, 1936	Aug. 16, 1936–Feb. 28, 1937	Mar. 1, 1937–Apr. 30, 1937	May 1, 1937–Apr. 15, 1938	Apr. 16, 1938 and after
On net demand deposits:					
Central reserve city	13	10½	22¾	26	22¾
Reserve city	10	15	17½	20	17½
On time deposits:					
All member banks	3	4½	5¼	6	5

APPENDIX

TABLE III
(From Rand McNally Bankers Directory, first 1939 edition, p. 69)
CONSOLIDATED CAPITULATION FOR DECEMBER 1938 STATEMENTS

State	National Banks	State Banks and Trust Companies	Private Banks	Other Banking Institutions	Total Banks	National Bank Branches	State Bank and Trust Co. Branches	Private Bank Branches	Other Banking Institution Branches	Total Branches Listed	Total Number Institutions Shown
Alabama	66	150	...	1	217	6	15	...	1	22	239
Alaska	4	8	1	...	13	...	2	...	...	2	15
Arizona	5	7	...	3	15	21	5	...	...	26	41
Arkansas	50	168	...	2	220	1	14	...	1	16	236
California	102	119	...	9	230	684	176	...	5	865	1,095
Colorado	78	66	...	2	146	...	...	...	1	1	147
Connecticut	54	138	4	11	207	4	10	...	...	14	221
Delaware	16	32	...	...	48	...	13	...	...	13	61
Dist. of Columbia	9	13	...	2	24	17	13	...	...	30	54
Florida	53	112	...	...	165	...	2	...	1	3	168
Georgia	52	232	64	6	354	16	8	...	1	25	379
Hawaii	1	10	...	...	11	12	22	...	...	34	45
Idaho	19	32	...	...	51	16	16	...	...	32	83
Illinois	317	540	...	5	862	...	*2	...	...	*2	864
Indiana	127	371	16	11	525	8	51	1	...	60	585
Iowa	109	541	12	4	666	...	155	...	...	155	821
Kansas	182	498	1	5	686	...	...	...	...	...	686
Kentucky	98	325	...	4	427	18	10	...	1	29	456
Louisiana	30	116	...	3	149	27	26	...	1	54	203
Maine	39	64	...	...	103	4	63	...	...	67	170
Maryland	63	128	...	2	193	8	80	...	1	89	282
Massachusetts	126	266	...	16	408	63	87	...	1	151	559
Michigan	82	374	18	1	475	55	103	1	1	160	635
Minnesota	192	492	...	6	690	6	...	...	1	7	697
Mississippi	25	180	...	...	205	1	41	...	...	42	247
Missouri	87	548	...	7	642	...	...	...	...	...	642
Montana	43	71	...	...	114	...	...	...	1	1	115
Nebraska	136	301	...	4	441	...	...	...	1	1	442
Nevada	6	5	...	...	11	11	...	...	...	11	22
New Hampshire	52	56	...	1	109	1	2	...	...	3	112
New Jersey	227	172	1	...	400	32	89	...	...	121	521
New Mexico	22	19	...	...	41	...	6	...	...	6	47
New York	438	445	12	9	904	184	499	...	†39	722	1,626
North Carolina	43	188	...	6	237	7	111	...	1	119	356
North Dakota	50	124	...	1	175	...	16	...	...	16	191
Ohio	246	448	13	2	709	35	135	...	1	171	880
Oklahoma	214	184	...	3	401	...	...	...	5	5	406
Oregon	28	48	...	2	78	65	3	...	1	69	147
Pennsylvania	695	387	17	5	1,104	41	71	3	2	117	1,221
Rhode Island	12	19	...	1	32	8	32	...	6	46	78
South Carolina	20	128	1	3	152	15	7	...	...	22	174
South Dakota	43	124	...	...	167	19	9	...	...	28	195
Tennessee	71	232	...	1	304	17	34	...	2	53	357
Texas	447	402	26	11	886	...	...	...	3	3	889
Utah	13	46	...	1	60	9	4	...	1	14	74
Vermont	42	42	...	...	84	2	19	...	...	21	105
Virginia	131	186	...	4	321	14	56	...	...	70	391
Washington	48	99	...	2	149	77	5	...	1	83	232
West Virginia	79	104	...	2	185	...	...	...	...	...	185
Wisconsin	105	481	...	...	586	14	107	...	...	121	707
Wyoming	26	32	...	1	59	...	...	...	...	...	59
Grand Total	5,223	9,873	186	159	15,441	1,518	2,119	5	80	3,722	19,163

* Canadian Agencies.   † Includes 38 Foreign Agencies in New York City.

TABLE IV

(From Twenty-Fifth Annual Report of the Board of Governors of the Federal Reserve System Covering Operations for the Year 1938, p. 59)

Maximum Rates on Time Deposits

Maximum rates that may be paid by member banks as established by the Board of Governors under provisions of Regulation Q

[Percent per annum]

	Nov. 1, 1933, to Jan. 31, 1935	Feb. 1, 1935, to Dec. 31, 1935	In effect beginning Jan. 1, 1936
Savings deposits.................	3	2½	2½
Postal Savings deposits...........	3	2½	2½
Other time deposits payable in:			
6 months or more..............	3	2½	2½
90 days to 6 months...........	3	2½	2
Less than 90 days.............	3	2½	1

NOTE.—Maximum rates that may be paid by insured nonmember banks as established by the Federal Deposit Insurance Corporation, effective February 1, 1936, are the same as those in effect for member banks. In some States the maximum rates established by the Board and the Federal Deposit Insurance Corporation are superseded by lower maximum rates established by State authority.

APPENDIX 473

TABLE V

(From Twenty-Fifth Annual Report of the Board of Governors of the Federal Reserve System Covering Operations for the Year 1938, p. 9)

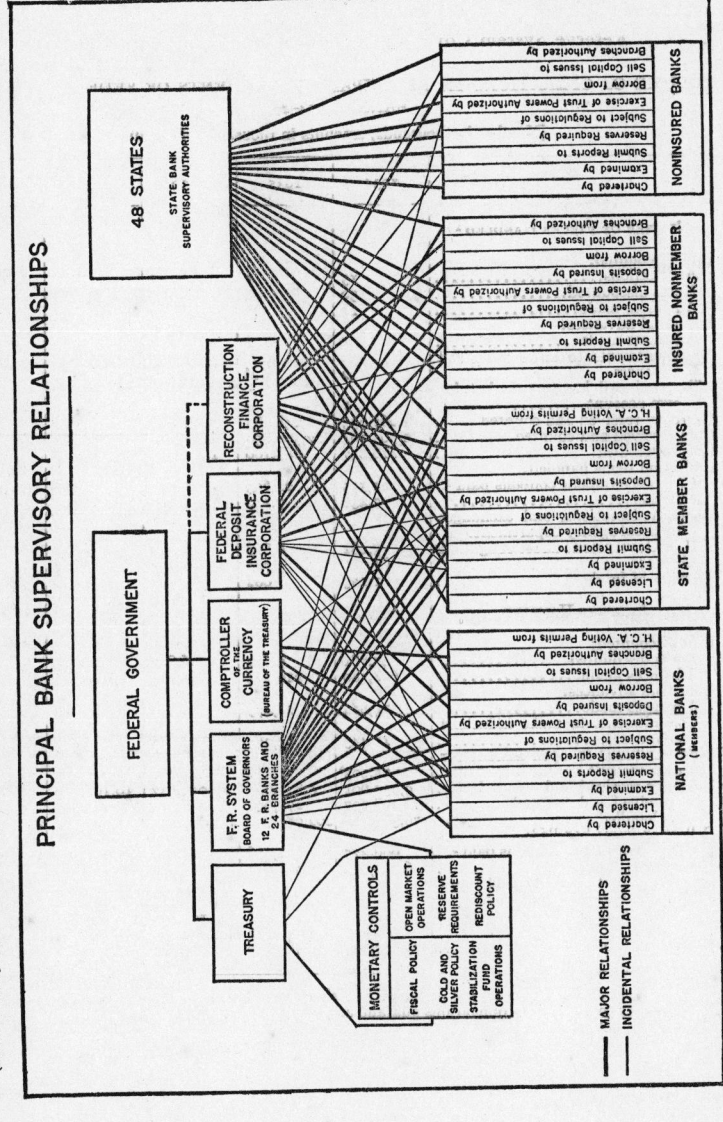

TABLE VI

(From Twenty-Fifth Annual Report of the Board of Governors of the Federal Reserve System Covering Operations for the Year 1938, p. 53)

VOLUME OF OPERATIONS IN PRINCIPAL DEPARTMENTS OF FEDERAL RESERVE BANKS, 1934–1938

[Number in thousands; amounts in thousands of dollars]

	1934	1935	1936	1937	1938
Number of Pieces Handled [1]					
Bills discounted:					
Applications	15	5	3	7	6
Notes discounted	30	8	4	7	6
Advances made	12	5	3	7	6
Industrial advances:					
Advances made	.5	1	.7	.2	.4
Commitments to make industrial advances	.2	.6	.3	.1	.2
Bills purchased in open market for own account	7	2	1	2	.2
Currency received and counted	2,067,835	2,148,485	2,232,980	2,257,892	2,089,987
Coin received and counted	2,565,164	2,599,859	2,665,190	2,730,387	2,676,248
Checks handled	818,847	885,190	1,009,264	1,044,553	1,098,115
Collection items handled:					
U. S. Government coupons paid [2]	21,555	22,633	18,806	18,566	17,802
All other	7,436	7,119	6,968	6,705	6,389
Issues, redemptions, and exchanges by fiscal agency department:					
U. S. Government direct obligations	5,281	6,838	27,919	3,892	3,456
All other	([3])	3,742	1,538	661	575
Transfer of funds	1,125	982	951	980	853
Amounts Handled					
Bills discounted:					
Notes discounted	45,781	9,622	6,886	16,187	10,472
Advances made	668,580	219,924	160,714	516,852	226,687
Industrial advances:					
Advances made	14,884	28,479	8,519	4,932	6,500
Commitments to make industrial advances	11,443	29,223	12,583	6,978	11,217
Bills purchased in open market for own account	75,903	31,446	25,207	25,252	2,781
Currency received and counted	9,932,601	9,837,681	10,059,637	10,199,559	8,883,728
Coin received and counted	298,297	275,608	276,323	287,708	271,128
Checks handled	179,544,488	202,989,742	234,417,787	255,453,609	232,090,217
Collection items handled:					
U. S. Government coupons paid [2]	699,325	751,916	798,925	865,465	854,273
All other	6,742,974	7,948,641	7,089,008	6,159,828	5,321,443
Issues, redemptions, and exchanges by fiscal agency department:					
U. S. Government direct obligations	29,941,049	30,755,611	25,196,825	19,304,020	24,450,791
All other	([3])	3,346,189	2,223,136	1,691,863	2,581,611
Transfer of funds	73,077,156	80,483,190	87,001,630	94,596,861	82,219,749

[1] 2 or more checks, coupons, etc., handled as a single item are counted as 1 "piece."
[2] Includes coupons from obligations guaranteed by the United States.
[3] Figures not available.

Illustrations

FIGURE		PAGE
1.	Bank Control	24
2.	Federal Reserve Districts	26
3.	External Control of National Banks	60
4.	Internal Control	65
5.	Time Schedule of Operations	74
6.	Trade Acceptance	82
7.	Certificate of Deposit Register	100
8.	New Account Form	102
9.	Signature Card	109
10.	Deposit Slip	119
11.	Advice of Credit	123
12.	Receiving Teller's Proof	131
13.	Batch System Operation	142, 143
14.	Stop-Payment Form	167
15.	Scratcher Form	177
16.	Individual Bank Sheet and Clearing House Proof	187
17.	Clearings Department Operation	197
18.	Clearing House Indorsement	198
19.	Return Slip (short form)	199
20.	Account Analysis Form	211
21.	Transit Letter	238
22.	Transit Department Organization of a Large Metropolitan Bank	250, 251
23.	Collection Operation	275

FIGURE	PAGE
24. Coupon Envelope	279
25. Savings Passbook	289
26. Savings Ledger Card	299
27. Bookkeeping Department Organization	337
28. Bookkeeping Department Operation	338
29. Time Schedule of Operations—Bookkeeping Department	339
30. Organization for Loaning Operations	372
31. Credit Department Organization	381
32. Process of Making a Loan	383
33. Discount Operation	395
34. Posting in the Discount Register	396
35. Posting in the Liability Ledger and in the Maturity Tickler	397
36. Collateral Note Operations	405
37. Investment Division Organization of the Trust Department	441
38. Trust Department Organization	444

Index

	PAGE
Acceptance	
Bank	81
Trade	82
Accommodation Paper	359
Accounting (*See* Accounts, Banks)	
Accounts	
Analysis of	181, 202
Association	114
Church	114
Club	114
Corporate	111
Individual	107
Kinds of	106
New	100
Partnership	110
Pay-as-you-go	219
Signature Card	117
Trustee	114
Administrator	427
Agents	427, 428
Alterations	162
American Bankers Association	63, 239
Analysis	
Cost Finding	203
Methods	205
of Accounts	181, 202
Operation of Department	214
Assets	93
Assistant Cashier (*See* Banks)	
Association Accounts	114
Attachment	165
Auditing (*See* Accounting, Accounts, Auditor, Banks)	
Auditor (*See* Banks)	

Banks

Acceptance 81, 84
Accounting 313
Accounting Records 315
and Banking 7
Application for Charter 42
Articles of Association 43
Assets 453, 459
Assistant Cashier 71
Assistant Vice President 70
Auditing 313, 344
Auditor 71, 313
Bookkeeping 317, 322, 328, 336
Branch 32
Building 458
By-Laws 46
Capital 52, 94, 462
Capital Requirements 51
Cashier 70
Cashier's Checks 461
Certified Checks 172, 461
Charters 40, 44
Checkings 377
Checks 327
Classification of 22
Clearing House Department 192
Collection Department 267
Commercial 30
Comptroller 71
Contracts 106
Control 24, 49, 61
Correspondent 234
Department Managers 62
Departments 342, 373, 387, 424
Deposits 459
Directors 46, 61, 67
Discounts 456
Double Entry Bookkeeping 317
Drafts 80
Due to Banks 460

Banks—(*Continued*)   PAGE
- Examination 10, 58, 448
- Executive Vice President 70
- External Control 61
- Failures 10
- Federal Reserve 23, 457
- Federal Reserve Bank Stock 457
- Filing 333
- Functions 15
- Furniture and Fixtures 458
- General Books 317
- Holds 329
- Income 210
- Individual Books 321
- Internal Control 61
- Investments 454
- Laws 59
- Ledgers 323, 331
- Liabilities 459
- Loans 350, 456
- Membership Requirements 51
- Mortgages 457
- National 23
- Offices 62, 69
- Operation 11, 34, 72
- Organization 11, 31, 39
- Overdrafts 334, 457
- Paying Checks 327
- Personal Loan 34
- Principles 13
- Private 33
- Powers of 48
- President 70
- Real Estate 459
- Regulations 59
- Reports 59
- Reserves 55, 461
- Resources 453
- Safe Deposit 267
- Savings 30, 33

Banks—(*Continued*) PAGE
   Savings Department 267
   Secretary 71
   Service 14
   Service Charges 205, 216
   State 23
   Statements 324, 333
   Statement Calls 59
   Statement of Condition 448, 451, 464
   Stockholders 45, 65
   Stock Payments 329
   Surplus 53, 463
   Time Schedule 74
   Trust Companies 30, 424
   Trust Officer 71
   Undivided Profits 463
   Unit 32
   Vice President 70
   See also Cash, Certificate of Deposit, Checks, Clearing, Collateral, Collection, Comptroller of the Currency, Customer, Deposits, Discount, Exchange, Federal Deposit Insurance Corporation, Federal Reserve Banks, Federal Reserve System, Float, Foreign, Loans, Safe Deposit, Savings, Teller, Transit, Trust.
Banker's Bill 419
Banking
   Act of 1935 .... 27, 44
   Associations 63, 64
   Chain 32
   Foreign 22
   Group 32
   Objectives 10
Banking Act of 1935 .... 27, 44
Bankruptcy 165, 430
Batch System 140, 249, 268
   See also Banks, Checks, Clearings, Collection, Deposit, Exchange, Teller, Transit.
Bill of Lading 366, 403
Bonds 363, 403, 428
   Hypothecation 404

Bonds—(*Continued*) PAGE
    Mortgage 429
    Power 403
Brokers' Loans 406
Business, New 104
Cable Transfer 419
Call Loan 361
Capital 94
Cash
    Bank's 154
    Items 123, 267, 276
    Protection of 151
Cashier (*See* Banks)
Central Proof Department 144
Certificate of Deposit 98
Certification 172
Chattel Mortgage 367
Checks 332
    Availability Schedule 240
    Cashier's 461
    Certified 172, 461
    Collection of 225
    Exchange of 225
    Holds 329
    In-Clearings 195
    Interdistrict Settlement Fund 246
    No Par Points 243
    Out-Clearings 192
    Paying 160, 327
    Post-dated 165
    Settlement of 245
    Stale 165
    Stop-payment 166, 329
    Travelers' 418
    Uncollected 236
    See also Banks, Clearing, Collection, Deposits, Discount, Exchange, Federal Insurance Deposit Corporation, Federal Reserve Banks, Federal Reserve System, Float, Teller, Transit.
Church Accounts 114

INDEX

Clearing   PAGE
    Assessments 189
    Department 226
    Float 208, 236
    Forms and Equipment 196
    Group Clearance 260
    House Association 62, 183, 189
    House Department 192
    House Teller 198
    In- 195
    No Par points 243
    Numerical System 239
    Operation of 184, 200
    Out- 192
    Principle 181
    Settlement 188, 225, 245
    Wire Transfer 261
    See also Banks, Checks, Collection, Deposit, Federal Reserve
        Banks, Federal Reserve System, Teller, Transit.

Club Accounts 114
Code Books 262
Collateral 357
    Care of 399
    Department 404
    Loan 362, 406
    Margin 401
    Records 400
    Teller 404
    Trust Bonds 429
    Verifying 402
    See also Banks, Loans, Federal Reserve System.

Collection
    Acknowledgment 276
    Advice of Credit 274, 276
    Audit form 274
    Availability Schedule 240
    by Messenger 276
    Channels 232
    Charges 281
    City Division 276

INDEX 483

Collection—(*Continued*) PAGE
    Country Division 273
    Coupon Division 278
    Coupon Envelope 279
    Credit Memorandum 274
    Debit Form 274
    Department 267, 272, 279
    Department Balance 282
    Department Operations 279
    Exchange Charges 242
    Federal Reserve Service 281
    Float 208, 236
    Items 123, 270
    Letter of Transmittal 273
    Maturity Tickler 276
    No Par Points 243
    Non-Cash Work 282
    of Checks 226
    Par 233
    Par Arrangement 282
    Permanent File Form 274
    Schedules of 226
    Special Instructions 241
    Tracer Form 274
    Tracing 242
    Uncollected Funds 236
    See also Banks, Checks, Clearings, Deposit, Federal Reserve Banks, Federal Reserve System, Float, Teller, Transit.
Commercial Letter of Credit 416
Comptroller (*See* Banks)
Comptroller of the Currency 23, 42, 58
Conservator 427
Contracts 79
    Authority to make 106
    Instalment 367
Corporate
    Accounts 111
    Agent 428
    Custodian 437
    Depository 428

Corporate—(*Continued*)   PAGE
   Fiscal Agent 428
   Receiver 430
   Registrar 428, 429
   Resolution 112
   Transfer Agent 428, 429
   Trust Department 425
   Trustee 428
   See also Directors, Stock, Stockholders.
Correspondent Banks 234
Cost
   Figures 221
   Finding 203
Credit Department 373
Currency
   Proving 170
   Service 157, 159
   Transfer of 19
Custodian 427
Customer
   Contact 12
   Deposit Relationship 105
   New Accounts 100
   New Business 104
   Relations 12
   See also Banks
Death of Maker 165
Debentures 429
Depository 428
Deposits 79
   Batch System 140
   Central Proof Department 144
   Certificate of 98
   Defined 92
   Demand 27, 95
   Distribution Department 144
   Duplicate Slip 121
   Function 16, 92
   Kinds of 95
   Mail Division 145

INDEX 485

Deposits—(*Continued*) PAGE
    Night 134
    Passbook 121
    Private 97
    Proving the 139
    Public 97
    Relationship 105
    Slip 118
    Time 27, 95
    Uses of 93
    See also Banks, Checks, Clearings, Collection, Federal Deposit Insurance Corporation, Federal Reserve System, Float, Teller, Transit.
Directors 46, 61, 67
    Building Committee 68
    Discount Committee 68
    Duties 56
    Examination Committee 68
    Executive Committee 68
    Liabilities 56
    Trust Investment Committee 68
    See also Corporate, Stock, Stockholders.
Discount 456
    Calculating 390
    Department 387, 406
    Register 391
    Teller 388
    See also Banks, Loans.
Distribution Department 144
Drafts 80
    Demand 80
    Documentary 81
    Time 81
Duplicate Deposit Slip 121
Examination (*See* Banks)
Exchange
    Charges 242
    Foreign 22
    Interdistrict Settlement Fund 246
    Medium of 15

Exchange—(*Continued*)   PAGE
    of Checks 225
    See also Banks, Checks.
Executor 427
Federal Deposit Insurance Corporation 27, 29, 41, 44, 95
Federal Reserve Banks 23
    Collection Service 281
    Currency Service 157
    Members 27
    Non-Members 27
Federal Reserve Districts 26
Federal Reserve System 23, 44, 154
    Availability Schedule 240
    Collections 225, 229, 281
    Examinations 448
    Interdistrict Settlement Fund 246
    Margin 401
    No Par Points 243
    Par Collection 233
    Rediscounts 351
    Settlement of Checks 245
    Wire Service 261
Financial Statements 376
Fiscal Agent 428
Float 208, 236
Foreign
    Banker's Bill 419
    Banking Transactions 413
    Cable Transfers 419
    Collections 420
    Department 387, 410, 419
    Exchange 412
    Identification 418
    Letters of Credit 415, 416
    Markets 413
    Traveler's Checks 418
Forgery 164
Funds
    Safety of 10
    Transfer of 19

INDEX

	PAGE
Guaranty	359
Guardian	427
Hypothecation	404
Identification	167, 248, 418
Income	210
Individual Accounts	107
Indorsements	88
Blank	89
Conditional	90
General	89
Irregular	89
Qualified	90
Restrictive	90
Special	89
Indorser	87
Identification Systems	248
Instalment Contract	367
Interdistrict Settlement Fund	246
Items	
Cash	123
Collection	123
Letters of Credit	415, 416
Liability, Double	45
Life Insurance	367
Loan Department	387, 406
Loans	
Accommodation	359
Accounting	391, 394
Agency Reports	378
Bank Checkings	377
Bill of Lading	366, 403
Bonds	363
Bookkeeping	391
Brokers	406
Call	361
Character	407
Chattel Mortgage	367
Collateral	357, 362, 399, 402
Credit Department	373, 380

Loans—(*Continued*) PAGE
Custodian Duties 391
Demand 360
Department 387, 406
Direct 368
Discount Register 391
Discount Teller 388
Filing 379
Financial Statements 376
Function 18, 350, 370
General Information 378
Guaranty 359
Indirect 368
Indorsed Paper 359
Instalment Contract 367
Interest 390
Interviews 375
Kinds of 356
Legal Limit 350
Liability Ledger 391
Life Insurance 367
Liquidity 353
Making 384
Margin 401
Maturity Tickler 392, 393
Past-due Notes 399
Personal 34
Promissory Notes 356
Records 375
Secured 357
Security Exchange Act 401
Small 407
Staff 370
Stocks 362
Statement Analysis 380
Substitution 406
Supplementary Records 393
Surety 359
Time 360
Trade Checking 377

INDEX 489

Loans—(*Continued*)   PAGE
  Two-Name Paper 359
  Warehouse Receipts 365, 403
  See also Banks, Collateral, Federal Reserve System, Stock.
Mail Division 145
Mortgage 403
  Bonds 429
  Chattel 367
  Loans 457
National Association of Mutual Savings Banks 33
National Bank Act 23, 239
National Monetary Commission 228
National Numerical System 239
Negotiable Instruments 79
  Indorsements 88
  Indorser 87
  Negotiation 85
  Payment 86
  Presentation 86
  Promissory Notes 85
  Protest 91
Negotiation 85
New Accounts 100
New Business 104
Notes
  Past-Due 399
  Promissory 85
Numerical System 239
Operations (*See* Banks)
Partnership Accounts 110
Passbook 121
Paying
  Function 151
  Teller 151
Paying Teller (*See* Teller)
Payment 86
Personal Loan Institutions 34
Power of Attorney 403
Presentation 86
President (*See* Banks)

INDEX

	PAGE
Promissory Notes	85, 356
Protective Work	153
Protest	91
Public Interest	8
Receiver	430
Receiving Function	79
Receiving Teller	126
Night Depository	134
Problems	132
Proof	130
Systems	134
See also Teller, Deposits.	
Reconstruction Finance Corporation	94
Registrar	428, 429
Reorganization	430
Reserves	96
Resolution, Form for Corporate Accounts	112
Safe Deposit	267, 303
Access Procedure	307
Accounts	307
Equipment	305
Identification	306
Operation	308
Responsibilities	304
See also Banks.	
Safekeeping	439
Safety of Funds	10
Savings	
Accounts	284, 290
Bank Drafts	296
Banks	30, 283
Bookkeeping	297
Cashier's Checks	296
Club Account	291
Coupon Account	291
Department	267, 283, 292
Deposits	95
Interest	300
Mutual	33

INDEX

Savings—(*Continued*)   PAGE
    National Association of Mutual Banks 33
    Operation 298
    Organization 298
    Overactive Accounts 286
    Passbooks 288, 298
    Paying Signatures 300
    Records 292
    Services 302
    Signatures 300
    Teller Systems 293
Secretary (*See* Banks)
Securities Exchange Act 401
Service Charges 205, 216
Settlement of Balances 225
Signature Card 117
Sinking Funds 429
Statement Analysis 380
Stock 362
    Exchange 363
    Delivery 403
    Hypothecation 404
    Indorsement 403
    Power 403
Stockholders 45, 65, 94
Surety 359
Surplus 94
Telautograph 178
Teller
    Alterations 162
    Attachment 165
    Bank's Cash 154
    Bankruptcy 165
    Batch System 140
    Cash 154
    Central Proof Department 144
    Certification 172
    Clearing House 198
    Death 165
    Department Operations 169

492 INDEX

Teller—(*Continued*) PAGE
    Distribution Department 144
    Equipment 170
    Forgery 164
    Handling Money 156
    Identification 167
    Mail Division 145
    Night Depository 134
    Organization 169
    Paying 151, 160
    Post-Dated Checks 165
    Problems 132
    Proof 130
    Proving Currency 170
    Proving the Deposit 139
    Qualifications 175
    Receiving 126
    Safeguards 175
    Special 174
    Special Payer 168
    Stale Checks 165
    Stop-payment 166
    Systems 134
    Telautograph 178
    Trust 435
    Unit System 169
    See also Banks, Checks, Clearings, Collection, Deposits, Federal Reserve System, Float, Receiving Teller, Transit.
Tracing 242
Trade Acceptance 82
Transfer Agent 428, 429
Transit
    Alphabetic Code 248
    Batch System 140, 249, 268
    Code Books 262
    Collection 226
    Correspondence Division 255
    Department 225, 252
    Earnings 258
    Equipment 257

INDEX

Transit—(*Continued*) PAGE
    Float 208, 236
    Group Clearance 260
    Indorser Identification Systems 248
    Letter 237
    Manager 252
    Numerical System 239
    Operations 258
    Pay-Off Division 255
    Personnel 257
    Routing Division 255
    Settlement of Balances 225, 245
    Special Instructions 241
    Tracing 242
    Uncollected Funds 236
    Wire Transfer 261
    See also Banks, Checks, Clearings, Collection, Deposits, Federal Reserve Banks, Federal Reserve System, Float, Teller, Transit.
Traveler's Checks 418
Trust
    Accounts 115
    Administrator 427
    Audit Control 438
    Companies 30
    Conservator 427
    Corporate 425, 428
    Custodian 427
    Department 429, 431, 440
    Functions 21, 424
    Indentures 428
    Investments 440
    Investment Committee 68, 440
    Life Insurance 428
    Officer 71
    Personal 426
    Records 433
    Safekeeping 439
    Securities 437

Trust—(*Continued*) PAGE
    Tellers 435
    Testamentary 428
Trustee 424
    Living Trust 427
    Under Life Insurance Trust 427
    Under Mortgage 428
    Under Trust Deed 428
    Under Wills 427
    Voluntary Trust 427
Undivided Profits 94
Unit System (*See* Teller)
Vaults 152
Vice President (*See* Banks)
Warehouse Receipts 365, 403
Wire Transfer 261